W9-CFV-112

JUVENILE JUSTICE

THEORY, SYSTEMS, AND ORGANIZATION

James Houston

Grand Valley State University

Shannon M. Barton

Indiana State University

Upper Saddle River, New Jersey 07458

Library of Congress Cataloging-in-Publication Data

Houston, James
  Juvenile justice : theory, systems, and organization / James Houston, Shannon M. Barton.
    p. cm.
  Includes bibliographical references and index.
  ISBN 0-13-907445-7
  1. Juvenile justice, Administration of—United States. 2. Juvenile delinquency—United States. I. Barton,
Shannon M. II. Title.

HD9104.H755 2005
364.36′0973—dc22

2004004465

Executive Editor: Frank Mortimer, Jr.
Associate Editor: Sarah Holle
Production Editor: Karen Berry, Pine Tree Composition
Production Liaison: Barbara Marttine Cappuccio
Director of Production and Manufacturing: Bruce
  Johnson
Managing Editor: Mary Carnis
Manufacturing Buyer: Cathleen Petersen

Creative Director: Cheryl Asherman
Cover Design Coordinator: Miguel Ortiz
Cover Designer: Steve Frim
Cover Image: Billy E. Barnes, PhotoEdit, Inc.
Editorial Assistant: Barbara Rosenberg
Marketing Manager: Tim Peyton
Formatting and Interior Design: Pine Tree Composition

Copyright © 2005 by Pearson Education, Inc., Upper Saddle River, New Jersey, 07458.
Pearson Prentice Hall. All rights reserved. Printed in the United States of America. This publication is protected by Copyright and permission should be obtained from the publisher prior to any prohibited reproduction, storage in a retrieval system, or transmission in any form or by any means, electronic, mechanical, photocopying, recording, or likewise. For information regarding permission(s), write to: Rights and Permissions Department.

Pearson Prentice Hall™ is a trademark of Pearson Education, Inc.
Pearson® is a registered trademark of Pearson plc
Prentice Hall® is a registered trademark of Pearson Education, Inc.

Pearson Education LTD.
Pearson Education Singapore, Pte. Ltd
Pearson Education, Canada, Ltd
Pearson Education–Japan
Pearson Education Australia PTY, Limited
Pearson Education North Asia Ltd
Pearson Educación de Mexico, S.A. de C.V.
Pearson Education Malaysia, Pte. Ltd

10 9 8 7 6 5 4 3 2
ISBN 0-13-907445-7

This book is dedicated to
Peggy Houston with much love
J.H.

To my loving husband Darin Bellessa and my parents
Gerald and Betty Barton. I could not have done this without you.
S.B.

And to all dedicated and underpaid youth workers

CONTENTS

7   Diversion   167

**8   Community-based Sanctions
and Juvenile Institutions   196**

III   Managing Processes in Juvenile Justice

9   Goals and Effectiveness of the Juvenile Justice System

12   Intergroup Relations and Conflict   304

IV Integrating the Juvenile Justice System   323

13 Power and Politics in Juvenile Justice   325

14 The Executive in Juvenile Justice   341

PREFACE

This book has been in progress for a long time and could not have been completed without a great deal of help and encouragement. It is our firm belief that students need to have a reasonably good grasp on how the juvenile justice system works and how it interfaces with other institutions in the community. Without that knowledge, the effective management of resources and programs is even more difficult. As a consequence, the book takes a different approach. That is, it is a blend of information about management and information about the juvenile justice system.

In the classroom we make artificial divisions and distinctions in order to facilitate discussion. This is a valuable approach, but hardly reflects the real world where everything depends on nearly everything else. Thus, we have attempted to not only educate the reader on the juvenile system, but also on how to bring the system together in order to serve the child and the community. This text is based on our combined field experience, education, training of juvenile justice practitioners, research, and teaching of juvenile justice during our careers. Our hope is that it will provide students with the theoretical foundation necessary to work with youth and also allow them to understand the interdependence between juvenile justice organizations and community institutions.

ORGANIZATION OF THE TEXT

Clearly juvenile crime is an issue that should concern us all. In addition, we must begin to develop programs and approaches to juvenile crime that will serve all children and protect the taxpayer. However, we cannot rely entirely upon repression and a "lock-'em up" approach. If we are going to be successful in our fight to reduce juvenile crime, we must take a different look at the juvenile system, recast its function, and gain a clearer understanding of how the system works.

Unfortunately, most texts on juvenile justice are nothing more than books on juvenile delinquency. That is fine as far as that goes, but few have made an attempt to integrate criminological theory and organizational theory in an attempt to explain the system. This is necessary because the juvenile justice system does not exist in a vacuum; it is a part of, and depends upon, the other social systems of which it is a subpart. However ambitious the task, it is necessary that we attempt to understand the juvenile justice system in light of how theory informs programs, how organizations work, and its dependency upon the legal subsystem.

One special feature of the book is that we attempt to use a spiraling approach. That is, we introduce a concept or idea at one point, perhaps in depth or briefly, and then return to it later on. For example, Chapter 4 is devoted to gangs. We return to the subject of gangs in Chapter 12. We talk about groups in Chapter 10 and in Chapter 12. We hope this approach will serve not only as learning reinforcement, but will reinforce the notion that juvenile justice is greatly affected by the environment and what goes on in the world as a whole.

Part I looks at delinquency in the twenty-first century. The scope and depth of the problem is probed in order to give the student an understanding of the real problem. Part II examines the system itself. The police, courts, the process of diversion, and community and institutions are discussed with a view towards how each works with the others. Part III is unique, in that the student is acquainted with the need to manage the juvenile justice system in order to maximize services to youth. Finally, Part IV looks at the executive in juvenile justice and how he or she can influence the system and related systems to serve the community and the youth. The final chapter is a discussion of the future of juvenile justice where we peer into our crystal ball and attempt to predict what the future holds for juvenile justice.

J.H. and S.B.

ACKNOWLEDGMENTS

In writing this book, it is difficult to acknowledge everyone who had a hand in its completion. We know that someone will be left off the list; for this we apologize. However, in particular we want to acknowledge the patience and guidance of Prentice-Hall, especially Sarah Holle, whose gentle manner guided the book to completion. We also thank Karen Berry of Pine Tree Composition for getting the book into production. John Hewitt deserves recognition for his assistance and willingness to listen to ideas and, along with Bob Regoli, for granting permission to borrow from their chapter on Diversion from a previous edition of their text as a starting point for our chapter on the same subject.

Furthermore, we would also like to acknowledge and thank all of those who wrote case studies highlighted at the beginning of each chapter. It is through their experience and tireless effort that we have gained knowledge and further understanding of the juvenile justice system.

Shannon Barton would like to personally thank all of her professors who encouraged her to obtain a Ph.D. and then guided and assisted her in becoming an academic. She feels a particular debt of gratitude to Ken Ayres, Ed Latessa, Frank Cullen, and Patricia VanVoorhis. She would also like to thank Velmer Burton and her former colleagues at Ferris State University for encouraging her to write and for giving her that first job. She also feels a debt of gratitude to Nancy Hogan, Eric Lambert, and co-author Jim Houston for their patience, input, and support during this process. And to her new colleagues at Indiana State University, thank you for your encouragement in completing the project.

The authors would also like to thank the following reviewers: Melton E. Beane, Tidewater Community College, Virginia Beach, VA; Tere Chipman, Fayetteville Technical Community College, Fayetteville, NC; J.L. Jengeleski, Shippensburg University, Shippensburg, PA; George Evans, Harper College, Palatine, IL; Brenda Bauch, Jefferson College, Hillsboro, MO; Alan Marston, Southern Maine Technical College, South Portland, ME; Christine Ludowise, Georgia Southern University, Statesboro, GA; and Beth Bailey, Charleston Southern University, Charleston, SC.

PART I
JUVENILE DELINQUENCY IN THE TWENTY-FIRST CENTURY

This section looks at the breadth and depth of delinquency in the United States and attempts to educate the student on the true scope of delinquency. Another aim of Chapter 1 is to expose the fallacy of a delinquency crime wave. Chapter 2 discusses explanations of delinquency and serves as the foundation for later chapters. Chapters 3 and 4 consider the external environment and how its impact influences delinquency. Gangs are dealt with in Chapter 4 because they have altered the fabric of many communities and must be accounted for in any discussion of juvenile justice.

PART I

JUVENILE DELINQUENCY
IN THE TWENTY-FIRST CENTURY

CHAPTER 1

DELINQUENCY AND THE JUVENILE JUSTICE SYSTEM

Uniform Crime Report
Delinquency
Open system
Closed system
Criminal offenses
Status offense

Juvenile justice system
Parens patriae
Illinois Juvenile Court Act
House of Refuge
Probation
Wedding Cake Model

National Crime
   Victimization Survey
   (NCVS)
Self-report studies

INTRODUCTION

For some time, we have witnessed the making of a tragedy in that the American public has become convinced that we are in the throes of a desperate fight against juvenile crime. The nightly news programs carry stories of murder, desperation, and violence that instill a fear of youth, particularly minority youth. In the past few years, aspirants to political office have attempted to outdo one another in suggestions for dealing with juvenile crime, and most rhetoric falls short on substance.

The truth about juvenile crime is ignored by most public officials as they seek election or reelection to public office. In addition, the result of the rhetoric is that it fosters contempt for the juvenile justice system by focusing on the symptoms and not the root causes of juvenile crime. The conditions fostered by poverty, single-parent families, and the resultant stress has caused an increase in some juvenile crime, but we have not witnessed an epidemic of juvenile crime in the past two decades.

The truth is, we can note a small increase in arrests of juveniles. For example, According to the **Uniform Crime Report** (UCR) from 1988 to 1999, arrests of juveniles increased from 1,280,260 to 1,348,731. This hardly qualifies as a crime wave, but it is cause for concern, particularly when we look at crimes of violence. For youth under the age of eighteen, murder and nonnegligent manslaughter decreased from 1,478 in 1988 to 665 to 1999.* Other crimes of violence have decreased as well.

The media has not helped matters at all. Especially violent and gruesome crimes are quickly seized upon by the media and politicians as examples of life in America and typical of our youth and are used by some legislators and policy makers to justify especially repressive and regressive measures to deal with juvenile crime instead of taking a hard look at the systemic causes of juvenile crime. The result has been a deep suspicion of the juvenile justice system and skepticism about the safety of life in America.

How much of what we are led to believe about crime in general and juvenile crime in particular coincides with reality? The truth is, not much. There are two different ideologies in the United States when it comes to crime. One confesses to a conservative ideology and the other a liberal ideology.

The conservatives assert that crime is destroying our nation and that could be prevented by getting rid of court decisions that "handcuff the police," appointing more conservative Supreme Court judges, and by having "get tough" prosecutors in charge of the fight against crime (Wilson, 1983). One need only recall every presidential election since 1964, particularly the elections of 1988 and 1992. In those elections in particular, crime was taken out of the realm of local issues and federalized. Conservatives asserted that solutions could be found in Washington under the direction of a conservative Supreme Court and Attorney General.

The liberal ideology is best articulated by Samuel Walker (1998), who points out that conservatives view the issue of crime as one of discipline and self-control. Liberals, on the other hand, view crime as a result of social influences; in other words, people commit crimes because family, peer group, or neighborhood, and so on influence their decisions and behavior.

Walker (1998) asserts that both subscribe to a theology that is based upon certain canons of faith, and facts do not alter that faith. Further, according to Walker, neither the crime control programs of the right or left have successfully confronted the problem of crime and **delinquency**.

Only a small proportion of delinquency is violent crime, but it is violent crime that concerns citizens most. That fear was highlighted in 1993 in Davenport, Iowa, when a seventeen-year-old high school senior was murdered for the keys to her car. The perpetrators were members of a notorious Chicago street gang, the Vice Lords. What shocked the region, and the nation, is that those who perpetrated the crime were white, effectively destroying the myth that violent juvenile crime, and juvenile street gangs were primarily a problem for minorities. What the citizens of Davenport and the surrounding region learned is that the large super-gangs subscribe to an equal opportunity philosophy, and

---

*The reader should note that there is some disparity in UCR tables; for example, "Numbers of persons arrested" (under 18) varies depending on the table one looks at. In 1999 (p. 218), the number of arrests are noted as 1,348,731; on page 216, arrests are noted as 1,294,513; and on page 231, arrests for those under age 18 are listed as 1,584,718.

Table 1.1 Juvenile Arrests by Total Arrests

By offense charged and age group, United States, 1991 and 2000
(6,422 agencies; 1991 estimated population 133,490,609; 2000 estimated population 149,828,555)

Offense Charged	Total All Ages			Under 18 Years of Age			18 Years of Age and Older		
	1991	2000	Percent Change	1991	2000	Percent Change	1991	2000	Percent Change
Total[a]	7,394,878	7,412,294	0.2%	1,214,753	1,255,623	3.4%	6,180,125	6,156,671	-0.4%
Murder and nonnegligent manslaughter	11,950	7,012	-41.3	1,811	641	-64.6	10,139	6,371	-37.2
Forcible rape	20,716	14,538	-29.8	3,211	2,364	-26.4	17,505	12,174	-30.5
Robbery	88,660	60,812	-31.4	21,504	15,310	-28.8	67,156	45,502	-32.2
Aggravated assault	270,787	265,385	-2.0	37,842	35,307	-6.7	232,945	230,078	-1.2
Burglary	248,292	157,665	-36.5	83,933	52,157	-37.9	164,359	105,508	-35.8
Larceny-theft	879,815	641,370	-27.1	265,806	202,933	-23.7	614,009	438,437	-28.6
Motor vehicle theft	118,867	77,070	-35.2	52,761	26,099	-50.5	66,106	50,971	-22.9
Arson	10,508	8,824	-16.0	5,068	4,712	-7.0	5,440	4,112	-24.4
Violent crime[b]	392,113	347,747	-11.3	64,368	53,622	-16.7	327,745	294,125	-10.3
Property crime[c]	1,257,482	884,929	-29.6	407,568	285,901	-29.9	849,914	599,028	-29.5
Total Crime Index[d]	1,649,595	1,232,676	-25.3	471,936	339,523	-28.1	1,177,659	893,153	-24.2
Other assaults	554,987	676,319	21.9	88,226	120,488	36.6	466,761	555,831	19.1
Forgery and counterfeiting	53,853	58,493	8.6	4,349	3,500	-19.5	49,504	54,993	11.1
Fraud	188,100	155,231	-17.5	4,891	4,755	-2.8	183,209	150,476	-17.9
Embezzlement	7,458	10,730	43.9	470	1,090	131.9	6,988	9,640	38.0
Stolen property; buying, receiving, possessing	91,166	66,772	-26.8	26,281	15,641	-40.5	64,885	51,131	-21.2
Vandalism	175,632	150,132	-14.5	77,182	60,951	-21.0	98,450	89,181	-9.4
Weapons; carrying, possessing, etc.	125,722	86,620	-31.1	27,360	20,133	-26.4	98,362	66,487	-32.4
Prostitution and commercialized vice	57,335	47,481	-17.2	832	727	-12.6	56,503	46,754	-17.3

(continued)

Table 1.1   Juvenile Arrests by Total Arrests (Continued)

By offense charged and age group, United States, 1991 and 2000
(6,422 agencies; 1991 estimated population 133,490,609; 2000 estimated population 149,828,555)

Offense Charged	Total All Ages			Under 18 Years of Age			18 Years of Age and Older		
	1991	2000	Percent Change	1991	2000	Percent Change	1991	2000	Percent Change
Sex offenses (except forcible rape and prostitution)	60,035	51,643	−14.0	10,162	9,707	−4.2	49,873	41,936	−15.9
Drug abuse violations	563,776	842,532	49.4	43,289	105,993	144.8	520,487	736,539	41.5
Gambling	7,124	4,020	−43.6	551	404	−26.7	6,573	3,616	−45.0
Offenses against family and children	50,869	68,740	35.1	2,088	4,015	92.3	48,781	64,725	32.7
Driving under the influence	971,628	775,392	−20.2	9,563	10,888	13.9	962,065	764,504	−20.5
Liquor laws	300,147	341,047	13.6	67,729	81,223	19.9	232,418	259,824	11.8
Drunkenness	492,720	358,041	−27.3	12,562	12,151	−3.3	480,158	345,890	−28.0
Disorderly conduct	336,418	295,597	−12.1	58,394	77,396	32.5	278,024	218,201	−21.5
Vagrancy	23,995	17,008	−29.1	1,937	1,296	−33.1	22,058	15,712	−28.8
All other offenses (except traffic)	1,534,628	2,000,927	30.4	157,261	212,849	35.3	1,377,367	1,788,078	29.8
Suspicion (not included in totals)	8,563	2,768	−67.7	2,614	640	−75.5	5,949	2,128	−64.2
Curfew and loitering law violations	50,472	91,453	81.2	50,472	91,453	81.2	X	X	X
Runaways	99,218	81,440	−17.9	99,218	81,440	−17.9	X	X	X

Note: See Note, table 4.1. This table presents data from all law enforcement agencies submitting complete reports for 12 months in 1991 and 2000 (Source, p. 405). Population figures are estimates calculated from U.S. Census Bureau data. For definitions of offenses, see Appendix 3.

aDoes not include suspicion.

bViolent crimes are offenses of murder and nonnegligent manslaughter, forcible rape, robbery, and aggravated assault.

cProperty crimes are offenses of burglary, larceny-theft, motor vehicle theft, and arson.

dIncludes arson.

Source: Ann L. Pastore and Kathleen Maguire, eds., Sourcebook of Criminal Justice Statistics 2001. U.S. Department of Justice, Bureau of Justice Statistics. Washington, D.C.: USGPO, 2002.

they are eager to include young people of all races. But gangs are only a small part of the total delinquency picture. Most juvenile crime is property crime and status offenses. However, we tend to think of delinquency as characterized by chronic, violent offenders, not the more mundane sort of delinquents seen by juvenile courts every day.

Part of the problem is that we live in a society dominated by information. Unfortunately, television is the major tool for the dissemination of information, and it relies on short, snappy one-liners that are short on analysis. These one-liners are known as "sound bytes" and fit into the thirty minutes usually allowed for the evening news, less commercials. The print media is also guilty of giving a skewed image of what is happening around the nation and also in one's local area. The need to increase readership generally means the rule of thumb is to lead with stories that appeal to human interest. The result is that the media is able to construct a sense of crisis, a belief that a problem is at hand and must be dealt with immediately. Soon, however, the issue plays out and the journalists all begin to look around for another "problem" to confront.

Abadinsky and Winfree (1992) point out that science and journalism differ a great deal. Science demands that the subject be approached cautiously and the scientist is enjoined to follow certain procedures in order to be assured that cautious and restrained conclusions are reached. Journalists, on the other hand, are not bound by the canons of scholarly research, and the overriding concern of the journalist is to produce exciting copy that may or may not be the result of painstaking investigation. As a result, truth and fact are often trampled in the pursuit of getting a byline and to boost sales. The result has been that the media is responsible for creating the general public's perception of crime and the juvenile justice system. The tendency of the media to feature "celebrity cases" causes us to view such occurrences as the norm, rather than aberrations in the total picture. In other words, myths are accepted as gospel in spite of the facts.

The construction of certain myths, according to Kappeler, Blumberg, and Potter (1996), serve at least three purposes:

- Myths tend to organize our views of crime, criminals, and the proper operation of the criminal justice system. This framework helps us identify certain social issues as crime-related and help us form opinions that allow us to apply ready-made solutions to complex problems.

- Myths support and maintain established views on crime. The reinforcement of established views of crime and what to do about it prevents us from defining the issues accurately, exploring new solutions, or searching for alternatives to existing socially constructed labels and crime control practices.

- Myths tend to provide the necessary information for the construction of a social reality of crime. Kappeler, Blumberg, and Potter point out that, "Myths of crime become a convenient mortar to fill gaps in knowledge and to provide answers to questions social science either cannot answer or has failed to address."

- Crime myths provide an outlet for emotionalism and channel emotions into action. They allow for interpretation of general social emotions and sentiment and direct those emotions to designated targets.

Fortunately most of us are not intimately acquainted with juvenile crime. We go about our daily business, raise our families, attend church, synagogue, or mosque, and hold jobs without having to deal with the kind of problems many families around the nation must contend with on a daily basis. On the other hand, there are neighborhoods in which the inhabitants cower in their homes or apartments each night because of juvenile crime and related gang activity. In many jurisdictions, the juvenile justice system has broken down; not because of a faulty philosophy, but rather because of inadequate resources and because of a breakdown in the traditional means to deal with illegal youthful behavior.

SYSTEMS DEFINED

There is a good deal of discussion of the juvenile justice system, but in fact it is more of a nonsystem. That is, it is a loose collection of agencies that often find it difficult to work together and which are autonomous and independently funded. This nonsystem is awkward at times and often fails to work smoothly. Still, it is designed to view the best interests of the child as its overarching philosophy. What may cause some of the problems is the fact that the juvenile justice system is an **open system**.

According the Ludwig von Bertalanffy (1950), there are two types of systems: closed and open. **Closed systems** do not interact with their environment; open systems interact with and are influenced by their environment. A good example of a closed system is a clock. If a continuous power source exists, the gears and other parts of the system do not require input from the external environment. On the other hand, a good example of an open system is that of a plant. The plant requires sunlight and CO_2 from the external environment to live and reproduce, and obviously without input from the external environment it would not survive.

Kast and Rosenzweig (1979, p. 98) define a system as "an organized, unitary whole composed of two or more interdependent parts, components, or subsystems and delineated by identifiable boundaries from its environmental suprasystem." Most texts of juvenile justice fail to emphasize that the juvenile justice system is made up of a number of parts. For example, the parts include police, courts, various public and private agencies, and residential institutions such as reform schools and group homes.

Each part affects the whole, and if one part fails to work properly, then the rest of the system feels the pain. For example, if a particular jurisdiction has an inadequate juvenile detention center and experiences a sudden increase in juvenile crime, other parts of the system are affected: The existing detention center is treading on thin ice because of overcrowding, and the jail must empty a cell block of adults in order to comply with the "out of sight and sound" requirement of the Office of Juvenile Justice and Delinquency Prevention (OJJDP). Probation officers may increase surveillance of those released on recognizance, probation officers and sheriffs deputies must spend valuable time transporting youths to far away detention centers who agree to hold the juvenile, and then more time is lost because of the need to transport the child back for court hearings. Finally the prosecutor's office must work harder and the juvenile magistrate or judge may need to hold hearings contesting the detention of the juvenile out of the county or in the jail.

In addition, most delinquency texts and texts on juvenile justice fail to point out that the juvenile justice system is connected to the larger environment in some way through education, government, and the public. That connection is made even stronger through the people who work in the system and who bring their values and attitudes to work with them every day. An institution for the long-term care and treatment of juvenile boys is an example of an open system. Employees bring their values and attitudes to work with them, the institutional inmate culture is constantly revitalized and sustained by the arrival of new inmates; the courts and legislature affect the institutions daily operations; and finally, food, water, and other necessities are brought into the institution on a daily basis. Clearly, the juvenile justice organization is an open system.

DELINQUENCY DEFINED

Defining delinquency is not difficult, as it is age-specific. That is, *a delinquent is a person who is found to have violated the criminal code and who is between the ages of seven and eighteen.* This is an important distinction because legally children under the age of seven are believed to be incapable of intent and therefore not capable of criminal or delinquent acts. Children between seven and fourteen, while assumed to be more capable of intent, are not as fully capable of intent as a child over the age of fourteen.

There are two types of delinquency, **criminal offenses** and **status offenses**, and both will be discussed in greater detail in a later chapter. Criminal offenses are those acts that if committed by an adult would be considered criminal such as burglary, robbery, and murder. On the other hand, there is a category of offenses that are peculiar to people under the age of eighteen—status offenses. A status offense is an offense that, if committed by an adult, would not be a crime. This includes offenses such as running away, truancy, and sexual promiscuity. Status offenses are handled differently from criminal offenses, and status offenders cannot be held in secure detention longer than 24 hours. The **juvenile justice system** can be defined as that loose confederation of agencies, both public and private, that work with delinquent and at-risk youth.

MOVING THROUGH THE SYSTEM

The juvenile justice system is a subsystem of independently funded, managed, and operated agencies that often have trouble talking to each other. The system is composed of law enforcement, juvenile courts, corrections agencies, schools, and private (both profit and not-for-profit) agencies interested in working with children and youth.

A number of factors that affect the juvenile justice system and have helped shape its course. First, a separate system for children is based upon the concept of **parens patriae**, that is, the state views itself as the benevolent parent. Under the doctrine of parens patriae, the state is to assume the role of parent and the responsibility for the care and

1600	1800	1824

Antiquity to late 1600s—children often died in infancy or early childhood, so adults distanced themselves from children. There was no difference in dress, etc, and children were expected to begin assuming adult responsibilities around age 5–7.

Church leaders and moralists began to promote idea that children were weak and needed protection, hence childhood began to be extended with schooling.

By 1800s, English common law had recognized a distinct set of rules regarding intent on part of children.

Emergence of Parens Patriae after 1800.

Laws of apprenticeship repealed.

First House of Refuge—New York.

Figure 1.1   Juvenile Justice in Historical Perspective

development of children (Regoli & Hewitt, 1994). In the case of children who exhibit criminal or deviant behavior, the early reformers saw their task as one of not only protecting children from the excesses of criminality, gambling, and drinking, but also of protecting society from "bad seeds capable of much harm" (Regoli & Hewitt, 1994).

Another factor is that the development of the juvenile court, and hence the entire juvenile justice system, was based upon the desire to shield the child from the harshness of the adult criminal court with its emphasis on adversarial procedures and a belief that a juvenile justice system should be based upon concepts of rehabilitation and care. A third factor was the desire to shield children from the predations of adults in prisons and jails. Until the advent of the juvenile court and its philosophy of rehabilitation and care, children were likely to be placed in prisons or jails with hardened criminals who exploited them in many ways.

The history of dealing with delinquents and wayward children is richly textured and often sordid, but recognition of delinquency as deserving special treatment did not begin to take hold until the 1600s when church leaders and others began to advocate protection and care of children (Thornton, Jr. & Voigt, 1992).

However, it wasn't until the early 1800s with the growth of the Child Savers Movement that children and delinquency began to be viewed as deserving special attention. In 1899, the movement to care for wayward and delinquent children culminated in the passage of the **Illinois Juvenile Court** Act. The provisions of the act included informal procedures for dealing with children. Finally, children were to be spared the harshness and adversarial proceedings of the adult court.

Prior to the Illinois Legislature approving a separate juvenile court in 1899, the **House of Refuge** had been conceived as a way of protecting children from a life of crime, but according to Regoli and Hewett (1994) they devolved into a means of saving society from the children. Punishment and harshness were the hallmark of most Houses of Refuge, and in spite of the intentions of the reformers responsible for the concept, they

1841	1850	1869	1872
Probation made its appearance—Boston.	Chicago Reform School founded.	Massachusetts requires that an agent attend all trials of children.	Massachusetts requires separate court trials for all children.

soon degenerated into places where older, more sophisticated youth would exploit and abuse younger children, along with the staff, who viewed the children incarcerated in them as deserving of their lot.

At the time the juvenile justice system was taking shape, the United States was evolving from an agrarian society to an urban society. In 1900 there were 75,994,575 people in the United States with 39 percent living in an urban area. In 1920, nearly 106,000,000 people lived in the United States with just over 51 percent living in an urban area (U.S. Census, 1999). Thus, in the two decades from the turn of the century, the United States added nearly 30 million citizens, many of them immigrants and many of whom settled in urban areas in order to be near jobs resulting from the rapid industrialization of the United States. Living conditions, illness, and death resulted in many children, usually orphans, living on the streets and their involvement in criminal behavior. Their idleness caused adults to become concerned, and they attempted to do something about their plight. Over time, the traditional means for dealing with homeless, abused, and delinquent children, which depended upon charity and the church, were recognized as inadequate. As a result, juvenile justice evolved over time through a series of steps and processes designed to protect the child.

Juvenile law violators move through the juvenile justice system in a less-than-orderly fashion. The average student and citizen knows very little about the system, except that they are told that it does not work well. In fact, the system works very well. Problems stem from misconceptions rooted in celebrity cases that grab the headlines and from unscrupulous politicians who lead us to believe that we are at the threshold of chaos.

Most delinquency and juvenile crime are petty offenses or status offenses. Quite often, children commit petty crimes or burglaries in addition to such offenses as being truant or under the influence of alcohol. Since the 1960s, the juvenile court hearing has changed a great deal. Prior to the Gault decision in 1967, juvenile court hearings were informal proceedings that focused on helping the child. After the excesses illustrated in the case of

1899	1904	1923	1944
Juvenile Court founded Cook County, Illinois.	19 states had juvenile court.	All states but Maine, Wyoming, and DC had juvenile court.	All states and DC had juvenile court.

Figure 1.1   Continued

Gerald Gault, the proceedings became formalized to the extent that they incorporate the same adversarial procedures from which the early reformers hoped to shield children.

The formal hearing at which the juvenile offender appears to settle the charges against him or her has several possible outcomes: dismissal of charges, informal probation, **probation,** and commitment (of which there are several possibilities). The single distinguishing feature of the juvenile court is that probation is a legitimate sentence, which it is not in adult court. In other words, the child can be sentenced to a period of probation and, if successfully served, will be discharged. An adult, on the other hand, is sentenced to a period of time in prison. But, the sentence is put aside and the offender is placed on probation subject to conditions imposed by the court. If he or she violates the probation, the offender must return to court where the judge may revoke probation and invoke the sentence to prison. In addition, if the probationer committed a new offense, he or she is also liable for an additional sentence to run consecutive (or concurrent) to the original sentence.

Figure 1.2 illustrates the progression of the child through the juvenile justice system. Note that there are a number of points at which the child can exit the system. In addition, there are a number of points at which the child's status can be validated or he or she can be placed in a more restrictive setting.

The diagram in Figure 1.2 emphasizes juvenile justice as a *system.* That is, what goes on in one part of the system affects the rest of the system. It's like hurting our foot. We limp around thinking the foot will get well, and soon the knee begins to hurt. Soon after that our back begins to hurt, and after that we begin to get headaches. All because we hurt our foot and ignored the injury. The juvenile justice system is like that, and Figure 1.2 shows how the child moves through the system, ideally at least. If the system is overloaded at one point, the rest of the system soon feels the stress.

While Figure 1.2 illustrates how we want the system to work, it works quite differently in reality. Samuel Walker (1998) describes what he calls the **Wedding Cake Model** in attempting to describe the adult criminal justice system. We can adapt the Wedding Cake Model to the juvenile justice system, and it makes just as much sense for juveniles as it does for adults. Walker states that the usual portrayals of the criminal justice system as a single model is misleading. In fact, there are fifty-one adult systems (fifty states and

1967	1974	1989	1997
In re: Gault, court case that revolutionized juvenile court and assured juveniles of constitutional protection.	Office of Juvenile Justice and Delinquency Prevention formed as provision of legislation.	In *Thompson v. Oklahoma,* Supreme Court ruled that it is unconstitutional to execute a 15-year-old. In *Stanford v. Kentucky,* Supreme Court ruled that it is constitutional to execute those who were 16 and 17 years old when they committed a capital offense.	Violent and Repeat Juvenile Offenders Act passed. This act made it easier to waive juveniles to adult court and cut many prevention programs.

one federal system) and each of these is divided into several informal layers. The juvenile justice system is much like the adult systems around the nation, and we can state with some certainty that there are at least fifty-one systems, but probably more because in states where the county is responsible for juvenile justice as an arm of a court of general jurisdiction, the juvenile judge, magistrate, or referee may manage his or her juvenile court autonomously with only minimal oversight by the local court of general jurisdiction or by the state.

In our juvenile justice model, there are four layers (Figure 1.3) made up of: the top layer—celebrated cases, the second and third layers—felonies, and the fourth layer—misdemeanors and status offenses.

The Top Layer—Celebrated Cases

These are the cases that usually make the papers and television. In 1995, a fourteen-year-old girl was murdered in Chicago by a boy eventually identified as "Yummy" Sandifer, age eleven years. If Yummy had been brought to trial the nation would have been riveted by the attention given to him, and the court proceedings would have informed us about how the juvenile court works and fails to work. Unfortunately, Yummy was murdered by his gang because the murder of the fourteen-year-old girl had brought on too much negative publicity. Gerald Gault is another example of a celebrated case. Gerald was arrested for making an obscene phone call and ultimately placed in the custody of the state training school for a period of time not to exceed his majority, twenty-one years of age. Thus, he received a sentence of six years for an offense if committed by an adult would have resulted in a short jail sentence and/or a fine. The U.S. Supreme Court ultimately overturned the conviction, and Gerald Gault lives on in criminal justice text books as a celebrity.

These cases are the type of drama that the media lives for. Into our living rooms come a steady parade of actors, and we are moved by the drama. The court process assures us that the defendants' constitutional rights are carefully guarded, and however indignant we might be over the offense, we learn quite a bit about evidence, investigations, admissibility of evidence, witnesses, cross examination, redress, briefs and so on.

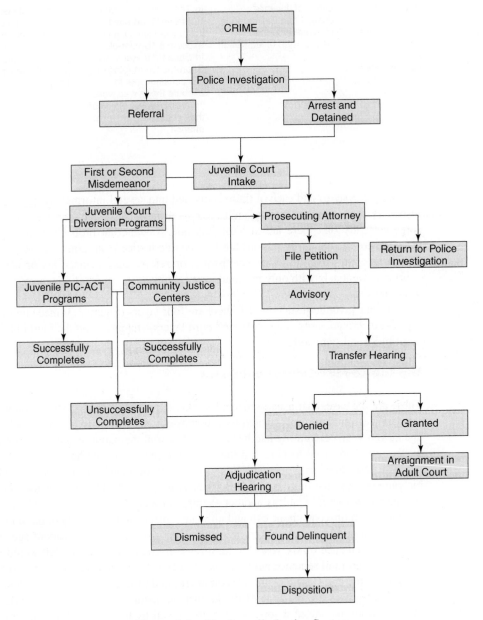

Figure 1.2   The Juvenile Justice System

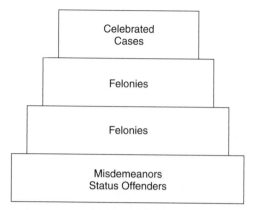

Figure 1.3   Wedding Cake Model of Juvenile Justice
Adapted from Samuel Walker. *Sense and Nonsense About Crime and Drugs:
A Policy Guide,* 3rd ed. Belmont, CA: Wadsworth Publishing Company, 1994.

Somehow after seeing or reading of the proceedings, we are reassured that we are safer and that the system somehow works.

The above cases, and others like them, are different from the majority of cases that come before the juvenile court. They sometimes involve famous or well-known children, or terrible crimes, or critical constitutional issues. But they are different in another way: They involve the full court process and today often involve waiver to adult court. Second, celebrated cases receive a lot of publicity and, as a consequence, heavily shape our perception of the juvenile court process.

The Second and Third Layers—Felonies

According to Walker, prosecutors routinely classify adult cases on the basis of three factors:

1. The seriousness of the crime.
2. The prior record of the suspect.
3. The relationship between the suspect and the offender.

In actuality, the prosecutor must ask, "How much is this case worth?" Prosecutors and the police classify cases into those that are "heavy" and "lightweight" by looking at such factors as seriousness of the offense, use of a weapon, prior record of the defendant, injuries incurred by the victim, and whether or not the defendant and victim were strangers.

The juvenile court is different from adult court. In contrast to the adult court, the philosophy of the juvenile court is one of benevolence, and the welfare of the child is of primary concern. Treatment and compassion are watchwords for prosecutor and judge alike. In spite of conventional wisdom, the juvenile court is tough on crime and very few of those who have violated the law get off without proper attention by the court. The problem is that the juvenile court does not have proper resources to deal effectively with nearly overwhelming caseloads. In actuality, juveniles who fit the top layer of Walker's Wedding Cake Model usually get sentences to the state reform school, or are waived to adult court, followed by supervision, called aftercare. Again, the problem boils down to one of too few resources available to serve the community and the child.

The third layer in the adult Wedding Cake Model is entirely different from layers one and two, according to Walker. Less serious cases committed by adults are routinely dismissed, offenders are allowed to plead guilty to less serious offenses, and if convicted, they are often placed on probation. However, for juveniles, those found guilty or who have pled guilty to offenses falling in this layer such as burglary and other relatively minor felonies, are most often given probation and assigned to a probation officer. The probation officer is responsible for supervision of the child and usually attempts to work with the family and devise a plan that attempts to keep the child out of trouble and prepares him or her to behave responsibly in school and at home.

The Fourth Layer—Misdemeanors

In the adult Wedding Cake Model, misdemeanants make up the fourth layer. The adult courts are overwhelmed by the numbers of misdemeanants, and justice is more or less a treadmill where due process takes a back seat to expediency. In the juvenile court, the fourth layer is composed of status offenders. This is a category that has no corresponding category for adults. A status offender is one who has committed an offense that if committed by an adult would not be an offense. Such transgressions as running away, incorrigibility, truancy, drinking underage, and promiscuity are offenses faced every day by juvenile court workers and are perhaps the most difficult with which to work.

The 1974 Juvenile Justice Act prohibits the secure detention of status offenders, and this makes sense, but it makes life more complicated for juvenile workers in that they must exercise creativity, and the community must be patient. For example, without being able to hold the many runaways in secure detention, it is often difficult to work with children who run away from the very people who are trying to help them.

CRIME AND DELINQUENCY

Before considering crimes committed by juveniles, it is instructive to look at the total crime picture. Index crimes, that is the crimes the F.B.I. considers the most serious—criminal homicide, forcible rape, robbery, aggravated assault, burglary, larceny/theft, motor vehicle theft, and arson—make up only about 20 percent of all offenses. In 1999, according to the F.B.I. (2001), there were 9,136,294 arrests (this is for 8,546 agencies reporting on a population of an estimated 171,831,000), out of which a little over 2 million were for the serious crimes just mentioned. The remainder (a little over 7 million crimes) were for what are called Part II Crimes, that means the lower courts handled a little over 7 million suspects. Regardless of whether or not the case went to trial, the individual had to be arraigned and the prosecutor and his or her staff needed to determine whether or not sufficient evidence was available for prosecution.

The volume of crimes coming before the misdemeanor courts demands that no one get too excited about due process and at least one study shows that most defendants did not have a jury trial and at least half did not have an attorney (Feeley, 1979). One feels that most defendants are just glad to get the process over with. That is just the point according to Feeley—the process is the punishment.

HOW MUCH DELINQUENCY

We should still be troubled by the number of arrests of young people under the age of eighteen, even though there has been a steady decline in arrests. In the period 1988 to 2000, the arrests of youth under the age of eighteen decreased 7.6 percent, that is, from 1,634,790 arrests in 1988 to 1,255,623 arrests in 2000. During the same period, total arrests declined nearly 30 percent (Pastore & Maguire, 2002), Table 1.2 illustrates the numbers, by offense, of juveniles arrested in 1988 and 2000.

We can see from Table 1.2 that arrests for all categories in Part I offenses except aggravated assault and arson are down from 1990, but where do these statistics come from? Crime statistics are notoriously unreliable, and it is necessary to briefly discuss how crime statistics are gathered. Generally speaking, crime statistics are obtained in three ways. The first is the Federal Bureau of Investigation's Uniform Crime Report (UCR). This report is the compilation of statistics from nearly all police agencies in the United States and represents about 98 percent of the U.S. population.

The second set of data is the **National Crime Victimization Survey (NCVS)** and is gathered by the Bureau of Census. It reports only victimizations, many of which are not reported to the police, in contrast to the Uniform Crime Report, which is reported crime. The third way is through self-report studies, usually conducted by college professors for one reason or another.

Abadinsky and Winfree report that all three ways of gathering statistics have problems. The Uniform Crime Report (UCR) collects only reported crime. That is, crimes unknown to the police are not entered into the total. The UCR is also subject to political manipulation. For example, if a mayor is running for reelection, he or she may not allow the chief of police to enter some of the known crimes for fear it may affect his or her chance for reelection. There are also some problems with recording practices. Let us say a man has been beaten, robbed, and his car stolen. The Hierarchy Rule requires that the offenses be classified and the most serious be recorded and the rest ignored. This rule applies to all offenses except arson. Still there are strengths, such as the data are easy to get at. In fact, we have nationwide data that covers approximately 98 percent of the population, and we can compare statistics over time because the statistics have been collected since 1930.

The National Crime Victimization Survey (NCVS) began in 1973 under the auspices of the Law Enforcement Assistance Administration. The survey is now conducted by the Bureau of Census and collects limited information from 59,000 households across

Table 1.2   Juvenile Arrests by Offense, 1988 and 2000

	1988		2000	
Offense Charged	Total All Ages	Ages Under 18	Total All Ages	Ages Under Age 18
Total	10,149,896	1,634,790	7,412,294	1,255,623
Murder and Nonnegligent Manslaughter	16,326	1,765	7,012	641
Forcible Rape	28,482	4,118	14,538	2,364
Robbery	111,344	24,337	60,812	15,310
Aggravated Assault	304,490	38,536	265,385	35,307
Burglary	331,758	111,284	157,665	52,157
Larceny-Theft	1,162,752	351,133	641,370	202,933
Motor Vehicle Theft	153,016	61,301	77,070	25,099
Arson	14,505	6,216	8,824	4,712
Other Assaults	687,928	97,634	676,319	120,488
Forgery and Counterfeiting	73,465	6,125	58,493	3,500
Fraud	260,848	12,135	155,321	4,755
Embezzlement	11,699	949	10,730	1,090
Stolen Property: Buy, Receiving/Selling	125,092	31,435	66,772	15,641
Vandalism	225,544	90,027	150,132	60,951
Weapons: Carry/Possession	163,480	26,986	86,620	20,133
Prostitution and Commercialized Vice	78,731	1,432	47,481	727
Sex Offenses/not Rape or Prostitution	78,239	12,585	51,643	9,707
Drug Abuse Violations	850,034	76,986	842,532	105,993
Liquor Laws	492,385	124,024	431,047	81,223
Drunkenness	606,053	17,886	358,041	12,151
Disorderly Conduct	573,580	25,738	295,597	77,396
Curfew and Loitering	55,327	55,327	91,453	91,453
Runaways	124,709	124,709	81,440	81,440

Source: U.S. Department of Justice. Federal Bureau of Investigation. *Crime in the United States, 1988 and 2000:* Uniform Crime Reports. Washington, D.C.

the nation. These households are constantly replaced after being surveyed every six months for three years. According to Abadinsky and Winfree, "In a normal year Census Bureau workers conduct two interviews each with 100,000 people aged twelve and older." There are some strengths associated with the NCVS such as it allows for comparisons with the UCR, the NCVS is not subject to political manipulation, and because of the questions and approach we can examine the psychosocial effects of victimization of crime, and finally a lot of information is gathered about a limited number of crimes. There are also weaknesses. For example, the survey only questions persons aged twelve years and older, crime against tourists and the homeless are not considered, and it is costly.

Self-report studies are the third way of gathering crime statistics. Usually they are in the form of anonymous surveys and confidential interviews. The shortcomings include the fact that respondents may tend to minimize criminal involvement and self-report studies have been applied to a limited population. Nevertheless, self-report studies do give criminologists a look at crime in a specific group and allows them to draw some conclusions.

In the world of journalism, self-report studies seldom are mentioned. Usually the Uniform Crime Report is most often cited as the authoritative source of crime statistics. However, the public is given a limited amount of information about crime because only the UCR is cited. On the other hand, data from the NCVS may be used if the reporter or person writing the story or report has a vested interest in playing down certain aspects of crime.

Still, even if the data is flawed to an extent, the decline in juvenile crime should not yet be celebrated. As pointed out earlier, the nation is not descending into a state of chaos, and our youth are not, in general, any worse than previous generations. Close examination of the arrests for youth reveals that 70 percent of all arrests for youth seventeen years of age and younger occurs in only eighteen states of which all (except for North Carolina and Indiana) are characterized by large urban populations. Leading the list are California and Texas; therefore, thirty-one states share the remaining 23.8 percent of all juvenile arrests. Table 1.3 depicts reported arrests of juveniles.

While delinquency occurs in all areas of the nation and in all social strata, it appears that some areas of our nation are more troubled than others. Clearly, we must not believe the sensationalized stories we read and hear in the media as representative of our nation's youth. From 1988 to 2000, arrests of juveniles declined considerably, according to the F.B.I. If we factor in the growth of the juvenile population, the fear of a juvenile crime wave is even more remote. According to the U.S. Census, the U.S. five to nineteen age group population grew from 45,299,989 in 1990 to 61,297,467 in 2000 (U.S. Census, 2000). Thus, any decrease in juvenile crime during the 1990s is remarkable in light of the numbers of youth in that age group. In addition, the high delinquency-prone years of fifteen to nineteen is represented by a little over 20 million youth, illustrating further that delinquency is the product of far fewer youth in our population than we are sometimes led to believe.

It seems clear enough that the "juvenile crime problem" is not evenly distributed across the nation. The juvenile crime that does exist should concern all citizens and policy makers, especially in the nineteen states that are responsible for three-quarters of all juvenile crime. How much juvenile crime is there in the United States? What is the juvenile

Table 1.3   Reported Arrests of Juveniles in 2001

National Total = 1,685,675 Reported Arrests*

Alpha Order				Rank Order			
Rank	State	Arrests	% of US	Rank	State	Arrests	% of US
33	Alabama	11,324	0.7%	1	California	239,109	14.2%
47	Alaska	4,726	0.3%	2	Texas	180,231	10.7%
7	Arizona	51,894	3.1%	3	Florida	127,179	7.5%
32	Arkansas	11,684	0.7%	4	Pennsylvania	95,281	5.7%
1	California	239,109	14.2%	5	New Jersey	62,339	3.7%
9	Colorado	46,389	2.8%	6	Ohio	53,807	3.2%
26	Connecticut	22,489	1.3%	7	Arizona	51,894	3.1%
41	Delaware	6,647	0.4%	8	North Carolina	50,266	3.0%
3	Florida	127,179	7.5%	9	Colorado	46,389	2.8%
21	Georgia	26,896	1.6%	10	Michigan	44,809	2.7%
35	Hawaii	10,196	0.6%	11	New York	43,460	2.6%
29	Idaho	16,598	1.0%	12	Washington	42,301	2.5%
13	Illinois	41,110	2.4%	13	Illinois	41,110	2.4%
18	Indiana	34,493	2.0%	14	Missouri	38,445	2.3%
31	Iowa	13,122	0.8%	15	Louisiana	37,382	2.2%
NA	Kansas**	NA	NA	16	Maryland	37,352	2.2%
45	Kentucky	5,493	0.3%	17	Minnesota	35,109	2.1%
15	Louisiana	37,382	2.2%	18	Indiana	34,493	2.0%
36	Maine	9,892	0.6%	19	Oregon	32,044	1.9%
16	Maryland	37,352	2.2%	20	Virginia	28,813	1.7%
28	Massachusetts	19,765	1.2%	21	Georgia	26,896	1.6%
10	Michigan	44,809	2.7%	22	Tennessee	26,061	1.5%
17	Minnesota	35,109	2.1%	23	Wisconsin	25,653	1.5%
34	Mississippi	10,946	0.6%	24	Nevada	25,249	1.5%
14	Missouri	38,445	2.3%	25	Oklahoma	22,632	1.3%
46	Montana	5,338	0.3%	26	Connecticut	22,489	1.3%
30	Nebraska	14,373	0.9%	27	Utah	21,803	1.3%
24	Nevada	25,249	1.5%	28	Massachusetts	19,765	1.2%
43	New Hampshire	6,416	0.4%	29	Idaho	16,598	1.0%
5	New Jersey	62,339	3.7%	30	Nebraska	14,373	0.9%
38	New Mexico	7,688	0.5%	31	Iowa	13,122	0.8%
11	New York	43,460	2.6%	32	Arkansas	11,684	0.7%
8	North Carolina	50,266	3.0%	33	Alabama	11,324	0.7%
39	North Dakota	7,478	0.4%	34	Mississippi	10,946	0.6%
6	Ohio	53,807	3.2%	35	Hawaii	10,196	0.6%
25	Oklahoma	22,632	1.3%	36	Maine	9,892	0.6%
19	Oregon	32,044	1.9%	37	South Carolina	8,689	0.5%

(continued)

Table 1.3   Continued

National Total = 1,685,675 Reported Arrests*

Alpha Order				Rank Order			
Rank	State	Arrests	% of US	Rank	State	Arrests	% of US
4	Pennsylvania	95,281	5.7%	38	New Mexico	7,688	0.5%
42	Rhode Island	6,511	0.4%	39	North Dakota	7,478	0.4%
37	South Carolina	8,689	0.5%	40	Wyoming	7,254	0.4%
44	South Dakota	5,924	0.4%	41	Delaware	6,647	0.4%
22	Tennessee	26,061	1.5%	42	Rhode Island	6,511	0.4%
2	Texas	180,231	10.7%	43	New Hampshire	6,416	0.4%
27	Utah	21,803	1.3%	44	South Dakota	5,924	0.4%
48	Vermont	1,773	0.1%	45	Kentucky	5,493	0.3%
20	Virginia	28,813	1.7%	46	Montana	5,338	0.3%
12	Washington	42,301	2.5%	47	Alaska	4,726	0.3%
49	West Virginia	1,242	0.1%	48	Vermont	1,773	0.1%
23	Wisconsin	25,653	1.5%	49	West Virginia	1,242	0.1%
40	Wyoming	7,254	0.4%	NA	Kansas**	NA	NA
					District of Columbia**	NA	NA

*Arrests of youths 17 years and younger by law enforcement agencies submitting complete reports to the F.B.I. for 12 months in 2001. See important note at beginning of this chapter.
** Not available.
Source: Federal Bureau of Investigation "Crime in the United States 2001" (Uniform Crime Reports, October 28, 2002)

justice system, and how does it work? What are the true costs of juvenile crime? These are important questions to the average American, and they deserve answers. This text attempts to answer those questions in light of the American experience and perhaps we can arrive at solutions that will serve the taxpayer and young people caught up in the juvenile justice system.

SUMMARY

Juvenile crime is a social problem of which we must all be concerned. However, it is not as great a problem as we are led to believe, but we must plan for the future, especially a future that accounts for a growing number of violent and increasingly pathological youth. The media, to a large extent is responsible for the crisis mentality that now exists in regard to juvenile crime. Clearly, overall juvenile crime is down, but crimes of violence are up and our youth, especially young African-American youth, are killing and maiming each other at alarming rates.

Part of our problem in determining how much juvenile crime exists lies in our desire for figures, and we look to the UCR and the NCVS. According to Biderman and Lynch:

> When the comparisons between the two series were confined to those components of each that can be identified as dealing with a common universe of events, when the same units were used for crime counts and when rates for the two series were calculated on an equivalent population base, the two indicators displayed the same directional changes . . . NCS-UCR differences in the magnitudes of rate changes and the general levels of crime also were greatly reduced. The trends for the two series converged rather than diverged over the period studied.

Juvenile crime may be down, but the real question is how much and for how long? Biderman and Lynch lead us to believe that the answer to a true crime figure lies somewhere between the two indicators.

STUDY QUESTIONS

1. How do science and journalism differ? Is the difference important when we talk about crime?
2. Why do you think urbanization and industrialization were important to the development of the juvenile court?
3. What are the three sources of crime statistics?
4. From 1988 to 1994 is juvenile crime up, down, or about the same?

BIBLIOGRAPHY

ABADINSKY, HOWARD, AND WINFREE, JR., L. THOMAS. (1992). *Crime and Justice: An Introduction,* 2nd ed. Chicago: Nelson-Hall, Inc.

VON BERTALANFFY, LUDWIG. (January 1950). "The Theory of Open Systems in Physics and Biology," *Science 111,* 23–29.

BIDERMAN, A.D., AND LYNCH, J.P. (1991). *Understanding Crime Incidence Statistics: Why the UCR Diverges From the NCS.* New York: Springer-Verlag New York, Inc.

BUREAU OF JUSTICE STATISTICS. (1992). *Criminal Victimization in the United States: 1973–90 Trends.* USDOJ. Washington, D.C.: USGPO.

BUREAU OF JUSTICE STATISTICS. (May 1995). *Criminal Victimization 1993.* U.S. Department of Justice. Washington, D.C.: USGPO.

BUREAU OF JUSTICE STATISTICS. (October 30, 1994). *Questions and Answers about the Redesign.* U.S. Department of Justice. Washington, D.C.: USGPO.

BUREAU OF JUSTICE STATISTICS. (October 30, 1994). *Technical Background on the Re-designed National Crime Victimization Survey.* Washington, D.C.: USGPO.

FEDERAL BUREAU OF INVESTIGATION. (2001). *Crime in the United States—2000.* Washington, D.C.: U.S. Department of Justice.

FEELEY, MALCOLM. (1979). *The Process Is the Punishment.* New York: Russell Sage Foundation.

FOX, JAMES ALAN, AND PIERCE, GLENN. (1995). "American Killers are Getting Younger," from *USA Today Magazine,* January, 1994, pp. 24–26, in *Criminal Justice 95/96,* 19th ed. John J. Sullivan and Joseph L. Victor. Guilford, CT: Duchkin Publishing Group.

KAPPELER, VICTOR E., BLUMBERG, MARK, AND POTTER, GARY W. (1996). *The Mythology of Crime and Criminal Justice,* 2nd ed. Prospect Heights, IL: Waveland Press.

KAST, FREMONT E., AND ROSENZWEIG, JAMES E. (1979). *Organization and Management,* 3rd ed. New York: McGraw-Hill.

MAGUIRE, KATHLEEN, AND PASTORE, ANN L., Eds. (1994). *Sourcebook of Criminal Justice Statistics 1993.* U.S. Department of Justice, Bureau of Justice Statistics. Washington, D.C.: USGPO.

PASTORE, ANN, AND MAGUIRE, KATHLEEN, Eds. (2002). *Sourcebook of Criminal Justice Statistics 2001.* U.S. Department of Justice, Bureau of Justice Statistics. Washington, D.C.: USGPO.

REGOLI, ROBERT M., AND HEWITT, JOHN D. (1994). *Delinquency and Society: A Child-Centered Approach,* 2nd ed. New York: McGraw-Hill, Inc.

THORNTON, JR., WILLIAM E., AND VOIGT, LYDIA. (1992). *Delinquency and Justice,* 3rd ed. New York: McGraw-Hill, Inc.

U.S. BUREAU OF COMMERCE, BUREAU OF CENSUS. (1999). *Statistical Abstract of the United States.* Washington, D.C.: Government Printing Office.

U.S. DEPARTMENT OF JUSTICE. Federal Bureau of Investigation. *Crime in the United States,* 1988 and 1992: Uniform Crime Reports. Washington, D.C.

WALKER, SAMUEL. (1994). *Sense and Nonsense about Crime and Drugs: A Policy Guide,* 3rd ed. Belmont, CA: Wadsworth Publishing Company.

WILSON, JAMES Q. (1985). *Thinking About Crime* (Rev ed.). New York: Vintage Books.

GLOSSARY OF KEY TERMS

Closed system.   A system that does not interact with the external environment.

Criminal offenses.   Those acts that if committed by an adult would be considered criminal.

Delinquency.   Behavior by a person between the ages of seven and eighteen who has violated the criminal code.

House of Refuge.   An institution of punishment and harshness for delinquent youth and in spite of the intentions of the reformers responsible for the concept, they soon degenerated into places where older, more sophisticated youth would exploit and abuse younger children along with the staff, who viewed the children incarcerated in them as deserving of their lot.

Illinois Juvenile Court Act.   An act passed by the Illinois legislature in 1899 to established a separate court for delinquent youth in order to remove them from the harsh adversarial nature of adult courts.

Juvenile justice system.   A loose confederation of agencies, both public and private, that work with delinquent and at-risk youth.

National Crime Victimization Survey (NCVS).   A random survey of 60,000 households in the United States every six months on victimization of the respondent. Another way to gather crime statistics.

Open system.   A system that relies on input from the external environment.

Parens patriae.   The state is to assume the role of parent and the responsibility for the care and development of children.

Probation.   A sentence for youth with the goal of rehabilitation and counseling.

Self-report studies.   Studies of groups of people asking them if they have committed criminal acts.

Status offense.   This category of behavior has no corresponding category for adults. A status offender is one who has committed an offense that if committed by an adult would not be an offense.

Uniform Crime Report (UCR).   A compilation of statistics from nearly all police agencies in the United States, which represents about 98 percent of the U.S. population. Reports only known crime.

Wedding Cake Model.   A illustration of how the criminal justice system works conceived by Samuel Walker.

CHAPTER 2
THEORETICAL EXPLANATIONS OF DELINQUENCY

KEY TERMS

Utilitarianism
Classical school of
  thought
Hedonistic calculus
Positivist school of
  thought
Medical model
Stigmata
Somatyping
Endomorphs
Mesomorphs
Ectomorphs
XYY chromosomal
  pattern
Psychological
  explanations

Id
Ego
Superego
Sociological explanation
Anomie
Conformity
Innovation
Ritualism
Retreatism
Rebellion
Labeling
Primary deviance
Self-fulfilling prophecy
Secondary deviance
Social control theory
Attachment

Commitment
Involvement
Belief
Differential association
Developmental
  perspective
Pathways
Chronic offender
Overt pathways
Covert pathways
Authority conflict
  pathways
Persisters
Experimenters

CASE STUDY

Delaware County, Ohio Juvenile Sex Offender Program
Coco J. Kneisly*

In 1993, the Delaware County Juvenile Court realized that they had a problem with the numbers of sex offenders committed to the Ohio Department of Youth Services (ODYS). Further, they questioned the value of treatment offered youth committed to the ODYS. As a result, in 1994 an intensive probation counselor was hired and trained to specifically work with juvenile sex offenders. The court and local mental health center collaborated in establishing a local juvenile sex offender treatment group. A multidisciplinary team was formed with members from the court, the local mental health center, and child protective agency in order to collaborate in creating protocols for assessment, treatment, and supervision of juvenile sex offenders. The program included a continuum of services designed to facilitate behavior change by focusing on the factors underlying the youth sex offending.

In March, 1995, a probation counselor—specializing in the treatment and management of juvenile sex offenders—and a specially trained clinician from the local mental health center began a community-based sex offender treatment group for adolescents adjudicated delinquent for sexual offenses. The group was developed with the premise that the majority of adolescent sex offenders could be more successfully treated in the community, while at the same time maintaining community safety. This approach allowed for greater family participation—a key component necessary for positive outcomes. In its first year, the treatment group served four adolescent males. The sex offender program, as a whole, provided supervision, treatment, and case management services to fourteen youth referred for sexual acting-out behaviors. None of the offenders were incarcerated, indicating that this high-risk population could indeed be treated and maintained successfully in the *community*.

The court has adopted a unique approach to dealing with sexual offenders in the community. Trained paraprofessionals provide one-to-one supervision of juvenile sex offenders in their homes, at school, or in their neighborhood. They shadow the offender daily, helping to identify high-risk situations and reinforcing the "messages" received during treatment. They help youth apply treatment "lessons" to daily situations. Staff also model appropriate interventions to parents of offenders in the family's natural environment. This helps strengthen the family's ability to safely maintain the offender within the community—and ultimately reduces the need for intervention by other child-serving systems.

Treatment foster homes are also used to assist in the treatment of juvenile sex offenders who would have unsupervised and dangerous access to victims if left in their own homes or neighborhoods. Treatment foster care maintains youth in their home community while substantially decreasing risk. This allows offenders to be maintained in a family en-

---

*Coco J. Kneisly graduated from Colombus State Community College and is in the process of completing her bachelor's degree in Criminal Justice Administration. She has been employed by the Delaware County (Ohio) Juvenile Court since 1995.

vironment while receiving treatment. According to the Center for Sex Offender Management, "one year of intensive supervision and treatment in the community can range in cost between $5,000 and $15,000 per offender; depending on treatment modality. The average cost for incarcerating an offender is significantly higher, approximately $22,000 per year, *excluding* treatment costs."[1] The Delaware County Juvenile Court's juvenile sex offender program has been funded through the Court's general operating funds (county and state subsidy dollars) and more recently through a Byrne Memorial Grant through the Ohio Office of Criminal Justice Services (OCJS).

The sex offender treatment group is based on a cognitive behavioral model. The treatment focuses on significantly altering an offender's thinking, problem-solving strategies, and coping mechanisms in order to substantially change behavior. The group meets as an education group once a week to focus on topics such as offense cycles, sex education, healthy relationship and anger management. It meets again later in the week for a "process" group that includes parents and significant support people. At this session offender dynamics are discussed within the context of the family. Parent education is seen as essential for the sustained progress of the offenders.

The juvenile sex offender program goals include:

- Breaking through denial and minimization by offenders and their families.
- Substantially altering how offenders approach relationships to reflect honesty and equality instead of coercion and exploitation.
- Identifying and expressing feelings.
- Identifying cognitive distortions or irrational thinking which support and trigger offending.
- Developing relapse prevention strategies.
- Having the offender accept responsibility without minimizing or external blaming.
- Identifying a pattern or cycle of abusive behavior.
- Interrupting the cycle before abusive behavior occurs.
- Having the offender understand the consequences of their offending behavior to self, family, and victims; and
- Dealing with any sexual abuse the offender may have suffered.

Prior to successfully completing the program, the youth will have made a full written and verbal apology (if appropriate) to his or her victim, taken full responsibility for the abusive behaviors, developed a plan to prevent relapse, and increased his or her internal and external supports to assist in maintaining a nonoffending lifestyle.

After successfully completing the juvenile sex offender program, the youth is placed in an aftercare program for six months for monitoring and support. Youth discuss risks, challenges, and/or changes that need to occur to maintain their relapse prevention plan. During this period, the youth remains on probation but on a nonreporting status

---

[1]Center for Sex Offender Management, "Myths and Facts About Sex Offenders," available on CSOM website (www.csom.org/pubs/mythsfacts.html).

involving limited court contact. Once aftercare is completed, a youth is successfully terminated from probation, and all restrictions are lifted.

Comprehensive research on juvenile sex offender recidivism rates is particularly lacking. However, a recent publication released by the Office of Juvenile Justice and Delinquency Prevention (OJJDP) entitled *Juveniles Who Have Sexually Offended*, indicates that the recidivism rates range between 8 and 14 percent, with one study showing a 37 percent recidivism rate.[2] The Center for Sex Offender Management reports that recidivism rates for juveniles responding well to cognitive-behavioral and/or relapse prevention treatment falls to as low as 7 percent.[3] Since 1995, the Delaware County Juvenile Court's juvenile sex offender program has served seventy juvenile sex-offenders with only three (4 percent) committing a new offense.

The Court has found that the community—including law enforcement, schools, employers, and church members—has been receptive and supportive of the juvenile sex offender programming efforts. Community education appears to be the key. When proactively informed about the program's treatment goals, commitment to keeping kids at home and within the community, and low recidivism rates, community members have shown great interest in being part of a juvenile sex offender's safety and support team. The reality is that juvenile sex offenders are part of our community, and the best way to ensure community safety is through changing the offender and reducing their risk—tasks that have been proven to be accomplished more effectively through community-based programs.

[2]Office of Justice Programs, "Juveniles Who Have Sexually Offended," U.S. Department of Justice, Washington, D.C.

[3]Center for Sex Offender Management, "Recidivism of Sex Offenders," available on CSOM website (www.csom.org/pubs/recidsexof.html).

INTRODUCTION

No other question is as troubling to normal, law-abiding citizens than the question of "Why do they do it?" The answers are many and varied. Before beginning a discussion of why people commit crimes, we need to acknowledge that in America a certain amount of crime, particularly violent crime, will unfortunately always be with us. These crimes include larceny, theft, fights, battering, and murders between people who are normally law-abiding. We cannot logically account for a spouse who suddenly murders the lover of his or her wife or husband. We cannot logically account for the desperate attempt of a businessman to save a business on the verge of bankruptcy through cheating or larceny. Nor can we adequately explain why a youth from an outwardly "normal" and law-abiding home becomes involved in delinquent activity. These kinds of criminal acts are a part of the human condition. Even the most reasonable of us are sometimes unable to keep a lid on our emotions or despair, but we seldom fall into criminal or delinquent behavior.

Both a certain amount and type of crime can be explained using scientific research. Intuitively some of the answers are known. Usually when crime is discussed most people have an opinion; however, typically this opinion is not formed by what is known on the subject. This is illustrated by the present approach to crime control used by the U.S. Congress and various state legislatures. Most crime control efforts and legislation assumes the value of punishment and also presumes that every criminal undergoes a form of mental calculus, informed choice, before committing a crime. That is, he or she will weigh the benefits of the crime versus the penalty and proceed if the calculated value of the pleasure derived is greater than the pain of being caught.

Following this line of reasoning for example, if a youth has a fight with another youth and wants to kill the other, he or she will calculate the value of benefits derived against the probability of getting caught and convicted of the crime. If the individual calculates that the probability of getting caught is too high, then he or she has been deterred from committing the offense. Under most current crime legislation, that line of reasoning is also followed for both property and violent crimes.

However, human beings are not that easy to predict. Research suggests that behavior can be predicted with some certainty based upon past behavior, but to say crime and delinquency can be prevented or deterred by simply making the penalties extremely severe is wishful thinking. This chapter leads the reader through a discussion of the two theoretical schools of thought (classical and positivist) and some of the more recent and enduring research and thinking on why youth and adults commit crimes.

No excuses are made for criminal behavior. What we do know, however, is that a close-knit family is the key to successful childrearing and that it takes more than one person to do an adequate job (Wilson & Herrnstein, 1985). If that job is done well, there is a high probability, not a guarantee, the child will grow up to be a responsible adult.

Crimes of passion aside, we can divide the various theories of criminal behavior found under the positivist school of thought into roughly three categories: biological, psychological, and sociological. These categories are presented simply as a tool for discussion. There is a good deal of overlap between the three, particularly between the psychological and sociological dimensions. Today most research by criminologists is within the sociological dimension and as a consequence most criminological theory is sociological criminology. The following is an incomplete, but illustrative review of explanations of delinquency and is included as a foundation for later chapters that attempt to shed light on managerial effectiveness and programs.

SCHOOLS OF THOUGHT

Before the development of scientific criminology, explanations of crime were found in religious principles and "concepts like sin, demonology, innate depravity, and **utilitarianism** (the idea that people calculated the relative likelihood of pleasure and pain in deciding how to act)" (Chambliss, 1988, p. 153). As Tennenbaum (1938) points out there was often a conflict between absolute good and absolute evil. Those who committed crimes were viewed as evil (Lilly, Cullen, & Ball, 2002, p. 11). Therefore, it was the responsibility of the community to ward off the evil spirits by punishing the evildoers.

Early Schools of Criminology

	Classical	Positivist
1. Central concern of model's founders	reform of criminal justice system	scientific study of criminal
2. View of humans	free-will; utilitarian	deterministic; biological, psychological, sociological
3. Responsibility for actions	yes	no
4. Way to stop crime	insure that the costs of crime outweigh the benefits	eliminate factors causing crime
5. Focus of social control	• the law: make penalties severe enough to outweigh the benefits of crime	the criminal and his/her condition: criminals are fundamentally different from the rest of us
	• no judicial discretion; to insure that costs outweigh the benefits, punishment must be certain for everyone; punishment fits the crime	• judicial discretion; since each criminal and his/her condition may be different, the judge needs the leeway to fit the penalty to the needs of the individual criminal
	• punishments fixed by law (implies the use of determinate sentences)	• indeterminate sentences
6. Purpose of social control	deterrence—if criminal is shown that the costs of crime outweigh the benefits (that "crime doesn't pay") then the person will not commit any more offenses; punishment of offender can also serve to deter public from crime	rehabilitate the criminal

Adapted from: Francis T. Cullen and Karen E. Gilbert (1982). *Reaffirming Rehabilitation*. Cincinnati, OH: Anderson Publishing, p. 35.

Responses to unacceptable behavior were often extreme and relied heavily on the use of physical punishments such as torture and death. Religious explanations of crime dominated the thinking until the eighteenth century. It was during this time period that thinkers such as Cesare Beccaria and Jeremy Bentham began to challenge the extreme forms of punishment. These teachings began the creation of what is known today as the **classical** school of thought. The classical school of thinking dominated criminological understanding of crime and delinquency until the early nineteenth century. It was during this time period that philosophers and scientists began to look for multiple factors to explain the existence of crime. This school of thought known as the positivist school sought to understand and explain the human condition as malleable. Each of these schools of thought has contributed to our understanding of and response to juvenile behavior and will be briefly discussed below.

Classical School

Classical school doctrine is based on the assumption that all criminals are motivated by the pleasure/pain principle and capable of free will. As free-will thinkers, individuals have the ability to calculate the benefits of their behavior versus the costs (likelihood of punishment). Therefore, if the offender is assumed to be a rational thinker who understands the cost and benefits of his or her behavior, the punishments should be based on the severity of the crime rather than the culpability of the offender. Classical criminology focuses on the offense rather than the motivation of the offender.

Mired in the works of Cesare Beccaria and Jeremy Bentham, whose philosophies were influenced by the social contract, that is individuals agree to forfeit some of their individual liberties to live in an orderly society, Beccaria argued individuals are inherently self-serving. Although individuals are self-serving and in need of punishment if they committed a crime they are also in need of legal protections from their government. He further believed that laws and punishments should be written in advance so members of society could have a better understanding of both the consequences and benefits of their actions. Further, Beccaria was more concerned about preventing future criminal activity and less concerned about reforming the individual offender (Lilly, Cullen, & Ball, 2002; Vold & Bernard, 1986).

Like Beccaria, Jeremy Bentham also argued that punishment should function to prevent crime or act as a deterrent and that behavior was a function of the principles of **hedonistic calculus**. The idea behind these principles is that the government must determine how much pain should be inflicted on the individual offender to prevent him or her from committing these acts in the future and to deter others from committing these acts. They established what we today know as the deterrence theory, which states that in order for punishment to be effective it must be administered swiftly, severely, and certainly (Lilly, Cullen, & Ball, 2002, p. 15; Chambliss, 1988, pp. 153–154).

Again these premises of the classical school can be seen in today's society. Our need to hold the offender, including juvenile offenders, accountable for their individual acts in addition to increasing the severity of sanctions points to the relative lack of concern for causes of crime and more concern towards the need to get tough.

Positivist School

The creation of the **positivist school of thought** is typically attributed to the creation and use of scientific methods. The biggest difference between the classical and positivist schools is that the positivist school looks for multiple factors to explain the existence of

---

Beccaria's Eleven Tenets

1. To escape war and chaos, individuals gave up some of their liberty and established a contractual society. This established the sovereignty of a nation and the ability of the nation to create criminal law and punish offenders.

2. Because criminal laws placed restrictions on individual freedoms, they should be restricted in scope. They should not be employed to enforce moral virtue. To prohibit human behavior unnecessarily was to increase rather than decrease crime.

3. The presumption of innocence should be the guiding principle in the administration of justice, and at all stages of the justice process the rights of all parties involved should be protected.

4. The complete criminal law code should be written and should define all offenses and punishments in advance. This would allow the public to judge whether and how their liberties were being preserved.

5. Punishment should be based on retributive reasoning because the guilty had attacked another individual's rights.

6. The severity of punishment should be limited and should not go beyond what is necessary for crime prevention and deterrence.

7. Criminal punishment should correspond with the seriousness of the crime; the punishment should fit the crime, not the criminal.

8. Punishment must be certainty and should be inflicted quickly.

9. Punishment should not be administered to set an example and should not be concerned with reforming the offender.

10. The offender should be viewed as an independent and reasonable person who weighted the consequences of the crime. The offender should be assumed to have the same power of resistance as nonoffenders.

11. The aim of every good system of legislation was the prevention of crime.

Adapted from: J. Robert Lilly, Francis T. Cullen, and Richard A. Ball (2002). *Criminological Theory: Context and Consequences,* 3rd ed. Thousand Oaks, CA: Sage Publications, pp. 14–15.

---

crime, whereas the classical is not concerned with causes of crime; rather it is concerned with responding to violations of law and preventing future criminal or delinquent activity (Lilly, Cullen, & Ball, 2002).

Positivist explanations of crime seek to understand human behavior through biology, psychology, or sociology. Cullen and Gilbert (1982) point out there are three central features to the positivist school of thought. "First, positivists, in seeking the source of criminal behavior, tend to assume that crime is determined by factors largely outside the control of the individual" (p. 33). These factors consist of multiple facets including psychology, biology, and sociology. Researchers may differ on the causes of behavior, but they agree there are factors outside of people's control that can explain the behavior.

Second, positivists argue "that since criminals did not freely choose their criminal behavior, it is inappropriate to punish them for their crimes" (Cullen & Gilbert, 1982, p. 33). Therefore, punishment should be based on the individual offender rather than focusing solely on the offense the offender committed. Using the **medical model**, criminal practitioners in conjunction with trained personnel (psychologists, social workers, etc.) should seek to find the underlying causes of the behavior. Once the causes have been ascertained, criminal justice professionals should seek to treat rather than punish these individual underlying factors. This treatment should focus on the rehabilitation of the offender. Furthermore, positivists argue there are very few offenders in society who deserve lifelong imprisonment.

Finally, in the "positivist scheme, more emphasis is placed on the offender than the offense" (Cullen & Gilbert, 1982, p. 34). Because offenders were believed to have committed crimes for varying reasons, it was believed that the punishments should be individually tailored to the offender. Therefore, judges and correctional personnel were given the task of determining when an offender was "cured" or prepared to reenter society.

Positivists sought to understand and respond to the human condition. Understanding of the human condition can be divided into three theoretical categories: biological, psychological, and sociological. Each of these theoretical categories will be reviewed below.

Biological Dimension

Man has searched for explanations for criminal conduct for nearly as long as civilizations have existed. Briefly speaking, we can divide our attempts to explain criminal behavior into three categories, or dimensions. Aside from supernatural explanations, one of the first attempts to explain why people commit crimes was linked to biological explanations. Form was linked to function, and even today we jokingly make remarks, such as, "He just looks like a criminal." Shakespeare even touches on the subject in *Julius Caesar* when Cais Cassius points out that Brutus "has a lean and hungry look." As a consequence, it seemed to make sense that physical abnormalities were related to criminal conduct.

The most complete explanation, and influential for its time, was Caesar Lombroso's book *The Criminal Man,* published for the first time in 1876. Lombroso, who is considered the father of criminology, attempted to explain criminal behavior by proposing that criminals are an evolutionary throwback to an earlier stage in human development. He referred to this degeneration as atavism. He identified a number of physical deformities, called **stigmata**, and by linking them to specific behaviors believed that he could explain criminal behavior. He began his work as a physician. Upon being called to perform an autopsy on a known criminal who had died in an Italian prison, Lombroso was struck by the number of physical anomalies this offender exhibited. As a consequence, he came to believe that criminals could be identified by such things as excessive facial hair in women, a lack of facial hair in men, large ears, long arms, supernumerary nipples, webbed toes,

Theoretical Dimensions

Theoretical Dimension	Explanation	Treatment Intervention
Biological dimension	Seeks to explain crime on the basis of form follows function.	Treatment interventions usually tend to focus on pharmacological or psychosurgery. However, treatments can be environmental in nature.
Psychological dimension	Seeks to explain crime as a function of personality problems.	Treatment interventions usually include some form of psychotherapy or counseling.
Sociological dimension	Seeks to explain crime in light of social pressures and influences.	Treatment interventions traditionally learned. Re-learning more appropriate behaviors and how to resist temptation. However, as the Just Deserts model has become more popular, programs have been abandoned, justified by the assumption that the sentence is a deterrent to future law-breaking behavior.

tattoos, and so on. Lombroso viewed tattoos as evidence that these individuals were insensitive to physical pain and immortality.

Lombroso divided criminals into three groups: the born criminal, insane criminals, and the criminaloid. The three categories attempted to explain criminal behavior by linking behavior to physical deformities, or by a criminal's passions getting the upper hand. Lombroso created a third group into which all others were thrust because they did not fit into the other two groups. Over the next twenty years, he gradually changed his thinking and came to rely more heavily on environmental factors (Vold & Bernard, 1986). He also admitted later in his life that the majority of criminals did not fit into the born criminal category.

Gradually the typologies of Lombroso lost favor as an explanation of criminal behavior. However, the notion persisted that there must be a biological explanation for crime and the idea of body type continued to hold some allure as a means to explain criminal behavior. William H. Sheldon was a proponent of body type explanations, also known as somatyping, in the late 1800s. **Somatyping** is the process of using an offender's physique and personal appearance to explain their participation in delinquent or criminal activity (Sheldon, 1949, pp. 15–30).

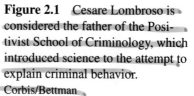

Figure 2.1   Cesare Lombroso is considered the father of the Positivist School of Criminology, which introduced science to the attempt to explain criminal behavior.
Corbis/Bettman

He posited that as the embryo developed in the womb, it was simply a continuous digestive tube composed of three layers of tissue. In his view, the inner layer of tissue was called the endoderm and gave rise to digestive viscera. According to Sheldon, individuals characterized by endoderm tissue were soft and round and had a tendency to put on fat. These individuals were classified as **endomorphs**. The middle layer was called the mesoderm and gave rise to muscle, bone, and tendon. Those individuals who had high levels of mesoderm were characterized as **mesomorphs**. These individuals had a tendency to be athletic, displayed a "solid" build, and typically had large hearts and blood vessels. The third layer was called the ectoderm and gave rise to connecting tissue, the nervous system, skin, and related appendages. These individuals were classified as **ectomorphs**. They were small in stature, had little body mass, and were characterized as lean. The point of his writing was that an excess of tissue of a particular kind gave rise to certain behaviors that led to deviant behavior. For example, based upon his observations of prison inmates, he believed that the mesoderm (mesomorphs) gave rise to behavior of most violent criminals because of their tendency to be muscular and physically active (Curran & Renzetti, 2001, p. 37; Sheldon, 1949, pp. 15–30). Although Sheldon's work is viewed as an expansion of criminological theory, it was met with much skepticism by both the academic community and policy makers. Further exploration of Sheldon's theory revealed problems with his sample size ($n = 200$) and his sample populations. In conducting his study, Sheldon identified two hundred youth at the Hayden Goodwil Inn for Boys in Boston, Massachusetts and compared this sample to four thousand male college students. His findings revealed that the population at the Inn were much more mesomorph and much less endomorph (Sheldon, 1949).

The idea of body types gradually fell by the wayside, but the idea that there was a physical explanation for criminal conduct still persisted. As a consequence, the idea of feeblemindedness caught hold. The reasoning was, and still is to an extent, that it takes a stupid person to commit a number of the criminal acts that came to light. This shift in thinking was given impetus by the increasing use of I.Q. testing in the classroom developed by Alfred Binet. Henry Goddard expanded the use of intelligence testing to the delinquent population. Goddard adapted a version of the Binet test to administer to boys and girls confined at the Vineland Training School for Feebleminded Boys and Girls. He further classified the results from the tests into categories with those scoring between the mental ages of eight and twelve being classified as feebleminded, morons, or high-grade defectives. He argued that these youths were not able to work in semi-skilled positions. Goddard further looked at the family histories of the youth. From this research he argues that feeblemindedness was hereditary (Curran & Renzetti, 2001). In addition, several studies were conducted that indicated that prison inmates had an average I.Q. score that was lower than the general population.

Interest in feeblemindedness theories began to decline by the 1930s when the results of several tests on WWI draftees and prison inmates were released. Those results indicated that the average prison inmate was smarter than the average WWI draftee. That research was flawed, and psychologists and criminologists came to the conclusion there is no difference in the distribution of individuals with low IQ whether in the Army or in the general population. As a result of further research, explanations of crime based upon intelligence fell by the wayside (Vold & Bernard, 1986).

More recent research on the relationship between IQ and crime has suggested that IQ and delinquency may be related. For example, Hirschi and Hindelang (1977) revisited the idea and found that as IQ increased, delinquency decreased. These findings were further supported by the controversial work of Herrnstein and Murray (1994). The work by Herrnstein and Murray suggested that IQ is directly related to race, therefore suggesting that non-white Americans are inferior and consequently are more likely to participate in delinquency. These findings have been disputed by a variety of researchers who have suggested the IQ tests themselves are flawed, as well as the demise of structural factors and social institutions such as poorly funded schools, breakdown in families, and an increase in poverty.

One interesting area of the study of biological influences on criminal behavior is the study of twins. Since identical twins develop from a single egg and have no hereditary differences, scientists can obtain a good idea of the influences of heredity and environment. Conklin (1998, p. 144) points out that results of twin studies in Japan, Europe, and the United States between 1929 and 1962 are "consistent with the idea that inherited factors influence criminal behavior." In these studies, it was found that the identical twins have a rate of between 60 percent and 70 percent for criminal behavior on the part of both. On the other hand, fraternal twins have a rate of between 15 percent and 30 percent criminal behavior for both.

In probably the most extensive twin study so far, Karl O. Christiansen (1974, 1977), investigated 3,586 pairs of twins born in a particular area of Denmark between 1881 and 1910. "He found that if one identical twin had a criminal conviction, the other twin also had a conviction in 35 percent of the cases. The rate of concordance was only 12 percent for fraternal twins" (Conklin, 1992). While we cannot see a consistent pattern in the influence of genetic influence on criminal behavior, clearly there is a factor, or factors, at work that precludes our dismissing the influence of genetics on criminal behavior.

Another explanation of criminal behavior is that of the **XYY chromosomal pattern**. Much of the interest in XYY is drawn from Richard Speck who brutally murdered eight nursing students in Chicago in 1966. A physical examination of Speck revealed that he had the XYY chromosome pattern. This anomaly, which occurs once in about every 400 to 500 live male births has been linked with antisocial behavior (Fox, 1971).

The XYY chromosomal pattern is relatively new and was only discovered in 1961. That person appeared to be perfectly normal, both behaviorally and physically. Shortly afterward a number of cases turned up in Australia, France, Great Britain, and the United States. There have been some attempts to use the XYY as a defense for criminal conduct, but to date no jury has accepted it. Research on the XYY is still ongoing, and it is too early to draw any conclusions. We can, however, conclude that the XYY is responsible for some abnormalities in the male population, but the sample is much too small to be considered a major factor in explaining crime. Besides, it does not explain female crime at all (Gibbons, 1992).

There are other efforts to link biological explanations to crime. For example, there are indications that delivery complications at birth are associated with violent episodes that may be linked to brain damage that reduce the inhibitory control of aggression. Research also has provided evidence that frontal lobe dysfunction has been found to be associated with adult violent behavior. Reduced spinal fluid levels have been found in people exhibiting impulsive aggression. Some antisocial individuals have been found to have reduced levels of autonomic reactiveness and poor conditioning of autonomic responses (Brennen, Mednick, & Volavka, 1995). Nutrition has also been investigated as a cause of criminal behavior with inconclusive results.

Psychological Dimension

Psychological explanations for criminal behavior are largely the product of psychiatry. Those explanations have had a lot to say about the treatment of criminals and other programs. Remember, positivists refer to this as the *Medical Model.* This approach to dealing with criminals and their conduct assumes that the individual is sick and that he or she must figuratively visit a "doctor" each day and receive a "pill." This pill is in the form of group counseling, individual counseling, or some other form of therapy in which an expert assists the individual to overcome a psychological problem that is at the root of his or her deviance.

According to Freudians, the personality is made up of three distinct components: the **id**, the **ego**, and the **superego**. The infant arrives in the world as simply a bag of protoplasm with eyes. The only instincts he or she has are sucking, blinking, sneezing, and coughing. It is dependent upon loving parents to care for it until it is able to survive by itself. This is the rub. Parents often do not do a good job, and the contamination of the personality by others is what may contribute to criminal behavior.

The id is a reservoir of instinctual energy that is basically uncontaminated, and in infancy the individual is prepared to behave only at the behest of pain or pleasure. Soon after birth, the ego begins to develop, and the infant begins to gain an awareness of self as distinct from its surroundings. In other words, the ego gradually assumes executive control of the young person's personality. The superego consists largely of morality or a conscience. The superego is formed out of the ego and is the sum total of standards and expectations of parents and significant others. In other words, it serves to "police" the individual and in a way punishes us for doing "wrong."

In a well-developed personality, these three components work well together, but in neurotic or otherwise disturbed individuals, problems arise. For example, the superego may become too rigid and powerful, and the person begins to have guilt feelings about repressed instinctual drives; or the superego may be underdeveloped and antisocial behavior may develop. The psychoanalytic interpretation of criminality is summed up very nicely by George Vold:

> Criminal behavior, under this general theoretical orientation, is to be understood, simply and directly as a substitute response, some form of symbolic release of repressed complexes. The conflict in the unconscious mind gives rise to feelings of guilt and anxiety with a consequent desire for punishment to remove the guilt feelings and restore a proper balance of good against evil. The criminal then commits the criminal act in order to be caught and punished. Unconsciously motivated errors (i.e., careless, or imprudent ways of committing the crime) leave "clues" so the authorities may more readily apprehend and convict the guilty, and thus administer suitably cleansing punishment (Vold, 1958).

According to Professor Don C. Gibbons (1992) psychoanalytic theory is deficient in several ways: (a) it assumes a biological motivation, particularly instinct; (b) it stresses the impact of infancy and early childhood; (c) it minimizes the influence of social factors on human behavior; and (d) it overemphasizes sexual aspects of behavior and motivation. In spite of the deficiencies of psychoanalytic theory, it gives us a clue about the importance of a strong family in raising a child.

For example, if a child is raised in a secure home where there are standards, limits on behavior, sanctions placed on negative behavior, and a consistent moral front posed to the child by all concerned, then in all probability the child will grow up to be a responsible adult. If, on the other hand, the child grows up in a home characterized by absent parent(s), discipline is nonexistent or erratic, where morality is absent, and available role models extol the virtues of deviant behavior, we should not be surprised at the results.

For the sake of understanding, think of the ego as an enclosure around the id. The id is a bundle of instincts that seek immediate gratification, and the ego is the buffer that prevents the illegal, illogical, or self-destructive behaviors from reaching into the external environment.

We can illustrate Figure 2.2 with the following example. A teenager is with a group of other youth when one of them suggests they steal a car and go for a ride. Everyone agrees but one whose parents have spent a lot of time reinforcing limits to behavior and explaining the importance of "right" behavior and "wrong" behavior. He tells the others that he is not interested and walks away and finds his way home.

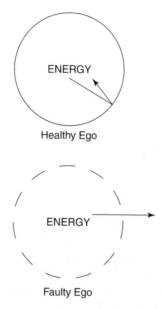

Healthy Ego

Faulty Ego   **Figure 2.2**   The Ego and You

The above scenario may seem a little far-fetched. But it illustrates that too many of our youth have been victimized by irresponsible parents, the media, and others to the degree that some neighborhoods are populated by an overabundance of people who are unable to stop their actions before they act upon them, thus we can begin to see the true dimensions of the crime problem. Even more lamentable is the fact that they seldom feel remorse for committing their crime—only for getting caught.

Samuel Yochelson and Stanton Samenow provide some unique ideas on "the criminal mind." In *The Criminal Personality* (1977), they relate that traditional psychiatric methods of working with criminals are ineffective and began a search for effective methods. Part of the problem, they state, is that all criminals have certain "thought patterns," whether they are from the inner-city or not, high school drop-outs or not and so on. They identify fifty-two specific errors of thinking that form the criminal personality. Among them are:

chronic lying

an attitude that other people's property is theirs

supreme optimism

great energy

fear of injury or being insulted

intense anger

manipulativeness

a high self-image that cannot be bent

Don C. Gibbons (1992) states that it is hard to take Yochelson and Samenow seriously because of flaws in their methodology. The research is the result of 255 interviews that are unrepresentative of even a part of the criminal population. Many of them had been adjudged not guilty because of insanity and had been sent to St. Elizabeth's Hospital instead of a regular prison. Nevertheless, the fifty-two "thinking patterns" identified by Yochelson and Samenow strike a chord with those who work in youth institutions and prisons and serve as a basis for a number of treatment programs.

Sociological Dimensions

As stated earlier, most criminology is sociological criminology. For the past 150 years beginning with philosophers/reformers and then sociologists trained in scientific methods, scientific attempts to explain crime and its causes have been made. We have to go back to the father of sociology to begin a **sociological explanation** of criminal behavior. Emile Durkheim is responsible for two main ideas about crime: The first is crime is "normal," and the second idea is the concept of normlessness, or as he called it "anomie."

To say that crime is normal usually raises the hackles of the average person. But in Durkheim's view, behavior exists along a continuum ranging from very bad to very good. He also maintained that "normal" behavior and the pathological are not different from each other, but are social distinctions that we place on certain kinds of behavior. A quick look at drinking and driving is a simplistic example of this concept. Twenty years ago, driving under the influence of alcohol and causing the death of another was viewed as reprehensible, but not criminal. Now it is viewed as both reprehensible and criminal, and a social stigma has been attached to drinking and driving. As a consequence, there has been a decline in the number of arrests for driving under the influence because of the relabeling of this behavior by the general public.

Anomie, or normlessness, states that "the social needs or desire of humans are potentially insatiable, so collective order (social organization) is necessary as an external regulating force to define and control the goal-seeking of men" (Gibbons, 1992). If, as Durkheim said, the social order is disrupted, then the aspirations of humans may increase to the point of outdistancing all possibilities of fulfillment. That is, when traditional rules have lost their ability to control behavior and when the regulatory functions of the normative order have broken down, then we have a state of anomie. Anomie is brought about, according to Durkheim by sudden depression or prosperity, rapid technological change and war, just to name a few causes.

Many neighborhoods are characterized by depression, have suffered from rapid technological change, and many inhabitants are unwilling to move or seek new training to keep up with the new economy, and so on: As a consequence, we avoid those neighborhoods when driving around town. We do so because often the inhabitants have a reputation for wanting "things," like our wallets or car; these are places where the normal order has broken down in that shame, guilt, nosy neighbors, and so on fail to keep behavior in check. These are places where the young people have no positive outlook for the future, where there are no decent jobs, where they have no investment in the city or neighborhood, and they simply don't care what anyone, other than peers, thinks.

Figure 2.3 Neighborhoods characterized by blight and anomie have higher than usual crime rates.
Scott Cunningham/Merrill Education

Emile Durkheim was observing events as he saw them in the late 1800s up to WWI. However, another sociologist by the name of Robert K. Merton continued this line of thinking by publishing a paper that embellished the idea of anomie. Mertonian anomie, as it is called, distinguishes between the *goals* that we are all told to pursue and the *means* to reach those goals. He points out that not all people have the same access to societally-approved goals. This goals/means disjunction is what causes a good deal of criminal behavior.

Durkheim observed that while all citizens are told to pursue the same goals—that is, an education, a good job, a house, and so on—not everyone has the same access to the means to achieve those goals as others. Consequently, humans have developed five ways of adapting to the conflict in achieving socially accepted goals. Those adaptations are: **conformity, innovation, ritualism, retreatism,** and **rebellion**. Figure 2.4 illustrates the adaptations to means.

We see in this figure that one who conforms to the goals and the means are living by the rules. He or she will learn a trade or go to college, and otherwise hold down a job and work hard to achieve a piece of "the American Dream." He or she has the support of all institutions in American life to pursue those goals: family; education; church, synagogue, or mosque; and so on. The person is able to achieve the goals that he or she set out to achieve.

	Goals	Means
Conformity	+	+
Innovation	+	−
Ritualism	−	+
Retreatism	−	−
Rebellion	±	±

Figure 2.4   Merton's Adaptation to Goals/Means
Adapted from Robert K. Merton. (1957). *Social Theory and Social Structure*. Glencoe, IL: Free Press, 131–160.

The innovation mode is one in which the individual accepts the goals that society has spelled out, but is blocked, or at least feels blocked, from achieving them. As a consequence, he or she finds another way. It isn't too hard to imagine how innovation occurs. There are a number of opportunities in the illegitimate opportunity structure of society. Sale of drugs is one example. We can take a small amount of comfort in that entreprenurialism is alive and well in the blighted areas of our cities and depressed areas of smaller towns and cities of our nation. Innovation by selling drugs is only one small example; burglary and robbery are others.

A research project (Knox et al., 1995) involving jail inmates in Iowa asked them to agree or disagree with the statement, "I believe in such things as education, having a nice home, and supporting my family." Over 93 percent of the respondents agreed with this statement. Respondents were also asked if they had ever felt shut out of an education or trade training. Nearly 50 percent (49.4 percent) said they had felt shut out of training or education. Whether or not one agrees with the respondent, we know that the consequences are real. They are in jail, and it costs us money.

The other forms of adapting to the means/goals disjunction are of a concern but are not as great a stimulant to criminal behavior. Ritualism refers to one who is more enamored with the means rather than the achievement. For example, a workaholic would be one who fits this mode and is rarely a concern to police and the courts. Retreatism is more of a concern in that one can retreat into drugs or alcohol, and the related offenses are of a concern to police and courts. The other choice is to retreat to a mountaintop and remain in seclusion. Rebellion is a concern in that those who fall into this mode reject both the means and goals of society and seek to replace them with other goals and means to achieve them. In this regard, organizations on both ends of the political spectrum cause a good deal of concern. In the 1960s, it was the Weather Underground on the left; today it is the Order, Posse Committatus, KKK, and other similar organizations on the political right that advocate the replacement of the existing order with their own view of society.

Labeling

How many times were we told as youngsters not to run around with others who were thought to be trouble-makers? Many times our parents were right, and we were lucky to be at home or on our part-time job when they were arrested for one thing or another. Labeling holds that if one is part of a group that is deemed undesirable, then regardless of the honesty or "goodness" of one or several of the members, all can be labeled with the same stigmatizing tag.

There are two views of deviance: (a) those who focus on the person who commits the act and the laws he or she violates, (b) and those who emphasize the audience who observe and react to rule breaking. The second group is called the labelers, and they insist that criminal conduct or deviance is the product of the social interaction between those who commit the act and those who label the behavior as deviant (Gibbons, 1992). Further delinquent or criminal behavior is said to continue once the youth has been labeled or stigmatized into believing he or she is deviant. Once youth are stigmatized, they ascribe the label of deviant to themselves and deviancy or delinquency becomes a product of the self-fulfilling prophecy.

According to Lemert (1952) the act of being labeled a deviant typically does not occur with one transgression. Many individuals in society participate in behavior that may be deemed as deviant. These behaviors may include alcohol consumption or acting out. In and of themselves, these acts alone, although not necessarily accepted by the larger community, may not be considered deviant; rather, they may be considered situational. For example, a child may act out in a loud or aggressive manner when his or her parent(s) are not paying attention to the child. A man may choose to consume an exorbitant amount of alcohol following the death of a loved one. These deviations are considered to be symptomatic of a larger problem rather than normal behavior. Responses to situations such as these or simple flirtations with deviance are known as **primary deviance**. This is not considered normal behavior from the individuals, and thus we can expect them to resume their normal lifestyle once they have overcome or dealt with their present situation. However, if the deviant acts are repetitive, or they illicit a strong negative societal reaction, and they begin to identify themselves with a given label, such as aggressive or alcoholic, then they may begin to adhere to the **self-fulfilling prophecy** of being a deviant. This process of being ascribed a label and fulfilling the negative connotations is known as **secondary deviance** (Lemert, 1952). Therefore, the process of ascribing the label leads to further and increased levels of delinquency. Lemert argues there is a specific sequence of interaction that leads to secondary deviance. This sequence includes: 1) primary deviation; 2) social penalties; 3) further primary deviation; 4) stronger penalties and rejections; 5) further deviation, perhaps with hostilities and resentment beginning to focus upon those doing the penalizing; 6) crisis reached in the tolerance quotient, expressed in formal action by the community stigmatizing of the deviant; 7) strengthening of the deviant conduct as a reaction to the stigmatizing and penalties; 8) ultimate acceptance of deviant social status and efforts at adjustment on the basis of the associated role (Lemert, 1952, p. 278).

This is what happened to drinking and driving. The same thing happened to LSD in the 1960s when LSD was not illegal along with other substances prior to 1964. The use of LSD was not considered a problem as long as a small group of people considered to be on the social fringe used it. But when the children of the middle class began to use LSD and became involved in bizarre behavior, even killing themselves as they attempted bizarre stunts, LSD use was labeled deviant and was declared illegal. This is an example of behavior that was tolerated for a while, but was eventually labeled deviant by a social audience.

The movie *Days of Wine and Roses* illustrates the point another way. Jack Lemmon's role was one of a heavy drinker whose behavior was tolerated within certain limits. When his behavior exceeded those limits, he was labeled a drunk, was shunned, eventually lost his prestigious job, and gradually spiraled downward to skid row. Along the way he was constantly searching for approval for his conduct. He became enmeshed in a deviant role and was excluded from resuming a normal social role.

It is labeling that often results in youth released from an institution that prevents them from rejoining the community. High school students experience this if they are labeled by "more popular" peers as undesirable. If youth are socially connected to a group of youth who have a reputation for deviant conduct, such as use of drugs, it is often very hard for a child to leave the group and be accepted by other, more socially acceptable, youth in the school. *He or she is excluded from resuming a normal social role.*

Social Control Theory

One of the more enduring theories of criminal behavior is that of **social control theory**, conceived by Travis Hirschi. Hirschi states that juveniles become free to commit delinquent acts when their ties to the conventional social order are severed (Gibbons, 1992). Obviously many delinquent acts are attractive, and most youth would engage in such things as playing hooky, drinking, promiscuity, and criminal acts for financial gain. However, most are constrained from such behavior because they have strong social links to others, particularly their family.

For others, no special motivation is necessary to participate in delinquent behavior because their links to others are nonexistent or, at best, weak. Hirschi identifies four dimensions along which the bond of the individual varies, and the stronger the bond, the less likely the individual will be involved in delinquent behavior. Those dimensions are:

Attachment.   **Attachment** refers to the bond between the child and parents and the child and school. According to Hirschi, children who have a significant attachment to parents will refrain from delinquency because they do not want to jeopardize that relationship. In regard to school, Hirschi states that incompetence in school leads to poor grades, which leads to a dislike of school, which leads to rejection of teachers and administrators as authorities, which leads to delinquency. Hirschi found that attachment to parents and school is more important than attachment to peers.

Commitment.   **Commitment** refers to the individuals investment in conventional activities. That is support of and participation in social activities that bind the individual to the morality and ethics of society.

Involvement.   This is the most important dimension for people as parents. **Involvement** is a dimension that stresses the importance of activities that promote the interests of society as a whole. Parents can foster this bond by encouraging participation in family activities, school activities such as sports, band, and/or service clubs. Hirschi points out that one who is busy with conventional things has little time for delinquent activities.

Figure 2.5 Participation in sports is one way to foster attachment to society as a whole.

Belief.   This dimension includes the **belief** in society's value system. This includes respect for the law, institutions, and the people who work in those institutions. Hirschi believes that if youth do not believe laws are workable or fair, their ties to society are weakened and there is a higher probability that they will become involved in delinquency.

One criticism of Hirschi's theory is that it explains delinquency and not adult crime (Adler, Mueller, & Laufer, 1995). However, it seems that if youth become involved in delinquency at an early age, then the probability of committing crimes as an adult is relatively high.

Differential Association

There is one more explanation of criminal behavior that needs to be discussed and that regards the way people learn to commit crimes. Edwin Sutherland is noted for his theory of **differential association** and states that crime is learned through social interaction. Sutherland drew heavily upon the ideas of others that delinquent values are transmitted from one person to another or from one group to another, and even from one generation to another.

He posited several propositions that attempt to explain criminal behavior.

1. Criminal behavior is learned.

2. Criminal behavior is learned in interaction with other people in a process of communication. That is, a person does not become criminal simply by living in an environment that has a lot of criminals. Crime is learned in participation with others.

3. The principal part of learning occurs in intimate personal groups.

4. When criminal behavior is learned, it includes how to commit the crime and how to rationalize the crime.

5. Depending on the primary reference group to which the individual belongs, he or she learns whether or not approval is forthcoming for breaking the law.

6. Becoming criminal or delinquent depends upon how many definitions one has that are favorable to violation of the law.

7. The differential associations may vary in frequency, duration, priority, and intensity. That is, how often one associates with criminals, how intense the contact is, the meaning those associations has for the individual are important to the learning process.

8. Learning law violating behavior is the same as learning law abiding behavior. The same mechanisms are at work (Sutherland, 1947, pp. 5–7).

Developmental Perspective

The **developmental perspective** addresses the existence and persistence of delinquent behavior over the life course and has developed out of the work of Sheldon and Eleanor Glueck. In their now-famous longitudinal study completed during the 1930s, the Gluecks matched five-hundred known delinquents to five-hundred nondelinquents and followed them until the age of thirty-two. They wanted to ascertain whether personal characteristics of youth could predict future delinquent and criminal involvement. Their findings revealed that the earlier the onset of juvenile delinquency the more likely youth are to persist in their criminal offending (Glueck & Glueck, 1950).

Interest in the Glueck study was renewed during the early 1990s. Modern-day developmental theorists have sought to understand why some youths delinquent behavior peaks at an early age and then levels off while others continue to persist throughout their life course. The Pittsburgh youth study sponsored by the Office of Juvenile Justice and Delinquency Prevention and led by Rolf Loeber and his colleagues has been instrumental in further understanding the developmental pathways into delinquency. A **pathway** is defined as "a group of individuals that shares a behavioral development that is distinct from the behavioral development of another group of individuals" (Thornberry, Huizinga, & Loeber, 1995, p. 222). In their longitudinal study of youth in the Pittsburgh area, they identified three major pathways to **chronic** and serious delinquency (see Figure 2.6 for an overview of the Pathways to Delinquency). These pathways are **overt pathways**, which range from minor aggression such as bullying and annoying others, to violence such as rape and attacks; **covert pathways** range from minor covert behavior, such as shoplifting to frequent lying, to moderate to serious delinquency such as fraud, burglary, and serious theft; the final pathway is **authority conflict pathway** which occurs before the age of

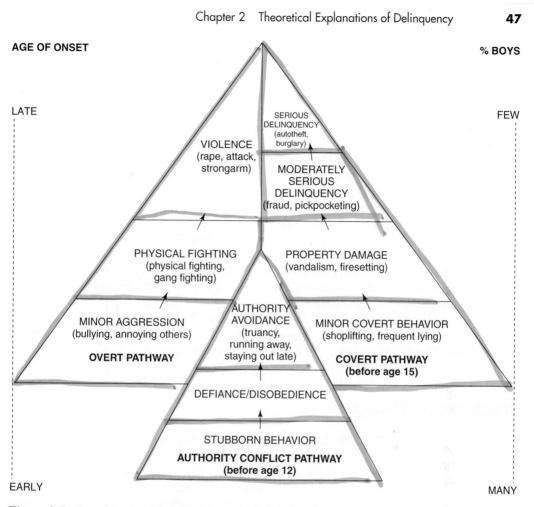

AGE OF ONSET

% BOYS

LATE

FEW

SERIOUS
DELINQUENCY
(autotheft,
burglary)

VIOLENCE
(rape, attack,
strongarm)

MODERATELY
SERIOUS
DELINQUENCY
(fraud, pickpocketing)

PHYSICAL FIGHTING
(physical fighting,
gang fighting)

PROPERTY DAMAGE
(vandalism, firesetting)

AUTHORITY
AVOIDANCE
(truancy,
running away,
staying out late)

MINOR AGGRESSION
(bullying, annoying others)

MINOR COVERT BEHAVIOR
(shoplifting, frequent lying)

OVERT PATHWAY

**COVERT PATHWAY
(before age 15)**

DEFIANCE/DISOBEDIENCE

STUBBORN BEHAVIOR
**AUTHORITY CONFLICT PATHWAY
(before age 12)**

EARLY

MANY

Figure 2.6 Developmental Pathways to Delinquency
Source: Howard N. Snyder and Melissa Sickmund. (1999 September). *Juvenile Offenders and Victims: 1999
National Report.* Washington, DC: Office of Juvenile Justice and Delinquency Prevention, p. 98.

twelve and ranges from stubborn behavior to authority avoidance such as truancy and running away (Loeber & Hays, 1994). Loeber and his colleagues found that delinquency was
highest for those boys who exhibited behavior in all three pathways and then for those
boys who displayed behaviors in both the overt and covert pathways (Loeber &
Stouthamer-Loeber, 1998; Loeber & Hays, 1994; Howell, Krisberg, & Jones, 1995).
Loeber et al. argued it was important to distinguish **persisters** (those who begin their
delinquent careers at an early age and continue on into criminal offending) from **experimenters** (those who commit delinquent acts but then stop their behavior). The key to this
perspective is if policy makers can identify the behaviors early on in a youth's life they
may be able to stop the behavior before it escalates into more serious violent behavior.

Programs in the community should attempt to prevent minor transgressions and to address delinquent behavior early on in the juvenile's career.

Further results from this study, as well as studies conducted in Rochester and Denver suggest that prevention and treatment programs should manifest three distinct characteristics: 1) early intervention; 2) comprehensive interventions; and 3) long-term interventions. First, the programs should focus on intervening early in the youth's life. As the research suggests, youth who begin their age of onset younger in life are more likely to persist into chronic delinquents. Second, programs should be comprehensive and should simultaneously address the prevention and treatment needs of youth. Thornberry, Huizinga, and Loeber (1995) point out that there are three areas that need to be addressed to maintain a comprehensive program: 1) the programs should address the multiple risk factors of youth not just one single factor; 2) chronic offenders appear to have co-occurring problem behaviors, therefore programs should have a variety of modules ready to deal with multiple problem behaviors such as teenage sexuality, drug use, and gang membership; 3) programs must also address the protective factors that keep youths from participating in future delinquent activity. Finally, prevention and treatment programs should attempt to be available on a long-term basis. These programs should be offered over a number of years rather than in a few months. These programs should seek to capitalize and enhance the number of protective factors within a youth's life over a number of years (Thornberry, Huizinga, & Loeber, 1995, pp. 233–234).

DRUGS AND JUVENILE CRIME

Elliott Currie (1993) states that we have made no headway on the drug problem and are in the midst of "the American nightmare." The news from the federal government is that we have made great headway on the drug problem, but this seems to be simply a justification for our present policies. To be sure, we have made some headway on middle-class drug use and the "crack epidemic" seems to have abated somewhat, but we are still the leading nation in the world for drug abuse. This fact has unleashed a terrible punitive streak that threatens the fabric of our society.

Because of our failure to get a grip on the introduction and use of drugs in our country:

- There are more cocaine-related arrests in our major cities than in most European nations in a single year.
- There are twice as many drug-related homicides in New York City in a single year than homicides for any reason in England.
- Nearly 25 percent of diagnosed AIDS cases are caused by intravenous drug use alone.
- Nearly one in eleven persons arrested are for drug abuse violations alone. This does not count those arrested for other crimes that can be attributed to drug abuse (Currie, 1993).

- Eleven percent (11.0%) of all cases adjudicated in juvenile court in 1998 were for drug offenses (Stahl, 2001).

- Results from the 2001 National Household Survey on Drug Abuse indicate that 10.8 percent of youth ages twelve to seventeen are current drug users, having used an illicit drug at least once in the month before being interviewed (ONDCP, 2003b, p. 1).

- For youth ages twelve to seventeen, an estimated 1.1 million persons (4.9 percent of this population) needed treatment for an illicit drug abuse problem in 2001. Of this group, only 10.2 percent of youths who needed treatment received any (ONDCP, 2003b, p. 5).

Drugs have permeated every level of our society, and we seem helpless to do anything about it. As a consequence, we can say with some certainty that drugs do cause crime. But this is like asking which came first, the chicken or the egg. Omitting casual marijuana use, it is a safe assumption that well-adjusted youth do not abuse drugs. However, the addictive personality will gravitate to whatever substance is available for use in order to "retreat" from the demands of family, society, and so on.

The Drug Use Forecasting Program was begun by the National Institute of Justice in 1987. It was designed to provide each of twenty-four cities with estimates of drug use among booked arrestees and information for detecting changes in drug use trends. In 1996, between 79 percent and 42 percent of arrestees showed positive for any drug. Today, approximately 55 percent of all citizens have ever used drugs. Clearly, drugs are a contributing factor to an individual getting in trouble with the law. In addition, a sizable number of high school seniors report drug use. Table 2.1 illustrates use of high school seniors.

Juvenile courts handled 192,500 cases in 1998. Of those cases, 11 percent were for drug-related offenses. Many of these delinquents appearing in front of the juvenile court are detained. For example, in 1998, 23 percent of all juvenile delinquency cases involving detention were for drug-related charges (ONDCP, 2003b, p. 5). One of the largest government-sponsored programs monitoring drug use among juvenile detainees is the National Institute of Justice's Arrestee Drug Abuse Monitoring (ADAM) Program. In 2002, the ADAM program tested juvenile male detainees at five sites across the nation: Birmingham, Alabama; Cleveland, Ohio; Phoenix, Arizona; San Antonio, Texas; and San Diego, California. Preliminary drug test results at these sites indicate that approximately 60 percent of juvenile male detainees were positive for drugs while 45.9 percent of females tested positive (ONDCP, 2003b, p. 5).

Data from the Bureau of Justice Statistics indicates that 78 percent of jail inmates in 1989 use drugs, 83.9 percent of state prison inmates were involved with drugs at the time of their arrest in 1999, and in 2001 55.5 percent of federal prisoners were drug offenders (ONDCP, 2003a). More sadly, 83 percent of all youth in long-term public juvenile facilities in 1987 had used drugs at some point in their lives (BJS, 1995).

Drugs and crime are related. According to the Bureau of Justice Statistics, 10 percent of federal prison inmates, 17 percent of state prison inmates, and 13 percent of all convicted jail inmates stated they had committed their crime to get money for drugs. Further,

Table 2.1   Drug Use by Adults and High School Seniors

Past illicit drug use, 2001

Respondent Age	Ever Used	Past Year	Past Month
12–17	28.4%	20.8%	10.8%
18–25	55.6	31.9	18.8
26–34	53.3	16.1	8.8
35 or older	38.4	6.3	3.5

Drug use among high school seniors, 2002

Drug	Ever Used	Past Year	Past Month
Amphetamines	16.8%	11.1%	5.5%
Cocaine	7.8	5.0	2.3
Crack	3.8	2.3	1.2
Hallucinogens	12.0	6.6	2.3
Heroin	1.7	1.0	0.5
Inhalants	11.7	4.5	1.5
LSD	8.4	3.5	0.7
Marijuana/hashish	47.8	36.2	21.5
MDMA (ecstasy)	10.5	7.4	2.4
Methamphetamine	6.7	3.6	1.7
PCP	3.1	1.1	0.4
Steroids	4.0	2.5	1.4

Source: Office of National Drug Use Control Policy. Drug Policy Information Clearinghouse: Fact Sheet. March 2003.

20 percent of Hispanic inmates, 15 percent of white inmates, and 17 percent of black inmates said they committed their present offense in order to get money for drugs (BJS, 1995).

Even more reprehensible is the fact that money spent on drugs by youth and adults represents a tax placed upon our society that flows into the pockets of a few corrupt, evil people who will stop at nothing to increase or preserve the flow of profits. The projected overall costs to society for drug abuse reached $106.7 billion in 2000 (ONDCP, 2003a, p. 2). In addition, drug money is spread around in a corrosive influence that rips away the integrity and honesty of public officials, bankers, and others who serve the needs of a few wealthy drug czars.

Are drugs and delinquency related? Yes, but not all delinquency is related to drugs. But, we can say that youth under the influence of drugs have committed nearly every crime possible from murder, bank robbery, and muggings to drug sales and public indecency. More than 9 percent of juvenile crime is known to be associated with drugs. Apparently youth learn from older, more sophisticated youth the techniques for drug use, as well as the rationalizations for drug use.

LEAPING FROM THEORY TO PRACTICE

Travis Hirschi remarked once that if we look at all the theories of criminal behavior one at a time, they don't seem to make much sense, but if we place them end to end they make a great deal more sense. This incomplete review of some of the reasons why youth commit crime sheds some light on the subject, but we need to place them end to end in order to make some sense out of them.

Let's begin with a worst-case possibility and examine a child born into a family characterized by a young unmarried mother. There are many possibilities in this example and not all of them lead to a life of deviance for the child. Nevertheless, if that child grows up neglected because the mother is out of the home for prolonged periods of time, the mother subsists on welfare and food stamps or by working two jobs, and if there are no other responsible adults in his or her life, there is little likelihood that the child will have an idea of what a "normal" family is supposed to be like. Assuming that the child lives in a neighborhood with an abundance of other families that are similar, where there are few external controls on the behavior of children, and the inhabitants of that neighborhood do almost as they please, we then have what we can term an anomic situation. In addition, if one, or several, of the young adults are criminal, they are available to teach the child, as he or she grows older, how to commit certain crimes, including ways to rationalize that behavior (that it is acceptable to steal, rob, or sell drugs).

At the same time, the child grows up with a television in the home, and it is used as a baby-sitting tool by the mother. The child learns what kind of material things are available if one has the money. This instills the desire to have nice things, but the opportunity to achieve them legitimately are closed because of class, opportunity, and perhaps race. Therefore, using Merton's scheme, he or she innovates and decides to take advantage of one, or several, of the illegitimate opportunities available to him or her.

We see in the above example several things at work. First, the bonds that attach the youngster to society are weak or nonexistent. There is no family, no school (or at least not an effective school), and no belief in the ethics and values of society. Second, a condition of anomie exists that fosters a means/goals disjunction, and since the child cannot achieve societally-approved goals legitimately, he innovates. Third, he or she has learned how to commit the crime or crimes through differential association. That is, he or she has learned the techniques and rationalizations for delinquent behavior.

This is all vastly simplified for example's sake, but we can see how some children do not have a chance from birth. The important thing to remember is that growing up in a single-parent home is not a guarantee that the child will grow up delinquent, and many dysfunctional homes are two-parent homes. By the same token, some homes have a child who grows up to be delinquent or criminal, and there appears to be no explanation for it. These are homes in which the parents tried to do all the right things: time with children, family activities, emphasis on education, church or synagogue, and so on. Sometimes we are at a loss to explain such behavior.

If we are going to make a dent in crime at the neighborhood level, we must begin by attacking the problems that breed delinquent conduct. It is axiomatic that if we have fewer delinquents, we will have fewer adult criminals. Research indicates that children imitate parental behavior, both conforming and criminal; antisocial behavior leads to rejection by teachers and peers leading to further alienation and more criminal behavior; programs that assist single parents in supervising their children and that free them to spend more time with their children may help to prevent delinquency. The above highlights point out that there is a lot of room for program innovation to prevent delinquent and criminal behavior and which draw upon the theoretical foundations found in this chapter.

IMPLICATIONS FOR TAX DOLLARS

During the debate over the 1994 Omnibus Crime Bill there was a great deal of controversy over "social pork." Some members of Congress stated that programs that attempt to deal with delinquency and crime are a waste of taxpayer's money and those funds can be better spent on prisons and police. The Midnight Basketball Program was held up as an example of "pork" without a discussion of its merits, even though the first President Bush hailed the program as a "point of light." There may be an issue here worthy of debate, but we do not need to read a book to tell us that there are dysfunctional families in every community. The important point in all of the rhetoric and debate is what to do with the product of dysfunctional families.

To simply send the individual off to reform school or prison after he or she has acquired an "attitude" is short-sighted. Criminological research indicates very strongly that the prison subculture is a reflection of the criminal subculture that exists on the street. It does not make sense to send a first-time offender to reform school or prison where he or she will be given approval for deviant behavior by other inmates. If the individual has a bad attitude going into prison, the deprivation, boredom, monotony, and the constant assaults on his or her psychological and physical self may well turn a marginal character into someone beyond redemption and we have an even greater problem when the individual is eventually released.

There is a history of programs that may have been ineffective either as controlling agents or with rehabilitative value. But that does not justify the refusal to implement programs altogether. This chapter reveals that there are too many variables to simply state that incarceration is the only alternative to law breaking. Clearly, if we seriously attack the problem of delinquency and criminal actions head-on before it becomes habitual behavior, we will save money in the long term. One answer to the problem is found in a review of social control theory.

We learned above that people commit crimes when the social bonds that unite families and communities are severed. These attachments, involvement, and belief in community rules allow civilized behavior to flourish. Therefore, efforts to prevent crime must include teaching conventional values, and ways must be found to strengthen individual bonds to society (Adler, Mueller, & Laufer, 1995).

SUMMARY

We can view criminological theories along three dimensions: biological, psychological, and sociological. The biological theories attempt to explain behavior in terms of form explaining function. Caesar Lombroso is important, in that he conceived the idea of the criminal man and was the first to make a scientific effort to explain criminal behavior. Included in this dimension are the body type theories, feeblemindedness, the XYY chromosome, as well as neurological problems and so on. While most biological explanations have fallen by the wayside, perinatal factors, neuropsychological and neurochemical factors appear to be connected to antisocial and criminal behavior.

The psychological explanations are largely the domain of psychiatry. Traditional Freudians hold that the personality is composed of an id, ego, and superego. When these three parts are working in harmony, the person is "normal." When there is an imbalance, problems result. Whether or not there is a "criminal personality" is open to debate, nevertheless, Yochelson and Samenow believe that they have identified a criminal personality and fifty-two "thinking patterns" that characterize the criminal.

The sociological dimension attempts to explain criminal behavior largely in terms of the impact of environment on the individual. Merton's anomie is important because it points out the disjunction between the goals that society approves of and, for a segment of the American population, the means to achieve those goals are often blocked. Hirschi calls our attention to the bonds that unite the individual to society: attachment, commitment, involvement, and belief. Hirschi states that if the bonds are severed the individual is free to commit delinquent acts. Finally, differential association was discussed as a learning theory. That is, one learns to commit crimes through the same mechanisms that we learn law-abiding behavior. Drugs play a role in crime in the United States, but to what extent drugs cause crime is difficult to determine because of the reporting practices of police agencies.

In spite of the image that the media conveys to us and the "sky is falling" attitude of many politicians, there are many nontraditional families in the United States that manage to raise law-abiding children. What is important to remember is that many variables enter into the life of the individual in determining whether or not he or she will enter into a life of deviance. There is hope, and programs exist that teach youth and adults conventional values and that strengthen the individual's bonds to society.

CASE STUDY WRAP-UP

Delaware County had a problem and wanted to serve juvenile sexual offenders in the best possible way. The authorities knew the youth sent to the State Training School did not receive adequate treatment for their offense and thus designed a program to meet the needs of the youth in the community. They began with the foundation that the family is the single best facilitator for treatment, as Hirschi points out. They then designed the program around the cognitive behavioral model for treatment groups, thus taking advantage of the notion that criminal behavior is learned behavior. Through therapeutic intervention, new behaviors could be learned by the offender and shed illegal behaviors that got him into trouble with the courts. The result has been a more effective program and substantial saving to the taxpayers of Delaware County.

STUDY QUESTIONS

1. Do you think we need to rethink our laws in regard to criminal intent in light of new knowledge about biological causes of crime? Why or why not?

2. Intuitively Merton's needs/goals dysjunction between means and goals is appealing. How do you think it informs programming possibilities?

3. In light of theory, how would you explain drug abuse by youth?

4. How do you explain Travis Hirschi's social bonding theory? Do you think it has implications for programs? Explain.

BIBLIOGRAPHY

ADLER, FREDA, MUELLER, GERHARD O.W., AND LAUFER, WILLIAM S. (1995). *Criminology,* 2nd ed. New York: McGraw-Hill, Inc.

BRENNAN, PATRICIA A., MEDNICK, SARNOFF A., AND VOLAVKA, JAN (1995). "Biomedical Factors in Crime," in James Q. Wilson and Joan Petersilia (Eds.), *Crime: Twenty-eight Leading Experts Look at the Most Pressing Problems of Our Time.* San Francisco: ICS Press.

BUREAU OF JUSTICE STATISTICS (1995). *Drugs and Crime Facts, 1994.* Bureau of Justice Statistics. Washington, D.C.: U.S. Department of Justice.

CHAMBLISS, WILLIAM J. (1988). *Exploring Criminology.* New York: Macmillan Publishing Company.

CHRISTIANSEN, KARL O. (1992). "Seriousness of Criminality and Concordance among Danish Twins," in Roger Hood (Ed.), *Crime, Criminology, and Public Policy: Essays in Honour of Sir Leon Radzinowicz.* New York: Free Press, 1974, in John E. Conklin, *Criminology,* 4th ed. New York: Macmillan Publishing Company.

CHRISTIANSEN, KARL O. (1992). "A Preliminary Study of Criminality among Twins," in Sarnoff A. Mednick and Karl O. Christiansen (Eds.), *Biosocial Bases of Criminal Behavior.* New York: Gardner Press, 1977, in John E. Conklin, *Criminology,* 4th ed. New York: Macmillan Publishing Company.

CONKLIN, JOHN E. (1998). *Criminology,* 6th ed. Boston: Allyn and Bacon.

CULLEN, FRANCIS T., AND GILBERT, KAREN E. (1982). *Reaffirming Rehabilitation.* Cincinnati, OH: Anderson Publishing.

CURRAN, DANIEL J., AND RENZETTI, CLAIRE M. (2001). *Theories of Crime,* 2nd ed. Boston: Allyn and Bacon.

CURRIE, ELLIOTT (1993). *Reckoning: Drugs, the Cities, and the American Future.* New York: Hill and Wang.

FOX, RICHARD G. (1971). "The XYY Offender: A Modern Myth?" *Journal of Criminal Law, Criminology, and Police Science, 62,* 59–73.

GIBBONS, DON C. (1992). *Society, Crime, and Criminal Behavior,* 6th ed. Englewood Cliffs, NJ: Prentice-Hall, Inc.

GLUECK, SHELDON, AND GLUECK, ELEANOR (1950). *Unraveling Juvenile Delinquency.* Cambridge: Harvard University Press.

HERRNSTEIN, RICHARD, AND MURRAY, CHARLES (1994). *The Bell Curve: Intelligence and Class Structure in American Life.* New York: Free Press.

HIRSCHI, TRAVIS (1969). *Causes of Delinquency.* Berkeley: University of California Press.

HIRSCHI, TRAVIS, AND HINDELANG, MICHAEL J. (1977). "Intelligence and Delinquency: A Revisionist Review." *American Sociological Review, 42,* 571–586.

HOWELL, JAMES C., KRISBERG, BARRY, AND JONES, MICHAEL (1995). "Trends in Juvenile Crime and Youth Violence." In James C. Howell, Barry Krisberg, J. David Hawkins, and John J. Wilson (Eds.), *Serious, Violent, & Chronic Juvenile Offenders: A Sourcebook* (pp. 1–35). Thousand Oaks, CA: Sage Publications.

KNOX, GEORGE W., TROMANHAUSER, EDWARD D., HOUSTON, JAMES G., MARTIN, BRAD, MORRIS, ROBERT E., MCCURRIE, THOMAS F., LASKEY, JOHN L., PAPACHRISTOS, DOROTHY, FEINBERG, JUDITH, AND WAXMAN, CHARLA (1995). *The Economics of Gang Life.* Chicago: National Gang Crime Research Center.

LEMERT, EDWIN M. (1952). "Primary and Secondary Deviance." *Social Deviance.* Reprinted in Francis T. Cullen and Robert Agnew (1999). *Criminological Theory: Past to Present* (pp. 276–278). Los Angeles: Roxbury Publishing Company.

LILLY, J. ROBERT, CULLEN, FRANCIS T., AND BALL, RICHARD A. (2002). *Criminological Theory: Context and Consequences,* 3rd ed. Thousand Oaks, CA: Sage Publications.

LOEBER, ROLF, AND HAYS, D.F. (1994). "Developmental Approaches to Aggression and Conduct Problems." In M. Rutter and D.F. Hays (Eds.), *Development Through Life: A Handbook for Clinicians* (pp. 488–516). Oxford, UK: Blackwell Scientific.

LOEBER, ROLF, AND STOUTHAMER-LOEBER, MAGDA (1998). "Development of Juvenile Aggression and Violence." *American Psychologist, 53,* 242–259.

MAGUIRE, KATHLEEN, AND PASTORE, ANN L. (Eds.) (1998). *Sourcebook for Criminal Justice Statistics 1997.* U.S. Department of Justice, Bureau of Justice Statistics. Washington, DC: USPGO.

OFFICE OF NATIONAL DRUG CONTROL POLICY (2003a, March). *Drug Data Summary.* Washington, DC: Office of National Drug Control Policy.

OFFICE OF NATIONAL DRUG CONTROL POLICY (2003b, June). *Juveniles and Drugs Fact Sheet.* Washington, DC: Office of National Drug Control Policy.

SHAH, SALEEM A., AND ROTH, LOREN H. (1974). "Biological and Psychophysiological Factors in Criminality," in Daniel E. Glaser (Ed.), *Handbook of Criminology*. Chicago: Rand McNally.

SHELDON, WILLIAM (1949). *Varieties of Delinquent Youth*. New York: Harper and Brothers.

STAHL, ANNE L. (2001, September). *Drug Offense Cases in Juvenile Courts, 1989–1998. OJJDP Fact Sheet*. Washington, DC: Office of Juvenile Justice and Delinquency Prevention. FS–200136.

SUTHERLAND, EDWIN (1947). *Principles of Criminology*, 4th ed. Philadelphia: J. B. Lippincott Co.

TENNENBAUM, FRANK (1938). *Crime and the Community*. New York: Columbia University Press.

THORNBERRY, TERRENCE P., HUIZINGA, DAVID, AND LOEBER, ROLF (1995). "The Prevention of Serious Delinquency and Violence: Implications from the Program of Research on the Causes and Correlates of Delinquency." In James C. Howell, Barry Krisberg, J. David Hawkins, and John J. Wilson (Eds.), *Serious, Violent, & Chronic Juvenile Offenders: A Sourcebook* (pp. 213–237). Thousand Oaks, CA: Sage Publications.

WILSON, JAMES Q., AND HERRNSTEIN, RICHARD (1985). *Crime & Human Nature: The Definitive Study of the Causes of Crime*. New York: Simon & Schuster.

VOLD, GEORGE B. (1958). *Theoretical Criminology*. New York: Oxford University Press.

VOLD, GEORGE B., AND BERNARD, THOMAS J. (1986). *Theoretical Criminology*, 3rd. ed. New York: Oxford University Press.

YOCHELSON, SAMUEL, AND SAMENOW, STANTON E. (1976, 1977). *The Criminal Personality: A Profile for Change, Vols. 1 and 2*. New York: Jason Aronson.

GLOSSARY OF KEY TERMS

Anomie.   The sense of normlessness that occurs when social order or moral values are disrupted. When traditional rules have lost their ability to control behavior and when the regulatory functions of the normative order have broken down, then we have a state of anomie.

Attachment.   Attachment refers to the bond between the child and parents and the child and school. Children who have a significant attachment to parents will refrain from delinquency because they do not want to jeopardize that relationship.

Authority conflict pathway.   This behavior occurs before the age of twelve and ranges from stubborn behavior to authority avoidance, such as truancy and running away.

Belief.   Belief includes a respect for law, institutions, and people who work in those institutions. This is a belief in society's value system.

Chronic offender.   These are youths who commit four or more offenses. They typically account for a significant portion of all offenses that are committed. Youth identified as chronic offenders typically begin offending early on in life and continue on into adulthood.

Classical school of thought.   This school of thought was predominant during the eighteenth century. During this time period, man was considered to be a rational free-will thinker who understood the consequences and benefits of his behavior. Therefore, punishment was based on the harm the offense caused society rather than the intentions of the offender.

Commitment.   Commitment refers to the individual's investment in conventional activities. Participation in social activities bind the individual to morality and ethics of society.

Conformity.   An individual desires conventional goals and accepts conventional means to obtain them. Conformists are most likely to be law-abiding citizens.

Covert pathway.   Delinquent behavior that ranges from shoplifting to frequent lying to moderate to serious delinquency such as fraud, burglary, and serious theft.

Developmental perspective.   This theoretical perspective seeks to explain the initiation and persistence of criminal and delinquent behavior throughout the life course.

Differential association.   Coined by Edwin Sutherland. This theory posits that criminal behavior is learned through social interactions like any other behaviors. Sutherland argued unlike previous theoretical explanations, differential association could be used to explain all criminal behavior.

Ectomorphs.   Individuals who are small in stature, have little body mass, and are characterized as lean.

Ego.   The portion of the unconscious that mediates or controls a person's personality.

Endomorphs.   Individuals who are characterized as soft and round and have a tendency to put on fat.

Experimenters.   Those who commit delinquent acts but then stop their behavior.

Hedonistic calculus.   The calculated ability of the offender to weigh the relative costs and benefits of his or her behavior.

Id.   The portion of the unconscious where an individual's wants and desires are located.

Innovation.   An individual desires conventional goals but rejects the conventional means to obtain them. Innovators are more likely to participate in delinquent or criminal behavior.

Involvement.   Involvement stresses the importance of activities that promote the interests of society as a whole. This refers to conventional activities a youth may participate in.

Labeling.   The process of participating in deviant activity once social control agencies ascribe the label of deviant to a youth. After this occurs, the youth becomes stigmatized by the label, and deviancy becomes a function of his or her normal behavior.

Medical model.   Criminal practitioners, in conjunction with trained personnel, such as psychologists, social workers, etc., seek to find the underlying causes of the criminal behavior. Once the cause has been ascertained, the offender should be placed in individualized treatment programs rather than punished.

Mesomorphs.   These individuals have a tendency to be athletic, display a larger build, and typically have large hearts and blood vessels.

Overt pathway.   Delinquent behavior that ranges from minor aggression, such as bullying and annoying others, to violence, which includes rape and attacks.

Pathways.   A group of individuals that shares a behavioral development that is distinct from the behavioral development of another group of individuals.

Persisters.   Those who begin their delinquent careers at an early age and continue on into criminal offending.

Positivist school of thought.   This school of thought has its origins in the early-nineteenth century. Using scientific methods, theorists looked for multiple factors to explain criminal behavior.

Primary deviance.   The initial participation or flirtation with delinquency that is considered to be situational or a normal response to a crisis. Typically the individual is not labeled deviant, and he or she does not continue the deviant behavior.

Psychological explanations.   Causal explanations of criminal behavior that attribute the causes of crime to psychological deficits such as lower I.Q., personality disorders, etc.

Rebellion.   An individual who rejects both the conventional goals and conventional means and adopts a new set of goals and means. Individuals who adopt alternative lifestyles or who attempt to overthrow the government are most likely to be rebels.

Retreatism.   An individual who rejects both the conventional goals and conventional means. Individuals such as alcoholics, psychotics, or vagrants are most likely to be retreatist.

Ritualism.   An individual rejects the conventional goals but accepts the conventional means to live by. An example of a ritualist would be someone who belongs to a cult.

Secondary deviance.   The initial flirtation with deviance that leads to being ascribed a label of deviant and committing future deviant acts in response to the label.

Self-fulfilling prophecy.   A condition in which one assumes that certain events will occur, thereby establishing a predisposition to engage in behaviors that will cause the event to occur.

Social control theory.   A theoretical explanation of crime put forth by Travis Hirschi. Hirschi attempted to explain why more individuals living in adverse conditions did not commit crime. He argued the stronger individuals bond to society and their community the less likely they are to commit delinquent or criminal offenses.

Sociological dimensions.   Explanations of crime and delinquency that look to an individual's environment including ecological factors as well as personal relationships that can explain and influence behavior.

Somatyping.   The process of using an offenders physique and personal appearance to explain their participation in delinquent or criminal activity.

Stigmata.   Physical deformities of offenders that were identified by Cesare Lombroso. These deformities included as enormous protruding jaws, large teeth, and sunken in eye sockets.

Super ego.   The portion of the unconscious that serves as the super moral compass.

Utilitarianism.   The idea that people calculated the relative likelihood of pleasure and pain in deciding how to act.

XYY chromosomal pattern.   The study of criminals that suggests violent male offenders have an extra Y chromosome, which makes them super-predators or extraordinarily aggressive.

CHAPTER 3
THE EXTERNAL ENVIRONMENT

KEY TERMS

Colonial period
Expansionist period
Urban growth period
Urban transformation
  period

Federal Aid Highway
  Transportation Act
Violent and Repeat
  Juvenile Offender Act

Four basic models for
  correction

CASE STUDY

The Frankenstein Effect*

Jeanette MacDonald Dillon identified a number of issues that she points out have created a Frankenstein in our midst. What, she wonders, will future citizens think of us when we did nothing to stem the numbers of crimes of violence in our world? Violence is an issue in modern society that has permeated every facet of our life with insidious effects. Ms. MacDonald Dillon calls to mind the school shootings in Arkansas and Kentucky where a fourteen-year-old boy shot up a prayer meeting of fellow students. Other incidents in Victoria, B.C, and London, Ontario, are also called to mind as she reminds us of terrible incidents we would like to forget. We are, she points out, hooked on violence.

Suicide is also mentioned as an alternative to despair and depression by the young. Kurt Cobain lived as a role model, not as one who believed in education or ethics or morality or hard work, but as one whom extolled the virtues of suicide. He talked about suicide, wrote about suicide, and sang about suicide. In the end, he killed himself, and in the following months numbers of young people attempted or accomplished suicide in sympathy.

*Source: Condensed from Jeanette MacDonald Dillon, *Juvenile Justice Magazine,* www.juvenilejustice.com/frank3.html. February, 2002

MacDonald Dillon spins a depressing litany of despair, and her conclusion is that the effects of urbanization contribute to the overall climate of youthful violence with which we are living. According to the U.S. House of Representatives, by age eleven a child of the Western world has witnessed in the various media more than 100,000 criminally violent acts, 8,000 of which are murders. Ted Bundy, who murdered more than fifty young women, was a first-rate Frankenstein, and MacDonald Dillon points out he was addicted to pornography, especially violent pornography.

The Internet is the final modern contrivance that adds to youthful violence. On the web, you can learn how to make a bomb, and you can "chat" about the best and most painless way to commit suicide. While the World Wide Web is a wonderful way to increase our learning, it also is important that we supervise our children in its use.

INTRODUCTION

The family is the most important social institution in our life, yet we often take it for granted. We abuse it, we fail to nourish it, and we combine it and recombine it in so many ways that we, especially many children, lose sight of the primary mission of the family: to care for and protect children until they are able to care for themselves physically and emotionally.

However, the family does not exist in a vacuum. It reacts to, and is a part of, events that operate in the community at large. For example, if the primary breadwinner loses his or her job and the family is at risk of depreciation in its lifestyle, the family as a unit bears the burden of the loss. Additionally, loss of employment by the primary breadwinner disrupts the family routine resulting many times in abuse of alcohol and drugs. Again, the family bears the burden of this loss.

This chapter explores the impact of the external environment on the family and the juvenile justice system. We will look at the family, politics, the urban and rural environment and attempt to understand how they interact to influence the family and children.

THE FAMILY

The family has the primary responsibility for the socialization of the child and is the vehicle for teaching the child right from wrong, expectations of others, that rules must be followed, what is appropriate behavior and what is not, the importance of deferred gratification, and how to appropriately satisfy desires (Thornton & Voigt, 1992). Today it appears that the family has broken down and that it is not accomplishing its primary task—the protection and socialization of children.

Probably there are no more dysfunctional families today than there were in 1950, but there are more of us, and, in addition, more incidents that would have been handled informally in previous years are now handled by the authorities, such as police and courts.

In Stephanie Coontz's book, *The Way We Really Are* (1997), a 1996 poll by the Knight-Ridder news agency is cited in which more Americans chose the 1950s as the single decade as the best time for children to grow up.

Coontz points out that there is nothing wrong with feeling nostalgic for the 1950s, because it was a period in which real wages grew more in a single year than in the entire decade of the 1980s, and it was a time in which a young family could purchase a median-priced home on less than 20 percent of the man's salary. But, as Coontz points out, it is more than a financial issue. It was a time when there were fewer choices for both children and parents; it was a time when there was more predictability in how people formed and maintained families, and there was a coherent "moral order" in the community for all to use as a reference point for family and personal norms. Even when people found the moral order to be unfair or repressive, its presence provided something concrete to push against.

Today it is quite different. Choices abound, not only in terms of what form the family will take, but also choices in behavior and responses to the behavior of others. As Coontz states, "nostalgia for the 1950s should be taken seriously, but it usually shouldn't be taken literally" (1997, p. 34). In her research on families, even those who hold the 1950s up as the ideal often go on to say that they do not like the way women were treated, that they wouldn't stay in a marriage like "so and so" had, and most point out that they have a great deal more communication with their children than they had with their parents or grandparents.

Life has changed, families have changed, and that is a difficult pill for many of us to swallow. In 1970, nearly 90 percent of families were two-parent families. Today about 75 percent of American families are two-parent families and about 16 million children live without their fathers. Poverty, however, has fluctuated with about 40 million people living below the poverty line in 1960 to 1963 when the poverty level for a non-farm family was $3,130 (Fisher, 1992) to about 32.3 million people in 1999 when the poverty line was $16,895 for a non-farm family of four including two children under the age of eighteen. Throughout the 1970s, the number hovered around 25 million people, but then began a slow rise to 35 million in poverty in 1983. It declined again to about 31 million in 1989, but began its slight rise to its present figure. In 1999, 12.1 million children were poor, down 1.4 million children in 1998. However, children make up 38 percent of the poor, but only comprise 26 percent of the population. Clearly children are a disproportionate number of the poor.

The structure of the family has also changed. *The United States Bureau of the Census* has changed its definition of family to include unmarried partners living together under one roof, and as a result, families that do not fit the traditional mother, father, children ideal no longer labor under the handicap of being abnormal. The shift has been driven by the increase of broken homes, that is homes whose structure has been altered by divorce, separation, or the death of either the mother or father. Families characterized by one parent, usually the mother, are more likely to live under the poverty line than those families with both parents in the household or with the father. But, according to Devine and Wright (1993), the rate of poverty among two-parent families has increased more rapidly than it has for single-parent families. In addition, according to Devine and Wright, during the decade 1978 to 1987 more than 3 million children, most of whom lived in working households, became impoverished. By 1987, 8 million children lived in an im-

poverished household where someone was working. Overall poverty among children increased from 12,275,000 in 1987 to 14,113,000 in 1997 and decreased to 12.1 million in 1999, reflecting the ups and downs of the economy (Statistical Abstract of the U.S., 2000).

The issue of poverty is important when discussing delinquency. The link between delinquency and poverty is tenuous at best, but conditions of poverty provide a fertile environment in which delinquency can occur (Gibbons, 1992). During the 1990s, a time of strong economic growth, income disparities in most states were even greater at the end of the decade than at the beginning of the decade (Bernstein et al., 2000). In their study, Bernstein and his colleagues found that from the late 1980s to the late 1990s, the average income of the lowest-income families grew less than 1 percent, the income of middle-income families grew by less than 2 percent, and the income of the wealthy grew by 15 percent. It seems that the wealthy continue to get even richer. From the late 1970s to the late 1990s, the average income of the lower and working class fell by over 6 percent, while the income of the top fifth income families increased by 30 percent. Clearly the gap between the lower and working class and the upper class is growing while the middle class is simply trying to hold on. The implications for the juvenile justice system are ominous indeed, including a higher percentage of alienated and disconnected youth that end up before the court.

The issue of broken homes as a contributor to delinquent behavior has been a theme for as long as can be remembered. However, the evidence is mixed on the impact of broken homes. Other factors must be at work because we all observe children who are raised in a single-parent home and are normal children who have no more problems than the average adolescent. Others, however, seem to experience one problem after another including problems with the police and courts.

As early as 1915, Healy (1915) reported that 36 percent of referrals to the Cook County (Illinois) Juvenile Court (and 49 percent of the repeat offenders) came from homes in which one parent was missing. Slawson (1926), in his investigation of children, found that 45 percent of the delinquents in the correctional schools he studied were from broken homes as opposed to 19 percent of nondelinquents in the public schools in the study. Karen Wilkerson (1980) studied Anglos and Mexican Americans, males and females, Catholics and Protestants in urban and rural settings and found that children from broken homes were consistently more delinquent than children from intact homes (see for example Shaw and McKay, 1931 and Monahan, 1957). Thus, the evidence is that a broken home can have negative effects on the child and that children from broken homes do show up in larger numbers than do their counterparts from intact homes.

The 1990s are recorded as a period of a booming economy. Citizens were constantly being told that the stock market was up, that home values were escalating, and that good times were projected at least through the end of the first decade of the new century. That is difficult to swallow for the working class who have suffered stagnating wages for most of the decade and who see no hope of getting out of an apartment in the inner city or out of the mobile home park in the small town. Frustration and anger are often taken out on children who are the victims of unfriendly governmental family policies and often adopt a fatalistic attitude with little hope for the future. This may be particularly telling on the nearly 50 percent of children who can expect to live in a single-parent home for a portion of their childhood. It is in this environment that children are now coming of age.

Hard Times Amid Plenty

With energy costs and unemployment rising, more and more Americans are falling behind on their mortgage payments. According to the *New York Times,* the increase is particularly worrisome because it suggests that many of the new homeowners, who were a part of the surge of new owners in the past decade of increased prosperity, may not be able to afford those mortgages during slow times. Increasingly liberal loan policies, which require smaller down payments than in years past, allowed first-time buyers to purchase a home, but the monthly payments are out of reach if one wage earner loses his or her job. Over the past year, a growing minority of new homeowners have struggled to make their payments.

In a popular government-insured program to help people purchase moderately priced homes, the percentage of owners whose loan payments are more than 30 days late exceed 10 percent for the first time ever at the end of 2000. Even during the recession-prone period 1980s and early 1990s, the percentage did not exceed 8 percent. Overall, about 400,000 more families were at least 30 days late on their mortgages in early 2001 than at the beginning of 2000.

The mortgage problems underscore one main reason policy makers and economists are so concerned with a recession in 2001. Americans have built up hundreds of billions of dollars in debt and should the current slowdown worsen, many more people will find themselves unable to pay their mortgage and other debts. The ups and downs of the economy underscore the impact the economy and the employment (or unemployment of parents) have on children. The stress and strains of an uncertain employment picture can have significant effects on youth impacting behavior in the community and school.

Portions of this essay are taken from, David Leonhardt, "More Falling Behind on Mortgage Payments," the *New York Times* on the web, www.nytimes.com/2001/08/12/business/12HOME.html.

THE EDUCATIONAL SYSTEM

School is important. After the family, school is the most important agent for the socialization of the child, and if it is faulty in any way, there can be serious consequences. It is in school that we all learn to work well with others, to share, and where we hone the social skills that will serve us for the rest of our lives. School is also important because it is in school that we acquire the intellectual skills necessary to assure adequate employment commensurate with our individual intelligence and aptitudes. School is where we often identify with our first role model outside of the family, meet our first sweetheart, and test the limits of authority. In spite of these distractions, most of us make it through these very awkward years and go on to become responsible adults who eventually hold down jobs, marry, and have families of our own. For some, however, school does not serve them well.

Academically some schools and children do not seem to get along. Teachers may spend the entire year and still not find the key to motivate a student. Other students are simply not to be reached academically because the family foundation is not there. The unfortunate aspect of today's schools is that they are asked to do many of the tasks the family should be doing and then are held accountable for the academic failure of the students. Many times teachers simply do not have adequate time to devote to proper instruction because they must attend to discipline and sundry matters as dictated by the state legislature.

In many cities, schools have become battlegrounds, and metal detectors and searches are common place. More and more, we are beginning to associate schools with youth crime. According to one survey of over sixteen thousand students conducted by the National Centers for Disease Control and Prevention, 11.8 percent of high school students reported that they had carried a weapon on campus, 24 percent reported that they were offered, sold, or given drugs on campus, 7.3 percent said that they were threatened or injured with a weapon in school, and 4.4 percent said they had skipped school in the previous month because they felt threatened (Levy, 1995, in Lawrence, 1998).

The above report is probably true for the population surveyed, but it may present a distorted picture. According to the *Sourcebook for Criminal Justice Statistics 2002,* members of the class of 2001 report that 83.3 percent of students have never been threatened with a gun, knife, or club by another student. Ninety-five percent have never been hurt by a student using a gun, knife, or club. Table 3.1 illustrates the victimizations of students in the United States. Still, even one student being hurt by another student is one too many, but schools cannot guard against faulty socialization on the part of parents. It is a safe assumption that the student who commits a transgression is just as much a victim in that he or she is the product of a dysfunctional family or neighborhood, and for that we all bear some of the blame.

Failure in school is associated with low income later in life and perhaps even raises the probability that the individual will rely on welfare in one form or another at some point in his or her life. It is important that students succeed in school and successful students seem to have many of the following characteristics: high motivation for learning, spend time on homework, parents or a parent who support the efforts of teachers, and who are connected to school through sports and extracurricular activities.

While delinquency is not just an urban phenomenon, we usually tend to think of delinquency in an urban setting. However, there are certain influences in the urban environment and characteristics that create a press for youth to be involved in delinquency. Before we attempt to move on to a more complete understanding of delinquency and the juvenile justice system, it may be instructive to gain an understanding of urban life. Traditionally, the city has been viewed as an unhealthy, unwholesome place where one is exposed to influences that are inimical to a healthy social and emotional life (Rothman, 1971). In the next part of this chapter we explore some of those themes.

THE URBAN ENVIRONMENT

Gideon Sjoberg (1960) estimates that the world population remained relatively stable from about 500 B.C. to A.D. 1800. However, with the beginning of the Industrial Revolution, cities began to grow and expand at an unprecedented rate. Today, much of the world population is concentrated in urban areas. City government struggles to keep pace with the demand for services but often fights a losing battle.

Table 3.1 High School Seniors Reporting Victimization in Last 12 Months

By type of victimization, United States, 1989–2001

Question: "During the last 12 months, how often . . ."

Type of Victimization	Class of 1989 (N=2,852)	Class of 1990 (N=2,627)	Class of 1991 (N=2,569)	Class of 1992 (N=2,690)
Has something of yours (worth under $50) been stolen?				
Not at all	56.3%	54.6%	55.4%	55.4%
Once	26.2	24.8	26.2	27.0
Twice	10.6	12.2	10.9	10.6
3 or 4 times	4.7	6.0	5.2	5.0
5 or more times	2.2	2.4	2.3	2.0
Has something of yours (worth over $50) been stolen?				
Not at all	79.4	77.9	77.2	77.5
Once	15.6	15.2	15.7	15.3
Twice	3.0	4.1	4.8	4.6
3 or 4 times	1.3	2.0	1.7	1.9
5 or more times	0.6	0.9	0.6	0.7
Has someone deliberately damaged your property (your car, clothing, etc.)?				
Not at all	66.7	66.3	65.8	68.4
Once	21.3	19.5	21.6	19.8
Twice	7.8	8.9	7.7	9.4
3 or 4 times	2.9	4.0	3.6	3.4
5 or more times	1.3	1.3	1.3	0.9
Has someone injured you with a weapon (like a knife, gun, or club)?				
Not at all	94.7	94.4	94.5	94.3
Once	3.9	3.7	4.1	4.0
Twice	0.8	1.1	0.7	1.4
3 or 4 times	0.3	0.4	0.4	0.1
5 or more times	0.3	0.4	0.3	0.2
Has someone threatened you with a weapon, but not actually injured you?				
Not at all	81.3	81.9	81.4	80.7
Once	12.2	10.4	11.1	10.9
Twice	3.1	3.9	3.9	4.0
3 or 4 times	1.7	2.0	2.0	2.4
5 or more times	1.7	1.8	1.6	2.1

Class of 1993 (N=2,770)	Class of 1994 (N=2,645)	Class of 1995 (N=2,656)	Class of 1996 (N=2,452)	Class of 1997 (N=2,638)	Class of 1998 (N=2,656)	Class of 1999 (N=2,322)	Class of 2000 (N=2,204)	Class of 2001 (N=2,218)
55.3%	56.6%	55.4%	52.5%	54.0%	54.7%	54.9%	54.6%	54.6%
25.6	25.3	25.7	27.0	26.8	25.6	27.1	25.2	26.7
11.0	11.0	10.7	11.0	11.0	11.1	10.9	10.8	10.2
5.7	5.1	5.2	6.4	5.3	5.9	4.8	6.1	5.2
2.4	2.1	3.0	3.1	3.0	2.6	2.4	3.4	3.2
75.1	76.8	76.0	73.3	74.2	73.4	74.3	74.3	74.3
17.2	16.8	16.4	17.0	17.2	17.3	18.2	16.6	17.4
4.0	4.1	4.7	5.7	5.5	5.5	4.8	6.1	5.3
2.6	1.6	2.1	2.5	2.3	2.3	2.0	2.1	1.7
1.0	0.7	0.7	1.5	0.8	1.5	0.7	0.9	1.3
66.1	67.0	66.4	65.6	67.4	67.5	69.2	69.7	67.4
19.1	19.6	19.5	20.9	19.9	19.3	19.5	17.7	19.6
9.2	8.5	8.6	8.8	8.2	7.6	7.7	7.8	6.9
4.2	3.8	3.7	3.0	3.4	3.8	2.5	3.4	4.4
1.4	1.2	1.8	1.6	1.1	1.8	1.1	1.3	1.8
93.9	94.9	95.0	95.0	94.9	95.0	95.2	95.5	95.0
3.6	3.5	3.0	2.9	2.8	3.0	2.5	2.8	3.3
1.4	1.1	1.1	0.9	1.1	1.0	1.0	1.2	1.1
0.7	0.3	0.5	0.5	0.8	0.6	0.6	0.3	0.3
0.4	0.2	0.3	0.6	0.4	0.4	0.6	0.2	0.2
79.6	80.9	82.1	81.0	81.8	82.3	84.2	83.8	83.3
11.5	11.3	9.3	10.7	11.1	9.8	9.3	9.6	11.0
3.8	3.7	4.5	4.6	3.3	4.2	3.4	3.2	2.5
2.8	2.4	2.2	1.9	2.3	1.7	1.8	1.6	1.9
2.3	1.7	1.8	1.9	1.5	2.0	1.3	1.7	1.3

(continued)

Table 3.1   **High School Seniors Reporting Victimization in Last 12 Months (*Continued*)**

By type of victimization, United States, 1989–2001

Question: "During the last 12 months, how often . . ."

Type of victimization	Class of 1989 (N=2,852)	Class of 1990 (N=2,627)	Class of 1991 (N=2,569)	Class of 1992 (N=2,690)
Has someone injured you on purpose without using a weapon?				
Not at all	84.2	83.3	83.8	84.0
Once	9.6	10.1	9.6	9.3
Twice	3.0	3.3	3.1	3.1
3 or 4 times	1.8	2.0	1.9	2.1
5 or more times	1.4	1.3	1.6	1.5
Has an unarmed person threatened you with injury, but not actually injured you?				
Not at all	69.6	66.8	69.1	69.3
Once	14.2	15.3	13.5	13.7
Twice	6.2	8.0	6.8	6.2
3 or 4 times	4.4	4.7	4.9	5.3
5 or more times	5.5	5.2	5.7	5.4

Note: These data are from a series of nationwide surveys of high school seniors conducted from 1975 through 2001 by the Monitoring the Future Project at the University of Michigan's Institute for Social Research. The survey design is a multistage random sample of high school seniors in public and private schools throughout the continental United States. All percentages reported are based on weighted cases; the Ns that are shown in the tables also refer to the number of weighted cases. Readers interested in responses to this question for 1976 through 1988 should consult previous editions of SOURCEBOOK. For survey methodology and definitions of terms, see Appendix 6.

Source: Pastore, Ann and Maguire, Kathleen. *Sourcebook of Criminal Justice Statatics, 2001.* U.S. Department of Justice, Bureau of Justice Statistics. Washington, DC: USGPO, 2002.

The Urbanization of the United States

The urbanization of the United States can be divided roughly into four periods: the **Colonial Period** (1609–1776), the **Expansionist Period** (1776–1900), the **Urban Growth Period** (1901–1960), and the **Urban Transformation Period** (1960–present). During the Colonial Period (1609–1776), the American wilderness was viewed as an area to be exploited for its wealth, and the first colonists were sent to establish outposts for the various empires that had claims on the continent. The first cities resulted from charters granted by the English and French Kings for purposes of mercantilism. As the population grew, so did the influence of the few settlements that had larger populations. By 1790, New York City had a population of 33,131, and the population of Boston was 18,320 (U.S. Bureau of Census, 1991).

During the Expansionist Period (1776–1900), the young United States grew from thirteen states huddled along the Atlantic Coast to a nation that stretched from the Atlantic to the

Class of 1993 (N=2,770)	Class of 1994 (N=2,645)	Class of 1995 (N=2,656)	Class of 1996 (N=2,452)	Class of 1997 (N=2,638)	Class of 1998 (N=2,656)	Class of 1999 (N=2,322)	Class of 2000 (N=2,204)	Class of 2001 (N=2,218)
83.6	84.9	84.1	84.4	85.4	85.3	85.6	85.7	84.8
9.2	9.3	9.0	7.9	7.8	8.6	8.3	8.2	7.5
3.4	2.7	3.7	3.2	2.7	2.6	2.6	2.1	3.4
2.0	1.7	1.8	2.6	2.1	2.2	2.1	1.8	2.3
1.8	1.4	1.4	1.9	2.0	1.3	1.3	2.2	2.0
69.0	70.1	70.2	69.9	71.7	71.5	72.1	71.9	70.8
13.1	13.2	12.8	13.4	13.5	12.4	11.3	12.8	14.0
7.6	6.8	6.4	6.2	5.3	6.4	6.3	5.5	5.5
4.2	4.5	4.5	4.0	3.8	4.1	5.1	4.3	4.5
6.1	5.5	6.1	6.5	5.8	5.5	5.2	5.5	5.2

Pacific Coasts. Settlers filled the spaces between, and during this period the population of the United States grew from 3.9 million in 1790 to 75,995,000 in 1900. We began to grow from an agrarian nation to an industrial nation, and during this period the stage was set for the United States to become the economic and industrial powerhouse that arose out of WWII. During this period, there was a great immigration, and the cities expanded and grew as they filled with immigrants who were willing to work. The cities were transformed as they were filled with different languages and customs that were often misunderstood by police and city authorities or were even met with hostility because they were "different."

As the settlers pushed the frontier back, the idea persisted that the city was an unhealthy place full of temptation. The general opinion was that "deviancy was primarily the result of the corruptions pervading the community and that organizations like the family and church were not counter balancing them . . ." (Rothman, 1971). Cities were unhealthy and often dangerous places and conventional wisdom stated that one was better off living outside of the city.

The Urban Growth Period (1900–1960) witnessed the continued growth of the cities, and by 1920 there had occurred a rural–urban shift in which more people now lived in cities than in the country. The city had developed as a way of meeting the manufacturing, finance, and trading needs of the particular region in which it was situated. It had been transformed by the huge numbers of immigrants who streamed in both from the countryside and from abroad. While it was still marked by contrasts of wealth and poverty, a new middle class was emerging that would soon fuel the engine of social progress. The city was also marked by its heterogeneity. In his description of the U.S. city with its different ways of life, Louis Wirth (1938) called it a "mosaic of social worlds." That is, while not exactly a melting pot, the city was composed of different neighborhoods whose sum total was the large city.

In about 1960, there began the fourth urban revolution, the Urban Tranformation Period. At this time, changes were occurring in cities all around the globe, but the event that began the transformation of the city in the United States was the passage by Congress of the **Federal Aid Highway Transportation Act**. This act, passed ostensibly to facilitate the transport of military supplies in time of national emergency, enabled the middle class to divide its time between the city and suburb. This trend began shortly after WWII, when suburbs such as Levittown, on Long Island, New York, were constructed to meet the pent-up housing needs of returning veterans and their families. Between 1950 and 1960, there was an 18 percent shift in population from the central cities to suburban rings (abu-Lughod, 1991) and the passage of the Highway Transportation Act just facilitated the trend.

Aided by the freeways that began to ring the larger cities and led to the countryside, the flight of the white middle class meant that housing was available for African Americans and their white brothers and sisters who were fleeing the farm because of a change in technology, which made farming less labor-intensive. Both black and white farmworkers were drawn to the city by the promise of jobs in manufacturing.

The loss of the middle class and its tax base, coupled with an influx of mostly poor immigrants from the farm, created a financial crisis for the cities and rendered them incapable of keeping up with the demand for services. Further complicating the situation was the increased loss of jobs as manufacturing employees began to follow the middle class to the suburban ring. At the same time, there began a subtle shift in population and jobs to the sunbelt. By 1980, the shift had crippled many cities, particularly in the heavily industrialized northeast and Great Lakes areas. As a further blow, the federal government has been unable, or unwilling, to establish policies and tax incentives that would stem the loss of manufacturing jobs to foreign countries.

Between 1980 and 2000, the population of the United States grew by more than 54 million people and by 2000, the urban transformation was nearly complete. There was a population shift from the heavily industrialized northeast and Great Lakes areas to the sunbelt. For example, California gained 25.7 percent in population between 1980 and 1990 and another 13.8 percent between 1990 and 2000. Between 1980 and 1990, Florida gained 32.7 percent and 23.5 percent between 1990 and 2000. Nevada has grown by leaps and bounds in the last twenty years, 50.1 percent between 1980 and 1990 and 66.3 percent between 1990 and 2000. The results of this shift are obvious: tremendous growth in major cities such as Atlanta, Miami, Dallas, Los Angeles. With that growth has come poverty,

Figure 3.1   Construction of the interstate highway system contributed to the breakdown of the inner city by providing an avenue for the middle-class to live outside the city and drive into the city for work.

despair, a permanent (mostly black and brown) underclass, and few meaningful jobs for a sizable number of citizens. Many city neighborhoods are battlegrounds, and the law-abiding inhabitants cry out for help while they attempt to hold on to a shred of dignity and security. In the meantime, the juvenile justice system has become so overloaded that it is virtually useless in many jurisdictions. The resulting cries for help have resulted in a re-vamping of the juvenile system. Many legislators have responded to this cry for help and have initiated reforms that reflect the harshness of the adult system in a misguided belief that harshness will solve the problem.

THE SUBURBS

As mentioned above, after WWII there began a population shift to the outer ring of the city and even beyond. That shift was facilitated by the construction of freeways that allowed the family to move out of the city a convenient distance and commute to work. As long as the mother stayed at home to look after children and home, there was no problem. However, as two-earner families became more the norm, some families began to experience more and more problems with children, such as increased truancy, delinquency, and rebelliousness.

At the end of WWII, approximately 70 percent of metropolitan citizens lived in the central city, but by 1990 only about 31 percent of metropolitan citizens lived in the central city. The suburbs have been criticized and castigated by many scholars and observers. Vice President Al Gore summed up the general attitude:

> Acre upon acre have transformed what were once mountain clearings and congenial villages into little more than massive parking lots. The ill-thought out sprawl that has developed around our nations cities has turned what used to be friendly, easy suburbs into lonely cul-de-sacs, so distant from the city center that if a family wants to buy an affordable house, they have to drive so far that a parent gets home too late to read a bedtime story (Postrel, 1999).

Wayne S. Wooden (1995) points out that "youth become deviant either out of a need for different experiences—for the thrill of taking risks—or out of unhappiness with themselves or with facets of society that they feel they have no control over." Absentee parents, broken homes, blended families, and in general a sense by youth that parents have no time for them litter the suburban landscape creating a cadre of alienated, often hostile youth.

These kids, according to Wooden, have been given everything from computers to cars. Still they are bored and, one suspects, are looking for structure not found in the home. In their search for excitement, they turn to peers and they become anomic, "broken by society." These youngsters become renegades, suburban "mall rats" and outlaws who cross the line between youth culture and delinquency.

THE RURAL ENVIRONMENT

Thomas Bender (1978), explores the notion of community lost, and he arrives at the conclusion that community has not been lost, but rather we have been looking in all the wrong places for it over the past hundred years. We still hold up the ideal of the rural community as the best place to raise children and as a place characterized by caring relationships and a place where one can live in emotional and physical safety.

Ferdinand Tonnies (1957, 1971) introduced the typologies of "*gemeinschaft und gesellschaft*" in his search for concepts that would explain the changes in relations associated with capitalism and the urbanization of society. Roughly speaking, *gemeinschaft* addresses the face-to-face relationships and relationships to primary reference groups. *Gesellschaft* refers to a society characterized by secondary relationships, competition, and impersonality. Emile Durkheim (1933) also viewed society as one that was in the process of evolving from "mechanical" to "organic."

However, it seems as if both men fell into the same trap, the same one into which nearly all of contemporary society has fallen; that is perhaps society is not moving from *gemeinschaft* to *gesellschaft* or mechanical to organic, but rather the two coexist side by side. There are parts of society (rural) that is characterized by primary, face-to-face relationships, and there are other parts (urban) characterized by secondary relationships and competition and impersonality. Each has its own values and norms and informal means of controlling behavior. Thus, community is not lost, perhaps it was and maybe it never existed so much as a place on the map, but in communities of people bound by similarities of race, ethnicity, interests, or blood.

As the United States moved from a rural, agrarian society to an urban, industrialized society, we began to look backward nostalgically. However, life in rural areas is not free from crime, nor is it always an idyllic life characterized by a lack of problems. Urban areas experience more crime specifically because of the higher density of the population. Rural areas have crime, and in addition there are a number of other problems (Weisheit, Falcone, & Wells, 2002) such as:

- Emergency response times are longer.
- Road maintenance and snow removal is a problem at times.
- Mail delivery is not available to all areas of the country.
- Telephone service can be a problem.
- Treated water may be nonexistent.
- Electric service may be interrupted.
- Trash removal is up to the homeowner.

Overall, rural crime decreased 1.9 percent in 2000 from 1999. We can look at the figures for Vermont and North Dakota to illustrate the numbers of violent crime. For example, Vermont in 2001 experienced a small drop in the violent crime rate from 113.8 violent crimes per 100,000 population. In 1993, they experienced 114.2 violent crimes per 100,000. North Dakota experienced 66.9 violent crimes in 2001, a drop from 82.2 violent crimes per 100,000 population in 1993. Thus, while rural crime has been dropping (as it has for all crime in the recent past) rural areas do experience crime.

THE POLITICAL SYSTEM

The American form of government is a difficult vehicle in which to accomplish anything. Working within our form of government means that one must contend with two houses of the legislature (except for Nebraska which has a unicameral legislature), three branches of government, interest groups, the media, individual personalities, and various bureaucracies. Thus, it sometimes seems unique if anything is accomplished at all.

Carl Cohen defines democracy as "that system of community government in which, by and large, the members of a community participate, or may participate, directly or indirectly, in the making of decisions which affect them all" (1971). For example, members of the U.S. Congress attempt to get involved in juvenile justice, as they did with the passage of the **Violent and Repeat Juvenile Offender Act of 1997**. The 1997 Juvenile Crime Bill directly affects juvenile justice policy and appears to equate accountability with stiffer sentences, provides for enhanced sentences for gang membership, and provides less money for prevention programs as opposed to suppression programs. In addition, after many acrimonious slurs being thrown about by conservatives over "social pork," money was appropriated for the states to "improve" juvenile offender programs, but the governor must certify the money is being spent in conformance with the Act requirements.

Traditionally, crime and delinquency have been thought of as a local matter, but the Juvenile Crime Bill clearly makes much juvenile crime a federal matter and coerces the states into doing the bidding of the federal government. Thus, the Juvenile Crime Bill may be a failure because many state legislators will object to the conditions contained in the bill.

The state can do anything not prohibited by the U.S. Constitution or preempted by federal policy and that is consistent with their own constitutions. This includes police power, that is those laws and regulations that promote health, safety, and morals, including those laws aimed at preventing and dealing with juvenile delinquency. The concept of *parens patriae* assumes the right of the state to intervene in natural family relationships and for the state to act as parent where necessary. Parens patriae is the underlying philosophy of the juvenile court. That is, a concerned judge will determine what is best for the child and work to treat, rather than punish the delinquent child. However, the philosophy of the juvenile court is being questioned, and efforts are being made to remold the court in the tradition of adult courts and thus weaken the tradition of parens patriae.

In 1999, the police made an estimated 1.3 million arrests for persons under the age of eighteen (Uniform Crime Report, 1999). Generally speaking, there has been a downward trend in juvenile arrests since at least 1996, but the media's focus on juvenile crime has raised the issue of youth crime to nearly epidemic proportions in the public mind. We learned in Chapter 1 that while youth crime has not risen nearly as much as the media would have us believe, the problem of violent crime committed by youth is still at levels that should cause us concern.

In Chicago, where the juvenile court began, juvenile judges find that they have on average six minutes per case or about sixty cases per day. In New Orleans, public defenders for juveniles must make do with the most primitive of conditions that hardly allow an adequate defense for their clients even if most youth are not represented by counsel (Butterfield, 1997). In Missouri, the Missouri Bar Association has prepared a pamphlet that is distributed to high school students on the first day of classes informing them of Missouri's tough new laws against delinquents. They are warned, "Your juvenile record can follow you forever" (Walters, 1995).

The above illustrations are an example of the conditions existing in the juvenile justice system, and at the same time, the average citizen pressures his or her representative for positive action. In addition, as noted in Chapter 1, the smart political candidate will take advantage of fear and exploit it to his or her advantage. As a consequence, forty-eight of fifty-one states (including the District of Columbia) have made substantive changes to the law, changes that target juvenile offenders who commit violent or serious crimes (Torbet et al., 1996).

That the political environment is very much a part of the juvenile justice system is beyond dispute. If it were not, there would have been fewer calls for harsher punishments by politicians. On May 8, 1997, the U.S. House of Representatives debated the Juvenile Crime Control Act of 1997. A number of representatives stood to denounce the juvenile justice system as a system out of control or as broken.

For example, Congressman Bill McCollum (R-FL) stated, "this bill focuses on the problems of a broken juvenile justice system, that is what the underlying bill is all about, which chronically fails to hold juvenile offenders acountable." Congressman Gekas (R-PA) asserted that,

The American people across the Nation are constantly shocked by the brutality and vicious-ness of some of the crimes that are being committed by thirteen- and fourteen- and fifteen-year-olds. And they are equally shocked, the American people are, when they see a system that treats these juveniles as something less than the predators that they seem to be even at that early age. And what happens? They produce this juvenile system which, as we know it today, produces a cycle of recidivism among the juveniles that commit these vicious crimes.

These comments are illustrative of the attitude and tone of attempts to do something about a juvenile justice system that is perceived as failing. The political environment can di-rectly affect the juvenile justice system, and it indirectly affects the quality of life of many children, and in many other ways it determines the lifestyle of families. The fact also remains that most children are not delinquent, but are able to step around temptations and go on to graduate from high school and eventually assume responsible positions in their community.

Torbet, et al. (1996) have identified five themes and trends in the new laws that target juveniles (see Figure 3.2). Nearly every state has taken some sort of action in response to es-calating arrests for juvenile violent crime and the public perception that juvenile crime has gotten out of hand. These five themes—jurisdictional authority, judicial disposition or sen-tencing authority, correctional programming, confidentiality of juvenile court records and proceedings, and victims of juvenile crime—significantly alter the way the juvenile court goes about its business. At present, there is a tidal wave of change sweeping the nation that has the potential to change the way juvenile corrections goes about its business for years to

Themes	**Trends**
Judicial authority	More serious and violent offenders are being removed from the juvenile justice system in favor of criminal prosecution.
Judicial disposition/ sentencing authority	More state legislatures are experimenting with new disposition/sentencing laws.
Correctional programming	Correctional administrators are under pressure to develop programs as a result of new transfer and sentencing laws.
Confidentiality of juvenile court records and proceedings	Traditional confidentiality provisions are being revised in favor of more open pro-ceedings and records.
Victims of juvenile crime	Victims of juvenile crime are being in-cluded as "active participants" in the ju-venile justice process.

Figure 3.2   Themes and Trends in New Laws Targeting Violent or Other Serious Crime by Juveniles
Source: Torbet et al. (1996). *State Responses to Serious and Violent Juvenile Crime.* Washington, DC: Office of Juvenile Justice and Delinquency Prevention.

Dealing with Juvenile Delinquency

During the May 8, 1997, debate on the Juvenile Crime Control Act of 1997, the following remarks were made by the Honorable Max Sandlin (D-CA) before the House of Representatives. The debate centered on an amendment offered by the Democratic minority to include more prevention incentives and to curb strong guidelines to states applying for federal block grant money to fight delinquency.

Mr. Chairman, in this country today, obviously we have a problem with juvenile crime. It seems to me that we must decide what to do about that problem and who should do it. The Democratic alternative addresses those issues.

As a former judge, I have heard thousands of juvenile cases. Many times we must deal seriously with juveniles. Some must be incarcerated. However, as the father of four children, as a former youth baseball, basketball, and softball coach, as someone active in the Boy Scouts of America, I can tell my colleagues that the children of America are worth saving.

Just like they must be responsible for their acts, we must be responsible, the U.S. Congress, for providing opportunities for children to stay out of the system. We know what does not work. We know that.

We know that spending more and more tax dollars to build facilities to lock up more and more children without hope is not the answer, but we have to provide alternatives. We need to incarcerate some juveniles, but we need to provide for education. We need to provide for intervention. We need to provide for community support, and the Democratic alternative does that.

Who knows best how to handle these problems? Who knows best how to handle things in Texas, in New York, in California, in Mississippi, in Iowa, in Illinois, in Massachusetts? People in those communities do, not Washington. Under the substitute legislation, local communities receive local grants to solve local problems. Let us let local teachers, local preachers, local parents, local friends handle local problems in our states.

One point I have not heard discussed is the fact our friends on the other side of the aisle are attempting to model the juvenile system after the adult system. Like it is some model. Is that not dandy? The adult system has not worked either. Treating juveniles and modeling the juvenile system after a failed adult system is certainly ridiculous.

It is time for a new approach. Our states do not need to change, our local communities do not need to change, Washington needs to change.

come. In a way, this is unfair in that if juvenile crime is escalating, it is escalating in response to the way adults manage the affairs of the nation and the lives of the children affected.

Inherent in many of the changes that Torbet et al. point out is the belief that juvenile offenders must be held accountable. This is a laudable sentiment, but in the mind of many legislators, accountability is the same as harsher punishment. And, just like the "Three Strikes" laws, the less serious offender is caught up in the reforms and must endure harsher punishments just like his or her older and more emotionally damaged brethren. Thus, for children, as for adults, punishment and not reformation is the goal.

A related problem is that many of the "reforms" are passed into law, but funding for increased facilities and related management problems are not forthcoming. The result is that juveniles who find themselves caught up in the juvenile justice or adult criminal justice net soon learn that there are few programs, facilities are overcrowded, and that to survive they must learn to survive in a very harsh environment, resulting in youth who are even more emotionally and psychologically damaged upon their return to their communities.

THE IMPACT OF THE EXTERNAL ENVIRONMENT ON THE JUVENILE JUSTICE SYSTEM

The impact of the external environment on the child and the juvenile justice system is substantial. The calls for "improvements" in the juvenile justice system are a result of a public concerned about children and their own safety. Daily life has taken on new challenges and under the influence of the media and cross pollenization of cultures, many people and groups lament a way of life that they feel has passed into history.

The beginnings of the juvenile court are founded in concern for youth and the way they were treated in a system perceived as adversarial, harsh, and with few opportunities for rehabilitation and self-improvement. Bartollas and Miller (1998) note that there are **four basic models for correction** of the delinquent: the rehabilitation model, the justice model, the crime control model, and the logical consequences model.

The rehabilitation model seeks to change an offender's behavior and attitudes, in other words, to somehow change the character of the juvenile and steer him or her away from a life of crime. According to Bartollas and Miller, the medical model is the primary expression of the rehabilitation approach. From the beginnings of the juvenile court, the medical model has been accepted as the approach to use. Delinquents are assumed to be "sick," and the probation officer or other court personnel serve as the "doctor" who will "treat" the offender and make him or her well again. The belief that delinquency is the result of factors that can be identified, diagnosed, and treated has driven the treatment approaches to probation and institutional programs. Events in the environment such as the rise of humanitarianism that fostered the Settlement House movement, improvements in health care, and interest in prisons and delinquency all contributed to the founding of the juvenile court. Today the steadfast belief that children and youth can be rehabilitated continues to inform the argument regarding improvements in the juvenile justice system.

The justice model asserts that punishment should be the primary purpose of the juvenile justice system. Bartollas and Miller cite several state crime bills as indications that the justice model is gaining currency with legislators as an approach to dealing with juvenile crime: the Omnibus Crime Bill of New York State (1978), the determinate sentencing law for juveniles in the state of Washington (1977), the California mandatory sentencing law, and the institutional release policy adopted for juveniles in the state of Minnesota.

The justice model asserts that juveniles have free will and are responsible for their behavior. This appears to make sense on the surface, but we must remember that juveniles are immature human beings who, regardless of age, still need the guidance and supervision of adults. A juvenile system that fails to account for the mistakes of adults in the lives of delinquents is a system that ultimately fails the youth.

The crime control model is based on the Classical School of criminology (see Chapter 2) and calls for quick, severe, and certain punishments based on a scale of punishments attuned to specific crimes, usually defined as months in institutions for specific crimes. The public is fed up with serious juvenile crime. They demand action but are short on information about the juvenile justice system and the causes for its apparent lack of success.

The logical consequences model makes five important assumptions: that juveniles have free will and should be held accountable for their behavior, delinquents know the system well enough to be able to manipulate it, delinquents will modify their behavior only when the costs for delinquent behavior become too high, required community service is necessary because juveniles do not take probation seriously, and finally it is possible to develop effective relationships with juveniles once they have decided to take probation seriously. Bartollas and Miller point out that the logical consequences model was derived from a logical consequences approach to disciplining children in society that gained acceptance in society in the 1970s and 1980s. That is, parents should give the child a choice and explain the consequences of negative behavior. Thus, the responsibility for behavior is placed on the child.

The four models described above have widespread support among members of society and, we might add, among members of Congress and the various legislators. However, the get-tough approach seems to have gained an edge, at least for the more serious offenders. Given the fragmentation of the juvenile justice system, practitioners and legislators seem to pick and choose a model to guide the design of programs and legislation.

The influences from the external environment that give rise to the four models described above impact the family in a variety of ways; there is an impact on employment of the primary breadwinner, on the quality of housing, education, and health care. Juvenile justice policy and legislation is often a symbolic issue for elected officials. We have heard campaign rhetoric that abounds with statements promoting a get-tough attitude on serious juvenile offenders. We need look no further than the 1997 Violent and Repeat Juvenile Offender Act for an example of symbolic action and a sure-to-fail piece of legislation. In the meantime, families, courts, schools, and recreation opportunities for youth suffer.

SUMMARY

The family has the primary responsibility for the socialization of the child and is the vehicle for teaching the child right from wrong, expectations of others, that rules must be followed, what is appropriate behavior, and what is not. If the family fails its primary responsibility, society must deal with a youth or adult who will come to the attention of the juvenile or adult justice system.

The educational system is primarily responsible for the education of the young and to prepare them to assume a place in society as informed citizens and capable employees. However, that task must often take a back seat to the discipline and control of students. In addition, more and more subjects are mandated by a symbolically motivated legislature that further takes time away from educational instruction.

The city is often blamed for much delinquency, and the unwholesomeness of city life is, in some people's mind, to blame for youthful crime. However, cities have always been blamed for unwholesome behavior, and there appears to be no prospect for a change in attitude. We must keep in mind that there is just as much rural crime as there is urban crime. It's just that urban crime has a greater probability of being reported. Clearly, the impact of the environment on the juvenile justice system is great and subject to many variables.

CASE STUDY WRAP-UP

Jeanette MacDonald Dillon covers a lot of material in her article summarized at the beginning of this chapter. To begin, it is apparent that something is wrong with the family constellation if it is unable to recognize when a child is about to do something drastically wrong. Clearly, we cannot attribute the problem to poverty. In fact, some of the youth involved in school shootings come from affluent homes. Likewise, we cannot attribute the apparent alienation and glorification of violence to broken homes only, as many of the youth involved in such atrocities come from intact homes. Suicide is also identified by MacDonald Dillon as an issue to be contended with, but in some instances we seem powerless to do anything.

Thus, there are a number of issues that must be monitored by the family and school if we are to do anything about the numbers of youth violence. The political system attempts to deal with youth crime, especially youth violence with harsh penalties and referring the youth to the adult court. On the other hand, little attention is paid to prevention and treatment as an alternative to harsher sanctions. We will delve into these issues at greater length in later chapters and perhaps arrive at solutions that better serve families, schools, and the youth.

STUDY QUESTIONS

1. How has the family changed over time, and has any change impacted the rate of delinquency experienced by the community?
2. How do you think urbanization affects delinquency?
3. Torbet identifies five themes and trends in laws that target juveniles. Can you identify three of them?
4. What is the medical model of rehabilitation as identified by Clemens Bartolas?

BIBLIOGRAPHY

ABU-LUGHOD, JANET (1991). *Changing Cities*. New York: HarperCollins.

BARTOLLAS, CLEMONS, AND MILLER, STUART J. (1998). *Juvenile Justice in America*, 2nd ed. Upper Saddle River, NJ: Prentice Hall Inc.

BENDER, THOMAS (1978). *Community and Social Change in America.* Baltimore: The Johns Hopkins University Press.

BERNSTEIN, JARED, MCNICHOL, ELIZABETH C., MISHEL, LAWRENCE, AND ZAAHRADNIK, ROBERT (2000). *Pulling Apart: A State-by-State Analysis of Income Trends.* Washington, DC: Center on Budget and Policy Priorities, Economic Policy Institute, January.

BUTTERFIELD, FOX (1997). "With Juvenile Courts in Chaos, Some Propose Scrapping Them." *New York Times.* Vol CXLVI. (M) July 21, p.1, col 1.

COHEN, CARL (1971). *Democracy.* Athens, GA: University of Georgia Press.

COONTZ, STEPHANIE (1997). *The Way We Really Are: Coming to Terms with America's Changing Families.* New York: Basic Books.

DEVINE, JOEL A., AND WRIGHT, JAMES D. (1993). *The Greatest of Evils: Urban Poverty and the American Underclass.* New York: Aldine de Gruyter.

DURKHEIM, EMILE (1993). *The Division of Labor in Society,* trans. George Simpson. New York: Free Press.

FEDERAL BUREAU OF INVESTIGATION (2000). *Crime in the United States—1999.* Washington, D.C.: U.S. Government Printing Office.

FISHER, GORDON (1992). *Social Security Bulletin* Vol. 55, No. 4, Winter.

GIBBONS, DON C. (1992). *Society, Crime, and Criminal Behavior,* 6th ed. Englewood Cliffs, NJ: Prentice-Hall.

HEALY, W. (1915). *The Individual Delinquent.* Boston: Little Brown.

LEVY, PAUL (1998). "Today's Lesson: Safety at School," *Minneapolis Star-Tribune.* Sepember, 3, p. 12A. 1995, in Richard Lawrence, *School Crime and Juvenile Justice.* New York: Oxford Univeristy Press.

MONAHAN, THOMAS P. (1957). "Family Status and the Delinquent Child: A Reappraisal and Some New Findings." *Social Forces, 35,* pp. 250–258.

POSTREL, VIRGINIA (1999). "The Pleasantville Solution," *Reason* online, March. Reason.com.

ROTHMAN, DAVID J. (1971). *Discovery of the Asylum.* Boston: Little Brown and Company, p. 82.

SHAW, CLIFFORD R., AND MCKAY, HENRY D. (1931). *Social Factors in Juvenile Delinquency.* No. 13, Vol 11. National Commission on Law Observance and Enforcement. Washington, D.C.: U.S. Government Printing Office.

SJOBERG, GIDEON (1960). *The Pre-industrial City.* New York: The Free Press.

SLAWSON, J. (1926). *The Delinquent Boy.* Boston: Badger.

THORNTON, JR., WILLIAM E., AND VOIGT, LYDIA (1992). *Delinquency and Justice,* 3rd ed. New York: McGraw-Hill, Inc.

TONNIES, FERDINAND (1957). *Community and Society: Gemeinschaft and Gesellschaft,* translated (1878) and edited by Charles P. Loomis, pp. 223–231 in Marcell. Fruzzi (1971). *Sociology: The Classic Statements.* New York: Oxford University Press, pp. 145–154.

TONNIES, FERDINAND (1963). *Community and Society,* trans. Charles P. Loomis. New York: Harper.

TORBET, PATRICIA, GABLE, RICHARD, HURST IV, HUNTER, MONTGOMERY, IMOGENE, SZYMANSKI, LINDA, AND THOMAS, DOUGLAS (July 1996). *State Responses to Serious and Violent Juvenile Crime: A Research Report.* Washington, D.C.: Office of Juvenile Justice and Delinquency Prevention.

U.S. BUREAU OF COMMERCE, BUREAU OF CENSUS, CENSUS OF POPULATION: 1920–1980. *Statistical Abstract of the United States.* Washington, D.C.: Government Printing Office, 1991, p. 7.

U.S. BUREAU OF COMMERCE, BUREAU OF CENSUS. (2000). *Abstract of the United States,* Washington, D.C.: Government Printing Office.

WALTERS, LAUREL SHAPER (1995). "State Try to Rewrite Crime and Punishment," *Christian Science Monitor,* December 5, p. 1, col. 3.

WEISHEIT, RALPH A., FALCONE, DAVID N., AND WELLS, L. EDWARD (2002). *Crime and Policing in Rural and Small Town America,* 2nd ed. Long Grove, IL: Waveland Press.

WILKERSON, KAREN (1980). "The Broken-Home and Delinquent Behavior," in *Understanding Delinquency,* Travis Hirshi and Michael Gottfredson, Eds. Beverly Hills, CA: Sage Publications, pp. 210–242.

WIRTH, LOUIS (1938). "Urbanism as a Way of Life," *American Journal of Sociology,* Vol. 44, July, pp. 8–20.

WOODEN, WAYNE S. (1995). *Renegade Kids, Suburban Outlaws: From Youth Culture to Delinquency.* Belmont, CA: Wadsworth Publishing Company.

GLOSSARY OF KEY TERMS

Colonial period.   During this period, the American wilderness was viewed as an area to be exploited for its wealth, and the first colonists were sent to establish outposts for the various empires that had claims on the continent. The first cities resulted from charters granted by the English and French Kings for purposes of mercantilism. During this period, the colonies were separated by distance and poor transportation and community institutions evolved along different tracks.

Expansionist period.   During this period, the young United States grew from thirteen states huddled along the Atlantic Coast to a nation that stretched from the Atlantic to the Pacific Coasts.

Federal Aid Highway Transportation Act.   An act signed by President Dwight D. Eisenhower that allowed the interstate highway system to be constructed. This is the public policy that urbanologists believe is responsible for the change in our cities.

Four basic models for correction.   The rehabilitation model, the justice model, the crime control model, and the logical consequences model.

Urban growth period.   The period in American history that witnessed the continued growth of the cities and by 1920 there had occurred a rural-urban shift in which more people now lived in cities than in the country. The city developed as a way of meeting the manufacturing, finance, and trading needs of the particular region in which it was situated and was transformed by the huge numbers of immigrants who streamed in both from the countryside and from abroad. While it was still marked by contrasts of wealth and poverty, a new middle class was emerging that would soon fuel the engine of social progress.

Urban transformation period.   Beginning in 1960, the cities began to change because of the impact of the Highway Transportation Act, and a population shift occurred that saw the out-migration of the middle class to the suburbs and a poor rural in-migration to the cities.

Violent and Repeat Juvenile Offender Act.   An act passed by Congress in 1997 designed to deal with juvenile delinquency, but critics agree that it is too harsh and focuses on repression rather than prevention and rehabilitation.

CHAPTER 4
GANGS

KEY TERMS

American Dream   People and Folks   Chronic poverty

CASE STUDY

A Police Officer Speaks Out
John Laskey, Lt. Chicago Police Department (ret.)*

By 1990, I had been fighting street gangs in Chicago for over twenty years. During most of that time I served as patrolman, homicide detective, or plainclothes tactical team supervisor for the Chicago Police Department, and I always thought every city had the same crime problem as Chicago; that is organized gangs of tough youth, many organized and managed by adults, who engaged in criminal activity. I used the "traditional" and accepted police tactics of the time: arrest, sweeps, and suppression. I never thought further about what I was doing or its effect, only to build a good case and prosecute the criminals.

*John Laskey retired in 2002 as a lieutenant in the Chicago Police Department after thirty-four years of service which included tours of duty as a patrolman, homicide detective, supervisor in tactical units, the FBI Task Force, Internal Affairs and Organized Crime Units. He participated in the prototype Community Policing Experiments in Chicago in 1992. He holds a masters degree in criminal justice from DePaul University and a BA from Loyola University. He has taught as an adjunct at the university and community-college level and has thirteen publications to his credit in the area of youth gangs and gang crime. In addition to over one hundred commendations, he was named as Illinois TOP COP and Honorable Mention for the National Police Organization's TOP COP award in Washington, D.C. In August 2001, he received a Life-Time Achievement Award for Excellence in Law Enforcement at Loyola University Law School.

However, over the years I couldn't help notice that the gang's power rose and fell across different neighborhoods and ethnic groups, but the gang always survived. Their symbols and clothing changed, and their criminal activity went from petty crimes, robbery, and assaults to organized drug sales and planned murder. But the gangs lived on.

Early in 1990, I started to teach at the college level as an adjunct and began to associate with people who had spent their lives researching gangs and the gang's impact on society. I started to question the effectiveness of what I was doing and of police policies in regard to gangs in general. I learned that smaller cities and towns did not recognize their gang problem and many denied having street gangs for political reasons. In addition, many local police officers received little or no training regarding street gangs, (Chicago included), and no police department that I was aware of had a systematic or reliable assessment of the effectiveness of their gang suppression strategy. Even today, police anti-gang tactics are not evaluated for their effectiveness and are not re-tooled or discarded based on objective evaluation. The same suppression tactics go on and on until a court challenge puts a halt to the program. In the meantime, the politicians can claim to community groups and other members of their constituency, which are eager for help, that they are proactive and anti-crime by proposing and supporting more police suppression procedures.

Regular street sweeps of suspected gang members, arrested for disorderly conduct and loitering, were ordered by command. Those arrested were out on bond within hours and regarded their arrest as a minor inconvenience and a badge of honor. Many of those arrested were not gang members, but innocent teens caught up in the sweeps that now were bitter with the police. Because our district police station was located within the boundaries of one street gang, opposing gang members leaving the station house after posting bond often had to run a gauntlet of gunfire to return to their home turf. Some didn't make it. After a time, the young tactical officers who were involved in the street sweeps questioned the tactic's effectiveness and legality. The officers usually did not appear in court to testify, and even when they did, the cases were dismissed. None of this fazed the police command staff that continued to order these sweeps until the court decisions and lawsuits stopped the programs.

I admit some street gangs are criminal organizations and need to be attacked through an efficient multiagency task force and gang tracking system. But even the effectiveness of a specialized police organization to implement a suppression strategy is being called into question. In 1992, Chicago, in response to an outside management study, decentralized their gang unit. Hundreds of gang specialists were absorbed into the district law enforcement teams across twenty-five police districts, leaving only a small central gang intelligence unit. In 2001, the remaining central gang intelligence unit was disbanded, the last of what once was a gang unit composed of over five-hundred officers. A decade of police and prosecution suppression tactics has failed to curb the growth of gangs. It seems the gangs never fail to have a pool of fresh recruits. Where do these new gang members come from? They come from our own neighborhoods and families, and many willingly join the gang, often in grade school. I have become convinced by thirty-four years of police work in the gang areas of Chicago that only a community-based police problem-solving approach will ultimately choke off the membership pool for the gangs. Don't get me wrong. I am not advocating a purely social response, but a community-based task force approach with police, prosecutor, community groups, social agencies, religious institutions, and educational institutions working in concert.

With little evidence that the various "hammer-like" police tactics are effective in reducing the gang problem in either large or small cities, the police should be at the forefront in developing community-based programs that work hand in hand with local grade schools. Teachers in grade schools should be the first to recognize troubled and disruptive children, many of whom are exhibiting all the signs of early gang vulnerability as young as nine years of age, many by age twelve. These kids come from troubled and dysfunctional families, many plagued with drug and alcohol abuse, physical and sexual abuse, and mental illness. Let us train our teachers to recognize these signs and refer the children and their families to our police-directed community-based program of investigation, referral, and prosecution if necessary. The police must place importance on suppression and social intervention, learn to communicate with the gang members and their families, not only emphasizing proper prosecution for gang crimes, but also expressing respect and concern for those who want to leave the gang and join society.

INTRODUCTION

The apparent disintegration of our inner cities and the violence that accompanies that disintegration has scorched the soul of America and led to a sense of impotence among our citizens. It has engendered fear of the streets, as well as anger and frustration with our elected officials. At times, we seem powerless to do anything about loss of jobs, crime, and street gangs, except perhaps to pass concealed carry laws. Many of our citizens and elected officials are in a state of denial about gangs and have not recognized, or refuse to recognize, law enforcement and social problems associated with the presence of street gangs. It is difficult to estimate the amount of delinquent behavior related to gangs, but there is no denying that street gangs have become a fact of life for many cities and smaller communities. However, during the prosperity of the middle-to-late 1990s and beyond, we saw a decline in the attractiveness of gang membership for some youth. It remains to be seen if this trend will continue to hold.

PUBLIC IGNORANCE

During the early 1980s, we rediscovered street gangs. Those of us in smaller cities and towns learned of their activities from newspapers or television and shook our heads in dismay. Our inclination was to deny their existence or to believe they had no impact on our immediate life.

How wrong we were. A survey of police chiefs and sheriffs (Knox et al., 1994a) reveals that street gangs are more than an inner-city problem. They estimated that nearly one in six crimes committed at that time were gang-related. This included murders, robberies, sexual crimes, drug offenses, and petty theft. Walter Miller (2000) reports that in 1995, all fifty states, 706 counties (23.2 percent of the total number of counties), and 1,487 cities and towns reported gang problems. Clearly, gangs have penetrated many cities and towns that previously thought they were isolated and safe from their predations.

Why has this phenomenon suddenly exploded upon our consciousness with the impact of a nuclear bomb? To begin, we have ignored the link between family and a steady paycheck for the primary breadwinner. The loss of opportunity for primary breadwinners to hold meaningful jobs has been sneered at or dismissed by "knowledgeable" business and financial executives whose lives are untouched by the despair and hopelessness brought on by prolonged unemployment, underemployment, and downsizing. To them, the bottom line has been most important. During the 1980s when the tax structure and economic conditions fueled the merger and acquisitions frenzy, many companies were looted and the employees discarded like yesterday's *Wall Street Journal*. Today, companies with a healthy bottom line are laying off employees, it seems, just to impress the barons of Wall Street.

Nowhere has the tragedy of job loss been acted out more disastrously than in the inner cities and to a lesser extent in nearly every town and city in America. Pamela Irving Jackson (1991) sheds light on the consequences of our lack of will to do something about gangs. After reviewing unemployment figures, crime statistics, gang crime statistics, and other demographic variables in all cities in the United States with a population over twenty-five thousand, she concludes that loss of jobs and the social dislocation caused by the transition of the American economy has harmed us far beyond what we thought could have been possible. Jackson asserts that the result has been a rise in street gangs. It is her contention that gangs serve a useful social purpose by providing acceptance, recognition, and a sense of belonging. It used to be that these were the things one gained from one's family or from one's employment or union. However, when there are no meaningful job prospects, a multitude of single-parent families, irresponsible parents, a glorification of violence, a supply of weapons, and a plentiful supply of cheap crack cocaine for use and resale, we should hardly be surprised at the consequences.

Our knee-jerk reaction has been to hire more police, build more prisons, and to send the gangster off to prison for longer periods of time. Few of us doubt the need for police, for evil people exist among us and we need protection. Few of us would quarrel with the existence of prisons; an orderly society must separate criminals from law-abiding citizens. However, we are compelled to ask how many people must we lock up before such tactics begin to offer a return? Today, according to the Bureau of Justice Statistics, we have nearly two million people in prisons and jails. Perhaps we will begin to experience success when we have three million people locked up; five million; ten million. Where does it end?

GANGS ARE AN ENDEMIC PROBLEM

If we believe the media, our nation is in trouble. In many cities, the inhabitants are assailed with daily accounts of violent gang activity and with the speculation that our nation's youth, particularly our African-American youth, are a lost generation. An article in *Newsweek* (Kantrowitz, 1993) is illustrative of media accounts: "Law enforcement and public-health officials describe a virtual 'epidemic' of youth violence in the last five years, spreading from the inner cities to the suburbs" (1993). Indeed, youth crime and violence and gang activity are two sides of the same coin. According to *The 1992 Law Enforcement Survey* (Knox et al.), police chiefs around the nation estimate that over 14 percent of total crime in their jurisdiction is caused by gang activity. County sheriffs estimate that over 11 percent of all crime is the result of gang activity. In addition, 89 percent of police chiefs and over 78 percent of county sheriffs throughout the nation state that youth gangs are a problem in their jurisdictions. In addition to violent crimes, they cite drug sales, burglary, robbery, drive-by shootings and car theft as the more troublesome activities of youth gangs (Knox et al., 1992).

A 1994 estimate of street gang activity by the St. Louis Police Department Intelligence Division (Gang Section) put gang membership in the United States between 240,000 and 400,000, with up to 9,000 gangs active in the United States. A report by the National Institute of Justice (1996) estimated that gang membership rose by 77 percent from 1991 and 1993. However, gang membership and gang crime figures are elusive indeed. The gang problem is so underestimated that according the National Institute of Justice (1996) there may be as many as 16,643 gangs nationwide with a membership that approaches more than 580,000.

There appears to be not one, but two gang problems in America. One is the problem that we read about in the media and of which we are all fearful: random violence. For example, we do not know who, or how many of the young people in the movie theater with us, are armed and ready to use weapons against others in retaliation for a real or imagined insult, thereby endangering us if we are caught in the resultant crossfire. According to the National Youth Violence Prevention Resource Center (2004), in 1999 9 percent of male students and 4.9 percent of all students reported carrying a gun at least once in the 30 days prior to the survey. While this figure is high, it still represents a decrease from 13.7 percent of male students and 7.9 percent of all students carrying a gun in 1993. The second problem is that our elected officials at the state and federal levels seem to be unwilling, or unable, to address the real issues that have brought about the formation of gangs. Instead, they attack the symptoms and ignore more fundamental and basic reasons for the spread of gangs.

It is not too late to attack the problem, but our list of options is growing smaller. It has become frighteningly apparent that gangs are not confined to the inner-city but have spread to smaller towns across America and that they follow a weakness in the social fabric composed of the socially and economically disadvantaged.

Until now, what energy federal, state, and local policymakers have devoted to gangs has been repressive in nature and has not led to the development of a long-term perspective in the fight against gangs and crime. Some jurisdictions have awakened to the need for strategic planning and *The 1992 Law Enforcement Survey* reveals that as the threat of gangs increase, so, too, does the likelihood that the police or sheriff's department will have a strategic plan to deal with the problem (Knox et al., 1992). Still, these strategic plans are for the police and rarely do they include not only plans for suppression, but also plans for the economic, social, medical, and educational needs of the community.

It should be clear by now that quick-fix approaches to crime and gangs are ineffective, as are repressive measures alone. Our prisons and youth institutions are full, probation caseloads are unmanageable, and valuable resources have been diverted away from programs that benefit the general good such as parks, education, medical care, and transportation. Unfortunately the "quick fix" mentality dominates crime policy generally, and methods for dealing with crime are merely a reflection of broader policy failure.

HOMEBOYS, GUNS, AND MOBILITY

Why young people join gangs may be a puzzle for some, but there are some well thought-out explanations. Knox (1994a) neatly summarizes the thoughts of various scholars on why young people join gangs. Thrasher (1936) called our attention to a lack of controls, a permissive environment, and the presence of criminals who have high status in the community as factors that promote gang activity. Whyte (1943), as did Thrasher, saw gangs arising from the continuous association of members over a long period of time. Cohen (1955) focused upon social class and pointed to the frustration of lower-class boys in their search for status in a world favoring middle-class boys.

Bloch and Niederhoffer (1958) recognized the importance of family and called our attention to the role gangs play as family substitutes, providing such things as support and recognition, which are not found in the existing social structure. Cloward and Ohlin (1960) stress the lack of opportunities in the legitimate opportunity structure and the corresponding presence of opportunities in the illegitimate opportunity structure. They point out that when there is no opportunity to be found legitimately, youth will turn to the illegitimate opportunity structure. Klein (1968) asserts that external realities such as poverty, poor job opportunities, and dysfunctional families, to name just three, drive young people together in a meager effort to make life more endurable.

Jackson (1991) calls our attention to the vacuum created by a lack of employment and suggests that youth join a gang in order to fill a need for self-esteem and a sense of belonging. A national survey of police and sheriff's deputies reveals a number of reasons why youth join gangs (Knox et al., 1994a). The respondent's report that in their opinion youth join gangs out of a need for self-esteem, a need for a sense of belonging, as well as in response to pressure from friends and acquaintances. Also cited as moderately important are a need for protection, family influence, and the ability to commit illegal acts for financial gain. One officer stated that white youths in his jurisdiction join gangs as an activity. This may be a particularly disturbing observation in that, as he observes, many of these youths are from intact families and have not suffered the privation common to inner-city youths. Finally, Yablonsky states that young people join gangs for protection and a sense of belonging (Houston, 1993).

Whatever the reasons for the youthful propensity to join gangs, it may well be that gangs as we know them today are the end result of technological advances, economic change, and social neglect. For example, the automobile has proven to be a mixed blessing. The automobile provides unparalleled mobility but at the same time gave birth to a variety of modern social problems including the ability of gangs to easily move around the city in pursuit of drugs, loot, or to commit drive-by shootings.

THE MODERN GANG

We can arguably trace the modern gang to the mid 1950s when the Federal Aid Highway Transportation Act was passed by the United States Congress. The intent of the sponsors of the legislation was to develop a highway system capable of moving supplies and military resources around the nation in the event of a national emergency. The unanticipated consequences of the act was that it enabled the middle class to drive out of the city a comfortable distance, build a home, and commute to work.

The consequence, once the interstate system was in place, was that the middle class left the central city and with them a stable tax base. Simultaneously, a demographic shift was occurring among rural residents, both black and white. Because of technological and social changes, farming became less labor intensive, and people began to be pushed off the farm and were lured to the cities by the promise of jobs. The available housing served the poor immigrants, and many were able to secure adequate employment.

For over a decade, cities were able to maintain services and an adequate tax base. Then in the 1970s, jobs began to leave the central cities and with them an erosion of the tax base began to occur. Thus, the cities were unable to keep up with the demand for services, resulting in a downward spiral to decay.

As the migration of rural workers and southern African Americans to northern American cities progressed, initially work was to be found in the city. However, beginning in the 1970s, jobs began to flow out of the northern cities to the suburbs, the sunbelt, and to foreign countries. As those jobs began to be lost, a slow decline occurred in the standard of living of those left behind. Unable to find employment, unable to keep up with the demand for greater skills, and unable to travel to the suburbs for employment, many inner-city workers began to take on an air of desperation and hopelessness. With the declining standard of living also went a declining tax base and the services normally paid for by a prosperous tax base.

The extent of the damage done to urban life as the United States transitioned from a manufacturing economy to a service economy is illustrated by noting that in 1970, 26 percent of our national income was derived from manufacturing; in 1987, that percentage had fallen to 20 percent. During the period 1970 to 1987, the number of manufacturing jobs in the United States remained relatively constant, that is, there was a net loss of approximately 100,000 jobs; a drop from 19 million jobs in 1970 to 18.9 million jobs in 1987, but between 1987 and 2001 the number of employees engaged in manufacturing declined to 11,235,111 (U.S. Census, 2002).

In addition, since 1970 many jobs have been relocated from the inner city to the suburbs and to the sunbelt. During the period 1970 to 1987, expenditures for new plants and equipment fell 6 percent, between 1987 and 1992, the new prosperity had begun to take hold, and expenditures and new capital expenditures grew from $103.1 billion to $150.2 billion, but in 2001 investment in manufacturing had declined to $143.6 billion. Thus, while manufacturing has realized its ups and downs, it continues to employ a sizable number of our citizens, even at lower numbers than thirty years ago. The reason this discussion is important is that jobs in manufacturing have traditionally been family sustaining. That is, the husband and father was the primary breadwinner, and the mother and wife spent much of her time at home supervising the children. However, as the economy transitioned from a manufacturing economy to a service economy, household wages declined when accounting for inflation.

This has been especially hurtful to minorities whose income traditionally lags behind that of whites. On the other hand, poverty respects no racial lines, and we are obligated to ask who benefited from the prosperity of the 1980s and 1990s.

Most economists and politicians will point out that there was a net increase of service-sector jobs during this time. That is true, but those jobs do not pay as well as jobs in manufacturing, and many inner-city inhabitants were, or are, ill-prepared to take these jobs as well. There appears to be a paradox here in that by 2001 manufacturing compensation totaled $593 billion (U.S. Census, 2002). Thus, gangs became a legitimate response to the declining opportunities in the legitimate opportunity structure, even as some areas of the nation and the upper social classes benefited from the greater prosperity.

With declining prospects for employment, declining funds available for training, and no incentives to keep employers near the available labor pool, the result has been a chronically high unemployment rate for healthy males, a spiraling crime rate, and gangs. The process has been repeated all over the nation to one extent or another. As employers left the cities and towns either by relocation or because of downsizing, a vacuum was cre-

Figure 4.1   The loss of family-sustaining manufacturing jobs contributed to the rise of contemporary gangs.
John Giordano/Corbis/SABA Press Photos, Inc.

ated that has been filled to a large extent by gangs. This is the point at which Pamela Irving Jackson (1991) steps in and correctly identifies the lack of employment prospects as a contributing factor in the rise of gangs.

The failure to adequately confront the proliferation of guns in today's society has also had a profound impact on how gang members do business. Formerly, disputes were handled with fists, knives, clubs, zip guns, and occasionally a "real" gun. Today in larger cities we regularly read accounts of guns used in drive-by shootings and other criminal activities. Thus the automobile and the gun are powerful tools used by gang members to intimidate competitors, enforce discipline, and to expand their influence. Over half of the respondents to a 1992 Law Enforcement Survey revealed that youth gangs in their jurisdictions were the perpetrators of drive-by shootings (Knox et al., 1992).

Beginning in the early 1980s, crack cocaine emerged as a cheap and profitable source of money for street gangs, and we seemed powerless to stem the flow of drugs of any kind into the country (Currie, 1993). As legitimate employment possibilities declined, entrepreneurs stepped into the void and offered relatively high-paying jobs to those willing to take the risk. We should not be surprised that young people in the inner city want the same access to the **American Dream** as do other youth, and that they are willing to innovate in order to obtain that dream. Gangs have supplied the organization, and willing workers have provided the labor to supply crack and other drugs to willing customers in an innovative approach to the American Dream.

A GANG TYPOLOGY

One misconception is that street gangs are confined to the mostly black or Hispanic inner city. It is true that minorities make up the bulk of gang membership, but the reasons are related to poverty and the inability of many minority members to become fully integrated into mainstream America. However, to think that all gangs are minority or that white children do not join gangs is not true. That fact was brutally brought to light in May 1993 in Davenport, Iowa, when four boys, purporting to belong to the Vice Lords, a well-known black Chicago Street gang, murdered a high school senior for the keys to her car (Terry, 1994). Cooper (1994) also found that white middle-class children were joining gangs as an activity and because they identified with black gang members.

In one research project by the National Gang Crime Research Center, 29.1 percent of the respondents stated that their gang is racially integrated (Knox et al., 1995). Subsequent research has documented that white youth join street gangs for the same reasons as minority youth. Clearly, variables are at work in American society that must be dealt with.

The definition of a gang is somewhat elusive, but most authorities agree that in order to avoid identifying members of the high school football team or a college fraternity as a gang, the following components must be present in a definition of a gang: (1) a group of two or more; (2) the group members must be in regular contact and identify with each other and identify themselves as a gang or organization; (3) group members must subscribe to a code of conduct and use certain colors, signs, and signals for identification; and (4) activities must revolve around illegal behavior.

Table 4.1   People and Folks (A Partial Listing)

Peoples Gangs	*Folks Gangs*
Bloods	Crips
Four Corner Hustlers	Almighty Ambrose
Black p Stone Nation	Brothers of the Struggle
Conservative Vice Lords	Black Disciples
Familia Stones	Black Gangster Nation
Honky Head	Black Souls
Insane Vice Lords	Gangster Disciples
Latin Counts	F.B.I.
Latin Kings	Harrison Gents
Loco Boys	Insane Spanish Cobras
Northsiders	Insane two-twos
Mickey Cobras	Simon City Royals
Traveling Vice Lords	Maniac Royals
Twin City Boys	Satan's Disciples
Unknown Vice Lords	Two six Nation
Vice Lords	Young Latin Organization
	Black Activitist Disciples
	Winged Disciples
	Washington Park Disciples
	Sons and Daughters of the Divine Temple of the Universal Star Inc.
	Insane Gangster Disciples
	15th Street Disciples
	89th Street Disciples
	Young Voters of Illinois Inc.

Source: National Gang Crime Research Center, Chicago State University. George W. Knox, Director, St. Louis Police Department, Intelligence Division (Gang Section). *Gang Manual* (1994).

Klein (1968) points out that a gang refers to any group of youngsters who (a) are generally perceived as a distinct aggregation by others in their neighborhood, (b) recognize themselves as a denotable group, and (c) have been involved in a sufficient number of delinquent incidents to call for a consistent negative response from neighborhood residents and/or enforcement agencies.

The California Youth Gang Task force definition of gangs is perhaps the most widely used definition of gangs. *The Guide for the Investigation and Prosecution of Youth Gang Violence in California* delineates the following factors as evidence of gang membership (Cozic, 1996):

1. Subject admits being a member of a gang.

2. Subject has tattoos, clothing, etc., that are only associated with certain gangs.

3. Subject has been arrested while participating in activities with known gang members.

4. Information that places the subject with a gang has been obtained from a reliable informant.

5. Close association with known gang members has been confirmed.

Street gangs break down into two basic groups, **People** (which includes the West Coast Blood gangs) and **Folks** (which includes the West Coast Crips gangs). Loyalty is prized very highly and both "nations" have a clannish form of identification including certain forms of jewelry, costume, and insignia. For example, Folk gang members all wear or indicate membership by wearing their identifiers on the right side such as rolling the right pant leg up or the cap tilted to the right. People gang members wear their identifiers to the left. Clearly we are not including white gangs such as the Aryan Brotherhood, the KKK, biker gangs, or other security threat groups who do not fit into this typology.

Knox et al. (1994b) found that basically there are no ideological differences between People and Folks. A few minor differences did show up: Folk gang members reported that their gang was racially mixed (70.4 percent compared to 59.7 percent of Peoples gang members); more Folks reported shoot-outs with police; and fewer Folks are deterred by the threat of a natural life sentence for committing a gun crime.

There are literally thousands of gangs across the nation. Some are designed more for social reasons, others exist primarily for the pursuit of violence, and others affect a corporate approach to the distribution of drugs. Table 4.1 illustrates a partial list of the types of gangs according to People or Folks allegiance. This list reflects a Chicago orientation and illustrates the migration of the gangs from Chicago out to the rest of the midwest.

GANGS AND THE AMERICAN DREAM

The American Dream is a part of our mythology and is a concept that captures the essence of the American spirit. It is a belief that if someone just works hard enough, he or she will overcome any obstacle and achieve material success. In turn, success will provide public testimony of that person's worth as an individual. The American Dream is promoted by our culture and our politicians, and our legends and lore all hold the rags to riches ideal up for emulation and adoration. We are encouraged to work hard and compete for material success.

Jennifer L. Hochschild (1995) found that blacks and whites both believe in the American Dream. In one survey of Californians, 70 percent of blacks and 80 percent of whites agree that "trying to get ahead is very important in 'making someone a true American.' " However, in her view, whites and blacks see "a barrier, if not an enemy, when they look at each other," in that many blacks see themselves as being denied a place at the table, and whites see blacks as making excessive demands.

Figure 4.2   Gangs have changed the social fabric of many cities.
Gangs mark their turf by graffiti.
Bruce Davidson/Magnum Photos, Inc.

In her research, she found that the percentage of blacks who perceived they had a shot at the American Dream had actually declined. In 1954, a survey question asked of blacks "Life will be better for you . . . in the next few years than it is now." Sixty-four percent (64 percent) agreed with this statement. In 1989, a similar question was asked, "My opportunities for promotion are high." Thirty-four percent (34 percent) agreed with this statement. Similarly, in 1991, the question was asked, "In the next five years, how likely are you to be promoted?" Forty-three percent (43 percent) stated likely or very likely. Thus, in her view, if blacks and whites continue to hold on to their views, a society based on belief in the American Dream is in jeopardy.

A unique look at crime in American Society is found in *Crime and the American Dream* (Messner & Rosenfeld, 1994). It is an excellent book that recasts an American aphorism in terms of opportunity and how we access that opportunity. According to the authors, the American Dream has been responsible for much that is good in American society: technological innovation, economic expansion, social mobility, and so on. However, it is also responsible for much on the dark side of the American psyche: It drives people apart, weakens a sense of community, and instills a drive to succeed at any cost.

Messner and Rosenfeld call another point to mind; that is the spirit of capitalism and its birth. The American Dream has its institutional underpinnings in the economy. A capitalist economy presumes an attraction to monetary rewards as a result of achievement, and property owners are profit oriented and eager to invest. The resultant competition demands that firms keep up with a changing market, and workers must keep up with changing skill requirements. As a consequence, "a capitalist economy cultivates a competitive, innovative spirit" (Messner & Rosenfeld, 1994).

Capitalism in America is different from that found in the rest of the world. In America, capitalism has an "exaggerated emphasis on monetary success and the unrestrained receptivity to innovation" (Messner & Rosenfeld, 1994). The goal of success overwhelms other goals and becomes the only measurement of achievement. This, according to Messner and Rosenfeld, tilts the balance of power towards the economy.

Capitalism in America developed free of preexisting institutions, as was not the case in other societies. As a result, American society was profoundly shaped by the requirements of capitalist economic development. Thus, a purity of form emerged in America that is unknown in other societies in which capitalism was imposed on social institutions whose roots and traditions go back several hundred years at least.

The result is a culture that both stimulates crime and fosters weak social control because of the dominance of the economy. The stimulation of crime derives largely from the content of the American Dream. That is, according to Messner and Rosenfeld, a strong, relentless pressure for everyone to succeed is defined in terms of monetary goals. This pressure fosters a willingness to substitute efficient but illegal means in the pursuit of success. At the same time, they argue, the American Dream does not contain within it strong injunctions against substituting more effective, illegitimate means for less effective, legitimate means in the pursuit of monetary success. Quite the contrary, the message is to succeed at any cost.

One reason the prosocial messages are not given credence at times is that certain tendencies in favor of the economy overwhelm the institutional balance of power. As a consequence, family, schools, churches and synagogues, and other institutional influences are devalued and play a subservient role to the economy. Thus, it becomes harder and harder for the controlling institutions in American society to do what they are supposed to do: control youthful impulses, socialize the young, and act as a leveling influence throughout society.

As Messner and Rosenfeld point out:

> Impotent families and schools are severely handicapped in their efforts to promote allegiance to social rules, including legal prohibitions. In the absence of strong socializing influences from these non-economic institutions, the cultural message that comes through with greatest force is the one most compatible with the logic of the economy: the competitive, individualistic, and materialistic message of the American Dream.

Clearly, the American Dream contributes to gang membership. Youth who feel that they are prevented from legitimate achievement pursue other avenues to success as measured in material terms. Some are successful, and some are not. We now turn to poverty as a contributor to gang membership.

POVERTY AND GANGS

Street gangs appear to thrive wherever poverty and normlessness exist, thus any discussion of gangs and crime is not complete without a discussion of poverty. The presence of poverty is not a necessary precondition for the existence of crime, but poverty does establish the conditions that breed crime (Gibbons, 1992). The viability of a strong democracy depends on a large middle class, and we must zealously guard against pressures that threaten its strength and vitality.

In 1991, 35.7 million Americans, or roughly 14 percent of the population, lived under conditions of poverty. The fact that our nation's cities have undergone a transformation caused by the erosion of their tax base in the last twenty-five years is worrisome enough, but add to that transformation the fact that many of our citizens who live in the inner cities and smaller towns appear to be trapped by endemic poverty, hopelessness, and despair is cause for even greater alarm.

Chronic poverty has increased dramatically since 1973 (Devine & Wright, 1993). Poverty had steadily decreased until 1973 when it began to track upward. Specifically they found that:

1. Nearly a third of black households (29.7 percent) have been poor in more than half of the nineteen years studied, while only 4.5 percent of white households have experienced ten or more years of impoverishment.

2. Attesting to the feminization of poverty thesis, female-headed households are more than five times as likely to have experienced five or more years of poverty and better than seven times as likely to have experienced ten or more years of poverty than male-headed households.

3. Only one in eight households (12.4 percent) headed by black females have not had a single year in poverty. The corresponding figure for households headed by white females, black males, and white males are 44.4 percent, 43.9 percent, and 79.6 percent respectively. Similarly, half of the black female-headed households were poor in ten or more years, while 21.6 percent of black male-headed households, and only 1.8 percent of white male-headed households experienced this degree of impoverishment.

While poverty continues to grip the lives of many of our fellow citizens, many minorities have been able to take advantage of opportunities that are the result of the civil rights movement. Those minority members who have taken advantage of opportunity and moved out of the inner city have done so leaving behind fewer legitimate opportunities and fewer positive role models to emulate. The result has been a higher degree of alienation and rebelliousness among those who see few opportunities.

The flight of upwardly mobile minorities left a vacuum waiting to be filled and gangs moved into the vacuum and provided a vehicle for those aspiring to better things (Jackson, 1991). During the 1980s, this drama began to be played out in smaller towns and cities throughout the United States, and the loss of opportunity suffered by minorities since the early 1970s also began to be felt by the white, working class.

The American Dream lived on in spite of endemic poverty and the loss of legitimate opportunity through manufacturing jobs. Those who use the phrase freely should take heart because in spite of rhetoric to the contrary, inner-city residents and their small-town brethren still subscribe to the American Dream. In one view, the twist is in the mode of adaptation to a dysfunctional opportunity structure. Drugs, weapons, extortion, fees, and purchase or start of small businesses with illegitimate profits are all instruments used by gangs to achieve the American Dream.

GANG RESEARCH

During the middle 1990s, the National Gang Crime Research Center conducted a number of projects including *The Economics of Gang Life* (Knox et al., 1995). The findings of this project shed light on a number of issues of gang economics and the American Dream:

- The gang appears to function much like a union guild.
- Gangs operate a wide variety of cash business enterprises.
- Gang members pay dues, which flow upward to the leadership.
- Organizationally sophisticated gangs have a number of economic functions.
- Gangs serve a welfare function in that they provide welfare payments for members who are in jail.

A questionnaire was administered to a sample of jail inmates, gang intervention programs, reform school inmates, and children in a juvenile detention center in a number of states across the nation. The results are somewhat startling and illustrate that the American Dream is alive and well in American cities.

Gang members believe in the same culturally acceptable goals as the rest of society. The survey asked gang members to agree or disagree with the statement "I believe in such things as education, having a nice home, and supporting my family." Over 93 percent (93.6 percent) agreed with this statement.

Collecting protection money on behalf of the gang. Approximately one-fifth of the gang members surveyed (21.2 percent) stated they had collected protection money on behalf of their gang. Additional information on how much money the respondent collected in protection money during the last year was available for $N = 155$ respondents. The 155 respondents report collecting from a low of \$1.50 to a high of \$12,000. The mean amount of protection money collected was \$8,696.

Parents of gang members are usually described as being employed. Respondents were asked "Which best describes your father: has a regular job or has no regular job?" Most of the gang members (70.8 percent, $N = 635$) described their father as having a regular job. However, nearly one-third (29.2 percent) described their father as not having a regular job.

In the same fashion, the survey also asked the respondent to describe their mother. Most gang members (72.7 percent) described their mother as having a regular job. On the other hand, a little over one-fourth described their mother as not having a regular job.

Family structure. Respondents were asked to describe their family of origin. Among gang members the largest group (42.1 percent) state that they come from an intact family, that is a family characterized by mother, father, and siblings. Nearly sixteen percent (15.9 percent) state they come from a family characterized by a mother, stepfather, and siblings, 3.4 percent state they came from a family characterized by a stepmother, father, and siblings. However, one-third of gang members state they come from a family composed of mother and siblings. Only 2 percent indicated a father and siblings.

The parent(s) of most gang members held or hold full-time employment according to gang members who responded to the questionnaire. This holds true whether or not the gang member is from a single-parent family or an intact family.

Number of close friends/associates who are gang members. Acceptance of criminal behavior and the learning of specific skills are conducted in intimate relationships, and as a consequence the researchers thought that it was important to determine the number of close friends who are gang members. The survey asked, "How many of your close friends and associates are gang members?" Possible responses were zero, one, two, three, four, five or more. The vast majority (76.9 percent) indicated they had five or more close friends and associates who are gang members.

Age when first entered a gang. The range of responses indicating the age when the respondent entered a gang was broad (1 year of age to age 35) but the mean age was 12.9 years.

Reasons for joining a gang. The survey asked, "What one reason comes closest to describing why you first joined any gang?" One-fourth (24.6 percent) claim they joined a gang to "make money." The largest response (37.9 percent) indicated they "just grew up in it." Other responses include being with friends (14.7 percent), because a family member was in the gang (9.7 percent), and for protection (2.7 percent).

Operation of legitimate businesses. The operation of legitimate businesses is important in that at the least it provides cover for the laundering of illegitimate profits. The question was asked, "Does the gang you belong to have any legitimate businesses?" Just less than one-half (47.5 percent) indicated that their gang does have legitimate businesses.

Older gang members manage the gangs. The stereotypical view of most Americans of street gangs is that they are loosely knit organizations that are managed by and for young people for a variety of purposes, mostly to meet social needs. The survey asked, "Does your gang have adult leaders who have been in the gang for many years?" Eighty-seven percent (87.8 percent) of the respondents answered yes, their gang has adult leaders who have been in the gang for many years. Thus, a reasonable conclusion is that these are not youth gangs.

Working as a "runner" in a retail drug operation. If one has accepted culturally accepted goals and legitimate opportunities are closed, the innovative person will seek out those opportunities in the illegitimate opportunity structure that meets his or her needs. The survey asked, "Have you ever worked as a runner in a retail drug sales operation?" Nearly one-half (43.8 percent) of the respondents stated they had worked as a runner. A follow-up question on income asked, "How much money do you get to keep on the average?" The results ranged from a low of $50 to a high of $25,000 with the mean at $1,631.

Committing crimes of financial gain with the gang. The survey asked "Have you ever committed a crime for financial gain with your gang?" Over one-half (61.3 percent) stated they had committed a crime for financial gain with their gang. Specifically, 75.2 percent sold drugs, 34.9 percent committed burglary, 48 percent robbery, 41.5 percent car theft, 16.4 percent arson, 28.9 percent shoplifting, and 48.6 percent transported guns, drugs, or a wanted person.

Views on work. A strong work ethic is important for success in the contemporary United States. The survey asked, "Which sentence best describes your thoughts on work?" Most gang members (74.3 percent) responded that "work is good and necessary." Eight percent (8.8 percent) state, "My mother/father worked their tails off and didn't get a thing for it"; 7.9 percent replied "I had a job once and didn't like it"; and 9 percent stated "There's no sense working for the man because he doesn't appreciate it."

The survey also attempted to determine if gang members had been exposed to role models who did have a regular job and were admired by the individual. The fact is, a little over three-fourths (78.2 percent) of responding gang members stated they do know working people they look up to and admire.

Views on racial oppression and poverty. Two questions attempted to get at the attitude of gang members in regard to poverty. About one-fourth of the gang members (27.7 percent) agreed with the statement "Being poor is mostly a racial thing." Nearly a fourth (23.7 percent) also agreed with the statement "I am poor mostly because of my skin color." An interesting caveat is that some white gang members complained about this item in the survey as being "offensive" to them, particularly those that identified themselves as skinheads, neo-nazis, and members of the Aryan Nation/Brotherhood.

Family economic backgrounds of gang members. A series of questions were included in the survey instrument that examines the economic conditions in which the respondents live. Over half (62.7 percent) of the gang members who responded stated that their family "sometimes used food stamps." Half (55.8 percent) stated their family "sometimes received public aid or welfare checks." Nearly half (47.8 percent) replied "their family had to take odd jobs just to get by."

A third (33.4 percent) said their family "sometimes received food baskets from churches, etc." Over one-fourth said their family "sometimes lived in a public housing project." Two-fifths (40.5 percent) said their family "sometimes had lights, gas, and telephone cut off because the bills could not be paid." Over one-third (35.6 percent) stated "sometimes there was very little if any food in the house." On the other hand, in a rather bizarre revelation, over half (61.5 percent) stated they "sometimes got a regular weekly allowance for spending money."

Regular employment and losing a job. Two-thirds (68.8 percent) of the professed gang members stated they had held a legitimate job at one time, and over one-fourth said they had been fired from any legitimate job.

Gangs serve a welfare function. The survey asked if the gang served needy members. Three-fourths (77.7 percent) stated that their gang does help needy gang members.

Extortion of protection money from small businesses. The survey asked, "Have you ever engaged in shakedowns of small businesses?" More than one-fourth (27.5 percent) stated they had done so. A follow-up question sought to determine which types of target preferences gang members had. Among those who claimed to extort from small businesses: 41.7 percent would choose white businesses, 44.6 percent would choose black businesses, 30.2 percent would choose Asian businesses, 32.5 percent would choose Arab businesses, and 31.5 percent would choose Hispanic/Latino businesses.

The economic study of gangs is valuable for several reasons. Padilla (1992) points out that there is a group of young men and women who have renounced the general culture and who

> have lost faith in the capacity of the society to work on their behalf. Because of this perception of society, many of these young people have organized and created counter-cultural structures that they believe are capable of delivering the kinds of emotional support and material goods the larger society promises but does not make available to youngsters like themselves.

One such structure is the gang (see Padilla, 1992; and Jackson, 1991). Gangs provide not only a unit with which to identify, a place for acceptance, and a family substitute, but also a chance for economic opportunity (see Jackson, 1991; Knox et al., 1992; Vigil, 1993; Knox, 1995).

Padilla (1992) illustrates the perception of "Diamond" gang members who "point out the poignant paradox between having culturally defined goals and ineffective but socially legitimate means for achieving them . . . the contradiction lies in the absence of avenues and resources necessary for securing the rewards that society most values and which it purports to offer its members." So it is with the majority of gang members interviewed for the cited project.

A positive attitude toward opportunity is important if one is to achieve a measure of success in later life. Merton points out that a dysfunctional opportunity structure promotes innovation (Merton, 1957; see also Cloward & Ohlin, 1960), and gangs have moved into the vacuum created by the loss of manufacturing jobs in many cities as a vehicle for innovation (Jackson, 1991). Table 4.2 illustrates the relationship between parents' employment and employment of gang members.

Table 4.2   Employment and Opportunity

	Father Has a Regular Job	*Mother Has a Regular Job*	*Gang Member Felt Shutout*
	% Yes	% Yes	% Yes
I believe in such things as education, having a nice home, and supporting my family.			
False	58.0%	53.8%	73.8%
True	71.8%	73.9%	47.8%
	$p = .02$	$p < .001$	$p < .001$
Which best describes your father?			
Has a regular job	n.a.	71.6%	
Has no regular job	n.a.	61.0%	
			$p = .003$
Have you ever held a part-time job?			
No	63.9%	67.6%	n.a.
Yes	74.0%	75.7%	n.a.
Which best describes the type of family you come from?			
Mother, father, and siblings	78.9%	n.s.	n.s.
Single mother and siblings	57.5%	n.s.	n.s.
Which sentence best describes your thoughts on work?			
Work is good and necessary.	74.1%	75.0%	45.0%
There's no sense in working for the man because he doesn't appreciate it.	50.7%	61.3%	55.0%
	$p < .001$	$p = .05$	$p = .005$
I am poor mostly because of my skin color.			
False	72.8%	n.s.	43.9%
True	63.1%	n.s.	63.0%
My family			
Sometimes used food stamps	66.4%	67.1%	n.s
Never used food stamps	78.2%	83.3%	n.s.
Sometimes received public aid or welfare checks	65.0%	65.4%	n.s.
Never received public aid or welfare checks	78.1%	82.8%	n.s.
	$p < .02$	$p < .001$	

(continued)

Table 4.2   Employment and Opportunity *(Continued)*

	Father Has a Regular Job	*Mother Has a Regular Job*	*Gang Member Felt Shutout*
	% Yes	**% Yes**	**% Yes**
Sometimes lives in a public housing project	66.6%	68.7%	n.s.
Never lived in a public housing project	73.3%	75.2%	n.s.
	$p = .05$	$p = .04$	
Has father ever been arrested?			
No	77.8%	n.s.	n.s.
Yes	60.6%	n.s.	n.s.
	$p < .001$		
Has mother ever been arrested?			
No	74.8%	75.7%	46.1%
Yes	52.0%	58.2%	58.5%
	$p < .001$	$p < .001$	$p = .004$

The data from the study by the National Gang Crime Research Center points out that the American Dream is alive and well. The majority of respondents report that work is good and necessary. Indeed, work provides a purpose and rhythm to our lives that is irreplaceable. It helps structure our time and provides a feeling of worthwhileness. Thus, if young people do not have a regular job or if they feel shut out of legitimate opportunities, they can structure their time and earn a good income by pursuing opportunities in the illegitimate opportunity structure.

Findings from the above study illustrate that gang members believe in the same things as everyone else in American society. In addition, they are first-rate consumers and entrepreneurs. A number of businesses have been started on profits from gang activities, and those businesses contribute to the overall economic blood of the community (Knox et al., 1995).

Poverty appears to play a part in gang membership as illustrated by the data. Nearly two-thirds of the respondents state that they have lived in public housing and had received welfare in one form or another. When coupled with the fact that of those reporting who felt shut out of legitimate opportunity (58.5 percent) and whose mother had ever been arrested, we have an explosive mixture.

There also appears to be a significant relationship between the employment status of parents on a variety of factors that affect the lives of gang members. Thus, it may be that family acts as an important buffer between the young person and continued gang membership. What is not entirely clear is what type of program can bolster these effects and what can juvenile courts, social service agencies, and the private sector do to be of assistance.

However, evidence is coming to light that there are approaches and programs that can work in separating individual gang members from gang activity (Palmer, 1994; Conly, 1993). Clearly, more research is needed if communities are going to successfully combat the allure of gangs.

FEMALE GANGS AND FEMALE GANG MEMBERS

Female membership in gangs has traditionally been limited to an auxiliary role. Over the past two decades, female membership in gangs and all-female gangs has remained relatively constant. Walter Miller (1975) estimated that 10 percent or less of gang membership in the cities he studied were female. Two decades later, the Office of Juvenile Justice and Delinquency Prevention (2000) found that female gang membership varies from 7 percent in large cities to 12 percent in small cities. Overall females account for 8 percent of all gang membership.

We have already documented that female heads of households are more likely than male heads of households to live below the poverty line. In addition, the role of poverty in

Table 4.3   Gang-Related Charges for Female Arrestees in Chicago, 1993–1996

Offense*	Female Arrestees with Gang-Related Charge (%)			
	1993	**1994**	**1995**	**1996**
Violent (total)	46.9	40.3	34.4	38.5
Homicide	0.2	0.1	0.0	0.1
Simple battery	17.6	16.1	14.1	14.9
Mob action	9.7	5.7	3.8	4.8
All other violent offenses	19.4	18.4	16.5	18.7
Drug (total)	36.4	37.9	44.4	37.7
Cocaine possession	14.3	9.8	8.8	2.6
Crack possession	7.0	11.6	13.9	15.6
All other drug offenses	15.1	16.5	21.7	19.5
Prostitution	0.8	1.5	4.1	9.8
Property	5.1	3.4	4.4	5.1
Weapons	3.7	4.3	2.5	2.8
Liquor	5.6	10.7	7.3	3.5
Other	2.2	1.7	2.7	2.3

Note: Percentages may not total 100 because of rounding. Total number (n) of cases per year: 1993, n=2,023; 1994, n=2,029; 1995, n=2,021; 1996, n=2,193.

*With the exception of vice offenses (drug, prostitution, and gambling), gang-related offenses are defined by referring to the motive of the offender. Vice offenses are considered gang-related if they involve a known gang member. Almost all liquor offenses involve underage drinking.

Source: Joan Moore and John Hagadorn. "Female Gangs: A Focus on Research." USDOJ, Office of Justice Programs, Office of Juvenile Justice and Delinquency Prevention. March 2001.

pushing youth into gang membership has been clearly documented. Is it little wonder that females are beginning to drift into gangs and either taking a major role in the life of the gang or forming all-female gangs in order to meet personal needs? Indeed, in regard to behavior in their gangs, Decker and Van Winkle (1994 and 1996) report that the roles of males and females are indistinguishable.

Generally speaking, female gang members commit fewer violent offenses than their male counterparts. They tend to gravitate toward property crimes and status offenses. Table 4.3 illustrates the type offenses for female gang members in Chicago.

Moore and Hagadorn (2001) call our attention to the fact that females join gangs because of deteriorating economic conditions in our inner cities. However, no research has been done that investigates the impact, if any, the improved economic climate has had on female gang membership in the cites. In addition, the movement to eliminate Aid to Families with Dependant Children may have created other problems in the midst of plenty, in regard to gangs. Beyond economic issues, females join gangs for friendship, solidarity, self-affirmation, and a sense of new possibilities (Moore & Hagadorn, 2001). Clearly, female membership in gangs has increased, causing another stress on the juvenile justice system. How does the probation officer or institutional case manager, for example, program female gang members when most programs are designed with a male model in mind? More on this issue in a later chapter.

SUMMARY

Gangs have certain signs, colors, and indicators that parents ought to be aware of in order to attempt to deal with a child who has a fascination with gangs. If one sign is crossed out and another sign appears over it, it should be taken as a warning that two rival gangs are present and violence is apt to occur in the near future.

Midwest and West Coast gangs have migrated to smaller cities and towns, and one research project found that 89 percent of police chiefs in a nationwide survey agreed that gangs are a problem in their jurisdiction (Knox et al., 1992). In another study, Jerome Skolnick, found that the Bloods and Crips of the West Coast had migrated as far as Kansas City by 1989 (Skolnick, 1989).

Gangs are a problem for nearly every city and town in the United States. However, the extent of gang membership and activity appears to be a function of general prosperity, cultural variables, and perhaps even the faddishness of belonging to a gang. Nevertheless, for some youth the gang still remains the closest they know of family and caring primary reference group. The concept of gang as family may be illusory at best; it speaks to the hopelessness experienced by the youth and the fact that basic community institutions have let the child down. The issues of poverty and single-parent families are central to the increasing numbers of females who join gangs.

How prosperity will influence gang membership remains to be seen. But it must be remembered that the tendency of youth to join gangs is a manifestation of problems with their home life. If those problems are addressed, then gang membership may decrease. In the meantime, adequate prevention programs must be implemented, and opportunities to succeed legitimately in life must be made available.

CASE STUDY WRAP-UP

John Laskey has seen a great deal of life as a Chicago police officer. During that time, he came to recognize that suppression alone is not the answer to street gangs and gang crime. Rather, as he points out, we need to begin to take advantage of what we know about criminal behavior and respond by drawing families and community agencies into our attempts to steer youth away from gangs. He believes that teachers can be the beginning of the process, and, with help, other agencies can be more effective.

STUDY QUESTIONS

1. Why do youth join gangs?
2. Are there effective programs to dissuade youth from joining gangs? What do you think would be an effective program?
3. How do you define a gang?
4. What differences are there between People and Folks?

BIBLIOGRAPHY

BLOCH, HERBERT, AND NIEDERHOFFER, ARTHUR (1958). *The Gang: A Study in Adolescent Behavior.* New York: Philosophical Press.

CLOWARD, RICHARD D., AND OHLIN, LLOYD E. (1960). *Delinquency and Opportunity.* New York: The Free Press.

COHEN, ALBERT K. (1955). *Delinquent Boys: The Culture of the Gang.* Glencoe, IL: The Free Press.

CONLY, CATHERINE H. (1993). *Street Gangs: Current Knowledge and Strategies.* Washington, D.C.: National Institute of Justice. Prepared by Abt Associates under contract #OJP-89-C-009.

COOPER, MARC. (July 1994). "Reality Check." *Spin* 10:4.

COZIC, CHARLES P. (Ed.) (1996). *Gangs: Opposing Viewpoints.* San Diego, CA: Greenhaven Press, Inc.

CURRIE, ELLIOT (1993). *Reckoning: Drugs, the Cities, and the American Future.* New York: Hill and Wang.

DECKER, SCOTT H., AND VAN WINKLE, BARRIK (1994). "'Slinging Dope': The Role of Gangs and Gang Members in Drug Sales." *Justice Quarterly* 11:583–604.

DECKER, SCOTT H., AND VAN WINKLE, BARRIK (1996). *Life in the Gang: Famiily, Friends, and Violence.* New York: Cambridge University Press.

DEVINE, JOEL A., AND WRIGHT, JAMES D. (1993). *The Greatest of Evils: Urban Poverty and the American Underclass.* New York: Aldine De Gruyter.

FOX, JAMES ALAN, AND PIERCE, GLENN (1994). "American Killers are Getting Younger" from *USA Today Magazine,* January, 1994, pp. 24–26, in *Criminal Justice 95/96,* 19th ed. John J. Sullivan and Joseph L. Victor. Guilford, CT: Duchkin Publishing Group, 1995.

FOX, S.J. (1970). "Juvenile Justice Reform: An Historical Perspective." *Stanford Law Review* 22: 1187–1239.

GIBBONS, DON C. (1992). *Society, Crime, and Criminal Behavior,* 6th ed. Englewood Cliffs, NJ: Prentice Hall.

HOCHSCHILD, JENNIFER L. (1995). *Facing up to the American Dream: Race, Class, and the Soul of the Nation.* Princeton, NJ: Princeton University Press.

HOUSTON, JAMES (1993). "The Violent Gang and Beyond: An Interview with Lewis Yablonsky." *The Gang Journal,* 1:2, 59–67.

JACKSON, PAMELA IRVING (1991). "Crime, Youth Gangs, and Urban Transition: The Social Dislocations of Postindustrial Economic Development." *Justice Quarterly,* 8:3, 379–397.

KANTROWITZ, BARBARA (August 2, 1993). "Wild in the Streets," *Newsweek* 40, 42–46.

KLEIN, MALCOLM (1968). *The Ladino Hills Project* (Final Report). Washington, D.C.: Office of Juvenile Delinquency and Youth Development.

KLEIN, MALCOLM (1983). "Violence in American Juvenile Gangs." A staff report to the National Commission on the Causes and Prevention of Violence, in Jerome A. Needle and William Vaughan Stapleton. "Police Handling of Youth Gangs." *Reports of the National Juvenile Justice Assessment Centers.* OJJDP. September, 1983.

KNOX, GEORGE W. (1994). *An Introduction to Gangs* (new rev. ed.). Bristol, IN: Wyndham Hall Press.

KNOX, GEORGE W., HOUSTON, JAMES G., LASKEY, JOHN A., MCCURRIE, THOMAS F., TROMANHAUSER, EDWARD D., AND LASKE, DAVID L. (1994a). *Gangs and Guns.* Chicago: National Gang Crime Research Center.

KNOX, GEORGE W., MCCURRIE, THOMAS F., HOUSTON, JAMES G., TROMANHAUSER, EDWARD D., AND LASKEY, JOHN A. (1994b). *The 1994 Illinois Law Enforcement Survey: A Report on Gang Migration and Other Gang Problems in Illinois Today.* Chicago: National Gang Crime Research Center.

KNOX, GEORGE W., TROMANHAUSER, EDWARD D., JACKSON, PAMELA IRVING, NIKLAS, DARN, HOUSTON, JAMES G., KOCH, PAUL, SUTTEN, JAMES R., AND WARD, DICK (1992). *The 1992 Law Enforcement Survey.* Chicago: National Gang Crime Research Center.

KNOX, GEORGE W., TROMANHAUSER, EDWARD D., HOUSTON, JAMES G., MARTIN, BRAD, MORRIS, ROBERT E., McCURRIE, THOMAS F., LASKEY, JOHN L., PAPACHRISTOS, DOROTHY, FEINBERG, JUDITH, AND WAXMAN, CHARLA (1995). *The Economics of Gang Life.* Chicago: National Gang Crime Research Center.

MERTON, ROBERT K. (1957). *Social Theory and Social Structure,* rev. ed. New York: Free Press.

MESSNER, STEVEN F., AND ROSENFELD, RICHARD (1994). *Crime and the American Dream.* Belmont, CA: Wadsworth Publishing Company.

MILLER, WALTER B. (1975). *Violence by Youth Gangs and Youth Groups as a Problem in Major American Cities.* Washington, DC: USDOJ, LEAA, National Institute for Juvenile Justice and Delinquency Prevention.

MILLER, WALTER B. (2000). *The Growth of Youth Gang Problems in the United States: 1970–98.* Washington, DC: OJJDP.

MOORE, JOAN, AND HAGADORN, JOHN (March 2001). "Female Gangs: A Focus on Research." USDOJ, Office of Justice Programs, Office of Juvenile Justice and Delinquency Prevention.

NATIONAL INSTITUTE OF JUSTICE, U.S. DEPARTMENT OF JUSTICE (Aug. 1996). Research in Brief, *Estimating the National Scope of Gang Crime from Law Enforcement Data 3.*

NATIONAL YOUTH VIOLENCE PREVENTION RESOURCE CENTER (2004). Rockville, MD: USGPO.

OFFICE OF JUVENILE JUSTICE AND DELINQUENCY PREVENTION (2000). *The 1998 National Youth Gang Survey.* Washington, D.C.: U.S. Department of Justice, Office of Justice Programs.

PADILLA, FELIX M. (1992). *The Gang as an American Enterprise.* New Brunswick, NJ: Rutgers University Press.

PALMER, TED (1994). *A Profile of Correctional Effectiveness and New Directions for Research.* Albany, NY: University of New York Press.

SKOLNICK, JEROME H. (1989). *Gang Organization and Migration.* Research undertaken for the Department of Justice, State of California.

SPERGEL, IRVING A. (1995). *The Youth Gang Problem.* New York: Oxford University Press.

TERRY, DON (1994). "Killed by Her Friends in an All-White Gang," *New York Times,* May 18.

THORNTON, WILLIAM E., JR., AND VOIGT, LYDIA (1992). *Delinquency and Justice,* 3rd ed. New York: McGraw-Hill, Inc.

THRASHER, FREDERICK (1936). *The Gang.* Chicago: University of Chicago Press.

TRACY, PAUL, AND FIGLIO, ROBERT (1985). "Chronic Recidivism in the 1958 Birth Cohort," Paper presented at the American Society of Criminology meeting, Toronto, Canada, October, 1982, in Larry J. Siegal and Joseph J. Senna. *Juvenile Delinquency: Theory, Practice, and Law,* 2nd ed. St. Paul, MN: West Publishing Co., 1985.

U.S. BUREAU OF THE CENSUS. *1987 and 2002 Census of Manufacturers.* Washington, D.C.: U.S. Government Printing Office, 1987 and 2002.

VIGIL, DIEGO (1993). "The Established Gang," in *Gangs: The Origins and Impact of Contemporary Youth Gangs in the United States,* Scott Cummings and Daniel J. Monti, Eds. Albany, NY: State University of New York Press.

WHYTE, WILLIAM FOOTE (1943). *Street Corner Society: The Social Structure of an Italian Slum,* 3rd ed. Chicago: University of Chicago Press.

GLOSSARY OF KEY TERMS

The American Dream.   A belief that if a person just works hard enough, he or she will overcome any obstacle and achieve material success. In turn, success will provide public testimony of that person's worth as an individual.

Chronic poverty.   The condition of poverty is intergenerational or an individual cannot break out of poverty because of certain variables such as a lack of skills, racism, or lack of opportunity.

People and Folks.   Major Chicago-based alliances with many sets or sub-gangs. The People Nation and Folk Nation are not gangs—they are alliances under which gangs are aligned. A simple comparison might be the National and American baseball leagues. The National League is not a team—it is the alliance under which teams like the LA Dodgers and Atlanta Braves are aligned. Both People and Folks have separate identifiers that law enforcement and social workers look for. For example, the People Nation's five-point star can be found in several People Nation set symbols. Similarly, the pitchfork is found in most Folk Nation set emblems and graffiti.

PART II
THE JUVENILE JUSTICE SYSTEM

Just as the external environment impacts the juvenile justice system, the organization it-self, be it the police, a small diversion program, a court, an institution, or group home, does not exist in a vacuum. Each functions according to its own standards and establishes goals and objectives. It is important to know how each part of the system works and what purpose each serves.

CHAPTER 5
POLICE AND THE JUVENILE OFFENDER

KEY TERMS

Crimes cleared by arrest
Role
Role conflict
Law enforcement role

Radical nonintervention
Order maintenance role
Community-oriented
  policing

Discretion
Chivalry hypothesis

CASE STUDY*

In June of 1995 at approximately 10:15 A.M., I was dispatched to a breaking and entering in progress. The caller said that a black male suspect kicked in the front door of a neighbor's home. Upon arrival a short time after the call with a back-up unit, we entered the home and announced our arrival. We searched the home and in a back bedroom located the suspect trying to hide behind a bedroom door. The suspect was searched, and no weapons were found although he had a number of coins in his pockets. I knew the suspect, Jimmy Smith (not his real name), from prior encounters. At that point, I asked Jimmy what he was doing in the home. He said that it was his friend's house and that he had permission to be in the house. After a few phone calls to the owner at his place of work and Jimmy's friend at school, we found that Jimmy did not have permission to enter the home. Also, it was determined that the coins were stolen.

I then transported Jimmy to the police department where Jimmy was listed as a runaway. I made contact with Jimmy's mother at work, advising her of the break-in and theft.

*Contributed by: David L. Greco, Community Policing Officer, Grandville Police Department, Grandville, Michigan. Officer Greco attended Grand Rapids Community College and graduated from the Grand Valley State University Police Academy. He worked road patrol for twelve years and for the last three years as the community policing unit.

Prior contact with Jimmy's mother offered an explanation of his home life. His parents were married, and Jimmy's mother seemed to really love her son. His father, on the other hand, did not demonstrate the same love and caring attitude that his wife did. His father's feelings about the police were not much better. I explained to Jimmy's mother that I would be lodging him at the county juvenile detention center for breaking and entering. Jimmy was lodged and spent approximately two weeks in the center.

As a police officer, I have the discretion of either locking up a juvenile offender or releasing him or her to a parent or guardian. In this case, I felt it was time for Jimmy to get a taste of what it was like when you break the law as a youth. Although Jimmy was only twelve years of age, he looked much older and was very big and streetwise.

Although I didn't know it at the time, this was just the start of Jimmy's juvenile career. From 1995 to 1997, Jimmy had thirteen more run-ins with the police. I befriended Jimmy in 1995 after the arrest for the break-in and tried to help as much as I could. He explained that he was adopted, and he hated his father. If Jimmy was not home when his father wanted him to be home, he would be locked out of the house for the entire night. When Jimmy got suspended from school, he was not allowed to be in the family home at all. As a consequence, Jimmy had a lot more time to get in trouble.

From 1998 to 2002, Jimmy has had twenty-one more contacts or arrests by our department, including drug-related offenses, indecent exposure, peeping Tom, and trespassing. Jimmy is now awaiting trial on a larceny from a building charge and may end up in prison. I am not alone in my efforts to work with Jimmy informally. Many officers went out of their way to befriend him and attempt to point him in the right direction, but to no avail.

Working with and dealing with juveniles is part of one's job as police officer. In some cases, the child you send to lock-up for whatever reason may or may not turn out to be a productive member of society. With this individual, I've made several attempts to help him make good decisions. In the end, perhaps we all have failed him.

INTRODUCTION

Police serve as the "gatekeepers" of the criminal justice system. Not only are they the most visible to the public, they are the most likely actors in the criminal justice system to receive criticism from the media, the public, and legislators. Although juveniles may be referred to juvenile court by their parents, teachers, guardians, social service agencies, victims, and schools, law enforcement agencies refer the majority (86 percent in 1996) (Stahl et al., 1999; National Research Council and Institute of Medicine, 2001). Police contacts may result in either official or unofficial or formal or informal dispositions/adjustments (Morash, 1984; Muraskin, 1998). This chapter explores the relationship between police and juvenile encounters. Specifically a review of the number and types of juvenile police contacts, the police officer role, use of police discretion, and attitudes of both police towards citizens and citizens toward police is presented.

POLICE–JUVENILE CONTACTS

Juvenile suspects have a variety of ways of coming to the attention of the criminal justice system. These encounters can be reports from a complainant to the police, parents directly referring youths to the court system, or police coming upon the offense themselves.

As Chesney-Lind and Sheldon (1998) points out police typically have five different options for dealing with juveniles when they are brought to their attention.

1. Simply warn and release, which is frequently done.
2. Release after filing an interview card.
3. Make a station adjustment where they are brought to the police station and either released to their parent or guardian or released with a referral to a community agency.
4. Issue a misdemeanor citation requiring the juvenile and their parent(s) to appear in court at a later date without detention
5. Transport back to juvenile court and make a formal arrest with detention (Chesney-Lind & Sheldon, 1998, p. 151; Krisberg & Austin, 1978, p. 83).

Typically police–juvenile contacts are measured through the use of the Uniform Crime Reports (UCR), which monitor the number of index crimes that come to the attention of the police (Snyder & Sickmund, 1999, p. 112). The UCR counts the number of **crimes cleared by arrest**. "A crime is considered cleared if someone is charged with the crime or if someone is believed to have committed the crime but for some reason (e.g., the death of the suspect) the arrest cannot be made" (Snyder & Sickmund, 1999, p. 113). There is a differentiation, however, between the percentage of persons who are arrested versus the percentage of crimes cleared by arrest. For example, in 1997 "the UCR data show 30 percent of all offenders were under eighteen but that 17 percent of all robberies in 1997 were cleared by arrests of persons under age eighteen" (Snyder & Sickmund, 1999, p. 113). The primary reason for the differentiation between the two statistics is juveniles are more likely to commit crimes in a group rather than alone (Snyder & Sickmund, 1999, p. 114).

In monitoring the arrest rates for offenders known as juveniles, the UCR defines five categories for juvenile arrest disposition:

1. Handled within the department and released
2. Transferred to another police agency
3. Referred to a welfare agency
4. Referred to a juvenile court
5. Referred to a criminal court (Pastore & Maguire, 2002, p. 381; Snyder & Sickmund, 1999, p. 113)

Research suggests however, that the majority of all police–juvenile encounters do not result in either an arrest or a referral to juvenile court. Estimates suggest that as many as

85 percent of the police juvenile contacts are resolved with unofficial adjustment (Muraskin, 1998, p. 152; National Research Council and Institute of Medicine, 2001). A national survey conducted in 1990 asked police departments to report how many youth taken into custody were placed in a temporary holding facility. On average, there were approximately six thousand youth arrested per day in 1990. Of those arrested, only one in ten were detained. Over the past ten years, law enforcement agencies have begun to refer more youths to either the juvenile or adult court systems. For example, in 1992 approximately 63 percent of all youths detained by police were referred to juvenile court, while 4.7 percent were referred to the adult court system. In 2001, approximately 72 percent of all youths taken into custody by police were referred to the juvenile court system while 7 percent were referred to the adult court system (see Tables 5.1, 5.2, and 5.3 for an overview of juveniles taken into custody) (Pastore & Maguire, 2002, p. 381; FBI, 2002, p. 291). This trend mirrors the movement towards getting touch on crime and a push towards the elimination of the juvenile court system.

In 2001, the UCR indicated that 1,558,496 persons under the age of eighteen were arrested by law enforcement agencies. This accounted for approximately 17 percent or near one in five of all arrests made by law enforcement agencies. The majority (55 percent) of these police contacts were for less serious offenses such as larceny theft, simple assault, drug abuse violation, disorderly conduct, liquor law violations, or curfew violations, although a greater percentage of violent crimes were cleared by arrest than property crimes. Juveniles (persons under the age of eighteen) represented approximately 19 percent of the total population. When compared to adult offenders, juvenile female and white offenders were disproportionately represented in the statistics. For example, juvenile females accounted for 23 percent of all female arrests, while juvenile males only accounted for 18 percent of all male arrests. Likewise 20 percent of all white arrests were for juvenile offenders compared to 16 percent of all black arrests (FBI, 2002, p. 232–233, 250; Snyder & Sickmund, 1999, pp. 113–117; Snyder, 2001).

THE POLICE OFFICER ROLE

The typical imagine of a law enforcement officer portrayed in the media is one of a crime-fighter, someone who is responsible for detecting and enforcing the laws by any means necessary. When dealing with juveniles, law enforcement officers oftentimes confront the need to enforce community standards while understanding there are alternative means for dealing with juvenile offenders.

In 1990, the U.S. Department of Justice surveyed a nationally representative sample of law enforcement agencies in the United States. Results from this study indicated that more than 90 percent of local police departments and 74 percent of state police agencies reported having some policy directive pertaining to the handling of juveniles (U.S. Department of Justice, 1993). Although most law enforcement departments have some policy directive describing how juveniles should be handled, they typically do not have specialized units responsible for responding to these cases (Muraskin, 1998; Goldstein, 1991).

Table 5.1   Percent Distribution of Juveniles Taken into Police Custody

By method of disposition, United States, 1972–2000ª

	Referred to Juvenile Court Jurisdiction	Handled within Department and Released	Referred to Criminal or Adult Court	Referred to Other Police Agency	Referred to Welfare Agency
1972	50.8%	45.0%	1.3%	1.6%	1.3%
1973	49.5	45.2	1.5	2.3	1.4
1974	47.0	44.4	3.7	2.4	2.5
1975	52.7	41.6	2.3	1.9	1.4
1976	53.4	39.0	4.4	1.7	1.6
1977	53.2	38.1	3.9	1.8	3.0
1978	55.9	36.6	3.8	1.8	1.9
1979	57.3	34.6	4.8	1.7	1.6
1980	58.1	33.8	4.8	1.7	1.6
1981	58.0	33.8	5.1	1.6	1.5
1982	58.9	32.5	5.4	1.5	1.6
1983	57.5	32.8	4.8	1.7	3.1
1984	60.0	31.5	5.2	1.3	2.0
1985	61.8	30.7	4.4	1.2	1.9
1986	61.7	29.9	5.5	1.1	1.8
1987	62.0	30.3	5.2	1.0	1.4
1988	63.1	29.1	4.7	1.1	1.9
1989	63.9	28.7	4.5	1.2	1.7
1990	64.5	28.3	4.5	1.1	1.6
1991	64.2	28.1	5.0	1.0	1.7
1992	62.5	30.1	4.7	1.1	1.7
1993	67.3	25.6	4.8	0.9	1.5
1994	63.2	29.5	4.7	1.0	1.7
1995	65.7	28.4	3.3	0.9	1.7
1996	68.6	23.3	6.2	0.9	0.9
1997	66.9	24.6	6.6	0.8	1.1
1998	69.2	22.2	6.8	0.9	1.0
1999	69.2	22.5	6.4	1.0	0.8
2000	70.8	20.3	7.0	1.1	0.8

Note: See Notes, tables 4.1 and 4.2. These data include all offenses except traffic and neglect cases.
ªBecause of rounding, percents may not add to 100.

Source: Pastore, Ann L. and Maguire, Kathleen (Eds.) (2002). *Sourcebook of Criminal Justice Statistics 2001* [online]. Available: http://www.albany.edu/sourcebook/1995/pdf/t426.pdf.

Table 5.2 Police Disposition of Juvenile Offenders Taken into Custody, 2001 (2001 estimated population)

Population Group	Total[1]	Handled within Department and Released	Referred to Juvenile Court Jurisdiction	Referred to Welfare Agency	Referred to Other Police Agency	Referred to Criminal or Adult Court
TOTAL AGENCIES: 5,813 agencies; population 122,154,066						
Number	781,813	148,238	566,187	5,703	10,568	51,117
Percent[2]	100.0	19.0	72.4	0.7	1.4	6.5
TOTAL CITIES: 4,277 cities; population 86,590,978						
Number	647,492	127,271	467,652	4,539	9,218	38,812
Percent[2]	100.0	19.7	72.2	0.7	1.4	6.0
GROUP I						
36 cities, 250,000 and over; population 20,512,259						
Number	139,394	33,419	98,890	300	2,960	3,825
Percent[2]	100.0	24.0	70.9	0.2	2.1	2.7
GROUP II						
91 cities, 100,000 to 249,999; population 13,416,737						
Number	90,048	14,617	69,992	1,195	1,114	3,130
Percent[2]	100.0	16.2	77.7	1.3	1.2	3.5
GROUP III						
228 cities, 50,000 to 99,999; population 15,529,044						
Number	115,891	25,762	82,359	465	2,040	5,265
Percent[2]	100.0	22.2	71.1	0.4	1.8	4.5
GROUP IV						
390 cities, 25,000 to 49,999; population 13,674,258						
Number	97,443	17,230	71,819	1,210	1,448	5,736
Percent[2]	100.0	17.7	73.7	1.2	1.5	5.9

	Total					
GROUP V						
848 cities, 10,000 to 24,999; population 13,584,903						
Number	107,935	18,260	77,809	770	815	10,281
Percent[2]	100.0	16.9	72.1	0.7	0.8	9.5
GROUP VI						
2,684 cities, under 10,000; population 9,873,777						
Number	96,781	17,983	66,783	599	841	10,575
Percent[2]	100.0	18.6	69.0	0.6	0.9	10.9
SUBURBAN COUNTIES						
604 agencies; population 23,751,585						
Number	95,266	15,566	70,747	716	944	7,293
Percent[2]	100.0	16.3	74.3	0.8	1.0	7.7
RURAL COUNTIES						
932 agencies; population 11,811,503						
Number	39,055	5,401	27,788	448	406	5,012
Percent[2]	100.0	13.8	71.2	1.1	1.0	12.8
SUBURBAN AREA[3]						
3,176 agencies; population 59,110,616						
Number	330,939	64,357	234,090	2,065	2,937	27,490
Percent[2]	100.0	19.4	70.7	0.6	0.9	8.3

[1]Includes all offenses except traffic and neglect cases.

[2]Because of rounding, the percentages may not add to total.

[3]Suburban area includes law enforcement agencies in cities with less than 50,000 inhabitants and county law enforcement agencies that are within a Metropolitan Statistical Area (see Appendix III). Suburban area excludes all metropolitan agencies associated with a central city. The agencies associated with suburban areas will also appear in other groups within this table.

Source: Federal Bureau of Investigation (2002). *Crime in the United States, 2001: Uniform Crime Reports.* Washington, D.C.: Department of Justice [p. 291] [online] http://www.fbi.gov/ucr/cius_01/01crime4.pdf.

Table 5.3   Arrests of Persons Under 15, 18, 21 and 25 Years of Age, 2001 (9,511 agencies; 2001 estimated population 192,580,262)

Offense Charged	Number of Persons Arrested					Percent of Total All Ages			
	Total All Ages	Under 15	Under 18	Under 21	Under 25	Under 15	Under 18	Under 21	Under 25
TOTAL	9,324,953	498,986	1,558,496	2,927,788	4,282,183	5.4	16.7	31.4	45.9
Murder and nonnegligent manslaughter	9,426	114	957	2,800	4,838	1.2	10.2	29.7	51.3
Forcible rape	18,576	1,180	3,119	5,719	8,433	6.4	16.8	30.8	45.4
Robbery	76,667	4,354	18,111	35,027	47,569	5.7	23.6	45.7	62.0
Aggravated assault	329,722	16,498	44,815	82,380	131,335	5.0	13.6	25.0	39.8
Burglary	198,883	23,287	61,623	98,747	124,231	11.7	31.0	49.7	62.5
Larceny-theft	806,093	92,317	238,605	363,342	452,469	11.5	29.6	45.1	56.1
Motor vehicle theft	102,607	8,425	33,563	53,121	67,298	8.2	32.7	51.8	65.6
Arson	12,763	4,048	6,313	7,610	8,690	31.7	49.5	59.6	68.1
Violent crime[1]	434,391	22,146	67,002	125,926	192,175	5.1	15.4	29.0	44.2
Property crime[2]	1,120,346	128,077	340,104	522,820	652,688	11.4	30.4	46.7	58.3
Crime Index total[3]	1,554,737	150,223	407,106	648,746	844,863	9.7	26.2	41.7	54.3
Other assaults	898,298	70,642	163,142	254,571	377,152	7.9	18.2	28.3	42.0
Forgery and counterfeiting	77,692	422	3,975	15,901	29,809	0.5	5.1	20.5	38.4
Fraud	211,177	958	5,830	28,285	63,249	0.5	2.8	13.4	30.0
Embezzlement	13,836	83	1,258	4,047	6,489	0.6	9.1	29.2	46.9
Stolen property; buying, receiving, possessing	84,047	4,982	18,467	34,933	48,149	5.9	22.0	41.6	57.3
Vandalism	184,972	31,597	71,962	102,124	125,719	17.1	38.9	55.2	68.0
Weapons; carrying, possessing, etc.	114,325	8,691	25,861	47,073	66,691	7.6	22.6	41.2	58.3

	Total								
Prostitution and commercialized vice	58,638	155	1,034	5,613	12,503	0.3	1.8	9.6	21.3
Sex offenses (except forcible rape and prostitution)	62,997	6,625	12,381	18,763	25,516	10.5	19.7	29.8	40.5
Drug abuse violations	1,091,240	24,061	139,238	346,532	532,881	2.2	12.8	31.8	48.8
Gambling	7,769	129	1,000	2,356	3,758	1.7	12.9	30.3	48.4
Offenses against the family and children	93,909	2,296	6,286	12,706	23,974	2.4	6.7	13.5	25.5
Driving under the influence	946,694	629	13,397	96,319	251,539	0.1	1.4	10.2	26.6
Liquor laws	408,203	8,879	92,326	284,045	315,053	2.2	22.6	69.6	77.2
Drunkenness	423,561	1,805	13,971	53,764	114,911	0.4	3.3	12.7	27.1
Disorderly conduct	425,751	47,043	117,635	176,429	240,405	11.0	27.6	41.4	56.5
Vagrancy	19,509	394	1,607	3,991	5,996	2.0	8.2	20.5	30.7
All other offenses (except traffic)	2,453,100	76,546	269,317	598,558	1,000,185	3.1	11.0	24.4	40.8
Suspicion	2,629	277	834	1,163	1,472	10.5	31.7	44.2	56.0
Curfew and loitering law violations	100,701	28,245	100,701	100,701	100,701	28.0	100.0	100.0	100.0
Runaways	91,168	34,304	91,168	91,168	91,168	37.6	100.0	100.0	100.0

[1] Violent crimes are offenses of murder, forcible rape, robbery, and aggravated assault.
[2] Property crimes are offenses of burglary, larceny-theft, motor vehicle theft, and arson.
[3] Includes arson.

Source: Federal Bureau of Investigation (2002). *Crime in the United States, 2001; Uniform Crime Reports.* Washington, D.C.: Department of Justice [p. 250] [online] http://www.fbi.gov/ucr/cius_01/01crime4.pdf.

Therefore, defining what role they should play in the handling of juvenile offenders can become quite confusing and lead to role conflict for the individual officers.

Walker (1992, p. 63) and Yinger (1965, pp. 99–100) define a **role** as "a unit of culture; it refers to the rights and duties, the normatively approved patterns of behavior for the occupants of a given position." Although this definition calls for a distinction in purpose, it is not always clear in addressing the needs of youths. Police officers are oftentimes asked to serve as both the enforcer of law and as a pseudo social worker relating with youths and their families in a supportive and friendly manner (Walker, 1992). It is these inconsistencies that lead to role conflict. **Role conflict** refers to the inconsistencies in the expectations officers may have of their job and the actual tasks they are asked to perform. This is particularly evident in the handling of juvenile offenders. Officers must turn to both departmental policies (informal and formal) and community standards to determine how to deal with juvenile offenders. In making these determinations, it is imperative that the officer work closely with the various other human service related agencies within the community to make an informed decision about whether to formally or informally process the juvenile.

When handling juvenile offenders, police officers typically take on either a law enforcement or order maintenance role. Although these roles are distinct, officers may choose to use both roles depending upon the particular call for assistance.

Law Enforcement Role

The **law enforcement role** requires the officer to strictly enforce violations of law regardless of seriousness of the offense. The law enforcement role is more likely to be found in departments that do not have specialized juvenile units. The reason for this that officers are trained to deal specifically with adult offenders with no specialized training for handling juveniles. Therefore, regardless of the reason for assistance they are more apt to treat juvenile offenders like adults and respond to any given situation in a legalistic manner. Even though officers are expected by society to strictly enforce the law, there is still an expectation that officers will use their discretionary ability to handle juveniles in an individualized manner. These inconsistencies in roles/purpose may lead to role conflict (Bynum & Thompson, 2002). Therefore, it is imperative police agencies work collaboratively with other local human service agencies to educate one another on the communities available resources. In doing so, this will allow officers more flexibility in not only strictly enforcing the law, but in doing so they will have more legal options available to them.

Order Maintenance Role

Historically, police have used both radical nonintervention and diversion programs to handle youth who come to their attention. During the 1960s and 1970s, theorist and policy makers emphasized the use of radical nonintervention with juveniles (Schur, 1973). As proposed by Edwin Schur (1973), **radical nonintervention** includes leaving youth out of the system as much as possible to avoid having them labeled delinquent. Just as the original founders of the juvenile justice system proposed, exposing youth to the system could lead to stigmatizing them and further contribute to their delinquent careers. Schur notes that once youth are labeled delinquent they are much more like to develop a self-fulfilling prophecy and further participate in delinquent activity. It was the belief that handling youths informally would eliminate the labeling of youths as delinquents/criminals, therefore stopping further involvement in the juvenile/criminal justice systems. Many agencies went so far as to create their own diversion units to keep youths out of the system. It wasn't until the 1980s and into the 1990s that agencies began to move towards the order maintenance or community models of policing. **Order maintenance** activities refer to the officers' ability to use discretion in ambiguous situations and decide to adjust formally or informally (Wilson, 1968; Langworthy & Travis, 1994, p. 292). Research suggests that order maintenance activities make people feel safer (Hickman & Reaves, 2003, iii).

Unlike the law enforcement role that requires the officer to have a true understanding of the state's penal codes, order maintenance requires the officer to be familiar with local/community resources, have a working relationship with a variety of community agencies, as well as having enhanced communication skills to deal with all different types of citizens in the community. Police work with juveniles today primarily consists of order maintenance and service activities. Diversion programs, such as informal community service and restitution, are used frequently by law enforcement officers. These programs require the officer to function as both a social worker and concerned adult.

Over the past twenty years, there has been a move towards incorporating more order maintenance and **community-oriented policing** activities. In 2000, 68 percent of local police departments employing 90 percent of all officers reported having some community-oriented policing initiatives in their department. These activities ranged from full-time community-oriented officers to meeting with various community groups on a regular basis (Hickman & Reaves, 2003, iii). Federal, state, and local initiatives have focused on instituting community-oriented policing in an effort to both prevent crime and hold communities responsible for individual behavior. These efforts further require police to be proactive rather than reactive. When dealing with juveniles, programs such as DARE, school liaison officers, shop with a cop, etc. have focused on the needs to enhance relationships between officers and the youth in the community.

Many of these programs using law enforcement officers working in conjunction with community members to reduce crime and delinquency have been shown to be effective in reducing delinquent behavior. For example, the Kansas City Missouri Police Department initiated the Kansas City (MO) Gun Experiment in an attempt to reduce the number of firearms on the streets. The police initially created a community workgroup, which included individuals from law enforcement, human service agencies, and community organizations. This workgroup was charged with creating a plan to eradicate crime particularly focusing on crimes committed with firearms. Ultimately the workgroup developed a plan to focus patrol efforts on high-crime neighborhoods by routinely stopping traffic violators, youth in violation of curfews, and individuals involved in other infractions of the law. The officers gained legal authority to search both cars and pedestrians for illegal guns once they found law violations during the course of the routine stops. Overall, an eighty-block high-crime area where the homicide rate was twenty times higher than that of the national average was targeted for these special intercept patrols. During the first six months of the program, crime was reduced by 50 percent. Furthermore, data indicated that crime was not displaced to other locations in the city. In working with the local community and religious leaders, the Kansas City Police Department were able to gain the acceptance and implementation of the program by community members. Other previous attempts had failed to accomplish this goal. These efforts had not included local leaders and had failed because they were typically viewed by community members as being racist. Overall, a study supported by the National Institute of Justice found that gun crimes in the neighborhood were reduced by 49 percent while drive-by shootings and homicides also dropped significantly (CCJJDP, 1996, p. 5).

These programs serve as examples of how the use of order maintenance activities placed in the community can work to reduce overall crime and delinquency. Additional efforts to incorporate community-oriented activities are being initiated throughout the United States. These efforts rely on coordinated responses by all agencies and community

---

Youth Focused Community-Oriented Policing Strategies and Programs that Have Demonstrated Promise or Effectiveness

There have been a variety of community-oriented policing programs that have shown promise of reducing delinquency or that have been shown to be effective at reducing delinquency. Below is a list of these programs that have been identified by the Coordinating Council on Juvenile Justice and Delinquency Prevention.

- Reintegrative Policing Strategies, in which law enforcement officers help juveniles make the transition into the community following secure confinement.
- Police Athletic Leagues (PAL), in which police provide a wide array of youth activities and programs that serve as alternatives to gang involvement, drug use, and other delinquency.
- Futures Programs in Philadelphia, PA, and other jurisdictions, in which police officers serve as mentors and role models, focusing on the academic achievement of at-risk students.
- Kids and Kops Day, part of the Santa Ana (C) Police Departments' youth-related activities, in which police offices spend a day with at-risk youth attending recreational and cultural events and participating in community activities.
- Multidisciplinary team building, such as the Family Assessment Services Teams of the Norfolk (VA) Police Assisted Community Enforcement project, which addresses the needs of multiproblem families in targeted neighborhoods and serves as a vehicle for information sharing and problem solving at the neighborhood level. The program led to a drop in violent crime in the targeted neighborhoods.

Taken from: Coordinating Council on Juvenile Justice and Delinquency Prevention (1996, March). Combating Violence and Delinquency: The National Juvenile Justice Action Plan. Washington, DC: Office of Juvenile Justice and Delinquency Prevention [online] http://www.ojjdp.ncjrs.org/action/sec3.htm (pp. 9–10).

members. By increasing the overall effectiveness of the departments and by increasing the community cooperation, police officers are better able to use their discretion to deal with minor violations in an informal manner. As we shall see, the use of police officer discretion is important in deciding how to handle cases, as well as how to potentially reduce the level of stigmatization a juvenile may experience at the hands of the criminal justice system.

POLICE DISCRETION

In any situation where a law violation may have occurred, police have a variety of options at their disposal. When dealing with juvenile offenders, these options include informal sanctions such as reprimanding and releasing youths either on their own or to their parent or guardian, or using more formal options such as referring youths to the juvenile or adult court systems. Each of these options requires law enforcement officers to use a certain amount of discretion or judgment to make their decision. As Samuel Walker (1992) denotes, the key elements to using **discretion** are: 1) A criminal justice official 2) acting in an official capacity who 3) makes a decision on the basis of individual judgment (Walker, 1992, p. 198). In spite of the ability to use their judgment in making decisions about how to respond to a particular case, law enforcement officers must still operate within the legal constraints of the criminal justice system.

The ability to effectively use discretion relies very heavily on the interdependence of criminal justice agencies. For example, law enforcement officers must be aware of the legal culture and climate of the court system. Operating within the constraints of the courtroom workgroup, it is their responsibility to understand and embrace the collaborative efforts of the system. As Kelling (1999) points out, discretion occurs within all levels of the criminal justice system. Particularly, low-level decision making by line personnel (both police and prosecutors) is influenced heavily by "real-life and practical considerations" (Kelling, 1999, p. 22). It is these considerations that ultimately impact the outcome of the police–citizen encounter. For example, two youths are fighting in a local convenient store parking lot. Two officers approach the scene in their squad car. Upon noticing the officers approaching, one youth stops fighting and remains calm. As the officer approaches the youth answers, the officers' questions in a cooperative manner. The other youth, however, upon seeing the officers approaching becomes afraid and runs. A chase ensues. The youth is caught and becomes belligerent. Based on this scenario, the youth who cooperates fully with the officers is more likely to be reprimanded and released than the youth who attempted to evade detention.

FACTORS INFLUENCING POLICE DISCRETION

Research suggests the following eight factors are most likely to influence the police decision to arrest regardless of whether it is an adult or juvenile offender: seriousness of the offense, citizen complaint, departmental policy, demeanor of subject, race, gender, age, and socioeconomic status.

Seriousness of the Offense

Although the majority of police–juvenile contacts (86 percent) do not result in a formal adjustment (National Research Council and Institute of Medicine, 2001; Muraskin, 1998), the seriousness of the offense is still the most important factor in determining whether a child will be released or whether he or she will be formally processed through the system (Black & Reiss, 1970; Lundman, Sykes, & Clark, 1978; Pilivin & Briar, 1964). This decision is primarily determined by the legal codes in the state, but can also be influenced by extralegal factors such as public sentiment and community concerns. For example, between 1992 to 2001, arrests for drug abuse violations for persons under the age of eighteen increased by 121.3 percent (FBI, 2002, p. 233). Although this offense is not counted as a Part I Index offense, it has been viewed as a serious law violation since the movement towards getting tough on drugs during the mid-1980s.

Victim Complaints/Wishes

Victims/complainants are present in half of all cases involving a police–juvenile encounter (Black & Reiss, 1970). Research assessing the impact of the presence of a complainant or victim suggests their wishes may strongly impact the outcome of the encounter (Black, 1980; Black & Reiss, 1970). For example, if a victim is not willing to

Figure 5.1 Police must work to foster positive relationships with youth for a variety of reasons.
Kent Meireis/The Image Works

cooperate with the police and the offense is of a less serious nature, the officer may not be willing to process the case formally. However, if the victim is insistent upon formal processing or filing of a complaint the officer may have no choice other than to respond formally. Furthermore, officers may actually encourage citizens to file a formal complaint merely by asking whether or not they wish to file a complaint (Bayley & Garofalo, 1989). Additionally, the nature of the relationship between the victim and the suspect may impact the outcome. For example, if the victim and the suspect know one another, police are less likely to arrest than if the victim and the suspect are strangers (Walker, 1992; Black, 1980). The status of the complainant in the community may also impact the outcome of the encounter. For example, individuals who hold status in the community may have a greater impact on the officer's decision than those who hold less status. Overall, in the majority of cases where both a complainant and a suspect is present the wishes of the complainant are often followed.

Departmental Policy

Written departmental policies impact the discretion of the officers in a variety of ways (Walker, 1992). Remember, as stated previously in this chapter, according to a 1990 LEMAS study over 90 percent of all local police department and 74 percent of state agencies indicated they had a departmental policy directive addressing the handling of juvenile offenders (U.S. Department of Justice, 1993). Although these policies are formal in nature, informal policies may also exist. These informal policies or practices typically reflect community standards and the styles of policing emphasized by the department. For example, an area that has experienced a high rate of vandalism may petition or place a request to a law enforcement agency to increase patrolling in an area. A department may further acknowledge the increase in vandalism by increasing patrols and handling juvenile offenders more formally when they are caught loitering or hanging on street corners. Therefore, the existence of both formal and informal departmental policies can and will impact the handling of juvenile offenders. More recently, statewide and local efforts have focused on eradicating particular controlled substances, such as methamphetamines and ecstasy or other drugs falling into the "date rape" classifications of narcotics. These efforts have led to increased enforcement and departmental responses to detection. Once again, these efforts reflect the "get tough on crime and drugs" mentality which began in the 1970s and has further grown into the new millennium.

Demeanor of Subject

Research suggests that the subject's demeanor toward police is instrumental in determining the response of the officer toward the suspect. For example, if youth are disrespectful, belligerent, or uncooperative toward the police then they are more apt to be formally processed through the system than youth who cooperate with the police (National Research Council and Institute of Medicine, 2001; Lundman, 1994).

Race

Issues related to racism and disproportionate minority confinement confront the criminal justice system on a daily basis. The issue of race and the impact on the decision to arrest or release is complex at best. Minorities, particularly blacks, are more likely to be involved in more serious offenses. Therefore, as previously mentioned, offense seriousness is a strong predictor of outcome. As the seriousness level increases, so does the probability of arrest. Additionally, some research suggests the race of the suspect and the officer may impact the decision to arrest. As Black (1980) reports, white officers are more likely to arrest black suspects when there is a black complainant. These encounters may be contributing to the dark figure of crime or the mistrust of minorities to both report crimes and follow through on filing complaints (Borrero, 2001).

Gender

Although women have made strides in equality in society as a whole, it is apparent that the criminal justice system still exhibits differential treatment of female suspects. Evidence suggests that girls are less likely to be arrested than boys but more likely to be processed formally through the criminal justice system for status offenses, whereas boys are more likely to be processed through the system for delinquent activity other than status offenses (National Research Council and Institute of Medicine, 2001). Some evidence suggests that girls are committing more serious offenses that they are not being held accountable for (Chesney-Lind & Shelden, 1998; Sampson, 1985). This phenomenon of differential treatment and processing is known as the **chivalry hypothesis**. This hypothesis purports that females being the weaker sex are in need of protection, therefore it is the duty of officers to treat less serious offenses more seriously as a way to prevent future delinquent or criminal involvement (Chesney-Lind & Shelden, 1998; Whitehead & Lab, 1996). Furthermore, girls are typically seen as less serious and more likely to be a victim of a crime rather than the suspect. However, if through the process of normal questioning the officer finds the girl(s) have committed some minor infraction such as violating curfew, they are more likely to process formally rather than reprimand and release or turning them over to the custody of their parents.

Age

State legal codes vary in terms of the minimum ages and maximum ages youth may be handled by the juvenile justice system. Sixteen states have established the youngest age for original court jurisdiction. These ages range from age 6 to 10 (see Table 5.4 for an overview of states) (Snyder & Sickmund, 1999). Likewise, all states have established a maximum age for court jurisdiction ranging from fifteen to seventeen (see Table 5.5 for an overview of states). Many states also set the upper age limit of twenty for status offenses (Snyder & Sickmund, 1999). Even for those states not establishing minimum ages for original court jurisdiction, common law has historically recognized age seven as the minimum age for culpability. Therefore, officers, either through their own detection or when

Table 5.4   Youngest Age for Original Juvenile Court Jurisdiction in Delinquency Matters

Age	State
6	North Carolina
7	Maryland, Massachusetts, New York
8	Arizona
10	Arkansas, Colorado, Kansas, Louisiana, Minnesota, Mississippi, Pennsylvania, South Dakota, Texas, Vermont, Wisconsin

Source: Snyder, Howard N. and Sickmund, Melissa (September, 1999). *Juvenile Offenders and Victims: 1999 National Report.* Washington, DC: Office of Juvenile Justice and Delinquency Prevention (p. 93).

Table 5.5   Oldest Age for Original Juvenile Court Jurisdiction in Delinquency Matters

Age	State
15	Connecticut, New York, North Carolina
16	Georgia, Illinois, Louisiana, Massachusetts, Michigan, Missouri, New Hampshire, South Carolina, Texas, Wisconsin
17	Alabama, Alaska, Arizona, Arkansas, California, Colorado, Delaware, District of Columbia, Florida, Hawaii, Idaho, Indiana, Iowa, Kansas, Kentucky, Maine, Maryland, Minnesota, Mississippi, Montana, Nebraska, Nevada, New Jersey, New Mexico, North Dakota, Ohio, Oklahoma, Oregon, Pennsylvania, Rhode Island, South Dakota, Tennessee, Utah, Vermont, Virginia, Washington, West Virginia, Wyoming

Source: Snyder, Howard N. and Sickmund, Melissa (September, 1999). *Juvenile Offenders and Victims: 1999 National Report.* Washington, DC: Office of Juvenile Justice and Delinquency Prevention (p. 93).

being called to a scene for assistance, consider age as a potential mitigating factor. Evidence suggests that younger children are more likely to be handled informally than older suspects. One explanation for this differentiation is that younger children are both typically experiencing their first encounter with police, as well as typically committing less serious offenses. Likewise, older youth (sixteen and seventeen year olds) oftentimes have had prior contact with either a law enforcement agency or with the juvenile justice system in general. Therefore, officers are less apt to reprimand and release. Additionally, it has been purported since sixteen and seventeen year olds are closer to the age of majority, they are somehow more culpable for their actions regardless of previous contact with the system (Bynum & Thompson, 2002).

Socioeconomic Status

Research shows juveniles from lower socioeconomic status (SES) communities are more likely to come in contact with police. Typically, these encounters reflect increased patrol responses in high crime or "hot spot" areas. This evidence further suggests lower-class youth are more likely to be formally processed than middle- or upper-class youths. This decision could be influenced by a variety of external factors, such as peer involvement in crime and the stability of the youths' home, meaning there may not be anyone available to take responsibility for the youth even if the officer wanted to handle the case informally (Sampson, 1986; Lundman, 1996).

Overall, these eight factors potentially impact an officer's decision to formally or informally process a youth through the juvenile or adult court systems. As stated, the most important factor is the seriousness of the offense and complainant wishes. Although still playing an important role in the making their decision the demeanor of subject, race, gender, age, and socioeconomic status are not as important.

ATTITUDES AND THE POLICE

Both police attitudes towards citizens and citizen attitudes toward police oftentimes shape the outcome of the encounter. Previous research has suggested that police oftentimes harbor suspicious or negative attitudes toward victims (Whitehead & Lab, 1996; Wilson, 1978). For example, as Wilson (1978) reports, law enforcement officers often categorize victims as legitimate or illegitimate, with middle-class victims of a street attack being viewed as the most legitimate and lower-class victims of assault being viewed as the least legitimate. Therefore, harboring these views may not only impact the legalistic interpretation of the event but it may also impact the amount discretion or judgments made in deciding whether to handle the juvenile formally or informally in the system.

As noted in the previous section, the amount of discretion used by the police in any given encounter is shaped not only by the type and seriousness of the offense but also by the attitude or demeanor of the suspect toward the police. Research has suggested that not only do these encounters shape the outcome but they also impact the likelihood citizens will cooperate with police during an investigation (Lieber, Nalla, & Farnworth, 1998; Decker, 1981). Although the majority of research has focused on adult attitudes toward the police, there is a growing body of literature that focuses specifically on juvenile attitudes toward the police. This is abundantly significant since police are typically the first and in many instances the only contact youths have with the criminal justice system (Taylor et al., 2001).

Research suggests adults and juveniles differ on their attitudes toward police. Overall, the majority of literature assessing adult attitudes toward the police suggests a favorable response. For example, research dating back to the 1960s to 1970s suggested that police do at least a "good or fairly good job" (Reiss, 1971). More recent studies have confirmed this finding. For example, overall satisfaction with citizen and police encounters have ranged from 65 percent of the respondents stating they were satisfied (Frank et al., 1996) to as high as 75 to 85 percent of the respondents (Hurst & Frank, 2000; Brandl, Frank, Wooldredge, & Watkins, 1997; Dean, 1980; Brandl & Horvath, 1991; Furstenberg & Wellford, 1973; Jacob, 1971). Other studies indicate citizens believe police do an overall good job of protecting them (Cao et al., 1996), while further studies suggest white respondents (46.7 percent) are more favorable than black respondents (30.9 percent) in reporting that police do a good job in prohibiting the sale of drugs in their community (Hurst & Frank, 2000; Frank et al., 1996).

A limited number of studies have been completed assessing juvenile attitudes toward police. Overall, research suggests juveniles have less favorable attitudes toward police than their adult counterparts (Borrero, 2001; Taylor et al., 2001; Hurst & Frank, 2000; Decker, 1981). Hurst and Frank (2000) administered a self-report survey to 852 urban and suburban students in the Hamilton County, Ohio, school system. Respondents were asked a series of questions regarding their attitudes toward the police, the extent of victimization suffered by the respondents, and constructs of the initiators of the police–citizen encounter. Overall, the findings suggest there was not widespread support for the police. Less than 40 percent of the respondents agreed with any of the general attitude items about liking the police, being satisfied with them, or trusting them. Support typically centered around the law enforcement efforts to keep their neighborhoods quiet at night. Results from this study further revealed that youths who had contact with police that was initiated by the police reported less positive attitudes than those who came in contact with the police for various other reasons. This finding was further supported by a study conducted by Taylor et al. (2001). Surveying eighth-grade students in eleven U.S. cities, the researchers concluded juveniles are indifferent on their opinions about their perceptions of police.

When assessing the attitudes of juveniles toward police and controlling for race, research suggests black juveniles have less favorable attitudes toward the police than white juveniles. In assessing the relationship between police surveillance and social control, Browning et al. (1994) found that blacks and youth were more likely to feel "hassled" by the police. Hurst, Frank, and Browning (2000) surveying 852 ninth- through twelfth-graders in the Cincinnati, Ohio, and Hamilton County area found that black youths' perceptions toward police were less positive than white respondents. However, when asked about "specific behavior involving the respondent and the police, their ratings of the police were quite similar" (Hurst, Frank, & Browning, 2000).

Overall, these findings do suggest that juveniles and blacks have much less positive attitudes toward the police than their adult counterparts. This finding is important since demeanor is an important factor in an officer's decision to formally or informally process a youth through the juvenile court system. Therefore, it is crucial that officers work in conjunction with community resources to eliminate some of the potential barriers that may be contributing to this distrust. The use of community resources such as school liaison programs, DARE programs, and community-oriented policing are a positive step in improving citizen's attitudes toward police and the overall citizens view towards the police.

SUMMARY

To summarize, this chapter explored the relationship between juveniles and the police. Overall, we see juveniles represent a significant portion of the criminal population. This chapter reviewed official statistics on the number of juvenile–police encounters. The police role was further defined and explored. As the literature suggests, officers dealing with juvenile offenders are often confronted with make discretionary decisions (order maintenance role) that are contrary to their police training (law enforcement role). Therefore, officers must be cognizant of the role conflicts that may potentially exist. Because police officers are the most visible actors in the criminal justice system, their response to a situation may impact the overall outcome of the case. Working in a collaborative arrangement with other human service agencies in the community will alleviate the overall role conflict that exists.

This chapter further examined the various factors that impact the discretionary decision-making abilities of officers. Eight factors were identified and reviewed. Overall, the literature suggests that the seriousness of the offense and the complainants' wishes were the most important factors impacting the decision to formally or informally process a case. Although departmental policy, age, gender, race, and socioeconomic status played a role in the decision-making process, these factors were not as strong as the previous two. Finally the chapter reviewed juvenile attitudes toward the police. As the literature suggests, juveniles display less favorable attitudes toward the police than their adult counterparts. This fact can play a role in the handling of a juvenile case.

CASE STUDY WRAP-UP

Officer Greco takes his job seriously and attempted to befriend Jimmy, as did a number of other officers. Officer Greco knows that he can divert a child out of the system by referring him or her to an agency for assistance and can work with family in the same way. In this case, perhaps Jimmy's attitude towards the police interfered with an opportunity to stay out of the system, and today, Jimmy is fully enmeshed with the system.

STUDY QUESTIONS

1. Law enforcement officers have five different options available to them once a juvenile comes to their attention. What are these options, and when would an officer elect to use one option over another?

2. According to the Uniform Crime Reports, how many arrests were made by officers in 2001? Why do we only use crimes cleared by arrests when assessing juvenile crime rates and trends?

3. Is the juvenile crime rate increasing or decreasing? Why is this statistic important for law enforcement personnel to understand?

4. When dealing with juveniles, law enforcement officers are asked to play competing law enforcement and order maintenance roles. What are each of these roles? When would an officer choose to adopt one role over the other? What are the costs and benefits of adopting one role over the other?

5. What is police discretion? How does the use of police discretion in handling juvenile offenders differ from the handling of adults?

6. There are eight different factors that are most likely to influence an officer's decision-making abilities. What are these eight factors and what role do they play in the decision-making process?

BIBLIOGRAPHY

BAYLEY, DAVID H., AND GAROFALO, JAMES (1989). "The Management of Violence by Police Patrol Officers." *Criminology, 27*(1), 1–15.

BLACK, DONALD J. (1980). *The Manners and Customs of the Police.* New York: Academic Press.

BLACK, DONALD J., AND REISS, ALBERT (1970). "Police Control of Juveniles." *American Sociological Review, 35,* 63–77.

BORRERO, MICHAEL (2001). "The Widening Mistrust Between Youth and Police." *Families in Society: The Journal of Contemporary Human Services, 82*(4), 399–408.

BRANDL, STEVEN, FRANK, JAMES, WOOLDREDGE, JOHN, AND WATKINS, R. COREY (1997). "On the Measurement of Public Support for the Police: A Research Note." *Policing: An International Journal of Police Strategy and Management, 20*(3), 473–480.

BRANDL, STEVEN, AND HORVATH, FRANK (1991). "Crime Victim Evaluation of Police Investigative Performance." *Journal of Crime and Justice, 19,* 293–305.

BROWNING, SANDRA LEE, AND CULLEN, FRANCIS T. (1994). "Race and Getting Hasseled by the Police: A Research Note." *Police Studies, 17*(1), 1–11.

BYNUM, JACK E., AND THOMPSON, WILLIAM E. (2002). *Juvenile Delinquency: A Sociological Approach,* 5th ed. Boston: Allyn and Bacon.

CAO, LIQUN, FRANK, JAMES, AND CULLEN, FRANCIS (1996). "Race, Community Context, and Confidence in the Police." *American Journal of Police, 15*(1), 3–22.

CHESNEY-LIND, MEDA, AND SHELDON, RANDALL G. (1998). *Girls, Delinquency, and Juvenile Justice,* 2nd ed. Belmont, CA: West Wadsworth.

COORDINATING COUNCIL ON JUVENILE JUSTICE AND DELINQUENCY PREVENTION (1996, March). *Combating Violence and Delinquency: The National Juvenile Justice Action Plan.* Washington, DC: Office of Juvenile Justice and Delinquency Prevention. [online] Available: http://www.ojjdp/ncjrs.org/action/sec3.htm.

DEAN, D. (1980). "Citizen Ratings of the Police: The Difference Police Contact Makes." *Law & Police Quarterly, 2,* 455–471.

DECKER, SCOTT H. (1981). "Citizen Attitudes Toward The Police: A Review of Past Findings and Suggestions for Future Policy." *Journal of Police Science and Administration, 9,* 81–87.

FEDERAL BUREAU OF INVESTIGATION (2002). *Crime in the United States, 2001: Uniform Crime Reports.* Washington, D.C.: Department of Justice. [online] Available http://www.fbi.gov/ucr/cius_01/01crime4.pdf.

FRANK, JAMES, BRANDL, STEVEN, CULLEN, FRANCIS, AND STICHMAN, AMY (1996). "Reassessing the Impact of Race on Citizens' Attitudes Toward the Police: A Research Note." *Justice Quarterly, 13*(2), 321–334.

FURSTENBERG, F., AND WELLFORD, C.F. (1973). "Calling the Police: The Evaluation of Police Service." *Law & Society Review, 8,* 393–406.

GOLDSTEIN, A.P. (1991). *Delinquent Gangs: A Psychological Perspective.* Champaign, IL: Research Press.

HICKMAN, MATTHEW J., AND REAVES, BRIAN A. (2003). *Local Police Departments 2000.* Washington, DC: U.S. Department of Justice, NCJ 196002.

HURST, YOLANDER G., AND FRANK, JAMES (2000). "How Kids View Cops: The Nature of Juvenile Attitudes Toward the Police." *Journal of Criminal Justice, 28,* 189–202.

HURST, YOLANDER G., FRANK, JAMES, AND BROWNING, SANDRA (2000). "The Attitudes of Juveniles Toward the Police: A Comparison of Black and White Youth." *Policing: An International Journal of Police Strategies & Management, 23*(1), 37–53.

JACOB, H. (1971). "Black and White Perceptions of Justice in the City." *Law & Society Review, 5,* 69–89.

KELLING, GEORGE L. (1999). *"Broken Windows" and Police Discretion.* Washington, DC: National Institute of Justice. NCJ 178259.

KRISBERG, G., AND AUSTIN, J. (1978). *The Children of Ishmael: Critical Perspectives on Juvenile Justice.* Palo Alto, CA: Mayfield.

LANGWORTHY, ROBERT H., AND TRAVIS, LAWRENCE F. (1994). *Policing in America: A Balance of Forces.* New York: Macmillan Publishing Company.

LIEBER, MICHAEL, J., NALLA, MAHESH, AND FARNWORTH, MARAGRET (1998). "Explaining Juvenile Attitudes Toward the Police." *Justice Quarterly, 15,* 151–174.

LUNDMAN, RICHARD J. (1996). "Demeanor and Arrest: Additional Evidence from Previously Unpublished Data." *Journal of Research in Crime and Delinquency, 33,* 306–323.

LUNDMAN, RICHARD J. (1994). "Demeanor or Crime? The Midwest City Police-Citizen Encounters Study." *Criminology, 32,* 631–653.

LUNDMAN, RICHARD J., SYKES, RICHARD E., AND CLARK, JOHN P. (1978). "Police Control of Juveniles: A Replication." *Journal of Research in Crime and Delinquency, 15,* 74–91.

MORASH, MERRY (1984). "Establishment of a Juvenile Record: The Influence of Individual and Peer Group Characteristics." *Criminology, 22,* 97–111.

MURASKIN, ROSLYN (1998). "Police Work and Juveniles." In Albert R. Roberts (Ed.), *Juvenile Justice: Policies, Programs, and Services,* 2nd ed. Chicago: Nelson-Hall Publishers.

NATIONAL RESEARCH COUNCIL AND INSTITUTE OF MEDICINE (2001). "Juvenile Crime, Juvenile Justice. Panel on Juvenile Crime: Prevention, Treatment, and Control." Joan McCord, Cathy Spatz Widom, and Nancy A. Crowell (Eds.), *Committee on Law and Justice and Board on Children, Youth, and Families.* Washington, DC: National Academy Press.

PASTORE, ANN L., AND MAGUIRE, KATHLEEN (Eds.) (2002). *Sourcebook of Criminal Justice statistics 2001.* [online] Available: http://www.albany.edu/sourcebook/1995/pdf/t426.pdf.

PILIAVIN, IRVING, AND BRIAR, SCOTT (1964). "Police Encounters with Juveniles." *American Journal of Sociology, 70,* 206–214.

REISS, ALBERT J. (1971). *The Police and the Public.* New Haven, CT: Yale University Press.

SAMPSON, ROBERT J. (1986). "Effects of Socioeconomic Context on Official Reaction to Juvenile Delinquency." *American Sociological Review, 51,* 876–885.

SCHUR, EDWIN M. (1973). *Radical Nonintervention: Rethinking the Delinquency Problem.* Englewood Cliffs, NJ: Prentice-Hall.

SNYDER, HOWARD N., AND SICKMUND, MELISSA (1999). *Juvenile Offenders and Victims: 1999 National Report.* Washington, DC: Office of Juvenile Justice and Delinquency Prevention.

SNYDER, HOWARD N. (2001). *Law Enforcement and Juvenile Crime. Juvenile Offenders and Victims: National Report Series, Bulletin.* Washington, DC: OJJDP. NCJ 191031.

STAHL, A.L., SICKMUND, M., FINNEGAN, T.A., SNYDER, H.N., POOLE, R.S., AND TIERNEY N. (1999). *Juvenile Court Statistics 1996.* Washington, D.C.: Office of Juvenile Justice and Delinquency Prevention.

TAYLOR, TERRANCE J., TURNER, K.B., ESBENSEN, FINN-AAGE, AND WINFREE JR., L. THOMAS (2001). "Coppin' an Attitude: Attitudinal Differences Among Juveniles Toward Police." *Journal of Criminal Justice, 29,* 295–305.

U.S. DEPARTMENT OF JUSTICE (1993). "LEMAS Reports—1990." In Roger G. Dunham and Geoffrey P. Alpert (Eds.), *Critical Issues in Policing: Contemporary Readings,* 2nd ed., pp. 33–71. Prospect Heights, IL: Waveland Press, Inc.

WALKER, SAMUEL (1992). *The Police in America: An Introduction,* 2nd ed. New York: McGraw-Hill, Inc.

WHITEHEAD, JOHN T., AND LAB, STEVEN P. (1996). *Juvenile Justice: An Introduction,* 2nd ed. Cincinnati, OH: Anderson Publishing.

WILSON, JAMES Q. (1968). *Varieties of Police Behavior.* Cambridge, MA: Harvard University Press.

WILSON, JAMES Q. (1978). *Varieties of Police Behavior: The Management of Law and Order in Eight Communities.* Cambridge, MA: Harvard University Press.

YINGER, J. MILTON (1965). *Toward a Field Theory of Behavior.* New York: McGraw-Hill.

GLOSSARY OF KEY TERMS

Chivalry hypothesis.   A view that the lower delinquency rates of juveniles refers to the differential and lenient treatment of girls within the criminal justice system.

Community-oriented policing.   A strategy of policing that relies on reducing fear of crime, organizing the community, and order maintenance activities rather than law enforcement.

Crimes cleared by arrest.   A crime is considered cleared by arrest if someone is charged with the crime or if someone is believed to have committed the crime but for some reason (e.g., death of the suspect) the arrest cannot be made.

Discretion.   Personal decision-making process law enforcement officers use in deciding how to handle a case. The more serious the offense the less discretion an officer has in enforcing the law.

Law enforcement role.   This role requires the officer to strictly enforce violations of law regardless of seriousness of the offense.

Order maintenance role.   This role refers to the officer's ability to use discretion in an ambiguous situation and decide to adjust formally or informally.

Radical nonintervention.   This form of intervention includes leaving the youth out of the system as much as possible to avoid having them labeled delinquent. The idea behind this nonintervention is that exposing youth to the system could lead to stigmatizing them and further contribute to their delinquent careers.

Role.   A unit of culture; it refers to the rights and duties, the normatively approved patterns of behavior for the occupants of a given position.

Role conflict.   The inconsistencies in the expectations officers may have of their job and the actual tasks they are asked to perform.

CHAPTER 6
THE COURTS AND JUVENILE JUSTICE

KEY TERMS

Parens patriae
Kent v. United States
In re Gault
In re Winship
McKeiver v. Pennsylvania
Teen courts
Breed v. Jones
Fare v. Michael C.
Schall v. Martin
Stanford v. Kentucky
Wilkins v. Missouri
Law-giver judges
Client-retained attorneys
Court-appointed attorneys

Legal aid or public
    defenders
Attorney consortiums
Guardian *ad litem*
Hearing officers
Courtroom workgroup
Shared decision making
Shared norms
Socialization
Sticks and carrots
Goal modification
Referral
Informal adjustment
Intake

Consent decree
Detention hearing
Adjudication hearing
Disposition hearing
Waiver hearing
Judicial waiver
Discretionary waiver
Presumptive waiver
Mandatory waiver
Direct file
Statutory exclusion
Reverse waiver
Once an adult/always an
    adult waiver

CASE STUDY*

I knew I wanted to enter the field of probation after completing an internship with the Vigo County Juvenile Probation Department during my senior year at Indiana State University. I enjoyed working with children who had challenging lives, parents who struggled to raise their families, and the community networking system involved in each probationer's life. A bonus with the internship was learning about juvenile law and being involved in the court system.

I found myself in the position of a juvenile probation officer sixteen months after graduation, and twenty years later, I'm still in the same department, serving as Chief Juvenile Probation Officer for the last fifteen. The Vigo County Juvenile Court is composed of five juvenile officers, including myself, and serves a county of approximately 100,000 people. Probation officers are involved with each case from beginning to end. We perform initial meetings, file cases with the prosecutor, attend all court hearings, place the child on probation and supervise that probation throughout his or her term. All together, the caseload numbers approximately fifty juveniles under supervision, but with various pending hearings, a probation officer can easily be working with over one hundred juveniles and their families at one time.

I believe we have a strong network of professionals in the local system with the same goals as the court has for the youth of our community. We work very closely with local schools, mental health facilities, community corrections, and the State Office of Family and Children. Together, agencies have created several programs and services that are designed to help children and families deal with the various stresses life can hold. I find it important that professionals need to pull together to be successful and that it is impossible for one agency to adequately handle all the issues a family may be dealing with. Our unwritten motto is to make each child's life the best it can be. The ability of the child and his/her family to change and better their situation is the guide used to develop goals for the family.

As a probation officer, it is our job to secure and implement whatever services are needed to reach those goals and to supervise that child and family, assuring they are participating in services and court-ordered programs. Many programs have been created with little to no cost to our families, keeping in mind most of them are at poverty level. We have programs from community corrections, such as home detention monitoring, day reporting, and supervised community service. One of our local mental health facilities provides several programs for drug and alcohol use, a family preservation program, and functional family therapy for families dealing with behavioral issues. We have a wraparound services program that serves families that are involved with several agencies.

Our Office of Family and Children provides some money for placement of children outside the home, which is needed when that child is not being successful on probation while living with his/her parent. One officer is assigned to work with the school corpora-

---

*Deborah Kesler was appointed chief probation officer after a series of administrators and a history of strife and political interference in the court. She has been successful as chief probation officer, and out of the twenty years she has been employed with the Vigo County Juvenile Court, Terre Haute, Indiana, for the past fifteen years she has served as chief probation officer.

tion, handling all truancy referrals. It is certainly a challenge to keep all services straight and what child is receiving what service. As probation officers, we have the challenge of the court and legal system. Although it gives us leverage other agencies don't have, it is a valuable tool that enables us to be more efficient in working with families and youth.

I find it interesting to watch our judicial system at work, learning the ins and outs of how laws work and how attorneys make those laws work. Juvenile law is a specialty, it is vastly different than adult law, and I believe one needs to consistently work in juvenile law to better understand it. The court is to be used, again, as a tool to help families better their situation, but also to enforce those orders the magistrate expects to be followed. In our county, the elected five superior court judges supervise the juvenile magistrate (which is not an elected office), who is my immediate supervisor. The building we are housed in is a county-owned building, so the county commissioners oversee our physical facility and the upkeep for the building itself. Our county councilpersons are directly responsible for all county office budgets, deciding yearly our salaries and how we are to spend our dollars. Because my agency is a government agency, supervised on many levels by local elected officials, our political elections and knowledge of how our county government is of interest to us. After twenty years, I am still challenged daily with new situations and problems, am always learning and looking to how to improve my performance as a juvenile probation officer. It is a very rewarding profession that I am proud to be involved with.

INTRODUCTION

Since the creation of the first juvenile court in 1899, the question of procedural justice and fairness has existed. What is the purpose of the juvenile court? What role does the Supreme Court play in determining procedural fairness? What roles do judges, attorneys, and other actors in the juvenile justice system play in assuring procedural fairness for youths? Is the purpose of the juvenile court to rehabilitate or punish? Or is it to provide age-appropriate punishments to those who violate the laws of the land, keeping in mind that rehabilitation should be a goal but not necessarily the primary goal of the juvenile court? Is a separate juvenile court necessary at all? Or, as opponents have suggested, does the existence of a separate juvenile court further restrict the ability of the court and system to appropriately punish and ultimately hold youths responsible for their problem behaviors? These questions and issues are all important for the sheer existence of the modern-day juvenile court. Therefore, it is appropriate to revisit the development of the juvenile court and overview the evolution of today's system.

As you recall from Chapter 1, prior to 1899, common law dominated our criminal justice system, therefore, youths were treated like adults. As a general rule, youth under the age of seven were immune from prosecution because they lacked moral responsibility, while youths between the ages of seven and fourteen were assessed for culpability. If they were found to be culpable for their actions, they would be tried as adults and therefore held to the same sentences and punishments as adults. Those youth fourteen and older were considered adults and held accountable for their actions (Shepherd, 1999).

During the late 1800s, the focus of attention on child behavior became a social rather than a familial issue. Spearheaded by a group of elitists who touted themselves as Progressives, these reformers targeted youth who were classified as "out of control" and suffering from pauperism. These reformers believed "poverty and bad parenting went hand in hand" (Guarino-Ghezzi & Loughran, 1996, p. 88). Therefore, they argued it was necessary to create a separate legal system aimed at addressing the issues of poverty and the resultant misbehavior of youth growing up in these homes. The plan for a separate court system was developed (Barton, 2000).

The passage of the Illinois Juvenile Court Act in 1899 called for the creation of the first court specifically designed to separate the handling of juvenile from adult cases in Cook County, Illinois. The original intent of the court was to function under the premise of *parens patriae*, which literally means "parent of the country." Under these ideas, the judge is to function as the pseudo parent of the child. Unlike the adult court, the juvenile court was designed as a non-adversarial, informal, civil system, focusing on rehabilitation rather than punishment. Acting as the benevolent surrogate parent of the child, judges were entrusted by the state with the responsibility of acting in the best interest of the child. They were ultimately responsible for providing moral training for youth since they were not receiving it at home (del Carmen, Parker, & Reddington, 1998; Shepherd, 1999). Courts were to hear all matters pertaining to troubled youth, including delinquency, as well as abuse, neglect, and dependency cases. This Act was one of the first attempts to distinguish delinquent children from neglected and dependent children (Barton, 2000). This nonadversarial, informal system ultimately negated the need for prosecutors and defense attorneys. Because all hearings were treated as civil rather than criminal matters, juveniles were not afforded the same constitutional and procedural safeguards as adults.

The original goal of the juvenile justice system was to investigate, diagnose, and prescribe treatment, not to adjudicate guilt or to fix blame (Simonsen, 1991). The juvenile courts wanted also to change the terminology used when dealing with juvenile offenders. First, the courts wanted to do away with any reference to a "trial." Since the juvenile was not being "tried" for a crime, the courts wanted any and all references to the word "trial" be changed to "adjudicated." And second, the courts wanted any and all reference to "guilty" to be changed to "adjudged" (Watkins, 1998). The optimistic goal of the juvenile justice system was "not so much to punish as to reform, not to degrade but to uplift, not to crush but to develop, not to make [the juvenile] a criminal, but a worthy citizen" (Besharov, 1974).

At the time of the creation of the juvenile court system, it was thought to become the center of society's efforts to help young people. With the help of social workers, psychologists, and psychiatrists, the juvenile court judge was to decide what the juvenile needed and see to it that it was provided (Besharov, 1974).

Within the next ten years, ten states had a juvenile court system in place; by 1925, all but two states, Maine and Wyoming, had a juvenile court system. However in 1945, both Maine and Wyoming created a juvenile court system (Simonsen, 1991). These new court systems were closely modeled after that of the original juvenile court set forth in Cook County, Illinois (Bernard, 1992).

While the idea of the new juvenile justice system blossomed, it was not without problems. In 1905, *Commonwealth v Fisher,* 213 Pa. 48, was brought before the Pennsylvania Supreme Court to discuss what due process protections were allowed juveniles. With this case, fourteen-year-old Frank Fisher was placed into the Philadelphia House of Refuge after being convicted of larceny. His father objected to this sentence, noting that Frank was given a sentence more severe than he would have received in a criminal court (Bernard, 1992). The Pennsylvania Supreme Court upheld the juvenile court's decision, noting that the State may place a juvenile into a house of refuge if the family is unwilling to control the juvenile's actions and that due process protections were unnecessary when the State acts under its *parens patriae* powers. Following this case, there were more challenges on the due process rights of juveniles. While supporters were pleased that a separate system was devoted to helping juveniles, many saw that it was often not serving the best interest of the child (Bernard, 1992). Nevertheless, the juvenile court continued to serve youth, and according to Zimring (2000) "the past thirty years have been the juvenile court's finest hour." However, critics abound on every side.

It wasn't until the mid-1960s with the passage of *Kent v. the United States* (1966) that courts began to question whether juveniles should be afforded constitutional protections. Since that time, the juvenile system has progressed into a more adversarial and less informal system.

The purpose of this chapter is to overview the legal transformation of the juvenile court since the 1960s, as well as the roles of the primary actors and the existence of the courtroom workgroup in the juvenile justice system. More specifically the chapter will overview eight constitutional questions addressed by the U.S. Supreme Court which have resulted in the modification of the concept of *parens patriae* in the juvenile justice system. These issues include: procedural due process, due process rights, burden of proof, jury trials, double jeopardy, representation by a youth probation officer, preventative detention, and death penalty. The roles of prosecuting attorneys, defense attorneys, judges, other hearing officers, and probation officers will be reviewed. The chapter concludes with a discussion of the courtroom workgroup and its role in the juvenile justice system.

LANDMARK SUPREME COURT CASES

Since the mid-1960s, the U.S. Supreme Court has significantly modified the original intent of the first juvenile court which focused on the concept of *parens patriae*. Four major U.S. Supreme Court rulings during the 1960s and 1970s covering the issues of procedural due process, due process, burden of proof, and jury trials modified the way juveniles are handled in the present-day juvenile justice system. (See Table 6.1 for an overview of these issues and their corresponding U.S. Supreme Court Cases.) The following is a brief discussion of the issue and the relevant cases.

Procedural Due Process

The question of procedural due process first came to the attention in the case of *Kent v. United States* (1966). In 1966 at the age of sixteen, Morris Kent was arrested in connection with housebreaking, robbery, and rape. In this case, the judge made an independent

Table 6.1   Summary of Relevant Supreme Court Cases

Year	Issue	Court Case
1966	Procedural Due Process	*Kent v. United States*
1967	Due Process	*In re Gault*
1970	Burden of Proof	*In re Winship*
1971	Jury Trials	*McKeiver v. Pennsylvania*
1975	Double Jeopardy	*Breed v. Jones*
1979	Representation by Youth's Probation Officer	*Fare v. Michael C.*
1984	Preventative Detention	*Schall v. Martin*
1989	Death Penalty	*Stanford v. Kentucky and Wilkins v. Missouri*

decision without full investigation to transfer Kent to the adult court system. Prior to being waived to the adult court system, Kent's mother met with the social service director of the juvenile court to discuss the possibility of waiver. However, she, Kent, and Kent's attorney opposed the waiver because the petitioner (Kent) was "a victim of severe psychopathology." In spite of their opposition, the juvenile court judge granted a waiver without full investigation, without consulting a psychologist, and without a hearing. Kent was then indicted in the district court for the District of Columbia on two instances of housebreaking, robbery, and rape, and one instance of housebreaking and robbery. His attorney moved to dismiss the charges on grounds that the waiver was invalid. However, this motion was denied. Kent was eventually found guilty of all charges and sentenced to a total of thirty to ninety years in prison. Furthermore, he was sentenced to a mental institution until sanity was restored. Kent appealed the motion to waive his case to the adult court based on the grounds he was denied a full investigation and a hearing. The U.S. Supreme Court ruled before youths could be waived to the adult court, they are entitled to a hearing "including access by his counsel to the social records and probation or similar reports which presumably are considered by the court, and to a statement of reasons for the Juvenile Court's decision" (Clement, 1997, p. 30; Kent v. United States, 1966; Siegel & Senna, 2000). Therefore, the U.S. Supreme Court upheld the ruling that youths are entitled to a procedural hearing prior to being waived to the adult court. This was the first time since the creation of the juvenile court in 1899 that the U.S. Supreme Court had ruled that juveniles were entitled to any such protections by the Constitution.

Due Process Rights

Although *Kent v. the United States* set the foundation for constitutional change, it was not until the passage of ***In re Gault*** that juveniles began to experience the full protections of the Constitution. Prior to the passage of *Gault,* it was fundamentally assumed there was no need for constitutional protection since the juvenile courts operated under the premise of *parens patriae,* therefore, the state entrusted judges with the authority to rule in the best interest of the child. However, this premise was challenged and refuted in the case of *In re Gault* (1967). This decision, in essence, transformed the juvenile court into a very different institution than originally envisioned by the Progressives (Feld, 1993). Recognized as the most significant Supreme Court case, *In re Gault* (1967) challenged the concept of *parens patriae* and the existence of the juvenile court as a completely separate entity. In 1964, fifteen-year-old Gerald Gault was taken into custody for making lewd telephone calls to a neighbor. Gault's parents were not informed he was taken into custody. The complainant did not appear in court to testify. After a hearing before the juvenile court judge, Gault was committed to the State Industrial School as a juvenile delinquent until he reached the age of majority (twenty-one), which translated into a six-year sentence. The same case tried in the adult court system carried a penalty of a $5 to $50 fine, or imprisonment for not more than two months. Gault appealed this decision based on the grounds that he was denied certain procedural due process rights afforded in the Fourteenth Amendment. The Supreme Court ruled in favor of Gault and stated that juveniles, like adults, have due process protections during the adjudication stage of the process when there is a possibility of confinement of the youth. These rights include:

1. Right to reasonable notice of the charges;
2. Right to counsel, his or her own, appointed by the state if indigent;
3. Right to confront and cross-examine witnesses;
4. Privilege against self-incrimination, including the right to remain silent (del Carmen, Parker, & Reddington, 1998, p. 175).

Therefore, in cases dealing with youth classified as Children in Need of Supervision (CHINS), Minors in Need of Supervision (MINS), or Persons in Need of Supervision (PINS) where the outcome will not result in the child losing their freedom, due process rights are not afforded (del Carmen, Parker, & Reddington, 1998). This case set the foundation for further appeals and expanding the rights of juveniles such that they resemble those of adults (Clement, 1997; Feld, 2000). Since the passage of *Gault,* the only rights that have not been afforded juveniles are "the right to a grand jury indictment, the right to bail, the right to a jury trial, and the right to a public hearing" (del Carmen, Parker, & Reddington, 1998, p. 177).

Burden of Proof

The original juvenile court was designed to hear cases as informal, civil matters where the preponderance of evidence was the only the burden of proof necessary for a guilty verdict. Because the court placed the ultimate fate of the child in the hands of the judge under the concept of *parens patriae,* it was believed that they only needed to be 51 percent sure the youth committed the offense to function in the best interests of the child. Therefore, trusting them with the ability to adjudicate a child delinquent and administer the appropriate disposition. The issue of the burden of proof was not challenged until 1970 in the case of *In re Winship*.

In the case of *In re Winship,* the U.S. Supreme Court was asked to address the issue whether "proof beyond a reasonable doubt was among the essential elements of due process and fair treatment required during the adjudicatory hearing when a juvenile is charged with an act which would constitute a crime if committed by an adult" where the disposition may include the child's commitment to a state institution. In this case, a New York Family Court judge found Winship, a boy who at the age of twelve broke into a locker and stole $112 from a woman's purse, guilty of committing the offense. This crime, if committed by an adult, would be classified as larceny. During the adjudicatory hearing, the judge recognized that if this case were heard in the adult court system, there may not be enough evidence to convict the juvenile. At the dispositional hearing the juvenile was ordered to be placed in a training school for eighteen months, subject to annual extensions of his commitment until the age of eighteen (del Carmen, Parker, & Reddington, 1998, p. 178). In this case, the Supreme Court ruled juveniles should be afforded the protection of proof beyond a reasonable doubt in an adjudication hearing when faced with the possibility of commitment to a state institution and if the act would be considered a crime if committed by an adult. Furthermore, they suggested that the informality of the juvenile proceedings would not be compromised because of increasing the burden of proof. Because this case deals specifically with crimes or delinquent acts that would result in institutionalization, other offenses not resulting in confinement still use preponderance of evidence as their burden of proof. Therefore, unless state law specifically requires proof beyond a reasonable doubt in minor violations, cases involving CHINS, PINS, and MINS or status offenses still rely on the preponderance of evidence as the burden of proof. In these instances, state law supercedes federal law.

Jury Trials

Researchers have argued that the creation of the juvenile court was, in part, an attempt to nullify jury trials (Shepherd, 1999). In doing so, the juvenile court negated the need for a jury of one's peers. Once again, it was the belief of the original framers of the court that the judge would act in the best interest of the child, therefore, it was unnecessary to clutter the system with jury trials. This practice was challenged in the case of *McKeiver v. Pennsylvania* (1971).

In the case of *McKeiver v. Pennsylvania,* the Supreme Court reviewed whether juveniles are afforded the Fourteenth Amendment right to a trial by jury in the adjudicative phase of a state juvenile court delinquency proceeding. In this case, sixteen-year-old Joseph McKeiver was charged with robbery, larceny, and receiving stolen goods (all felony offenses). His counsel requested a trial by jury, which was subsequently denied. His case was heard by the presiding family court judge, Judge Theodore S. Gutowicz of the Court of Common Pleas of Philadelphia County, Pennsylvania. He was found delinquent and placed on probation. In his appeal, his counsel argued that all persons had the right to an impartial jury trial. However, the Supreme Court ruled that juveniles do not have a right to a trial by jury. Rather, they ruled that the adversarial component of a trial by jury was not appropriate for juvenile proceedings. As del Carmen, Parker, and Reddington (1998) point out, the Court gave a number of reasons for not extending the jury trial to juvenile proceedings. These reasons may be divided into four areas:

1. Compelling a jury trial might remake the proceeding into a fully adversary process and effectively end the idealistic prospect of an intimate, informal, protective proceeding;

2. Imposing a jury trial on the juvenile court system would not remedy the system's defects and would not greatly strengthen the fact-finding function;

3. Jury trial would entail delay, formality, and clamor of the adversary system and possibly a public trial; and

4. Equating the adjudicative phase of the juvenile proceeding with a criminal trial ignores the aspects of fairness, concern, sympathy, and paternal attention inherent in the juvenile court system (p. 181).

Thus far, the Supreme Court of the United States has not extended the right to a trial by jury during the adjudicatory phase or any other phase of juvenile proceedings. Although this right is not constitutionally guaranteed, some states have given juveniles the right to sit in front of their peers at different stages of the proceedings. These proceedings are typically referred to as **teen courts** or peer and youth courts (Godwin, 1996). These courts are alternatives to the traditional juvenile court system, and they are normally used during the dispositional phase. However, some courts allow for the determination of guilt or innocence. Typically these courts are designed for younger juveniles (ages ten to fifteen), those with no prior arrest records, and those charged with less serious law violation (e.g., shoplifting, vandalism, and disorderly conduct) (Urban Institute, 2000, p. 1). The juveniles who participate in the teen court process do so on a voluntary basis. The youth participating in the process take on the roles of prosecutor, defense attorney, jurors, court clerks, and bailiffs. Typically, the juvenile will appear in front of the juvenile court judge for the adjudication portion of the hearing. However, adults are typically responsible for overseeing the administration of the program, such as ensuring the disposition that is given is followed through, as well as overseeing budgeting and personnel issues.

The Urban Institute has identified four potential benefits for teen courts:

1. **Accountability:** Teen courts may help to ensure that young offenders are held accountable for their illegal behavior, even when their offenses are relatively minor and would not likely result in sanctions from the traditional juvenile justice system.

2. **Timeliness:** An effective teen court can move young offenders from arrest to sanctions within a matter of days rather than the months that may pass with traditional juvenile courts.

3. **Cost Savings:** Teen courts usually depend heavily on youth and adult volunteers. Therefore, they can process a large number of offenders at a substantial cost savings to the community.

4. **Community Cohesion:** A well-structured teen court program may affect the entire community by increasing public appreciation of the legal system, enhancing community–court relationships, encouraging greater respect for the law among youth, and promoting volunteerism among both adults and youth (Urban Institute, 2000, p. 2).

Overall, teen courts serve as a viable alternative to the traditional courts. Although the research on the effectiveness of these courts is limited, they are being implemented increasingly across the United States.

OTHER RELEVANT SUPREME COURT CASES

In addition to the four major Supreme Court rulings in the 1960s and 1970s, there have been other more recent developments in how we handle youth pertaining to the protection against double jeopardy, the right to representation by probation officers, the need for preventative detention, and the imposition of the death penalty. The following is a summary of these issues and relevant cases.

Double Jeopardy

Prior to the mid-1970s, juvenile court judges had the authority to try a youth in juvenile court and then upon further consideration waive that youth to the adult court to be tried for the same case. This practice continued on until 1975 when the case of ***Breed v. Jones*** (1975) appeared in front of the Supreme Court. In the case of *Breed v. Jones,* the Supreme Court established that the double jeopardy clause of the Fifth Amendment does extend to juvenile offenders. In this case, a seventeen-year-old, Jones, was accused of committing a robbery with a deadly weapon. At the adjudication hearing his allegations were substantiated, and he was ordered to stay in detention. He was adjudicated in the juvenile court and proceeded to the dispositional phase. During the dispositional phase, the court ruled that he was not suited for treatment in the juvenile court and therefore should be waived to and prosecuted in the adult court. At the subsequent trial in the adult court, he was found guilty for robbery and ordered to be committed to the California Youth Authority. The Supreme Court ruled that once a youth is found to be under the jurisdiction of the juvenile court he or she cannot be tried in adult court for the same offense. To do so violates the double jeopardy clause of the Fifth Amendment (del Carmen, Parker & Reddington, 1998, p. 139; *Breed v. Jones,* 1975, 421 U.S. 517).

Representation by a Youth's Probation Officer

In the case of ***Fare v. Michael C.*** (1979), the Supreme Court took issue with whether a juvenile's request to see his or her probation officer held the same weight as a request to see his or her attorney, as provided by Miranda v. Arizona. In this case Michael C., a sixteen year old, was accused of murder. He was taken to the police station and advised of his rights. At the time he was on probation, and he asked to see his probation officer. His request was denied. He proceeded to relinquish his right to remain silent, and he talked to the police without an attorney. The Supreme Court ruled that Michael C. because of his age, past contact with the police and the juvenile court, and his intelligence, was able to weigh the totality of his circumstances and understood the ramifications of speaking without representation, therefore his testimony was admissible in court. This ruling in effect suggested that a juvenile's request to see his or her probation officer did not have the same impact as his or her request to see an attorney.

Preventive Detention

Schall v. Martin (1984) answered the question of whether it was appropriate to preventatively detain a youth prior to an adjudicatory hearing. In this case, Gregory Martin, a fourteen year old was detained and charged by police with first-degree robbery, second-degree assault, and criminal possession of a weapon for hitting another youth over the head with a loaded gun and stealing his jacket and sneakers. Because of his age, Martin fell under the jurisdiction of the New York Family Court. Martin was placed in preventative detention pending his fact-finding hearing because he lied to the police about where he lived. In this case, the Supreme Court ruled it is permissible to preventatively detain a youth to protect both the juvenile and society from criminal acts the youth might commit while released in society. The judge is, therefore, required to keep the best interests of the child in mind while protecting society by preventing crime.

Death Penalty

Prior to 1900, at least ten children were executed for their crime committed before the age of fourteen (Shepherd, 1999, p. 13; Streib, 1987). With the creation of the juvenile court, juvenile sanctions were less severe than adults. It was common practice that juveniles were not to be sentenced to death for their action. This practice continued on until 1989 with the simultaneous rulings in two Supreme Court cases: **Stanford v. Kentucky** and **Wilkins v. Missouri** (1989)

The U.S. Supreme Court considered the applicability of the death penalty for juveniles ages sixteen and seventeen in the cases of *Stanford v. Kentucky* and *Wilkins v. Missouri* (1989). In the case of *Stanford v. Kentucky,* Stanford was a seventeen-year-old male who repeatedly raped, sodomized, and shot a woman during the course of robbery of a convenience store. Stanford was convicted of murder, first-degree sodomy, first-degree robbery, and receiving stolen property. He was sentenced to death and forty-five years in prison (Payne, 1998).

In another similar case, Heath Wilkins committed murder while he was approximately sixteen years old. Wilkins stabbed a convenience store clerk, stealing liquor, cigarettes, rolling papers, and approximately $450 in cash and checks. Wilkins pled guilty to first-degree murder, armed criminal action, and carrying a concealed weapon (Payne, 1998). In both these cases, the defendants were sentenced to death. Appealing based on the grounds of Eighth Amendment violations of cruel and unusual punishment, the U.S. Supreme Court ruled that the death penalty was not unconstitutional. Furthermore, the death penalty could be imposed on youth who committed their crimes between the ages of sixteen and eighteen.

ACTORS IN THE JUVENILE COURT SYSTEM

The actors in the juvenile court system are the same as those found in the adult system. However, the level of participation will differ by court structure as well as courtroom workgroup dynamics. Primarily though, the judge, the prosecutor, the defense attorney, and probation officer are responsible for collecting information on the social history or background of the juvenile appearing before the court, proving guilt or innocence, and making recommendations on the appropriate disposition. The following is a brief discussion of the roles of each of these actors as it relates to the juvenile justice system.

Juvenile Court Judges

Arguably, the juvenile court judge is the most powerful actor in the juvenile court process. Operating under the concept of *parens patriae,* the judge is responsible for working towards the best interests of the juvenile. Typically juvenile court is held in the court of limited jurisdiction, oftentimes referred to as district court, or in the family courts, which are typically some combination of district and circuit courts.

Judges come to the bench in a variety of manners. In some states/jurisdictions, judges are elected to serve as juvenile court judges. Therefore, they campaign for the par-

Figure 6.1   Juvenile court judges and magistrates must take the needs of the child and the community into consideration.
Michael Newman/Photo Edit

ticular judgeship according to the laws of their state. Other judges may be appointed to the bench on a rotating basis ranging anywhere from the typical one to three years or there is a move towards having judges serve indefinitely (Knepper & Barton, 1996; Cox & Conrad, 1996; Elrod, & Ryder, 1999). In many counties where the rotation method is used, newly elected/appointed judges are assigned to the juvenile court during their first year on the bench and then rotated out after another new judge is elected. Oftentimes, in rural communities the concept of one judge–one court prevails. In these cases, judges are responsible for hearing all matters pertaining to both juvenile and adults violations of law. Therefore, these judges do not specialize in juvenile matters (Knepper & Barton, 1996).

Juvenile court judges may be best viewed in the context of a continuum of care with those judges maintaining the majority of the focus on *parens patriae* (playing the role of the parent figure), and those judges who are most interested in maintaining a law-giver approach to handling youth. For those judges playing the role of the parent figure, they are most concerned with talking to the juveniles and establishing the best method for dealing with their case. Those judges identified as **law-giver judges** are most concerned with following procedural guidelines and procedural fairness (Yablonsky, 2000).

Yablonsky (2000, pp. 38–39) identified six primary duties and responsibilities of the juvenile court judge:

1. To conduct a judicial proceeding in a fair and equitable manner. If the proceeding is perceived to be arbitrary and unfair by the children who appear in court, the judge may be contributing to disrespect for law and, in a very real sense, to the future delinquencies of children.

2. To decide, after a fair hearing, whether or not the child committed the offense alleged in the petition. The judge also has traditionally had the power to make a finding of delinquency if it is determined that the child committed some infraction other than the one alleged.

3. To protect society. The judge must determine whether allowing the child to remain in the community would be dangerous to society or to the child.

4. To determine whether the child will remain with his or her family or be taken from the family and (a) placed in a foster home, (b) sent to a psychological treatment center, or (c) sent to a custodial institution.

5. To decide what measures will be taken to rehabilitate the child.

6. If the judge decides to place the child in an institution, he or she must determine the one most appropriate to the needs of the child and the protection of society.

Prosecutor

The prosecuting attorney serves as the gatekeeper for the juvenile justice system. Their primary role is to ensure that justice is served while maintaining the safety and well-being of the community. As in the adult system, they review cases that are referred to them either by police, schools, or the community to determine whether to forward the case on to court, dismiss the case, what charges and dispositions are appropriate, and whether a waiver should be used. In essence, the prosecutor plays the most powerful role in the courtroom workgroup. The prosecutor, in conjunction with the probation officer and judge, can determine whether the case should be tried formally or informally. The prosecutor has an inordinate amount of discretion to determine whether to proceed with the case or dismiss it outright (Cox & Conrad, 1991). Since the passage of *In re Gault* (1967), the role of the prosecutor has changed significantly. Where once the system was established as a nonadversarial environment, now the role of the prosecutor resembles that of the adversarial role played in the adult system.

According to Cox and Conrad (1991, p. 158), prosecutors have the following duties in juvenile proceedings:

- investigate possible violations of the law.
- cooperate with the police, in-take officers, and probation officers regarding the facts alleged in the petition.
- authorize, review, and prepare petitions for the court.
- play a role in the initial detention or temporary placement process.
- represent the state in all pretrial motions, probable cause hearings, and consent decrees.
- represent the state at transfer and waiver hearings.
- may recommend physical or mental examinations.
- seek amendments or dismissals of filed petitions if appropriate.
- represent the state at the adjudication of the case.
- represent the state at the disposition of the case.
- enter into plea-bargaining discussions with the defense attorney.
- represent the state on appeal or in habeas corpus proceedings.
- are involved in hearings dealing with violation of probation (see also Siegel & Senna, 1981, pp. 439–440).

Defense Attorney

The Supreme Court's landmark *In re Gault* (1967) decision extended due process protections to juvenile defendants and established a right to the assistance of counsel. Since the passage of *In re Gault,* the role of the defense attorney has become ever more important. There are two primary categories of defense attorneys: private counsel and public defender. These attorneys may be client-retained; court-appointed; legal aid or public defenders; or part of an attorney consortium (Cox & Conrad, 1996; Elrod & Ryder, 1999). **Client-retained attorneys** are those attorneys who are hired by the juvenile to represent him or her in the court proceedings. **Court-appointed attorneys** are typically placed on a list with the juvenile court judge and appointed on a rotating basis to represent youth. Placement on these lists varies by court jurisdiction. In some jurisdictions, placement is voluntary and in others it is mandatory (Elrod & Ryder, 1999; Knepper & Barton, 1996). **Legal aid or public defenders** oftentimes appear in juvenile court because of their contract with the adult court system. **Attorney consortiums** are composed of a group of attorneys who have joined together to work in the best interests of the children in their community. These private attorneys preestablish their attorney fees. Furthermore, they have a special interest in working in the juvenile court (Elrod & Ryder, 1999). Whether private counsel or a public defender, the role of the defense attorney is the same: to ensure their client receives adequate representation in court. Because the juvenile justice system is still designed as a nonadversarial system, zealousness of the defense attorney is not appreciated (Rubin, 1998). The nonadversarial process is maintained formally through the passage of court cases, and informally through dispositional findings. Research suggests youth represented in court by an attorney typically receive more severe sanctions than those who are unrepresented (Feld, 1988).

Seven years after the passage of *In re Gault,* the courts extended the right to representation to children in child protection cases with the creation of the **guardian *ad litem*** (GAL) requirement with the passage of the Child Abuse Prevention and Treatment ACT (CAPTA) of 1974. This Act requires that states seeking federal funds must appoint guardians *ad litem* to represent children in proceedings related to abuse, neglect, or dependency (Barton & Knepper, under review; Sagatun & Edwards, 1995, p. 52). In spite of this requirement, research suggests that only 4 percent of GAL attorneys provide effective representation of children in these cases (Puritz, Burrell, Schwartz, Soler, & Warboys, 1995, p. 23). As more states move towards the creation of family courts, the role of the guardian *ad litem* is being expanded to include representation for both delinquency and dependency issues.

Overall, the role of the attorney, whether public or private, remains the same: They are responsible for representing juveniles through all stages of the process, to ensure their rights are not violated, and present their client in the most favorable light regardless of their involvement in the alleged case. In theory, the system is to remain nonadversarial. However, in practice the defense attorney must take on some adversarial qualities to ensure the best representation of their client.

Other Hearing Officers

Juvenile court cases may also be heard by quasijudicial officers known as "referees in Michigan, masters in Delaware, commissioners in Missouri, and magistrates in Hamilton County (Cincinnati) Juvenile Court" (Rubin, 1998, p. 213). These **hearing officers** are typically attorneys who are empowered with the authority of the court to hear all types of juvenile cases with the exception of waiver hearings and jury trials. These officers are usually appointed by the presiding juvenile court judge but may also come to the bench through popular election. In some jurisdictions, the quasijudicial officer is responsible for hearing the majority of cases. They are also typically viewed as experts in juvenile court legal matters.

Juvenile Probation Officer

The juvenile probation officer plays a key role at all stages of the juvenile justice system. The juvenile probation officer is responsible for gathering all of the information to be included in the youth's social history file. This information includes, but is not limited to, personal information such as date of birth, names of parents and siblings, residence, school, known peers, and delinquency history. As Elrod and Ryder (1999, p. 249) note, probation officers are responsible for six basic roles in juvenile court:

1. Performing intake screening.
2. Conducting presentence investigations.
3. Supervising and monitoring youths' adherence to their rules of probation.
4. Providing assistance to youths placed on probation.
5. Providing ongoing assessments of clients' needs.
6. Completing a variety of job-related administrative tasks.

Overall, juvenile probation officers are involved with the youth in a variety of capacities. They typically have the most contact and most control over youth that come to the attention of the court. Probation officers are responsible for supervising both formal and informal probation, making recommendations to the court, and overseeing the completion of their community disposition.

COURTROOM WORKGROUPS

As previously suggested, it is unclear whether the roles of actors in the juvenile justice system are clearly defined. Therefore, the role of the informal **courtroom workgroup** is instrumental in the handling of all cases that appear before the court. The workgroup is defined as, "A collective of individuals who interact in the workplace on a continuing basis, share goals, develop norms as to how activities should be carried out, and eventually establish a network of roles that serves to differentiate the group from others" (Cole & Smith, 1996, p. 212). In juvenile court, the courtroom workgroup is typically comprised of the judge, prosecutor, defense attorney, probation officer, and to some extent police officers and social service workers. Although research suggests actors in the juvenile justice system have distinct roles they adhere to in the system, it is unclear whether these roles are clearly defined or are one area impacting the processing of juvenile delinquency or status cases.

David Neubauer identifies five categories of the informal court workgroup: 1) shared decision making; 2) shared norms; 3) socialization; 4) sticks and carrots; and 5) goal modification. **Shared decision making** involves the judges reliance on other members of the workgroup sharing information about this case. This allows for the judge to remain the informal leader of the workgroup but allows the judge to diffuse blame to other members should something go wrong. **Shared norms** represent the informal understanding among the members of the workgroup concerning how they should and should not behave. The most important consideration here is shielding one another from outside influences, such as witnesses, or other elements the group cannot control. Other shared norms include adherence to professional standards, and policies. **Socialization** refers to the process of breaking in new members. Since most judgeship and prosecuting positions are elected, there is a process of socialization that must occur. It is the responsibility of the other members of the workgroup to advise and communicate the informal rules of the workgroup to new members. **Sticks and carrots** refer to the process of rewarding and penalizing adherence to the informal court rules. Those who abide by the rules are given carrots (rewards), while those who do not abide by the rules are given sticks (sanctioned). Conformity is secured by both means. Finally, **goal modification** refers to the process of doing justice. Although it is difficult to measure this concept, goal modification assists in achieving the organizational objectives such as disposing of cases (Knepper & Barton, 1997, p. 294; Neubauer, 1996, pp. 77–75).

Each courtroom has its own unique personality, "character," or "community" that is distinctive from all of the others. However, each courtroom has one "dominant" person that is determined by "personality, professional skills (or reputation), political power, longevity, or some other attribute" (Walker, 2001, pp. 53–54). In the juvenile justice system, the existence and power of the courtroom workgroup is supported and even encouraged by the nonadversarial nature of the system. In practice, there is a high degree of consensus among all of the members of the workgroup. The existence and adherence to the informal norms can work to expedite or frustrate the most valiant of efforts at reform. Therefore, for any manager to effectively work towards managing caseloads and seeking justice, it is imperative that the manager become familiar with the working of the courtroom workgroup and, if possible, join.

JUVENILE COURT PROCESS

As pointed out earlier, the first juvenile court was started in Cook County, Illinois in 1899. The principles of the court are basically the same as they were nearly one hundred years ago: to protect the child from the harshness of the adversary system and to provide treatment and guidance to wayward youth. To be sure, American culture and events have overwhelmed the capacity of the juvenile court to fully accomplish that mission, and many legislatures are moving to make it easier to try juveniles in adult court for more serious crimes. However, this discussion is restricted to the handling of children in juvenile court.

Referral

Before a child can be brought into juvenile court, he or she must be referred. That is, a formal complaint must be made by an adult, and the adult must sign a petition. The **referral** can come from a police officer, teacher, parent, or anyone else who has firsthand knowledge that a crime has been, or may have been, committed by the child in question. If a police officer has made the referral and signed a petition, it is accompanied by an arrest report and other supporting documents.

As noted in Chapter 5, once an offense is committed, the police officer has one of four choices: a) the officer can take the juvenile into custody; b) he or she can issue a citation, refer him or her to juvenile intake and release the juvenile to his or her parents; c) the officer can counsel and release the juvenile to his or her parents; or d) the officer can release the juvenile and refer him or her to community resources (Chesney-Lind & Sheldon, 1998, p. 151; Krisberg & Austin, 1978, p. 83).

Many of the cases appearing before law enforcement officers are handled through **informal adjustment**. The process of informal adjustment allows the law enforcement officer the opportunity to reprimand and release juveniles into the custody of their parent or guardian or on their own accord, or the officer may require program involvement or some task be completed rather than turning the youth over to detention or intake. If the officer issues a citation or takes the juvenile into custody, the juvenile then enters into the intake or booking stage. Here, the juvenile is fingerprinted, photographs are taken, and all personal information is gathered on the individual. Federal regulations discourage holding juveniles in adult jails for an extended period of time. "Federal regulations require that the juvenile be securely detained for no more than six hours and in an area out of sight or sound of adult inmates" (Sickmund, 2003, p. 2). (See Chapter 8 for a broader discussion of the federal requirements.) Also, a written report is taken regarding the arrest or detention. The referral is then sent on to the juvenile court where an intake officer will review it. The intake officer must give the child and parents at least twenty-four-hour notice of an initial hearing and notice of the charges, in writing.

Intake

The **intake** function is usually the responsibility of the juvenile court probation department. During the intake phase of the process, also known as preliminary hearing, the probation officer will interview the juvenile to ascertain background information on the youth such as basic demographic information, names of parents, education level and school, and elements of the specific referral. It is during this interview that the officer will collect the information to forward onto the prosecutor, who will make a decision to dismiss the case, handle the case informally, or to process the case formally. If a decision is made to process the case formally, then the prosecutor will decide whether the case should be heard in the juvenile court or forwarded on to an adult court. It is important for the probation officer to be aware of the elements of the case and the appropriateness of handling the case in juvenile court. Should a case be waived to the adult court system, in most states, the probation officer becomes a witness to the case, and the officer may be called to testify in the criminal trial. Thus it is imperative the probation/intake officer understand both the laws of the state and the process.

About half of all cases are handled informally in the system and then subsequently dismissed. If the youth enters into an informal agreement with the probation officer, the youth is typically subject to similar types of requirements and restrictions as those youth who are placed on formal probation. These written agreements, typically called **consent**

decrees, would generally include conditions such as curfew, attending school, restitution, and counseling (Sickmund, 2003). Most states and juvenile jurisdictions only allow the youths to enter into informal agreements if they admit to the charges. Youth are normally supervised by a probation officer, and they never appear in front of the judge. However, if they violate their informal conditions of probation, they will be terminated and sent on for formal processing in front of the juvenile court judge. At that time, the judge will be notified that the youth was placed on informal probation, and he or she did not successfully complete the terms of his or her conditions. If the youth does successfully complete the conditions of his or her informal probation, the youth is removed from supervision and the youth's records are only maintained in the juvenile probation office, or they may be destroyed altogether.

If at intake the intake officer, in conjunction with the prosecutor, decides to formally process the case, one of two petitions will be filed: a delinquency petition or a petition requesting a waiver hearing. "A delinquency petition states the allegations and requests the juvenile court to adjudicate (or judge) the youth a delinquent, making the juvenile a ward of the court" (Sickmund, 2003, p. 2). If a delinquency petition is filed, the court will set a date for an adjudicatory hearing where the youth with the presence of his or her parent or guardian will stand before the judge to hear the petition stating the charges put forth against him or her (see below for a discussion of the adjudicatory hearing).

Detention Hearing

If a juvenile is not released to his or her parents or guardian shortly after being taken into custody or detained, a **detention hearing** must be held. Juveniles may be detained in a juvenile detention facility awaiting the adjudication phase if the court determines the child is a threat to him or herself or his or her community. If the child is released, pending a formal hearing, he or she must be released to a parent or a guardian, which can be problematic. Oftentimes, it is difficult to locate the parent, and if located some parents refuse to cooperate or appear with the juvenile. All state statutes mandate a specified time period for either release from detention or holding a detention hearing. In most states, this time period does not exceed twenty-four hours. Some states distinguish the time period for holding juveniles by offense type. For example, the state of Indiana requires status offenders to be released within a twenty-four-hour time period. However, delinquent offenders can be detained for up to forty-eight hours before holding a detention hearing, but the prosecutor has several days to file a petition.

In many instances, the detention hearing is the initial contact between the court and the child and parent(s). Reasonable notice of the hearing must be given to all parties. The hearing begins with the judge advising the child and parents of his or her constitutional rights. The child is then made aware of the charges against him or her, and the youth is given a chance to explain or to speak on his or her own behalf. The hearing is informal and is tailored with the child's best interests at heart. After the intake officer, in conjunction with the prosecutor, has determined that an offense has occurred, further decisions must be made. At this point, the hearing becomes a detention hearing. Often a matter is informally adjusted by referral to a community agency such as a child guidance clinic or, in less serious matters, the child and parents may agree to a period of informal probation.

Once formal charges are made, bail may be determined. Although bail is not constitutionally guaranteed (del Carmen, Parker, & Reddington, 1998) and not all states have this as an option, many states do provide the option for juveniles to be released into the custody of their parents with the promise to return or released on bail. If the juvenile is eligible for bail, he or she is released into the care of his or her parents to await trial. However, if the juvenile is not eligible for bail, he or she is sent back to detention to await the formal hearing.

If formal charges are brought against the juvenile, his or her attorney can go through the process of plea-bargaining. The use of plea bargaining in the juvenile justice system is controversial since plea-bargaining assumes that an adversarial process is in existence. However, if a formal delinquency petition is filed against the juvenile, a probable cause hearing will be held. Here, both the prosecutor and the defense will present evidence to establish probable cause. The juvenile will be arraigned with a parent or guardian present. During the arraignment, the juvenile is once again advised of his or her rights. At this time, the juvenile can secure a private attorney or request a public defender normally known as a guardian *ad litem*. Also during the arraignment, juveniles may enter into a plea agreement or have the case deferred pending successful completion of informal probation or community program. In addition, the juvenile is informed of the specific charges being brought against him or her, a formal plea is entered, and a formal hearing or an adjudicatory hearing date is set. If a probable cause hearing is held, evidence is established. If the prosecution has no case, the charges will be dropped, and the juvenile will be released. The judge in the detention hearing could also drop the charges and release the juvenile.

Adjudicatory Hearing

If the child's case is not handled informally, he or she will be given notice of an **adjudication hearing**. Since the passage *In re Gault* in 1967, the juvenile court has undergone a number of changes. The child must be accorded the same rights as adults, particularly the right to counsel, notice of the charges, cross-examination of witnesses, and protection against self-incrimination in cases where the proceedings may result in commitment of the juvenile (del Carmen, Parker, & Reddington, 1998).

Today the adjudicatory hearing is more formal than it was prior to the *Gault* decision. The judge begins the hearing by advising the child of his or her rights and the charges against him or her, and the judge again asks the child how he or she pleads. The prosecutor begins by presenting the case and witnesses are called, cross-examined by the defense attorney, and so on. Closing arguments will be made, and the judge will either order the child held in detention or released to the custody of parent(s) or guardian pending the completion of a predisposition report. The judge will determine whether the juvenile is responsible for the offense. In some states, juveniles now have the right to a jury trial. This right, however, is not a constitutional right. It is only afforded through state statute (Sickmund, 2003).

Disposition Hearing

Following the adjudication hearing, the probation officer is responsible for completing the predispositional plan. This plan includes the social history of the youth, the youth's role in the crime, any addiction or mental health assessment that may have been completed, a recommendation for disposition, and a review of the available resources that may be used to assist the youth. The **disposition hearing** is typically held a few weeks after the adjudicatory hearing because the judge will order the probation department to complete a predisposition report prior to the disposition hearing. Once released, the child will be assigned to a probation officer for a predisposition investigation. The prehearing investigation is the same as the presentence investigation for adults except for a child. The probation officer will gather the facts and make a recommendation to the judge who will determine the sanction to be applied.

With the predisposition hearing report in hand, the judge will ask the child, the child's attorney, and often the parent(s) to stand before him or her to hear the disposition. Many factors come into play in making the disposition: age of the child, seriousness of the offense, prior record, school achievement, and so on. The options before the judge vary depending upon the location. All jurisdictions can place the child on probation or continue the use of probation, send him or her to state reform school, or send the child to a private residential facility. Beyond that, the options begin to narrow depending upon the progressiveness of the jurisdiction, available money, and local attitudes and values.

Here, the juvenile will learn of his or her "punishment." This could be detention, community service, electronic monitoring, probation, or other types of sanctions as the magistrate sees fit. Figure 6.2 illustrates the juvenile court system.

Waiver Hearing

It is informative here to briefly comment on the **waiver hearing** of juveniles to adult court. As mentioned previously, the intake officer has the option of filing a delinquency petition or filing a petition for waiver to the adult court system. This practice is the

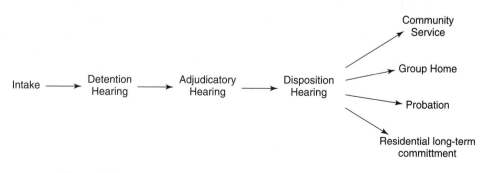

Figure 6.2   The Juvenile Court System

traditional safety valve that permits serious or chronic offenders to be transferred after a hearing in juvenile court. However, since the late 1970s, the "get tough" attitude regarding juvenile offenders has resulted in reforms aimed at ensuring accountability on the part of juveniles and the vilification of the juvenile court. In the last decade, almost every state has modified its laws relating to juvenile court reform, and in nearly every instance the direction of reforms has been in the direction of shifting away from the rehabilitation model to the punishment model (Bishop, Frazier, & Henretta, 1989).

Waivers to the adult court system can be classified into five categories: judicial waiver, direct file, statutory exclusion, reverse waiver, and once an adult/always an adult. (See Chapter 15 for a more in-depth discussion of the waiver process.)

Judicial waiver provisions leave the decision-making process up to the individual courts. There are three different types of judicial waivers that may be used: discretionary, presumptive, and mandatory. The **discretionary waiver** (also known as "certification," "bind-over," "remand," or "transfer") provides a lot of flexibility to the individual courts. It is entirely at the discretion of the judge within specified criteria whether to transfer or not. These criteria, which are outlined by state statute, typically include a minimum age, offense type or level, record of previous delinquency, or a combination of all three. The majority of all states (forty-six) use some form of discretionary judicial waiver. In seventeen of the states, discretionary waivers can be used for any offense category within specified age ranges (Griffin, Torbet, & Szymanski, 1998).

The **presumptive waiver** transfers the burden of proof onto the juvenile to prove why he or she should not be transferred to the adult court system. Currently fifteen states use the presumptive waiver provision. If the juvenile meets the minimum age, offense type or level, and the record of previous delinquency criteria the onus is on the juvenile to make an adequate argument as to why he or she should not be transferred. If the juvenile fails to make this argument, then the juvenile court must send the case on to the criminal court (Griffin, Torbet, & Szymanski, 1998).

The **mandatory waiver** statute requires that cases meeting certain age, offense type or level, and/or previous delinquent records be waived automatically to the adult court system. Unlike the statutory exclusion waiver that automatically bypasses the juvenile court system entirely, when the mandatory waiver provisions are used, the youth must first appear in the juvenile court where he or she has some form of a preliminary hearing to determine probable cause and the appropriateness of the transfer to the adult court. Fourteen states currently use the mandatory waiver provision (Griffin, Torbet, & Szymanski, 1998).

The **direct file** method of waiver transfers the discretion of the court from the judge to the prosecutor. In these cases, it is up to the prosecutor to decide whether there is enough evidence and whether the case meets the specified criteria to transfer the case to the adult court system. This method of transfer gives both the juvenile and adult court systems concurrent jurisdiction over the juvenile matter. Currently, fifteen states allow for the use of the direct file method (Griffin, Torbet, & Szymanski, 1998).

As previously mentioned, states maintaining **statutory exclusion provisions** use specific offense-based criteria to exclude someone from being considered a child. Therefore, if juveniles fall within a specified age range and meet the identified age criteria, they will bypass the juvenile system altogether and have their case heard directly in the adult court system. Twenty-eight states have this provision written into their state statute (Griffin, Torbet, & Szymanski, 1998).

Unlike the other waiver provisions, the **reverse waiver** allows for juveniles who have been transferred to the adult court system to petition the court to have their case transferred back to the juvenile system regardless of the provision that may have placed it in the adult court initially. There are various mechanisms in place to allow juveniles in states that have both direct file and reverse waivers to have their cases reheard or reconsidered by the juvenile courts. A total of twenty-three states have reverse waiver statutes. "Twenty of the thirty-five states with direct file or statutory exclusion also have reverse waiver provisions" (Griffin, Torbet, & Szymanski, 1998, p. 10).

The final waiver provision is the **once an adult/always an adult waiver**. In its truest sense, this waiver requires that once a juvenile has been waived and tried in the adult court system, all subsequent offenses will be heard by the adult court. Although some states have provisions allowing for subsequent cases to be tried in the juvenile court system, typically in these instances, criteria outline which cases should remain in the adult court system and which cases can be transferred back to the juvenile court system. A total of thirty-one states maintain the once an adult/always an adult provision.

The concern over juvenile crime by the American public has led to an increase in both the existence and frequency with which these provisions are used. As you will see in Chapter 15, in spite of their popularity, they oftentimes fail to achieve both a reduction in recidivism and the harshness that is implicitly implied by the mere existence and use of a waiver provision.

Thus far, we have discussed juvenile court as an organization designed to deliver services for the treatment and care of juvenile offenders. How those resources are allocated and delivered greatly depends upon how the court is organized. The next few pages briefly summarize the principle of organization necessary to efficiently process youth through the system.

PRINCIPLES OF COURT ORGANIZATION

The juvenile court or institution, just like any organization, contains social units constructed to achieve some purpose. Chapters 9 to 14 will discuss in more detail that open organizations are influenced by their environment. However, it is important to briefly explain management concepts at this point in order for the student to grasp the importance of order and organization as the intent of the courts and public are carried out. Generally speaking, organizations are characterized by five elements:

1. **Purpose.** Organizations exist to achieve some purpose, be it to run a supermarket, keep youth locked up in an institution, or serve the community by dealing with delinquent youth in a court setting. Sometimes the purposes of the organization are not entirely clear and that creates problems, such as role ambiguity.

2. **Participants.** People make up the organization. As such, organizations are subject to the whims, values, and foibles that make up the human condition.

3. **Resources.** Organizations must acquire and allocate resources to meet established goals. Resources include people, time, money, raw materials, knowledge, and skills.

4. **Structure.** In order to accomplish goals, organizations require a structure to divide and coordinate activities. Effective organizations can be highly structured, bureaucratic, and hierarchical such as the military. They can also be relatively unstructured, flat in organizational appearance, such as a think tank or university academic department, or informal such as a community activist organization.

5. **Leadership.** In order to be effective, organizations rely upon certain members to provide the leadership necessary to identify goals, achieve those goals, and direct the efforts of other organizational members. Leaders also oversee planning, influence members in one way or another, and act as the visible sovereign in order to interface with those outside of the organization (Certo, 1986).

Henri Fayol made a significant contribution to organizational theory with his "general principles of management." Several of those "general principles" are most important to organizational structure in the juvenile court. These principles include: division of work, unity of command, centralization, and scalar chain. Each of these principles will be discussed below.

Division of Work

According to Fayol, the object of division of work is to produce more and better work with the same effort. In a juvenile court, there must be division of work if youth are to be effectively supervised and paperwork attended. For example, in a large court, there may be a specialized unit for writing prehearing reports or for supervising those with a history of substance abuse or sexual crime. They are specialized in nature and require a degree of special training in order to best serve the youth. Still, if necessary, personnel assigned to those units can work effectively in other less specialized units.

Unity of Command

Fayol made a special point in that employees should receive orders from one superior only. If this rule is violated, discipline and authority are undermined, and order and stability are threatened.

Centralization

Fayol believed that centralization is a part of the natural order. In small organizations, centralization is greater, but in larger organizations the scalar chain is interposed between the court administrator and those lower down in the organizational hierarchy.

Scalar Chain

The scalar chain is the chain of command ranging from the highest authority to the lowest rank. The line of authority is the route followed by all formal commands and communications. Suppose, for example, that the chief probation officer receives a call about a particular offense and youth who is involved. The chief probation officer will call the appropriate supervisor, who in turn will contact the appropriate probation officer. There are exceptions, of course. In a small rural department, the chief probation officer will contact the probation officer himself or herself. Nevertheless, the scalar chain allows for clear channels of communication without outside interference.

SUMMARY

To summarize, there have been a variety of issues that have plagued the development of the juvenile court since its inception in 1899. Although in theory the Progressives envisioned a nonadversarial, informal system where the judge could be trusted to act in the best interest of the child, the reality is the system has not fully supported this concept. The U.S. Supreme Court began taking issue with the constitutional protections of youth during the mid-1960s and have continued to modify the system on into the 1990s and 2000s. This chapter reviewed the relevant Supreme Court cases that modified the juvenile court system. Although it is not exhaustive in its review, it does serve as a foundation for overviewing the rights of juveniles.

Furthermore, the chapter reviewed the roles of judges, prosecutors, defense attorneys, and probation officers. Because of the informal nature of the juvenile court, it is imperative that these primary actors work as part of an informal collective known as the courtroom workgroup. As suggested, the roles and responsibilities of each of these actors in the system will differ by the community in which they live. They will also differ by the individual power and status that is maintained within that community. Other external factors such as employee turnover and elections may contribute to the stability of the workgroup.

Today's juvenile court system is burdened with two conflicting obligations. The juvenile court system is expected to carry out its original purpose as a welfare agency for the rehabilitation of wayward youths, and also it is expected to protect society from the foul deeds of the juvenile delinquent (Simonsen, 1991). While neither purpose will ever be carried out to society's expectations, all involved with the system are striving to protect the ones who enter into the system. Clearly, if rehabilitation and community protection is to be achieved, there must be some way to endure accountability and effective communication within the court if it is to effectively carry out its mission.

CASE STUDY WRAP-UP

Ms. Kesler is dedicated to her job and is genuinely interested in serving the youth of her community. As both the chief probation officer and as a working probation officer with a caseload, she knows the issues youth face in the community and in their families. She must be aware of community resources, various case management approaches, subscribe to a therapeutic approach, be familiar with several others, and be able to converse with juvenile workers in mental health, education, and academe. She has a tough job.

STUDY QUESTIONS

1. Where was the first juvenile court located?

2. Is *parens patriae* still alive and well?

3. What are the main points of *In re Gault?*

4. Who are the actors in the juvenile court, and what are their jobs?

5. Waivers are being used increasingly. What do you think of them? Does a waiver to adult court guarantee harsher punishment?

6. Do you think a child can be diverted at the time of his or her detention hearing? (Think ahead.)

7. Why is it important to organize a juvenile court effectively, and how would you organize a court?

BIBLIOGRAPHY

BARTON, SHANNON (2000). *Love Me, Hate Me, Beat Me: The Impact of Child Maltreatment on Delinquency.* Unpublished Dissertation. Ann Arbor, MI: UMI Dissertation Services.

BARTON, SHANNON, AND KNEPPER, PAUL (under review). "The Role of the Guardian *Ad Litem* in Juvenile Delinquency Court: Implications for Training." Paper under review.

BERNARD, THOMAS J. (1992). *The Cycle of Juvenile Justice.* New York: Oxford University Press.

BESHAROV, DOUGLAS J. (1974). *Juvenile Justice Advocacy.* New York: Practicing Law Institute.

BISHOP, DONNA M., FRAZIER, CHARLES E., AND HENRETTA, JOHN C. (1989). *Crime & Delinquency,* 35(2), 179–201.

CERTO, SAMUEL C. (1986). *Principles of Modern Management: Functions and Systems,* 3rd ed. Dubuque, IA: Wm. C. Brown Publishers.

Breed v. Jones, 421 U.S. 519, 95 S.Ct. 1779, 44 L.Ed.2d. 346 (1975).

CLEMENT, MARY (1997). *The Juvenile Justice System: Law and Process.* Boston: Butterworth-Heinemann.

COLE, GEORGE F., AND SMITH, CHRISTOPHER E. (1996). *Criminal Justice in America.* Belmont, CA: Wadsworth Publishing Company.

Cox, Stephen M., and Conrad, John J. (1991). *Juvenile Justice: A Guide to Practice and Theory,* 3rd ed. Dubuque, IA: Wm Brown Publishers.

Cox, Stephen M., and Conrad, John J. (1996). *Juvenile Justice: A Guide to Practice and Theory,* 4th ed. Dubuque, IA: Brown and Benchmark.

del Carmen, Rolando V., Parker, Mary, and Reddington, Frances P. (1998). *Briefs of Leading Cases in Juvenile Justice.* Cincinnati, OH: Anderson Publishing, Co.

Elrod, Preston, and Ryder, R. Scott (1999). *Juvenile Justice: A Social, Historical, and Legal Perspective.* Gaithersburg, MD: Aspen Publication.

Fare v. Michael C., 442 US 707, 99 S.Ct. 2560, 61 L.Ed.2d 197 (1979).

Fayol, Henri (1984). "General Principles of Management," in D. S. Pugh, Ed., *Organization Theory,* 2nd ed. New York: Penguin Books.

Feld, Barry C. (2000). *Cases and Materials on Juvenile Justice Administration.* St. Paul, MN: West Group.

Feld, Barry C. (1988) "In re Gault revisited: A cross-state comparison of the right to counsel in juvenile court." *Crime & Delinquency, 34,* 393–424, cited in H. Ted Rubin (1998). *The Juvenile Court Landscape* (p. 214). In Albert R. Roberts (Ed.), *Juvenile Justice: Policies Programs and Services,* 2nd ed. (pp. 205–230). Chicago: Nelson-Hall.

Feld, Barry C. (1993). "Juvenile (In)Justice and the Criminal Court Alternative." *Crime & Delinquency, 39* (4), 403–424.

Godwin, Tracy M. (1996, August). *A Guide for Implementing Teen Court Programs.* Washington, DC: Office of Juvenile Justice and Delinquency Prevention.

Griffin, Patrick, Torbet, Patricia, and Szymanski, Linda (1998). *Trying Juveniles as Adults in Criminal Courts: An Analysis of State Transfer Provisions.* Washington, DC: Office of Juvenile Justice and Delinquency Prevention.

Guarino-Ghezzi, Susan, and Loughran, Edward J. (1996). *Balancing Juvenile Justice.* New Brunswick: Transaction Publishers.

Illinois Juvenile Court Act, 1899 Ill. Laws 132.

In re Gault, 387 U.S. 1, 87 S.Ct. 1428, 18 L.Ed.2d 527 (1967).

In re Winship, 397 U.S. 358, 90 S.Ct. 1068, 25 L.Ed.2d 368 (1970).

Kent v. U.S., 383 U.S. 541, 11 Ohio Misc. 53, 86 S.Ct. 1045, 16 L.Ed.2d 84 (1966).

Knepper, Paul, and Barton, Shannon M. (1996). *Kentucky Court Improvement Project: First Year Assessment and Recommendations.* Frankfort, KY: Kentucky Administrative Office of the Courts.

Knepper, Paul, and Barton, Shannon M. (1997). "The Effect of Courtroom Dynamics on Child Maltreatment Proceedings." *Social Service Review, 71* (June), 288–308.

McKeiver v. Pennsylvania, 403 U.S. 528, 91 S.Ct. 1976, 29 L.Ed.2d 647 (1971).

Neubauer, David (1996). *America's Courts and the Criminal Justice System.* Pacific Grove, CA: Brooks/Cole.

PAYNE, PATRICIA (1998). "Juvenile Law and Landmark U.S. Supreme Court Cases." In Roberts, Albert R. *Juvenile Justice: Policies, Programs, and Services,* 2nd ed., pp. 194–204.

PURITZ, PATRICIA, BURRELL, SUE, SCHWARTZ, ROBERT, SOLER, MARK, AND WARBOYS, LOREN (1995). *A Call for Justice: An Assessment to Counsel and Quality of Representation in Delinquency Proceedings.* Washington, DC: American Bar Association.

RUBIN, H. TED (1998). "The Juvenile Court Landscape." In Albert R. Roberts (Ed.) *Juvenile Justice: Policies Programs and Services,* 2nd ed. (pp. 205–230). Chicago: Nelson-Hall.

SAGATUN, INGER J., AND EDWARDS, LEONARD P. (1995). *Child Abuse and the Legal System.* Chicago: Nelson Hall.

Schall v. Martin, 467 U.S. 253, 104 S.Ct. 2403, 81 L.Ed.2d 207 (1984).

SHEPHERD, ROBERT E. (1999). "The Juvenile Court at 100 Years: A Look Back." *Juvenile Justice Journal, VI* (2), 13–21.

SICKMUND, MELISSA (2003, June). "Juveniles in Court." *Juvenile Offenders and Victims National Report Series.* Washington, DC: Office of Juvenile Justice and Delinquency Prevention.

SIEGAL, LARRY J., AND SENNA, JOSEPH J. (1981). *Juvenile Justice: Theory, Practice, and Law,* 2nd ed. St. Paul, MN: West Publishing Company.

SIEGEL, LARRY J., AND SENNA, JOSEPH J. (2000). *Juvenile Delinquency: Theory, Practice, and Law,* 7th ed. Belmont, CA: Wadsworth.

SIMONSEN, CLIFFORD E. (1991). *Juvenile Justice in Action,* 2nd ed. New York: Macmillan.

Stanford v. Kentucky and Wilkins v. Missouri, 492 U.S. 361, 109 S.Ct. 2969, 106 L.Ed.2d 306 (1989).

STREIB, V. (1987). *Death Penalty for Juveniles.* Bloomington, IN: Indiana University Press.

URBAN INSTITUTE (2000). *Teen Courts: A Focus on Research.* [online] http://www.ncjrs.org/html/ojjdp/jjbul2000_10_2/page2.html.

WALKER, SAMUEL (2001). *Sense and Nonsense About Crime and Drugs: A Policy Guide.* Belmont, CA: Wadsworth Publishing.

WATKINS, JOHN C. (1998). *The Juvenile Justice Century: A Sociological Commentary on American Juvenile Courts.* Durham, NC: Carolina Academic Press.

YABLONSKY, LEWIS (2000). *Juvenile Delinquency into the 21st Century.* Belmont, CA: Wadsworth Publishing.

ZIMRING, FRANKLIN E. (2000). "The Common Thread: Diversion in Juvenile Justice." *California Law Review,* 88 (6) 2477–2495.

GLOSSARY OF KEY TERMS

Adjudication hearing.   This hearing is more formal than it was prior to the *Gault* decision. The judge begins the hearing by advising the child of his or her rights and the charges against him or her and the judge again asks the child how he or she pleads. This phase of the process is analogous to the trial phase in the adult court system.

Attorney consortiums.   These consortiums are composed of a group of attorneys who have joined together to work in the best interests of the children in their community. These private attorneys preestablish their attorney fee.

Breed v. Jones.   A 1975 U.S. Supreme Court case that established the double jeopardy clause of the Fifth Amendment does extend to juvenile offenders.

Client-retained attorneys.   Attorneys who are hired by the juvenile to represent them in the court proceedings.

Consent decree.   A written agreement between the youth and the intake officer. These agreements would generally include conditions such as curfew, attending school, restitution, and counseling.

Court-appointed attorneys.   Attorneys are typically placed on a list with the juvenile court judge and appointed on a rotating basis to represent youth. Placement on these lists vary by court jurisdiction. In some jurisdictions, placement is voluntary and in others it is mandatory.

Courtroom workgroup.   A collective of individuals who interact in the workplace on a continuing basis, share goals, develop norms as to how activities should be carried out, and eventually establish a network of roles that serves to differentiate the group from others.

Detention hearing.   This is the initial hearing between the court and the child and their parent(s). During this hearing the child is advised of his or her constitutional rights. The child is made aware of the charges against him or her, and the child is given a chance to explain or to speak on his or her own behalf.

Direct file.   This method of waiving a youth to the adult court system transfers the discretion of the court from the judge to the prosecutor. This method of transfer gives both the juvenile and adult court systems concurrent jurisdiction over the juvenile matter.

Discretionary waiver.   Also known as "certification," "bind-over," "remand," or "transfer," this provision provides a lot of flexibility to the individual courts.

Disposition hearing.   This hearing is analogous to the sentencing hearing in the adult system. This hearing occurs a few weeks after the adjudicatory hearing. Many factors come into play in making the disposition: age of the child, seriousness of the offense, prior record, school achievement, and so on.

Fare v. Michael.   The U.S. Supreme Court in 1979 ruled that Michael C. because of his age, past contact with the police and the juvenile court, and his intelligence, was able to weigh the totality of his circumstances and understood the ramifications of speaking without representation, therefore his testimony was admissible in court.

Goal modification.   Part of the informal courtroom workgroup refers to the process of doing justice. Although it is difficult to measure this concept, goal modification assists in achieving the organizational objectives such as disposing of cases.

Guardian *ad litem.*   The Child Abuse Prevention and Treatment Act of 1974 requires that states seeking federal funds must appoint guardians *ad litem* to represent children in proceedings related to abuse, neglect, or dependency. Attorneys in this role seek to represent the best interests of the child during all phases of the juvenile court process.

Hearing officers.   Also known as referees, masters, commissioners, or magistrates, these officers are typically attorneys who are empowered with the authority of the court to hear all types of juvenile cases with the exception of waiver hearings and jury trials.

Informal adjustment.   The process of informal adjustment allows the law enforcement officer the opportunity to reprimand and release the juvenile into the custody of their parent or guardian or on their own accord or the officer may require program involvement or some task be completed rather than turning the youth over to detention or intake.

In re Gault.   The U.S. Supreme Court in 1967 ruled in favor of Gault and stated that juveniles, like adults, have due process protections such as the right to counsel, notice of the charges, cross-examination of witnesses, and protection against self-incrimination.

In re Winship.   The U.S. Supreme Court in 1970 ruled that juveniles should be afforded the protection of proof beyond a reasonable doubt when faced with the possibility of commitment to a state institution.

Intake.   During the intake phase, probation officers will interview the juvenile regarding their demographic information including names of parents and education as well as background information on the specific referral. Once the information is collected the probation/intake officers will discuss the case with the prosecutor to determine whether the case should be handled informally, formally, or referred to the adult court system.

Judicial waiver.   These waiver provisions leave the decision-making process up to the individual courts. There are three different types of judicial waivers that may be used: discretionary, presumptive, and mandatory.

Kent v. United States.   In 1966 the U.S. Supreme Court ruled before a youth a could be waived to the adult court, they are entitled to due process protections such as access by counsel to the social records and probation or similar reports, which presumably are considered by the court, and to a statement of reasons for the juvenile court's decision.

Law-giver judges.   These judges functioning under the concept of *parens patriae,* play the role of the parent figure in the courtroom. They are most concerned with talking to the juveniles and establishing the best method for dealing with their cases. These judges are most concerned with following procedural guidelines and procedural fairness.

Legal aid or public defenders.   Attorneys representing the best interests of children oftentimes appear in juvenile court because of their contract with the adult court system.

Mandatory waiver.   This form of judicial waiver provision requires that cases meeting certain age, offense type or level, and/or previous delinquent record be waived automatically to the adult court system.

McKeiver v. Pennsylvania.   The U.S. Supreme Court in 1971 rules that juveniles do not have a right to a trial by jury. Rather, they ruled that the adversarial component of a trial by jury was not appropriate for juvenile proceedings.

Once an adult/always an adult waiver.   This waiver provision requires that once a juvenile has been waived and tried in the adult court system, all subsequent offenses will be heard by the adult court. Although some states have provisions allowing for subsequent cases to be tried in the juvenile court system.

Parens patriae.   Literally translate as the "Parent of the Country." This refers to the doctrine of the state overseeing the welfare of the child.

Presumptive waiver.   This form of judicial waiver provision transfers the burden of proof onto the juvenile to prove why they should not be transferred to the adult court system.

Referral.   A formal complaint must be made by an adult and the adult must sign a petition. The referral can come from a police officer, teacher, parent, or anyone else who has firsthand knowledge that a crime has been, or may have been committed by the child in question.

Reverse waiver.   This waiver provision allows for a juvenile who has been transferred to the adult court system to petition the court to have their case transferred back to the juvenile system regardless of the provision that may have placed it in the adult court initially.

Schall v. Martin.   In 1984, the U.S. Supreme Court ruled it is permissible to preventatively detain a youth to protect both the juvenile and society from criminal acts the youth might commit while released in society. The judge is, therefore, required to keep the best interests of the child in mind while protecting society by preventing crime.

Shared decision making.   Part of informal courtroom workgroup. This category involves the judges reliance on other members of the workgroup sharing information about this case.

Shared norms.   Part of the informal courtroom workgroup. This category represents the informal understanding among the members of the workgroup concerning how they should and should not behave.

Socialization.   Part of the informal courtroom workgroup that refers to the process of breaking in new members.

Stanford v. Kentucky and Wilkins v. Missouri.   In 1989, the U.S. Supreme Court ruled that the death penalty was not unconstitutional. Furthermore, the death penalty could be imposed on youth who committed their crimes between the ages of sixteen and eighteen.

Statutory exclusion.   This method of waiving a youth to the adult court system uses specific offense based criteria to exclude someone from being considered a child. The juveniles case bypasses the juvenile system altogether and goes directly to the adult court.

Sticks and carrots.   Part of the informal courtroom workgroup that refers to the process of rewarding and penalizing adherence to the informal court rules by the courtroom workgroup members.

Teen courts.   These are alternative courts used in the juvenile justice court system. These courts are alternatives to the traditional juvenile court system they are normally used during the dispositional phase. However, some courts allow for the determination of guilt or innocence. Typically these courts are designed for younger juveniles (ages ten to fifteen), those with no prior arrest records, and those charged with less serous law violation (e.g., shoplifting, vandalism, and disorderly conduct).

Waiver hearing. Cases meeting certain age, offense type or level, and/or previous delinquent record may be waived to the adult court system. In instances in which youth are not automatically transferred to the adult court system, they are entitled to a hearing in front of the juvenile court where they are provided their due process protections including notice of charges and reasons for transfer to the adult court system.

CHAPTER 7
DIVERSION

KEY TERMS

Diversion

Net widening

Diversion without referral

Internal referral

External referral

Informal adjustment

Mediation

Youth service bureau

Community youth board

Wilderness program

CASE STUDY

Persistence and Love Creates a Place of Peace*

In a ravine between the turfs of two Hunters Point gangs, scores of city workers and volunteers converged Friday to spruce up two dilapidated buildings where thousands of children have found a haven in the past three decades. With roots going back to 1966 when the area blew up after a police officer shot and killed a fleeing sixteen-year-old black youth suspected of stealing a car, Julia Middleton saw a need to create a place to provide a sense of safety and programs to help neighborhood youth.

On this bright day in June 2003, they came from every corner of the Hunters Point Community Youth Park—where gunfire is often heard—to lay down paint, hack away at weeds, tinker with plumbing and electricity, and sweep the concrete-covered playground.

Moving in the midst of this hubbub was Marian Jones, the new director of the program where children find a playground, snacks, sports, dance, choir, computer classes, and tutoring—and leave behind a realm in which guns, drugs, and violent death are too often commonplace.

*Source: Adapted from Susan Sward (June 14, 2003). "A Patch of Peace." *San Francisco Chronicle,* A, p. 1,3.

"We want all the kids to get on together as they should," said Jones, a sixty-five-year-old Louisiana-born woman who has worked in the program since the early 1970s and knows most of the young men slain in the gun battles between the Big Block and West-mob gangs in recent years. "If we can just get to the young kids before they fall into those traps."

All the activity at the park site Friday came a month and a half after the death of the program's longtime director Julia "Aunt Bea" Middleton, and three days before Mayor Willie Brown's office of community development staff was to arrive for a routine inspection. Jones, who was Middleton's assistant for three decades, is a well-loved, respected figure in the community, and she grasps clearly the enormity of what she wants to see change. In the corner of one classroom, Jones keeps a poster board covered with funeral notices of slain young people from Bayview–Hunters Point.

"We can't know what these children have been through—so we have to come to them with an open heart and mind: In every child is some good," said Jones, whose park program serves about 250 kids from low-income families—many of whom live in government-subsidized housing.

Called "Aunt Marian" by many she cares for, Jones knows the Hunters Point Hill so well she can say which boy lost his father and which girl lost her cousin in the killings. Children dashing around the playground stop long enough to recount some of what she gives them. She always has time to listen to their problems; she gives then free snacks and provides flavored, homemade ices for twenty-five cents each, and she lets them bring and play their own CDs.

This island of safety exists between Big Block turf and Westmob turf around West Point Road. The two turfs are only a few hundred yards apart.

From 2000 to the present, police say sixty-four homicides have occurred in the area that encompasses Bayview–Hunters Point and stretches from Pac Bell Park to Candlestick Park. Many killings were gang-related.

Over the years, the youth park has escaped being a spot where much violence occurred in part because "most of the older kids have grown up here, and they respect us enough not to bring the violence here," Jones said. She added that recently the killings have tapered off somewhat following the arrest of many gang members by an FBI–police task force.

The park program now operates under a five-year lease from the San Francisco school district, which owns the land, and Jones said its buildings "are falling down."

In the future, Jones and other supporters hope to win approval to construct a new facility at the site for the program, which Mayor Willie Brown called "one of the finest community service organizations in San Francisco." But so far, approval hasn't come.

In 1999, Brown met Middleton at one of the mayor's open-door Saturday office sessions, and when he heard her plea for a new building he told his aides to seek donated help from the building trades unions. He asked for a monthly update and said: "I want to cut the ribbon."

Since then, Richard Bailin, president of the Hunters Point Community Park Foundation, says he has been told by the Mayor's office of community development, which has supported the program with federal funds since the 1970s, that it can't approve funding for a building until the program owns the land or has a long lease. He said the school district has told him it wasn't turning over the land without assurances that funding is in hand for the new building.

Roger Sanders, director of the mayor's office of community development, said, "The city is committed to building some type of facility for children and families in Bayview–Hunters Point, but whether it occurs at that site hasn't been decided." In the immediate future, Jones has a basic wish list—including new playground equipment, a pool cue rack, pool cues and balls for a pool table donated by a neighborhood resident.

INTRODUCTION

Diversion is a controversial issue. The intent of those in favor of diversion is laudable; to shield youth from the effects of contact with the system when it may not be necessary to involve them in the system. However, critics point out that it is simply widening the net. In regard to adults, Shover and Einstadter (1988) question the value of developing and expanding traditional correctional programs for the same reason, and further, they believe that many recent structural and technological developments in adult corrections have led to increasing control over citizens. Can this control be extended to juveniles? This chapter takes up this issue and many others as we strive to make some sense of diversion and its usefulness.

Are programs administered by the juvenile court extending state control over youths? Many experts would answer affirmatively and say we expect too much of the juvenile court system. It is overloaded with cases involving difficult and complex behavioral and social problems but does not have the resources it needs to handle them. Similarly, others note that there are limits to the extent to which courts can be transformed entirely into therapeutic organizations. On the other hand, Zimring asserts that the past thirty years have been the juvenile courts' finest hour as a diversion project (2000). He sees the attacks on the juvenile court over the past decade as a tribute to the ideals of the reformers who conceived the juvenile court and to its success as a diversion project.

The official processing of youths in the courts and the subsequent stigmatization of minor juvenile offenders have frequently been criticized. Removing minor offenders from court jurisdiction to avoid the effect of labeling is viewed by many as a way to reduce the likelihood of an adolescent's moving from *primary* to *secondary* deviance (Hinshaw, 1993; Frazier et al., 1983) Consequently, some criminologists now think the juvenile court should restrict its efforts to hard-core, chronic offenders (Krisberg et al., 1986; Lundman, 1984). They suggest that agencies outside the juvenile justice system be utilized to shift less serious cases away from the courts. These agencies should provide services to address the many individual and collective needs of children today.

This chapter draws heavily on Robert M. Regoli and John D. Hewitt. *Delinquency in Society*, 3rd ed. New York: McGraw-Hill Companies, Inc. 1997. With permission of the authors.

The shifting or moving of juveniles away from official processing is a means of diverting youths into more positive alternatives. However, there is a wide spectrum of opinion concerning what diversion should entail and how to implement it. At a minimum, diversion involves *doing something* with the offender, that is involvement in some sort of program such as drug counseling or a program to decrease truancy. This has resulted in extending the concept of diversion to include policies of benign neglect, judicious nonintervention, decriminalization, and release of offenders on their own recognizance (Lundman, 1984). Clearly, we need to minimize the number of youths admitted into the juvenile justice system, but we must address a number of questions about juvenile diversion before we can assess diversion programs. First we must define diversion.

WHAT IS DIVERSION?

The term "diversion" has several different meanings. Broadly defined, **diversion** is a process whereby a child is referred to a program (usually external to the official system) for counseling or care of some form in lieu of referral to the juvenile court. This can happen at several levels, Figure 7.1 illustrates the possibilities. Cases are removed from the juvenile justice system after they have been admitted at some level. But the term also refers to a set of informal hearings and subsequent dispositions that circumvent the juvenile justice system altogether.

The President's Commission of Law Enforcement and Administration of Justice describes diversion as a process of referring youths to an existing community treatment program in lieu of further juvenile justice processing at any point between apprehension and adjudication. Diversion is "designed to suspend or terminate juvenile justice procession of

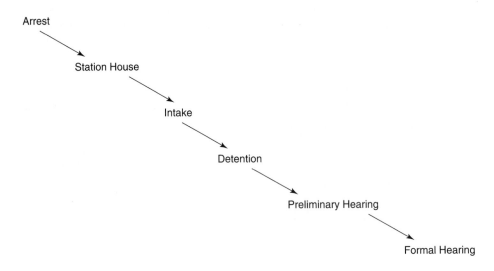

Figure 7.1   Diversion out of the Juvenile Justice System

youth in favor of release of referral to alternate services" (OJJDP, 1977). Another view is that diversion is simply a means of informal procession. For John Kenney and Dan Persuit, it is "an exercise in discretionary authority to substitute an informal disposition prior to a formal hearing on an alleged violation" (Kenney & Persuit, 1975). Similarly, Richard Sundeen argues that diversion

> is the return of the offender by the police to the community (the family or a referral agency) rather than referral to an official sanctioning agency, such as the probation department and juvenile court. (Sundeen, 1974)

And Albert Roberts sees diversion as "any process that is used by components of the criminal justice system (police, courts, corrections) whereby youths avoid formal juvenile court processing and adjudication" (Roberts, 1989b). Finally, Charles Frazier and John Cochran suggest that diversion be defined as

> the earliest possible cessation of official intervention with delinquent youth following the point of initial contact with law enforcement authorities. In its "pure" form, diversion also implies that no sanction of treatment (i.e., no intervention) is imposed on the juvenile offender by either official or nonofficial agents. (Frazier & Cochran, 1986)

To many, diversion means referral to programs *outside* the justice system. Frazier and his colleagues believe that "diversion refers to efforts aimed at reducing state control over youth by decreasing the number of juveniles processed through official justice channels" (Frazier & Cochran 1986). Arnold Binder and Gilbert Geis add that many juveniles would benefit from diversion programs that provide services, such as employment, family, and substance abuse counseling; require that the youths make restitution to victims; or enable the youths to become involved with a Big Brother or a Big Sister. (Binder & Geis, 1984) Clearly, the exact meaning of diversion is ambiguous and potentially contradictory. As Dean Rojek and Maynard Erickson note, "Diversion may entail the avoidance of the juvenile justice process through an outright release, or it may consist of diverting offenders away from the justice system through placement in an alternative program" (Rojek & Erickson, 1981/1982).

WHO SHOULD BE DIVERTED?

Rosemary Sarri and Robert Vinter (1975) argue that diversion should be automatic for "first offenders charged with status offenses or minor misdemeanors, repeated status offenders, or youth known to be receiving service [treatment] in community agencies." It has also been suggested that juveniles who are referred to the court because they have problems at school or because social service agencies do not want to handle them should be diverted to programs that can deal with them more appropriately.

One major recurrent fear is that diversion programs will produce a **net widening** of the juvenile justice apparatus. That is, diversion might be used primarily as a disposition for youths who would be screened out of the system if diversion programs did not exist (Hinshaw, 1993; Fuller & Norton, 1993; Pratt, 1986). Each stage of juvenile justice reform in recent years has resulted in more juveniles being brought into the juvenile justice net, as well as increased "capacity for surveillance, regulation and intervention in the lives of young people" (Pratt, 1986). Binder (1989) sees the concern over net widening as rather ironic. During the late 1960s and early 1970s, because of critical attacks on the juvenile justice system, the diversion of youth was expanded in order to avoid labeling. Now, many critics suggest that diversion itself has produced an increase in negative labeling. More on this later.

Each community is different. Thus, who is screened out of the system, diverted, or referred on to juvenile court differs from community to community. In addition, the nature of the delinquency problem varies widely by setting, both in terms of levels of community concern and in terms of patterns of juvenile misconduct. But the subjective and unofficial nature of diversion programs may also lead to bias in the screening process. Thomas Blomberg (1984) suggests that "diversion program clients tend to be drawn from groups that are predominantly middle-class . . . As a result, many lower-class youth who might benefit from diversion's family services are being denied these services."

The sex of the offender may also affect case handling. Christine Adler (1984) found that girls are more likely than boys to be referred to diversion agencies than to be handled by the formal juvenile justice system. Boys, on the other hand, who engage in similar minor misbehaviors are more likely to end up in juvenile court.

Edward Latessa et al. (1984) and his colleagues point out that when nonlegal factors such as race, social class, age, and sex are taken into consideration in the decision to refer juveniles to diversion programs, or when juveniles are subjected to supervision and other nonvoluntary treatment without having been adjudicated delinquent, adherence to important due process rights of juveniles may be ignored.

S. Lee Hinshaw (1993) suggests that because juvenile diversion programs are more of a supplemental, rather than an alternative, form of processing cases in the juvenile court, they may violate certain due process rights of juveniles. By widening the net through diversion, the juvenile justice system not only brings juveniles further into the net but typically brings them in unadjudicated, that is they are placed under court supervision without ever having been found guilty or able to take advantage of their due process rights. There may have been no formal adjudicatory hearing, charges may not have been filed, and youths may not have had an opportunity to meet with an attorney. According to Hinshaw, when police or the prosecutor initiate the procedures to place a youth in a diversion program, the youth is very likely to be subjected to subtle coercion to enter the program. If the youth refuses to participate, he or she faces a strong possibility of a formal court hearing and a potentially more severe sanction.

In the end, we are left with a conundrum: To eliminate bias, we must formalize the system, but with formalization comes official labeling, which endangers the ideal upon which diversion is based. Yet, regardless of this issue, one thing is clear; however the pool of youths eligible for diversion in a particular community is defined, care must be taken to ensure that juveniles are really diverted out of official system processing rather than just being put on hold until they are older.

WHEN SHOULD YOUTH BE DIVERTED?

Different communities are going to have different standards for answering the question on when youth should be diverted. Some communities will have a very tolerant attitude, while others will have little patience for those youth who do transgress. However, we should always be concerned with the long-term effects of ensnaring youth in the justice net. Thus, a rule of thumb is that of "the sooner, the better." There are several points in the juvenile justice system process where diversion can occur—during apprehension, court intake, or adjudication. Thus, if the goal of diversion is to minimize penetration into the system, then "the sooner, the better."

Diversion at different points requires that juveniles be differentiated in terms of seriousness of offense and other related factors: those diverted from the system at the time of initial police contact are more likely to be less serious offenders than those diverted at court intake. Similarly, programs to which diverted youth are sent at the various diversion points will also differ. For example, those diverted at court-intake may require a more detailed, complex program than youths diverted at initial contact.

WHERE SHOULD YOUTH BE DIVERTED?

Most observers argue that diverted youths should receive the benefit of positive life experiences that will open up legitimate roles for them in society. This includes such diverse programs such as shelters, treatment programs, education, and mentoring. While there is no single formula for creating a diversion organization, the possibilities are nearly unlimited. Still, some broad goals for diversion programs can be identified. They should stress youth involvement and participation; they should endeavor to include youths in various aspects of decision making; and, most important, they should regard juveniles as an integral part of the program, not merely as clients.

Diversion programs should offer an innovative approach to treatment and rehabilitation. Research efforts on the effectiveness of traditional treatment models—intensive counseling, therapy, and other change-the-offender types of programs—have been found lacking. In assessing delinquency prevention programs, the President's Commission on Law Enforcement and Administration of Justice noted that intervention strategies such as an individual and group counseling, social casework, and the use of detached workers have consistently failed to either prevent or reduce juvenile delinquency (PCLEAJ, 1967).

However, there is still no compelling evidence showing that intervention into the lives of delinquent youths, even by means of programs based on highly sophisticated theoretical rationales, is any more effective than are policies of minimal interference.

However, if one agrees that truancy, drinking and drugs, promiscuity, and running away are detrimental to the future, and even the health and safety of youth, then one must agree that something must be done. As a result, it is crucial that programs be tested against both conventional justice system processing and minimal interference with juveniles.

SOME EARLY DIVERSION PROGRAMS

The early innovative diversion programs had two goals in common: to intervene with youthful first-time offenders prior to court processing or possible commitment to a correctional facility and to keep youths in a local community treatment program if possible. In Chapter 4, we discussed the sexual offenders program of Delaware County, Ohio, and its success in the treatment of youthful offenders by keeping them in the home. Four others are highlighted below as examples of programs of excellence.

- **Project Crossroads:** Project Crossroads was a highly structured community treatment program established in Washington, D.C., in the late 1960s. The program was funded by the Department of Labor and had as its primary objective the provision of vocational services to youthful first-time offenders between the ages of sixteen and twenty-six. People selected for the program had to have no prior convictions, had to be currently facing charges for a nonviolent offense, and had to be unemployed or underemployed. Project Crossroads combined counseling, vocational training, and academic development to enhance the youth's feelings of self-worth and thereby increase the likelihood of the juvenile's becoming a productive member of society.
- **St. Louis Diversion Program:** Established in 1971, the St. Louis Diversion Program provided home detention as an alternative to incarceration in the city's already-overcrowded detention center. Because their caseloads were small, probation officers could work directly and intensively with juveniles, their family members, and school representatives.
- **Baltimore Diversion Project:** Baltimore's diversion program, like Project Crossroads, was funded by the Department of Labor. Eligibility in the program was restricted to juveniles between fifteen and seventeen years of age who were not currently charged with a serious violent crime. Drawing upon the unique experience and expertise of adult ex-offenders, the program focused its efforts on job counseling and placement.
- **Sacramento County 601 Diversion Project:** Started in 1970 as an experiment to reduce court costs and recidivism rates, "Project 601" provided crisis intervention and counseling for families that had problems. Many juveniles selected for the program had already been identified as truants, habitual runaways, or incorrigible youths who were beyond the control of their parents.

TYPES OF POLICE DIVERSION PROGRAMS

Most state juvenile codes are so broad in scope that almost every youth could be arrested at some point. Moreover, children are generally accountable to the adult world for virtually everything they do, so the range of surveillance exceeds even the broad limits required for what is by law prohibited juvenile conduct (for example, alcohol consumption). While most misconduct goes unnoticed by the authorities, when problem behavior is detected, it is police who serve as the major source of diversion away from the application of the juvenile code.

Of the juveniles taken into police custody in 2000, over 70 percent were referred to the juvenile court, 20 percent were handled in the police department and released, and 7 percent were referred directly to criminal (adult) court (Ferro, 2003). In 2001, approximately 72 percent were referred to juvenile court, about 7 percent were referred to criminal or adult court, about 2 percent were referred to another police or welfare agency, and the remaining 19 percent were handled within the department and then released (FBI, 2002, p. 291). In other words, police make diversionary decisions in a little less than one-third of the juvenile cases they encounter.

Diversion without Referral

The most basic form of juvenile diversion by police is **diversion without referral**. Typically, this involves an informal adjustment (for example, warn, counsel, and release), whereby the juvenile is immediately diverted from the system without further significant action. This is one of the most common police diversion practices. This option, especially if exercised in the field, is the purest form of diversion because the youth's exposure to the juvenile justice system is kept to a minimum.

Diversion with Referral

A second type of diversion by police is diversion with referral. In this case, the youth is referred to a program administered by an agency other than the juvenile justice system. Diversion with referral is generally dictated by departmental policy or by written agreement between police and community agencies. It involves filing reports and sometimes officially transferring jurisdiction from police to some other agency.

Internal Referral

An **internal referral** (in-house diversion) is the referral of a case from one branch of the police department to another branch better equipped to handle it. In-house programs can be organized in different ways. In many departments, an officer administers the program and supervises a team of full-time professional counselors (usually civilians). In a variation of this approach, an officer serves as an administrator and directs the efforts of a team of volunteer counselors. The degree to which specialized counseling skills are required depends on the assessed needs of the juveniles who are being targeted, as well as on overall program goals. Typical internal referral programs include community volunteer programs, recreation programs, and probation programs.

Community Volunteer Programs

The goal of community volunteer programs is to identify and recruit individuals from within the community to assist problem youths. Potential candidates contribute by serving as Big Brothers or Big Sisters or by providing educational tutoring or employment opportunities. Police officers are responsible for identifying and developing liaisons with the appropriate community members.

One example of this type of approach is the Firefighter-Counselor Program. On the basis of the premise that firefighters often project a positive, nonthreatening image to many youths, some police departments (including those in Dallas and Los Angeles) have organized interested volunteers from the local fire department to serve as Big Brothers and Big Sisters and as part-time counselors to troubled youths. Volunteers are trained in the objectives of the diversion program (for instance, counseling about drugs, alcohol, and sex) and receive additional training in adolescent development and in crisis intervention techniques. The value of community volunteer programs is that they increase the number of available resources at minimal cost and can provide long-range follow-up to initial counseling and work.

Recreation Programs

Generally called Police Athletic League (PAL) Clubs, recreation programs are found in almost all large and medium-sized cities. Through athletic activities, especially team sports, PAL programs attempt to channel the energy of delinquent youths into socially constructive activities. Such programs are based on the assumption that if youths are exposed to the benefits of sportsmanship, playing by the rules, and healthy competition, they will internalize these values and apply them to other spheres of life. Also associated with recreation programs is the belief that improved health and attitude will result in a beneficial modification in behavior. Direct police personnel involvement in the programs is believed to have a positive influence on the attitudes of youths and the community towards police officers.

Prohibition Programs

Based on informal police probation, diversionary probation programs are designed to make it clear to the youth that he or she is to stay out of trouble and that the police officer is there to see that he or she does. Generally, the police department requires that the juvenile report to an officer at the police station or elsewhere on a regular basis. The juvenile reports on his or her activities since the last visit and receives encouragement, advice, or warning (as warranted) from the officer. This approach is authoritarian and intentionally coercive. If the juvenile is involved in subsequent misconduct, he or she is threatened with removal from the diversion program and referral to juvenile court. The program explicitly incorporates a negotiation process through which the officer and the youth work out a deal that "gives the child a break" this time, but not the next.

External Referral

External referral is the diversion of youths to available outside community resources for assistance. These resources can range from general family services to specific drug treatment programs. External diversion programs stress the organization and cultivation of local community agency resources to meet the needs of troubled youths in lieu of traditional processing through the juvenile justice system. In a more formalized type of external referral, a police department may contract with professional service agents (such as a child psychologist or drug therapist) when a service is unavailable through public agencies or is deemed especially critical in addressing the needs of a particular youth.

Police departments examine four criteria when referring youths to community service agencies: acceptability, suitability, availability, and accountability. (Klein, 1976).

Acceptability

Police officers have a tendency to stereotype certain service agencies as soft, lenient, coddling, and permissive. Free clinics, runaway shelters, and crisis centers are examples of endeavors that are sometimes successful in helping troubled youths but are viewed with suspicion by police. Police tend to see these programs as catering to the vices of youths rather than controlling or preventing them.

Suitability

Many community service agencies are unsuitable for use by the police as potential referral sources. An agency may accept only certain cases, or its policies and practices may conflict in some way with those of police. Other practical considerations that affect suitability are restrictive costs, long waiting lists, and insufficient personnel. Furthermore, many service agencies are open only between 9:00 A.M. and 5:00 P.M. Police officials can adapt to these conditions, or they can begin to work with the agencies in question to resolve whatever problems stand between them.

Police should be careful to select a referral agency whose resources match the needs of the individual youth. Referral agencies sometimes begin accepting a wide variety of clients on the basis of past successes in one particular area. For example, an agency that has been effective in treating juveniles who have drug or alcohol problems may expand its services to include counseling runaways and incorrigible youths. Expansion may be inappropriate and detrimental to the youths, as well as the agencies: The quality of service may decline, and, if so, the credibility of the agency will probably follow.

Availability

Over the years, various recommendations have been made in an attempt to provide community resources where none exist. There are two problems that may arise regarding such resources. First, availability of resources is no guarantee of quality. This problem must be dealt with on a community-by-community basis; where weaknesses are known and acknowledged, police may have a responsibility to demand high-quality services.

Second, there is often a low level of resource awareness among police, a problem that both police and community agencies must address. Malcolm Klein interviewed officers in six California cities on the availability of community resources; he found an almost total lack of knowledge on the subject. (Klein, 1976) Juvenile officers are not required to seek out referral services as a normal part of their job, officers often do not live in the communities they serve, and private agencies often do not make their services available to police. Police and resource people must actively and regularly meet to discuss youth needs and ensure that there are available resources.

Accountability

The appropriateness of a referral can never be known without formal procedures for follow-up. By actively soliciting comments from referral agencies, police are better equipped to make future referrals and improve communication with service agencies. Better communication, in turn, improves coordination and the ability of agencies to respond to police needs.

COURT DIVERSION ALTERNATIVES

Although police divert many juveniles from further formal processing within the juvenile justice system, most diversion occurs after youths have been brought into court. A youth may be diverted through *informal adjustment* of the case, and thus never face a formal court hearing. In addition, a court may choose from a variety of *diversion alternatives* that effectively keep an adjudicated youth from facing a correctional institution placement.

Informal Adjustment

Many state juvenile codes permit the suspension of the formal juvenile court process prior to the filing of a petition so that a juvenile can be handled informally by community agencies. This process is called **informal adjustment**. In most states, statutes specify provisions that must be met for diversion through informal adjustment. The Iowa juvenile code, for example, requires that the child voluntarily admit that he or she committed a delinquent act. The admission must be based on the intelligent consent of the child to advice given by his or her attorney. In addition, the terms of the informal adjustment must be clearly stated and signed by all parties, Finally, there is a six-month limit on the duration of the adjustment, and the child has the right to terminate the agreement at any time.

States are beginning to adopt provisions that allow for intake screening by community agencies. In Pennsylvania, for instance, in the probation officer deems such screening to be in the best interest of the child and the public, the officer refers the child and his or her parent to any willing public or private agency that reports to the officer. This child and parent must voluntarily consent to this referral, and a six-month limit is put on the screening process. The agency can send the case back to the juvenile court for further informal adjustment at any time, but no petition can be filed.

Mediation

As discussed in Chapter 6, the Supreme Court rulings in *Kent, Gault,* and *Winship* require that the juvenile court adhere to basic due process considerations. As a result, juvenile court proceedings have become more formal and adversarial, and many cases that come before the court are not well-suited for this atmosphere. Cases involving ongoing personal conflicts between disputants, for example, may be inappropriate for a court whose primary concern is the specific complaint at hand. One emerging alternative for the resolution of such conflicts is mediation. In a typical **mediation** program, problems are worked out at meetings attended by the complainant, the respondent (the accused juvenile), and a neutral hearing officer who facilitates communication between the disputants and helps them reach a mutually acceptable resolution. Mediation can involve varying degrees of intervention, ranging from providing the disputing parties with a meeting place to establishing ground rules for discussion and actively recommending possible solutions.

The advantages of mediation are many. Disputants have more time in a mediation session than they would before a judge and are more relaxed. They are able to explore the aspects of their dispute more thoroughly, not just the particular complaint at issue. In addition, the informal process of mediation is more likely to help resolve the problem than formal court proceedings, and it is generally faster and less expensive than working through the legal system (Shover & Einstadter, 1988). As a result of being brought into mediation, the parties are more likely to consider compromises and to uphold the terms of any settlement reached.

Cases may be referred to a mediation program at three different points during case processing: (1) Noncourt referral (such as by police or social service agencies) occurs prior to the filing of a petition; (2) court-intake referral, by an intake officer, takes place either before or after the filing of a petition; and (3) court referral follows a hearing by a judge. While mediation programs vary in format and procedure, the following description of a session is typical of the basic operation.

The hearing officer (mediator) begins the mediation session with a brief opening statement that describes the nature of the proceedings. The complainant speaks first and presents his or her evidence and witnesses; then the respondent is given the same opportunity. After these initial presentations, the disputants may question each other and any witness present. The mediator helps pinpoint relevant facts, tries to identify possible areas of agreement, and helps compensate for any unequal bargaining abilities the parties may have. If the mediator discovers that the disagreement goes beyond the specific complaint at hand, the discussion can be broadened into an attempt to resolve the full dispute. If a settlement is reached, the mediator writes out the specific terms of the agreement and asks both parties to sign it. If they cannot agree on the appropriate settlement, the mediator informs them of their remaining options for resolving the dispute (such as initiation of formal court proceedings).

When a dispute has been referred to mediation following the filing of a petition, the settlement is typically reviewed by a judge before it is converted to an order of the court. Cases referred to mediation prior to formal court intake are not subject to judicial review or enforcement.

Two important, related issues surround the use of mediation in juvenile court: the type of information given to parties about the referral to mediation and the degree of choice afforded parties in determining whether they will use it. Parties cannot make an informed choice unless they understand the differences between court adjudication and case resolution through mediation. At a minimum, disputants need answers to the following questions:

- How quickly can the hearing be scheduled?
- Can the respondent be forced to attend, or is participation voluntary?
- Do the parties waive any legal rights by accepting the alternative forum?
- What is the format of the hearing?
- What is the role of the hearing officer?
- What options are available if the attempt at mediation fails?
- Is the mediated settlement enforceable by the court?

To guarantee that disputants are properly informed about the mediation process, the program coordinators should prepare a written description that addresses these questions, either for the parties to read or for intake officers or judges to use as a guide in explaining the program to potential clients. The disputants should be allowed to decide for themselves whether a mediation session or a court hearing will best serve their interests. For information on mediation programs within schools, see the box on p. 181.

Youth Service Programs

One of the more specific diversion recommendations of the President's Commission on Law Enforcement and Administration of Justice was the establishment of **Youth Service Bureaus (YSBs)** as community diversion agencies. (Roberts, 1989a) According to Sherwood Norman, the primary objective of Youth Service Bureaus was to divert children from the justice system by:

1. Mobilizing community resources to solve youth problems.
2. Strengthening existing youth resources and developing new ones.
3. Promoting positive programs to remedy delinquency-breeding conditions. (Norman, 1972)

Between 1967 and 1973, 150 YSBs were established in states around the country. These YSBs provided diversion programs ranging from drop-in centers and temporary shelter for runaways to crisis hotlines and school outreach programs. Some YSBs in larger cities offered special programs for pregnant teenagers and provided employment for high school dropouts (Bartollas & Miller, 1994).

Unfortunately, almost any type of youth program could call itself a "youth service bureau." In fact, many YSBs were nothing more than extensions of the juvenile justice

DELINQUENCY PREVENTION
Young Peacemakers—Mediation in the School

When two former friends were about to get into a fight in school because one refused to return a music tape to the other, they were quickly brought into the Tucson school's peer mediation program. Student mediators began by getting the two to agree on the ground rules, which included no name calling, no physical violence, and no walking out of the session. According to Christina St. Charles, a Tucson High School junior, "You have to ask some questions, and you've got to find out what's at the bottom of it. You just ask them, like, 'What are the consequences going to be if you get in a fight and get suspended?' or 'What happens if you get suspended and your grade goes down?' "

Mediation can be requested by the disputants, by other students, or by teachers. After a request for mediation is made, student mediators make all the arrangements and then bring the disputants together, out of the way of other students, teachers, and administrators.

Student mediators are nominated by fellow students and must have good abilities for sitting and listening. One principal commented that student mediators need not be "ideal students," A-plus students, or even ones that teachers think might be best for the job. However, Velma Castaneda-Titone, a social worker and Manzo Elementary School, said that schools should not have unrealistic expectations of what student mediation programs can accomplish, especially when young children are involved: "To look at children as mediators and expect that they'll never get into conflicts is unrealistic. It takes years to internalize skills and for the skills to become a part of who we are."

So far, school administrators feel that the program has had about 85 percent success rate. Not only are conflicts getting resolved, but school counselors and advisers do not have to spend time working on the problems handled by mediation.

Currently, more than two thousand conflict resolution programs operate in schools across the country. Many have student-mediator components built into them. Mediation in school settings is increasingly viewed as a valuable alternative to formal action and possible referral to the police or juvenile courts. According to one program coordinator:

> . . . When we let kids watch "Teenage Mutant Ninja Turtles" and all this other stuff, it shows them that the best way to solve your problems is to be stronger and have some really good weapons. We're taking kids when they're ready to be taught and teaching them an alternative skill in terms of handling a conflict.

system, adopting similar service patterns, relationships to other official agencies, and, most important, coercive practices (Polk, 1971).

The effectiveness of Youth Service Bureaus has not been ignored by criminologists studying the role of diversion programs. An evaluation of YSBs prior to 1980 led to the conclusion the YSBs "do not appear to be a viable mechanism for reducing delinquency" (Haapanen and Rodisill, 1980). Researchers who evaluated a YSB in Wisconsin noted that there were no apparent differences in the postrelease delinquency rates of youths participating in the program and those not participating. (Venezia & Anthony, 1978) Furthermore, Ronald Quincy reported that his evaluation of a USB diversion program led to the conclusion that "no strong inference can be made that the YSB had a significant impact on the youths' subsequent delinquent behavior" (Quincy, 1981).

On the other hand, Albert Roberts found that whatever success YSB programs did achieve was often related directly to their specific location and accessibility to targeted populations. (Roberts, 1989a) If the number of referrals is used as the empirical measure of success, then YSBs located in areas frequented by youths, near high schools, or near police departments were more successful because they had greater numbers of referrals (Roberts, 1989a).

Chicago's Omni Youth Services, one of the few remaining YSBs, has been operating on the city's north side since 1972. It was established as the Omni House Youth Service Bureau and given a mandate to provide services for police-referred youths who otherwise would have been processed by the juvenile courts. Magnus Seng and Gad Bensinger examined the Omni program in the twenty-year period between 1972 and 1992 to evaluate whether it had accomplished its primary goal of diverting youths from official police and court processing. (Seng & Bensinger, 1994) They concluded that although LEAA (Law Enforcement Assistance Administration) funding had declined during the two decades, the data indicated the Omni House was able to serve "a population referred by the police and the courts for behaviors normally addressed by justice system agencies" (Seng & Bensinger, 1994). However, not many YSBs have lasted as long as Omni House. By the end of the 1980s, all but a few had closed down their operations.

Community Youth Boards

An *involuntary* system of diversion from the traditional juvenile court process involves the use of **community youth boards**. These agencies are informal hearing boards that determine what, if any, services should be provided to children referred by schools, police, the juvenile court, parents, or the children themselves. Their goals are the same as those of the first juvenile courts—to help children in trouble to become useful and healthy citizens, not to determine fault. While some boards accept only status offender referrals, others allow referral of all juvenile offenders. Children must obey the board's orders regarding the services they are to receive unless they choose to ask for a juvenile court review, in which case the court has the power to revoke the board's orders.

Wilderness Programs

Early outdoor **wilderness programs** (as alternatives to incarceration) were modeled after the Civilian Conservation Corps camps, which operated between 1933 and 1943. Forestry camps provided an open-air environment for treatment rather than the traditional fenced-in prison setting. The camps of the 1940s and 1950s were generally either senior forestry camps for youths between the ages of sixteen and eighteen or junior probation camps for boys between ages thirteen and fifteen. Senior forestry stressed such work as reforestation, brush clearance, fire suppression, and maintenance and construction of park facilities. The focus of junior probation camps was on education, athletics and counseling (Roberts, 1989).

Today's wilderness programs grew out of both forestry camps and the Outward Bound program created in Wales during World War I. Outward Bound was established as a training experience for merchant seamen in which they could gain success and confidence in meeting physical challenges and develop a sense of group pride (Roberts, 1989d). Building on the Outward Bound model, wilderness programs attempt to take streetwise youths, with their well-developed skills at conning and manipulating people and place them in a setting where they cannot avoid taking responsibility. Wilderness programs generally include the following components:

- *An orientation phase,* during which the youth is introduced to the rules and expectations of the program.
- A series of *physical challenges* that cannot be conned or manipulated.
- An *educational component* that is integrated into the camp experience.
- A *solo* (usually from one to three days in length), in which the youth must survive alone in the wilderness, drawing upon skills and knowledge gained earlier in the program.
- A *final event,* which is frequently a group run of many miles.
- A *celebration ceremony,* which signifies successful completion of the wilderness program (Roberts, 1989).

While most wilderness programs are private enterprises, the Stephen French Youth Wilderness Program (known as Homeward Bound) is run under the jurisdiction of the Massachusetts Division of Youth Services. Originally established as a youth forestry camp, Homeward Bound has evolved into an experience designed to increase participants' self-respect by fostering self-discipline and the ability to overcome both physical and psychological challenges through individual and group efforts (Roberts, 1989d). Boys between the ages of fourteen and seventeen are brought into the twenty-six-day wilderness experience.

The first few days in the program are largely limited to physical fitness activities, such as running, hiking, and completing obstacle courses. After being introduced to a variety of survival skills, the boys pursue wilderness challenges that include rock climbing, canoeing, rappelling, and cross-country skiing. The culmination of the Homeward Bound experience is a three-day solo into the wilderness with only the barest of essentials (matches, plastic sheet, cooking pail, and water). While the wilderness experience combines physical and mental challenges, boys are also provided with individual and group counseling at every stage of the program to prepare them for their eventual release back into their communities and families (Roberts, 1989d).

Florida's Associated Marine Institute (AMI), funded by state, federal, and private donations, is a nonresidential treatment program for youths referred by the juvenile courts. For a youth to participate at one of the five AMI centers, he or she must be between fifteen and eighteen years old, have basic math and reading skills, and have no

Figure 7.2   Wilderness programs serve as diversion programs and treatment programs. Participants have the chance to work together, accomplish tasks through cooperative effort and gain in self-esteem by completing a rigorous program.
Richard Frear/United States Department of the Interior

repeated involvement with either drugs or assaultive behavior. Most youths live at home or with foster families during the nine-month training period. The AMI program involves a diversity of activities, including training in boat repair, diving, ship handling, marine biology, lifesaving, and first aid. AMI also operates the Florida Environmental Institute (FEI), a wilderness program. In the FEI program, youths are taken to isolated settings in the Florida Everglades, where they engage in productive environmental work. The experience helps rebuild both the Everglades and the youth's self-image. (Krisberg & Austin, 1993). (See the box on p. 185 for a look at another innovative diversion program.)

It is arguable whether wilderness programs reduce future delinquency. Meda Chesney-Lind and Randall Shelden reported no significant difference in recidivism after five years between juveniles participating in an Outward Bound program in Massachusetts and those receiving some other type of disposition. Publicity, however, has centered on some of the more unfortunate incidents that have occurred in the course of some wilderness programs. For example, in Hawaii, an employee of a wilderness program was charged with child abuse. In Utah, the director of a wilderness program was charged with negligent homicide of a female. And in California, a sixteen-year-old boy had to have parts of both feet amputated after being forced to sleep outside in the snow (Chesney-Lind & Sheldon, 1992).

DELINQUENCY PREVENTION

Shipping Out Delinquents

Fort Smallwood Marine Institute in Maryland is an innovative youth diversion program that uses swimming, scuba diving, boat handling, and other nautical activities to build self-esteem, confidence, and a sense of teamwork as an alternative to traditional correctional treatment. "Most of the kids [in the program] come from neighborhoods with drugs and violence. They've been kicked out of public schools, and their families have lost control of them. When they arrive, usually on court order, they have a big chip on their shoulders." Because few of the youths have been around water before, the water activities are designed to build confidence and self-discipline. As the youths feel more confident and focused in their efforts, their work in school activities also improves.

When their behavior in the institute reaches a certain level, the youths are challenged with additional activities. "Most have been told all their lives that they're stupid or can't do anything right. All of the sudden, they achieve simple goals, including showing up every day, and they begin to believe in themselves."

Currently, there are about thirty boys at Fort Smallwood. The total cost to the state for the eight-month program is less than $10,000 per boy, which is much less than the $60,000-per-year cost of incarcerating a juvenile in Maryland youth correctional facility.

More than twenty thousand delinquent youths have completed the program at Fort Smallwood during its twenty-four years of operation. Fewer than 20 percent have been rearrested after leaving the program. A unique graduation requirement is that the youth must obtain a job, enter college, or enroll in a vocation training program when he graduates.

"For a lot of these kids, who have known only failure, success is very scary," says Ron Hauswald, past community coordinator at Fort Smallwood. "All of the sudden, they're in the real world—making money, handling their own decisions. That's when the positive values that we've tried to teach them really count. What you learn at sea you apply on land."

Source: Adapted from, Al Santoli (1992). "A New Course for Life," *Parade Magazine,* March 8:14–15.

Aside from boosting self-esteem, it is unclear how wilderness skills apply in urban settings. It might be argued that such programs are influenced by the turn-of-the-century belief that the city was an evil environment and children could be reformed only by taking them into the purifying setting of the countryside.

THE IMPACT OF DIVERSION ON THE JUVENILE JUSTICE SYSTEM

Diversion programs were viewed by many in the late 1960s and 1970s as innovative and less expensive alternatives to traditional police and court interventions with juvenile delinquents. Advocates argued that diversion programs would increase both the efficiency and the effectiveness of the juvenile justice system. The following discussion examines these two claims.

Increased Efficiency

Efficiency is usually thought of as the difference between costs and benefits, but it is rarely possible in the public sector to measure costs (or inputs) and benefits (or output) in the same units. Conclusions about efficiency often depend on the value assigned by the analyst. Partly because there is no consistent definition of efficiency, diversion's impact on efficiency is more often attributed than demonstrated. Diversion's efficiency is based on three claims:

- It reduces court caseloads and police agency costs.
- It reduces the amount of time officers spend on case processing.
- It reduces the length of time during which the juvenile is involved in the juvenile justice system.

While it may seem that, by definition, diversion will reduce court caseloads, this is not necessarily true. Some studies indicate that because diversion programs handle some individuals who would not otherwise come into contact with police, diversion may actually *increase* the number of cases sent to court. Malcolm Klein (Klein, 1976), as well as Don Gibbons and Gerald Blake (Gibbons & Blake, 1976), have suggested that diverted youths are drawn from a group traditionally released after initial contact or arrest without further police action. That is, officers may now become formally involved with juveniles who would have been released without arrest if no diversion program existed.

In an evaluation of a juvenile court liaison program in a large Ohio city, Edward Latessa and his colleagues examined the stated diversionary program goals of avoidance of stigma and reduction of court caseloads (Latessa et al., 1984). Juveniles brought into the program had been referred for minor criminal offenses, drug involvement, and status offenses. While the diversion of youths from the court caseload may have reduced the number of cases the court faced, Latessa and his associates suggest that negative consequences also resulted. (Latessa et al., 1984) They noted that extralegal factors (age, race, neighborhood, and sex) influenced the court's decision to refer juveniles to the diversion program. Perhaps more importantly, they state that, on the basis of follow-up supervision, "the delivery of treatment services to those referred by the diversion program appears to have had the effect of worsening the behavior pattern of the referred youth" (Latessa et al., 1984).

Mark Pogrebin and his colleagues reported that while findings from an experimental juvenile court diversion program in Colorado showed that diversion reduced court caseloads and lowered recidivism rates for juveniles in the experimental group, some net widening occurred. (Progrebin et al., 1984) Of 848 referrals, 179 of the juveniles who were brought into the diversion program would probably have only been lectured and then released prior to the court experiment: "Hence, those 179 juveniles became more involved in the system processing than they would have otherwise experienced" (Progrebin et al., 1984).

Similar findings were observed by William Barton and Jeffery Butts in their evaluation of juveniles assigned to a new in-house program over the four-year period between 1983 and 1986 (Barton & Butts, 1990). They noted that while the new program did enable juveniles who would have otherwise been committed to an institution to remain at home, the actual number of youths sent to court prior to the diversion screening increased. They suggest that these youths would have been less likely to be committed to an institution prior to the introduction of the programs. Barton and Butts argue that a number of factors probably contributed to the widening of the net in this diversion program. These factors included "the court's increased propensity to commit cases; prolonged lengths of stay in the intensive probation programs; and the use of wider discretion in screening committed cases for diversion to the intensive probation programs" (Barton & Butts, 1990).

After reviewing the evidence of a wide variety of diversion projects, Kenneth Polk concluded that the positive goal of diversion, to keep the juvenile from moving further into the juvenile justice system, often fail" (Polk, 1984). Instead of removing juveniles from the system, the machinery simply expands to handle larger numbers who have engaged in behaviors that would not previously have come under the control of the juvenile justice machine.

However, findings contradicting those discussed above were reported by Finn-Aage Esbensen in an evaluation of police diversion programs over a six-year period in three cities. According to Esbensen, with the introduction of police diversion programs, "fewer youths should penetrate into the system and fewer still should receive formal sanctioning" (Esbensen, 1984). Only in one of the three cities did penetration rates increase during the six-year period. In the other two cities, fewer youths penetrated the system, and those who did come into contact with police were less likely to receive formal dispositions from the courts.

Charles Frazier and his colleagues found conflicting evidence regarding the issue of net widening. (Frazier et al., 1983) They examined a diversion project in Florida for the period between 1977 and 1979. The program was aimed at youths who would have been referred for official handling by the juvenile court if the diversion alternative had not existed. At each stage in the diversion process, minority youths, more serious offenders, and younger offenders were found in the diversion group. According to Frazier,

> This diversion program may have widened the juvenile justice nets by processing young Blacks with no previous agency contacts but who could be charged as having committed serious offenses. Without a diversion alternative, such youth may have been seen as predelinquent and needing only a warning. Diversion programs, then, may offer an attractive option to police for dealing with youth who have attributes interpretable as predictors of future delinquency but whose cases do not warrant full official processing. (Frazier et al., 1983)

The second contention regarding diversion and efficiency—that diversion reduces the amount of time officers spend counseling citizens, making arrests, or appearing in court, thereby freeing them for other duties and ultimately reducing agency costs—is neither supported nor refuted by scientific data. Malcolm Klein (Klein, 1976) and Paul Nejelski (Nejelski, 1976) argue that diversion decreases the costs of processing individuals through the criminal justice system. Yet Peter Pitchess (Pitchess, 1974) reports (without supporting data) that a diversion program operated by the Los Angeles County Sheriff's Department has reduced agency costs.

John Stratton studied a diversion program operated by the San Fernando Police Department, in California (Stratton, 1975). Status offenders and first-time misdemeanor offenders were randomly assigned to two groups: one was diverted, and the other was admitted into the justice system. Stratton found some evidence showing that expenditures for the processed group were higher than those for the diverted group, although his sample size was very small.

The third contention—that diversion reduces the length of time spent by the juvenile in the juvenile justice system—also appears to have little support. Frazier and Cochran suggest that the nature of intervention can be measured in three ways: (1) Intervention may vary temporally (from short to long periods of time); (2) intervention may vary according to the degree of restrictive control imposed; and (3) intervention may vary by the level of formality used in dealing with the juvenile (Frazier & Cochran, 1986). According to Frazier and Cochran, when measured in these ways, diversion programs should result in the following:

- Official intervention for shorter periods of time.
- The application of less restrictive controls on the juvenile.
- Less formal interaction between the juvenile and system officials at each stage of the juvenile justice process (Frazier & Cochran, 1986).

After reviewing data gathered from a volunteer services program operated in eight north Florida counties between 1977 and 1980, Frazier and Cochran concluded:

> Diversion status is negatively related to all three measures of the length of intervention. That is, diverted youth are in the system longer than nondiverted youth regardless of whether the measure is total time in the justice system, the time involved in prosecution and subsequent processing, or the total time in the intake stage (Frazier & Cochran, 1986).

Such surprising outcomes were viewed as being the result of a subtle labeling process pervasive within the juvenile justice system. Most of the diversion staff had prior training in counseling or social work that strongly predisposed them towards more intervention in people's lives rather than less. As a consequence, the staff tended to believe more positive outcomes were likely if more attention was given to the youth over a longer period of time.

Increased Effectiveness

Whether diversion is considered effective depends upon the goals of the juvenile justice system and community agencies. Effectiveness is a measure of what an agency achieves, but agency goals are rarely defined or may be so general that they are difficult to measure. Juvenile justice experts and program planners usually list reduction in delinquency and improved treatment for juveniles as primary goals of diversion. While recidivism rates are one measure of the former, the latter is determined by subjective evaluation.

Dean Rojek and Maynard Erickson argue that the claim of many diversion advocates that diversionary treatment of less serious offenders will reduce the potential development of delinquent careers is not well supported (Rojek & Erickson, 1981/1982). In their study of 766 juveniles diverted from the Pima County, Arizona, juvenile court, they observed that while delinquents arrested for property and other crimes showed an escalation into more serious crimes, status offenders (those overwhelmingly referred to diversion programs) demonstrated no pattern of escalation at all. Furthermore, there was little evidence suggesting any significant attitude or behavior change among the juveniles diverted to the various community-based programs.

In an analysis of fifty-five studies of correctional treatment programs for juveniles, Steven Lab and John Whitehead compared nonsystem diversion programs, system diversion programs, probation, parole and other community intervention programs, institutional-residential intervention programs, and Outward Bound and Scared Straight programs in the period between 1975 and 1984. The studies involved a total of eighty-five comparisons between experimental groups and comparison or control groups. Both system and nonsystem diversion programs were found to have more positive effects on reducing future recidivism (Lab & Whitehead, 1988).

In a ten- to twenty-five-year follow-up study of youths referred to two Pennsylvania juvenile courts, Waln Brown and his colleagues examined the effectiveness of early diversion (Brown et al., 1989). Postponement of court adjudication appeared to increase the likelihood of subsequent adult criminal conviction, while early juvenile court adjudication reduced that probability. In both counties, juveniles who spent thirteen months or longer on probation or court placement as a result of their first adjudication were significantly more likely to avoid later adult conviction and incarceration. According to Brown and his associates, "Based upon these findings, it is our belief that the worst thing to do concerning juvenile delinquents is to do nothing" (Brown et al., 1989).

Richard Wiebush believes that intensive probation supervision as a diversion from institutional placement is effective. Wiebush compared eighteen-month offense-related outcomes of three groups of juveniles adjudicated delinquent for felony offenses (Wiebush, 1993). These groups included (1) felony offenders originally sentenced to the Department of Youth Services (DYS) but instead diverted to intensive probation supervision, (2) felony offenders sentenced to DYS but not placed in the intensive supervision program, and (3) felony offenders placed on traditional court-assigned probation. Wiebush observed that there were no significant differences between youths placed on intensive supervision and the other youths in the average number of new offenses or the seriousness of new offenses. According to Wiebush, "These results demonstrate that an intensive supervision program—if properly implemented—poses no greater threat to public safety than does a traditional incarceration/parole strategy" (Wiebush, 1993).

Ensuring Due Process

Diversion programs may or may not be significantly effective in reducing juvenile delinquency. However, there is no question that when youths are diverted into programs prior to formal judicial action, issues of due process arise. According to S. Lee Hinshaw,

Due process problems in diversion programs occur primarily because the juvenile is diverted from the juvenile court before appearing in front of a judge. Diversion was not created to be, and should not be, a method of circumventing the procedures designed to protect a child's constitutional rights (Hinshaw, 1993).

Hinshaw argues that diversion should not be confused with the plea bargaining that occurs in criminal court. Admission of guilt by a youth should not be a requirement for participation in a diversion program. Furthermore, he suggests that if a youth's case is one that would typically have been dismissed, it should be dismissed if the youth refuses to enter a diversion program. Finally, Hinshaw states that juveniles should retain the right to return to court for an adjudicatory hearing at any stage in the diversion process and that there should be no disadvantage to the youth for having tried diversion.

Many youths enter diversion programs prior to formal court hearings, a stage similar to the pretrial proceedings in criminal court. If there is to be any consideration of diversion at this point, the juvenile should have access to an attorney. Although a youth may waive the right to an attorney, Hinshaw believes that "this right should be non-waivable for juveniles under sixteen" (Hinshaw, 1993). This will help ensure that younger juveniles make better-informed decisions about accepting participation in a diversion program.

SUMMARY

The word "diversion" has been applied loosely and sometimes indiscriminately to so many approaches for dealing informally with delinquent youths that it may be futile to try to define in any useful way. Nevertheless, the *principle* of diverting youths from the juvenile justice system is supported by the feeling that (1) traditional strategies for dealing with juvenile offenders have not worked, (2) diversion has been used widely and effectively, and (3) the most humane treatment of troubled youths is based on the *parens patriae* philosophy of justice.

The diversion movement grew in magnitude for nearly 20 years in spite of relatively little scientific data supporting its claims. The enthusiasm engendered by the diversion movement may best be seen in the following statement from Arnold Binder:

> Diversion remains a thriving enterprise in the 1980s—as indeed it must if one assumes that youths in trouble frequently need such services as employment counseling, family counseling, tutoring, substance abuse education, or a relationship with a "big brother or sister" (Binder, 1989).

Clemens Bartollas and Stuart Miller, on the other hand, argue that diversion programs have actually declined in recent years and identify three reasons for their decline. First, most diversion programs depend on federal funding. With the end of LEAA (and its locals-grants program) in the late 1970s, federal funding ceased. Second, by the late 1970s and early 1980s, politicians, as well as the public in general, had become more supportive of get-tough policies, and diversion programs were not viewed as compatible with the new harsher climate. Finally, evaluation studies of diversion projects produced few findings supportive of the claim that diversion was *more* effective than doing nothing. Instead, concern began to grow about how diversion might be widening the net of the juvenile justice system (Bartollas & Miller, 1994).

There are three major criticisms of diversion

1. The concept's ambiguity allows many to promote expansion of the juvenile justice system in the form of diversion to other programs, while true diversion *away from* the system is nonexistent.

2. The goals of diversion programs—such as elimination of stigmatizing labels and formal duplication of existing informal processes—are unattainable.

3. Informal diversion practices are incompatible with due process ideals.

Although in principle diversion should be used to redirect youths who otherwise would be processed through the juvenile justice system, in practice this has often not been the case. Many youths selected for diversion would formerly have been screened out or dismissed after brief contact with police. Also, an important unintended consequence of the diversion movement has been the concept's substantial adoption by police and probation departments. This development is diametrically opposed to the main idea of diversion—that is, to shift cases *away from* the juvenile justice system.

Diversion from juvenile justice processing also raises fundamental issues of fairness: selection for diversion may be arbitrary or biased, procedural rights may be overlooked or ignored, eligibility requirements may violate due process, and long-term effects may hinder the juvenile's return to society. It is important for people in the field of juvenile justice to be aware of the protections needed in diversion and how they can be made available.

Diversion should be evaluated according to its success in reducing recidivism or balancing costs and benefits. But its future more likely will hinge on sociopolitical developments in various branches of the juvenile justice system. What began as an effort to establish alternative methods for handling problem youth became a warrant to increase discretion and extend control to areas where there had been none before. Many see diversion as yet another coercive social control system with low visibility and accountability. If we learn nothing else from the current state of diversion, at least it has given us a better understanding of the extent of the *de facto* power of the police and court officials in the American juvenile justice system.

CASE STUDY WRAP-UP

The Bayview–Hunters Point school program is an important prevention and diversion program for the area. Mayor Willie Brown has hailed it as "one of the finest community service organizations in San Francisco." However, it has its troubles. Ms. Jones wants to expand and improve the facilities, and even though the program has been operating for more than thirty years, she must still rely on community volunteers to do a lot of the work.

This is good to a point, but at some point, the city and county must begin to assume some responsibility for the financial life of a proven program.

Further, bureaucratic red-tape prohibits the school district from turning over the land until the future of a building can be assured. These are all issues that the effective juvenile justice executive can become involved in. Later chapters on planning, decision making and role of the executive help the reader to understand how he or she is a part of community life and has a stake in the continued existence of proven programs outside of the juvenile court or residential unit.

STUDY QUESTIONS

1. How may the use of diversion widen the net of juvenile justice processing?
2. What are the problems police face when referring youths to community service agencies?
3. Why were Youth Service Bureaus described in the text as "extensions of the juvenile justice system"? Explain your answer.
4. What evidence exists to suggest that diversion programs are effective in reducing juvenile recidivism? What findings contradict this evidence?
5. Discuss the available evidence regarding the impact of diversion programs in reducing court caseloads.

BIBLIOGRAPHY

ADLER, CHRISTINE (1984). "Gender Bias in Juvenile Diversion." *Crime and Delinquency*, 30, 400–414.

BARTOLLAS, CLEMENS, AND MILLER, STUART J. (1994). *Juvenile Justice in America*. Upper Saddle River, NJ: Prentice Hall.

BARTON, WILLIAM, AND BUTTS, JEFFERY (1990). "Viable options: Intensive supervision programs for juvenile delinquents." *Crime and Delinquency*, 36: 238–246.

BINDER, ARNOLD, AND GEIS, GILBERT (1984). "*Ad populum* argumentation in criminology." *Crime and Delinquency*, 30, 309–333.

BINDER, ARNOLD (1989). "Juvenile Diversion." In Albert Roberts (Ed.), *Juvenile Justice*. Chicago: Dorsey Press, p. 183

BLOMBERG, THOMAS G. (1984). *Juvenile Court and Community Corrections*. Lanham, MD: University Press of America.

BROWN, WALN, MILLER, TIMOTHY, JENKINS, RICHARD, AND RHODES, WARREN (1989). "The Fallacy of Radical Nonintervention." *International Journal of Offender Therapy and Comparative Criminology*, 33, 177–182.

CHESNEY-LIND, MEDA, AND SHELDEN, RANDALL (1992). *Girls, Delinquency, and Juvenile Justice*. Pacific Grove, CA: Brooks/Cole Publishing Co.

ESBENSEN, FINN-AAGE (1984). "Net Widening? Yes and No: Diversion Impact Assessed through a Systems Processing Rate Analysis." In Scott Decker (Ed.), *Juvenile Justice Policy*. Beverly Hills, CA: Sage Publications, pp. 115–128.

FEDERAL BUREAU OF INVESTIGATION (2002). *Crime in the United States 2001: Uniform Crime Reports*. Washington, DC: U.S. Department of Justice. [online] http://www.fbi.gov/ucr/cius_01/01crime4.pdf.

FERRO, JEFFREY (2003). *Crime: A Serious American Problem*. Detroit, MI: Information Plus® Reference Series, Thomson/Gale.

FRAZIER, CHARLES, RICHARDS, PAMELA, AND POTTER, ROBERTO (1983). "Juvenile Diversion and Net Widening." *Human Organization*, 42, 115–122.

FRAZIER, CHARLES, AND COCHRAN, JOHN (1986). "Official intervention, diversion from juvenile justice system, and dynamics of human services work." *Crime and Delinquency*, 32, 158–159.

FULLER, JOHN, AND NORTON, WILLIAM (1993). "Juvenile diversion: The impact of program philosophy on net widening." *Journal of Crime and Justice*, 16, 29–45.

GIBBONS, DON, AND BLAKE, GERALD (1976). "Evaluating the impact of juvenile diversion programs." *Crime and Delinquency*, 22, 411–420.

HAAPANEN, R., AND RODISILL, D. (1980). *The Evaluation of Youth Service Bureaus*. Sacramento: California Youth Authority.

HINSHAW, S. LEE (1993). "Juvenile diversion: An alternative to juvenile court." *Journal of Dispute Resolution*, 2, 305–321.

KENNEY, JOHN, AND PERSUIT, DAN (1975). *Police Work with Juveniles and the Administration of Justice,* 5th ed. Springfield, IL: Charles C. Thomas.

KLEIN, MALCOLM (1976). "The explosion in police diversion programs." In Malcolm Klein (Ed.), *The Juvenile Justice System*. Beverly Hills, CA: Sage Publications.

KRISBERG, BARRY, SCHWARTZ, IRA, LITSKY, PAUL, AND AUSTIN, JAMES (1986). "The watershed of juvenile justice reform." *Crime and Delinquency*, 32, 5–38.

KRISBERG, BARRY, AND AUSTIN, JAMES F. (1993). *Reinventing Juvenile Justice*. Newbury Park, CA: Sage Publications.

LAB, STEVEN, AND WHITEHEAD, JOHN (1988). "An Analysis of Juvenile Correctional Treatment." *Crime and Delinquency*, 34, 60–83.

LATESSA, EDWARD, TRAVIS, LAWRENCE, AND WILSON, GEORGE (1984). "Juvenile Diversion." In Scott Decker (Ed.), *Juvenile Justice Policy*. Beverly Hills, CA: Sage Publications, pp. 145–165.

LUNDMAN, RICHARD (1984). *Statistics on Delinquents and Delinquency*. Springfield, IL: Charles C. Thomas.

NEJELSKI, PAUL (1976). "Diversion." *Crime and Delinquency*, 22, 393–410.

NORMAN, SHERWOOD (1972). *Youth Service Bureau: A Key to Prevention.* Paramus, NJ: National Council on Crime and Delinquency.

OFFICE OF JUVENILE JUSTICE AND DELINQUENCY PREVENTION (1977). *Federal Juvenile Delinquency Programs.* Washington, DC: U.S. Government Printing Office.

PITCHESS, PETER (1974). "Law enforcement screening for diversion." *California Youth Authority Quarterly*, 27, 49–64.

POGREBIN, MARK, POOLE, ERIC, AND REGOLI, ROBERT (1984). "Constructing and implementing a model juvenile diversion program." *Youth and Society*, 15, 305–324.

POLK, KENNETH (1971). "Delinquency prevention and the youth service bureau." *Criminal Law Bulletin*, 7, 490–511.

POLK, KENNETH (1984). "Juvenile diversion." *Crime and Delinquency,* 30: 648–659.

PRATT, JOHN (1986). "Diversion from the juvenile court." *British Journal of Criminology*, 26, 212–233.

PRESIDENT'S COMMISSION ON LAW ENFORCEMENT AND ADMINISTRATION OF JUSTICE (1967). *Task Force Report: Juvenile Delinquency.* Washington, DC: U.S. Government Printing Office.

REGOLI, ROBERT M., AND HEWITT, JOHN (1997). *Delinquency in Society,* 3rd ed. New York: McGraw-Hill.

ROBERTS, ALBERT (1989a). "Community Strategies with Juvenile Offenders." In Albert Roberts (Ed.), *Juvenile Justice.* Chicago: Dorsey Press, pp. 40–55.

ROBERTS, ALBERT (1989b). "The Emergence and Proliferation of Juvenile Diversion Programs." In Albert Roberts (Ed.), *Juvenile Justice.* Chicago: Dorsey Press. pp. 56–76.

ROBERTS, ALBERT (1989c). "Treating Juveniles in Institutional and Open Settings." In Albert Roberts (Ed.), *Juvenile Justice.* Chicago: Dorsey Press, pp. 21–39.

ROBERTS, ALBERT (1989d). "Wilderness Experience: Camps and Outdoor Programs." In Albert Roberts (Ed.), *Juvenile Justice.* Chicago: Dorsey Press.

ROJEK, DEAN, AND ERICKSON, MAYNARD (1981/1982). "Reforming the Juvenile Justice System." *Law and Society Review*, 16, 241–264.

SARRI, ROSEMARY, AND VINTER, ROBERT (1975). "Juvenile Justice and Injustice." *Resolution*, 18, 45.

SENG, MAGNUS, AND BENSINGER, GAD (1994). "Juvenile Diversion as Agency Policy: A Twenty-year Perspective. *Journal of Offender Rehabilitation*, 21, 65–182.

SHOVER, NEAL, AND EINSTADTER, WERNER (1988). *Analyzing American Corrections.* Belmont, CA: Wadsworth Publishing Company.

STRATTON, JOHN (1975). "Effects of Crisis Intervention Counseling on Predelinquent and Misdemeanor Juvenile Offenders." *Juvenile Justice*, 26, 7–18.

SUNDEEN, RICHARD (1974). "A Four-dimensional Perspective on Police Typologies." *Criminology*, 12, 328–337.

VENEZIA, P. AND ANTHONY, D. (1978). *A Program Level Evaluation of Wisconsin's Youth Service Bureau.* Tucson: Associates for Youth Development.

WHITEHEAD, JOHN, AND LAB, STEVEN (1989). "A Meta-analysis of Juvenile Correctional Treatment." *Journal of Research in Crime and Delinquency*, 26, 276–295.

WIEBUSH, RICHARD (1993). "Juvenile Intensive Supervision: The Impact on Felony Offenders Diverted from Institutional Placement." *Crime and Delinquency*, 39, 68–89.

ZIMRING, FRANKLIN E. (2000). "The Common Thread: Diversion in Juvenile Justice." *California Law Review*, 88(6), 2477–2495.

GLOSSARY OF KEY TERMS

Community youth board.   These agencies are informal hearing boards that determine what, if any, services should be provided to children referred by schools, police, the juvenile court, or by parents of the children themselves.

Diversion.   A process whereby a child is referred to a program (usually external to the official system) for counseling or care of some form in lieu of referral to the juvenile court.

Diversion without referral.   This involves an informal adjustment (for example, warn, counsel, and release), whereby the juvenile is immediately diverted from the system without further significant action.

External referral.   The referral of an at-risk youth to an agency or program outside of the agency.

Internal referral.   The referral of an at-risk youth from one department of the agency, such as the police department, to another department within the agency.

Mediation.   Problems are worked out at meetings attended by the complainant, the respondent (the accused juvenile), and a neutral hearing officer who facilitates communication between the disputants and helps them reach a mutually acceptable resolution.

Net widening.   A process whereby a youth might be diverted just to get the youth involved into the system from which it is then difficult to get out of the system.

Wilderness program.   An outdoor experience designed to develop self pride, confidence, and the ability to work with others. Patterned after the forestry camps of the 1930s and early 1940s.

Youth service bureau.   Begun in the late 1960s, Youth Service Bureaus are designed to mobilize community resources to solve youth problems, strengthen existing youth resources and develop new ones, and promoting positive programs to remedy delinquency-breeding conditions.

CHAPTER 8

COMMUNITY-BASED SANCTIONS AND JUVENILE INSTITUTIONS

KEY TERMS

Juvenile detention
Deinstitutionalization
Boot camps
Group homes
Day reporting centers
Reception and diagnostic
  centers

Training schools
Aversion therapy
Token economy systems
Behavioral modification
Cognitive therapy

Group therapy
Guided group interaction
Reality therapy
Therapeutic communities/
  milieu therapy

CASE STUDY

Gibault School for Boys: A Chance for a New Life
James M. Sinclair, M.S.S.W., J.D.*

Managing a residential school for delinquent boys is difficult, but quite rewarding, and without the assistance of dedicated staff, it would be impossible. The Gibault School for Boys has always had a sound reputation as a well-managed, effective school for delinquent boys. Gibault was founded in 1921 by the Indiana Knights of Columbus as a "refuge for wayward boys," and since that time, the school has undergone many changes and continues to change with the times. The main campus in Terre Haute, Indiana, occupies 60 of the original 347 acres of farm, woodland, streams, and ponds and is located three miles south of the city Terre Haute, Indiana. Our residential capacity is 147, and

*James M. Sinclair, M.S.S.W., J.D. is the Executive Director/CEO of Gibault School for Boys, Terre Haute, Indiana, and is responsible for the total operation of the school and its programs.

Gibault is licensed by the State of Indiana and accredited by the Council on Accreditation (COA). Today, we serve children between the ages of eight and seventeen—male and female—from all over the state of Indiana and the Midwest. Since our founding, we have served more than 7,500 children and adolescents. Our clients come to Gibault through the Indiana Division of Family & Children, the juvenile courts, Department of Education, other childcare agencies, the Department of Correction, and private placements. Gibault's residential programs consist of long-term, on-site programs designed to fit the specific needs of the individuals we serve.

The Main Campus program consists of Children's and Adolescent's Residential Environment (CARE). One of the living units within CARE specializes in Adventure-Based Programming, and another addresses chemical dependency issues. The Residential Program also includes the Intensive Sexual Intervention Systems (ISIS), and the Intervention System for Sexually Abusive Children (ISSAC). The treatment is based on life skills and making the right choices.

Gibault is accredited by the Indiana Department of Education through Performance-Based Accreditation and the North Central Association of Colleges and Schools. The on-grounds school operates a year-round education program for students in grades one through twelve. Students are placed into classes based on their ability and educational need rather than age or grade. Classes include math, reading/literature, science, history, language arts/English, computers, developmental physical education, and industrial technology.

Gibault awards high school diplomas to students who meet all credit requirements from the Indiana Department of Education. The diploma is issued from our on-grounds Holy Cross High School. Parents and agencies are invited to attend the graduation ceremony. Gibault also offers the General Educational Development (GED) Program. Additional academic opportunities include public school enrollment within the Vigo County School System, enrollment at IVY TECH State College or Indiana State University and college correspondence course work.

The Recreation Program at Gibault offers a variety of activities and special events. The clients can participate in an active, well-organized intramural program campus-wide. Emphasis is placed on sportsmanship and helping each client experience success in sports and recreational, leisure-time activities. Gibault is a member of the Indiana High School Athletic Association.

Gibault also offers a Transitional Living Program and an Independent Living Program. The Transitional Living Program transitions a client from a rigorously structured residential setting back to the home and community environments. The Independent Living Program serves two groups of clients. The first group generally lives on-campus and in our own group home in Terre Haute before moving into an apartment. Members of the second group are at least fourteen years of age and need independent living skills to benefit them when returning to their families after discharge.

Whenever possible, Gibault works closely with each client's family. Our therapists hold at minimum a masters's degree in social work, counseling, or psychological services, and services to families include family therapy, transportation for home visits/passes, regular parenting skills classes, an array of visitation opportunities. At Gibault, our child and adolescent psychiatrist, clinical psychologist, and licensed (or license eligible) therapists provide clinical services within our residential programming. Typically, therapists hold master's degrees in the fields of clinical social work, mental health counseling, and/or marriage and family therapy.

Each client's therapist participates in a weekly clinical staffing with the clinical psychologist and other therapists on the team. The staffing provides opportunities for the exchange of therapeutic strategies, diagnostic updates, and treatment plan revisions. Group therapy is specific to a particular problem such as anger management/conflict resolution, sexual abuse, physical abuse, or chemical dependency. In group therapy, clients learn the skills necessary to support and confront one another in the group setting as efforts are made to change self-defeating patterns of thoughts, feelings, and behavior.

Gibault offers aftercare services to ensure that each client who leaves Gibault has a plan to allow a successful transition back into the community. Gibault's Aftercare program starts while the client is still in placement. The aftercare coordinator uses information gained from working directly with the client, therapist, case manager, placing agency, and parents to determine what services will be needed in the home community upon discharge. Gibault has outreach offices in Gary and Evansville, Indiana, and Terre Haute, Indiana.

INTRODUCTION

What happens to a youth once he or she has been adjudicated delinquent? Our response to juveniles has been evolving over the past four hundred years. We have advanced from a society that once did not recognize the existence of children as a separate person in need of protection, to a society that believed they were in need of full protection. In today's society, we continue to recognize the concept of childhood, but we are debating the age at which youths are responsible for their own actions. This shift reflects ever-changing community and societal values ranging from our desire to rehabilitate to our desire to punish wrongdoers.

This chapter provides a brief overview of community-based corrections for juveniles and the evolution of the juvenile institutional system. A discussion of the modern short-term versus long-term confinement options follows. In addition, a brief discussion on the role of correctional officers in a juvenile correctional setting, as well as the inmate's response to the setting will follow. We conclude the chapter with a brief overview of different types of treatment options available in the juvenile institutional setting.

PROBATION AS AN ALTERNATIVE TO INCARCERATION

As previously mentioned, probation is a community-based sanction that allows the juvenile to remain in the community. While in the community, the youth is supervised by a probation officer and ordered to follow a variety of different rules or requirements put forth by the court and the probation staff. These requirements may be general (standard), such as do not commit any additional status or delinquent offenses, or they may be specific to the offender such as "drug counseling, weekend confinement in the local detention center, or restitution to the community or victim" (Sickmund, 2003, p. 4). The term of probation can vary from a specified amount of time to an open-ended sentence dictated by the upper-level age limit of disposition determined by the state. Periodic review hearings are typically held with the judge to determine whether youths are successfully completing the terms of their probation. The frequency of the hearings will be determined by the judge working in conjunction with the probation officer and the prosecutor. These hearings will continue until the youth is released (terminated) from probation (Sickmund, 2003).

Probation is the most severe sanction given in approximately one-third of all juvenile cases (38 percent). In 1998, for example, 1.8 million youths were arrested, and of those, 665,500 were placed on some form of probation. Furthermore, of those youths who were adjudicated delinquent more than half (55 percent or 366,100) were placed on formal probation. The remaining 45 percent were placed on informal probation. Property offenses made up the majority of the offender caseload (45 percent property; 23 percent person; 12 percent drug offense; 21 percent public order offenses) (Black, 2001).

One of the ongoing debates in the present-day probation system is what the purpose or the focus of the probation department should be. Should it be as originally intended—treatment- or rehabilitation-focused—or should the focus shift to a more punitive or custody orientation? Despite the conflict that may arise amongst staff, the underlying philosophy of *parens patriae* and rehabilitation still exists. As the following discussion will show, many of our recent innovations, such as house arrest or electronic monitoring, have been punitive in nature.

As stated previously, probation is an alternative that allows for the supervision of an offender in the community. Juvenile probation, however, allows for a variety of different levels of supervision. These levels include informal adjustments, informal probation, formal probation, and intensive supervision probation. Each of these will be discussed.

The informal adjustment is typically given by the intake officer to a child who has committed a less serious or status offense (Bartollas & Miller, 1998). In these cases, the intake or probation officer may choose to just warn the child and release him or her; the officer may refer or divert the child to another social service agency (see Chapter 7 for a more in-depth discussion on juvenile diversion); or the officer enters into an informal agreement with the youth, such as requiring the youth to pay restitution and the case is never processed through the system. In this instance, because there is typically no official paperwork filed on the youth, rather there may be a chart or form maintained by the probation staff, the intake officer will file a petition with the court, and the youth will be formally processed. At this point, the judge may decide to either adjudicate the youth a delinquent or status offender or the may again place the youth on a more organized form of informal probation. In either case, the youth will appear in front of the judge and a determination or adjustment will be made.

Informal probation refers to the supervision of the court without a formal determination of guilt (Clear & Dammer, 2003; Bartollas & Miller, 1998). Although the child appears in front of the judge, the child is not adjudicated delinquent. While in the community, the youth is given a set of requirements he or she must adhere to. Like formal probation, these requirements typically include a curfew, staying away from or not associating with other known delinquents or criminals, attending school, and other rules specific to the youth. The length of time spent under supervision will differ by the youth and the offense the youth committed. The advantage to using informal probation is if the juvenile completes all of the requirements, when the youth is released from supervision his or her case will be removed from official record. If the juvenile fails to complete the requirements, the judge will revoke the agreement and a petition is filed. The youth is then formally processed through the system and adjudicated a delinquent or status offender. There is some evidence to suggest that in these cases where the youth is given an opportunity to reform but fails to respond, the judge is harsher in his or her disposition.

Formal probation resembles the adult system. Once youth are adjudicated delinquent, they may be placed on formal probation. Typically formal probation is given in conjunction with a suspended disposition. The suspended disposition is when juveniles receive a sentence of institutionalization, but that sentence is suspended as long as the conditions put forth during formal probation are met. Should these conditions not be met, the suspension will be revoked and youth will be sent to a formal institution where they will serve either their entire original disposition or the remainder of the original disposition. As previously mentioned, a set of formal requirements are established by the youth and the probation officer. Most of the requirements are standard, but some may be created to address the specific needs of the youth. These needs will be determined by the present offense, past history, and the information collected during the formation of the social history. The social history is an extensive and hopefully exhaustive assessment of the youths' home life, academic attainment, peers, mental health status, and skills.

The differences between adult and juvenile probation are very subtle. Juvenile probation officers are much more inclined to develop relationships with the youth. In addition, the family is much more likely to be involved in any rehabilitation efforts. In some instances, the judges disposition will require both the juvenile and his or her immediate family members to attend counseling or treatment. As Clear and Dammer (2003) point out adults and juvenile offenders sentenced in the community differ in five important ways:

1. Juveniles are young and may easily change.
2. Juveniles have a high rate of desistance from crime.
3. Juveniles' families are an important part of their lives.
4. Juveniles are easily influenced by their peers.
5. Juveniles have little responsibility for anyone other than themselves (Clear & Dammer, 2003, p. 430).

The most frequently used dispositions are restitution and intensive supervision probation. Restitution is the monetary repayment of losses incurred by the offense (Clear & Dammer, 2003; Bartollas & Miller, 1998). Intensive supervision probation programs include the use of increased contacts and controls over the youths while in the communities

(Palmer, 1992). Development of these programs began in the 1980s as a way to reduce overcrowding in institutions but yet maintaining a high level of supervision over the youths while in the community.

Intensive supervision programs may be used in conjunction with house arrest and electronic monitoring. House arrest or home confinement is an alternative that requires the youth to remain in the home except for attending school or other preapproved functions such as doctor's visits or work (Ball, Huff, & Lilly, 1988). Electronic monitoring may be used in conjunction with house arrest (Petersilia & Turner, 1993). This option requires the youth to wear an ankle or wrist bracelet that monitors their movement in and out of their home. These devices send a signal to a computer box, which is located in the youth's residence. If that signal is broken, the computer device contacts a central location and the police or probation staff are then notified that the youth has more than likely left the residence. A supervisory probation officer typically responds to these calls to see whether the youth has violated the conditions of probation (Ball, Huff, & Lilly, 1988). If it is determined the youth has violated the conditions, the probation officer may choose to reprimand the youth or to begin revocation proceedings where the youth may ultimately be found in contempt of court and sent to a confined institution. As we will see in Chapter 11, electronic monitoring incorporates elements of behavior modification to improve and alter the juvenile's behavior.

Electronic monitoring has been criticized for a variety of reasons. One of the largest criticisms is that the electronic monitoring system discriminates against the poor. To be eligible for the system, youths must not only have a permanent residence, but they must also have access to a telephone. If they do not have either of these then they will not be eligible. The devices have also been criticized because they sometimes fail to work or the response time between the recording agency and the probation staff is sometimes lengthy extending as long as one hour. In addition, although difficult, the devices may be removed by youth (Clear & Dammer, 2003).

As one can see, these community-based alternatives are a very viable option to institutionalization. Although we are continuing to use more punitive measures in our sentencing dispositions, these options are treatment-oriented by nature.

SHORT-TERM CONFINEMENT

Short-term confinement refers to the detention or housing of a youth for a short (usually no more than twelve months) period of time. These facilities can be divided into two different types of holding facilities: pre-adjudication and post-adjudication. The following section of this chapter reviews both pre-and post-adjudication strategies.

Pre-adjudication Short-term Confinement

When juveniles are taken into custody by the police (arrested), three options are typically available to law enforcement officers: lock-up, jail, or detention facilities. The following section will discuss each of the different options.

Lock-up Facilities

Lock-up functions as a short-term holding facility for youth (usually no more than six hours). Lock-ups are typically found at the local police department. They are ordinarily used as a holding facility where youth will wait for their parents or guardians to take custody (Wordes & Jones, 1998; Howell, 1998).

Jails

Jails are typically used for adults. However, in some areas, usually rural communities, law enforcement officers have no other options but to hold youths in an adult jail facility for a short period of time, usually until detention bed space is available in a detention facility. Youth may also be held in jails when they have committed a very serious offense that carries an automatic waiver to an adult court system. Because jails were designed as holding facilities for adults awaiting court appearance, there are usually no services offered in the facility.

Our first efforts to address the needs of juveniles in confinement can be traced back to the early 1960s. In 1961, California created a special category in their criminal code for status offenders. In 1962, New York created a new "family court act that separated delinquents from 'persons in need of supervision' (PINS)." Other states such as Florida, Ohio, Georgia, and Colorado created new statutory provisions, while other states such as Pennsylvania, Iowa, and Indiana moved status offense violations to the dependency section of their legal codes (Maxson & Klein, 1997, p. 26).

In 1966, the President's Commission on Law Enforcement and the Administration of Justice commissioned a survey of state and local correctional facilities in the United States. This study assessed the number of juveniles in juvenile detention and correctional facilities. Results from the 1967 study found that nearly 325,000 youths were admitted to **juvenile detention** facilities. This study further indicated that 93 percent of all juvenile court jurisdictions do not have a specific juvenile detention facility. Rather the majority of youth being detained were held in either a local jail or police lock-up. More disturbing findings from this study suggested that juveniles were not being well-supervised. They were falling victim to a variety of atrocities such as sexual assaults, suicides, and even murders (Howell, 1998; Parent et al., 1994). These findings led to the creation of the Juvenile Justice and Delinquency Prevention Act of 1974. This mandate focused primarily on the prevention of delinquency rather than punishment and the **deinstitutionalization** of youth (Holden & Kapler, 1995).

There were four primary findings or areas that were mandated to the states. First, states receiving federal funds were to deinstitutionalize status offenders from adult lock-up. Remember status offenders are youth who have committed crimes that if committed by an adult would not be considered illegal. These violations include offenses such as running away, truancy, or incorrigibility. They were originally given two years to meet this mandate. A 1980 mandate, allowed states an exception to this ruling. Juveniles who were found in violation of a status offense and placed under the court's supervision but failed to meet the requirements of a valid court order (VCO) could be found in contempt of court. This provision allowed judges to adjudicate the status offender as delinquent, which allowed them to confine the status offender in secure detention for a short period of time (Holden & Kapler, 1995). So for example, if a youth is failing to attend school and is found truant, the youth is by definition a status offender. A typical VCO would be to order the youth to attend school. If following the order the youth still fails to attend school, the judge could then adjudicate the youth delinquent for contempt of court and detain him or her where the youth would be required to attend school in the institutional setting. This is not an uncommon practice in areas where bed space is available.

Second, states were required to completely separate juveniles from adult offenders. Therefore, juveniles were to be kept out of complete sight and sound of adult offenders. This included sleeping quarters, educational and recreational facilities, booking areas, dining facilities, and health care areas (Howell, 1998; Holden & Kapler, 1995). Because of the design and structure of most local jails, this mandate was almost a near impossibility, therefore, causing many jurisdictions to be in violation of the JJDP Act.

The third mandate was given in 1980, five years after the initial passage of the JJDPA. This addendum to the original mandate called for the complete removal of juveniles from adult jails and institutions. This modification called for complete separation of juveniles from adult offenders in areas such as police lockups or any holding facilities where both juveniles and adults might be (Howell, 1998). Many state, county, and local jurisdictions found themselves in noncompliance because of the constraints of both not having a separate facility and not having the monetary support to create a separate facility. In some instances, police and probation officers would resort to detaining youth in separate offices in the probation department or other areas of the court house so that they would not be in violation of the JJDP Act.

The final amendment to the original JJDP Act was made in 1988. At this time, through further statistical analysis, courts began to recognize there was a disproportionate number of minority youth detained in both detention and institutions. Therefore, the Act called for assurances that states would seek to minimize the overrepresentation of minority youth in the system (Howell, 1998).

Although this particular legislation is a move in the right direction to alleviate the burdens caused by detaining youth with adult populations, many states are still not in full compliance. For example, mid-year 2001, there were 7,613 juveniles under the age of eighteen held in local jails. Of those 89 percent (6,757) were held as adults or those who were either convicted of or those awaiting trial for an adult offense. This suggests that 11 percent of those juveniles held in adult jails are there for juvenile offenses. Trends from the past ten years reveal that the number of youths detained in an adult jail have decreased from 2,301 mid-year 1990 to 856 mid-year 2001 (a 37.2 percent decrease) (Beck, Karberg, & Harrison, 2002, p. 9). These figures suggest that although 11 percent of all youth being held in adult jails are there for juvenile offenses, there is still an effort being made to meet the guidelines established by the JJDPA of 1974 and amended in 1980 and 1988. These figures also reflect efforts by the states to use legislation to ensure juveniles are kept out of adult jails. For example, states such as California and Utah have made it unlawful to jail a juvenile (Bartollas & Miller, 1998, pp. 316–317; Schwartz, Harris & Levi, 1988; Steinhart, 1988), while states such as Illinois, Missouri, North Carolina, Tennessee, and Virginia have enacted legislation either prohibiting the jailing of juveniles or restricting the number of admissions (Bartollas & Miller, 1998, p. 317; Steinhart & Kris-berg, 1987).

Juvenile Detention

Juvenile detention facilities were designed to specifically house juvenile offenders await-ing their court appearance. Detained youth are supposed to be given detention hearings within one or two days of being taken into custody. As Wordes and Jones (1998) point out, detention generally only has two purposes: "to ensure a youth appears for all court hear-ings and to prevent a youth from reoffending prior to disposition" (p. 546). Detention may also be used to ensure the youths' and the communities' safety as well as to evaluate youths (Puzzanchera, et al., 2003). Although detention is supposed to be used primarily as a holding facility, research reveals detention facilities suffer from a variety of problems such as extreme forms of overcrowding, misuse of confinement, and geographic disparity (Barton & Schwartz, 1994, pp. 1–3).

The number of youth detained in these facilities continues to increase, yet the num-bers of available bed space does not. For example, in 1997 there were 327,700 youths de-tained for delinquent offenses. The number of youths detained increased 25 percent between 1988 and 1998 (see Table 8.1). "Person cases had the largest percent increase in the number of detained cases (63 percent), followed by drug cases (55 percent) and public order cases (44 percent). In contrast, the number of detained property cases declined 6 percent" (Puzzanchera et al., 2003, p. 22).

Over one-third (36 percent) of all delinquents are detained for a property offense, while just over one-fourth (27 percent) are detained for a person offense, 13 percent are detained for a drug offense, while almost one-fourth (24 percent) are detained for a public order offense (Puzzanchera, 2003, p. 8). In 1997, the majority of all status offenders de-tained were detained for running away (40 percent), while 22 percent were detained for

Table 8.1   Offense Profile of Detained Delinquency Cases

Most Serious Offense	1989	1994	1998
Person	21%	27%	27%
Property	48	42	36
Drugs	11	10	13
Public Order	21	21	24
Total	100%	100%	100%
Number of Cases	261,500	308,000	327,700

Note: Detail may not total 100% because of rounding.

Taken from: Puzzanchera, Charles, Stahl, Anne L., Finnegan, Terrence A., Tierney, Nancy, and Snyder, Howard, N. (2003). *Juvenile Court Statistics 1998.* Washington, DC: Office of Juvenile Justice and Delinquency Prevention.

incorrigibility, 9 percent for truancy, 8 percent for underage drinking, 6 percent for curfew violation, and 15 percent for other status offenses (Snyder & Sickmund, 1999, p. 207).

In today's system, there are a variety of issues that continue to confront not only the need for juvenile detention facilities but also the appropriateness of confining youth. Several studies have been conducted assessing the issues of overcrowding, inadequate staffing, and poorly managed and antiquated facilities. Results from these studies suggest these inadequacies are primarily driven by policies ranging from intake to judicial decision-making (Schwartz, 1994; for an overview of the studies see Schwartz & Barton, 1994). Overall, findings from these studies indicate that there needs to be some serious attention paid to intake criteria. For example, are there other less restrictive alternatives that could be used for youth. One example can be found in the state of Colorado where attention facilities were created versus detention facilities. These facilities were designed with the intent of offering youth attention to their problems rather than focusing reactively on what they had already and responding accordingly (Bartollas & Miller, 1998). Other recommendations include creating objective detention criteria so all actors in the system, such as police and intake officers, understand who should be detained and who may be released on their own recognizance or into the custody of their parents (Schwartz, 1994).

Post-adjudication Short-term Confinement

The juvenile justice system provides short-term post-adjudication options for the juvenile court system. These options include boot camps, group homes, and day reporting centers. Each of these options will be discussed below.

Boot Camps

One short-term confinement alternative to the use of incarceration is a boot camp. **Boot camps** are a military-style intermediate sanction used to both punish and rehabilitate offenders who have violated the law. Recall intermediate sanctions are those alternatives that exist somewhere between prison and probation. The use of a military-style boot camp to address the institutional needs of the juvenile justice system is a relatively new phenomenon. Dispositional boot camps became popular during the early 1990s. Originally designed for use with young adult offenders, the use of boot camps for juveniles was created in an effort to reduce overcrowding, which ultimately reduces costs, and rehabilitate offenders. Using a paramilitary style, the purpose of the boot camp will differ by state and program, but the basic ideology and routine of the facility is similar. A drill instructor is in charge of administering the program. Juveniles are put through a rigorous, regimented physical program. Punishment typically includes having to do pushups (MacKenzie et al., 2001). The Office of Justice Programs 1995 has indicated that the following definitions should be used for the development of any boot camp program:

- Participation by nonviolent offenders only.
- A residential phase of 6 months or less.
- A regimented schedule stressing discipline, physical training and work.

- Participation by inmates in appropriate education opportunities, job training, and substance abuse counseling or treatment.
- Provision of aftercare services that are coordinated with the program that is provided during the period of confinement (Peters, Thomas, Zamberlan, & Caliber Associates, 1997, p. 3).

The program guidelines also recommend that the following components should be used to maximize the effectiveness of boot camps:

- Education and job training and placement.
- Community service.
- Substance abuse counseling and treatment.
- Health and mental health care.
- Continuous, individualized case management.
- Intensive aftercare services that are fully integrated with the boot camp program (Peters et al., 1997, p. 3).

The purpose of the boot camps will vary not only by state but also by jurisdiction. Therefore, the goals emphasized will vary as well. There are typically five goals commonly expressed:

- Deterrence—to discourage or stop by fear; anything that impedes or has a tendency to prevent.
- Incapacitation—to make legally incapable or ineligible; disable.
- Rehabilitation—restoring person to a former capacity; reinstating.
- Punishment—any fine, penalty, or confinement inflicted upon a person by the authority of the law and the judgment and sentence of a court, for some crime or offense committed by him or her. A deprivation of property or some right.
- Cost control—keeping the operating cost low (Zaehringer, 1998, p. 2).

Most juvenile boot camps attempt to incorporate some form of rehabilitation into the boot camp process. Rehabilitation can include a variety of things such as altering the offenders' attitude or changing their behavior (Peters et al., 1997). The issue of cost control is a major one for most juvenile boot camps. A 2000 study conducted by the Koch Crime Institute, they reported that there was at least one boot camp for juveniles currently in operation in twenty-one states (see Table 8.2 for a complete listing of states with boot camps and a summary of the program selection criteria).

The majority of these boot camps were designed for male offenders, ages fourteen to seventeen, who had committed nonviolent offenses. The average reported costs were approximately $87.00. The range however, was from a reported low of $20.00 in one nonresidential program in Florida to a high of $134.25 per day for a residential program in New York. Overall, six states reported costs of over $100 per day, five reported costs be-

Figure 8.1 Boot camps are designed to be short-term alternatives to incarceration. Cadets are confronted with their shortcomings and self-destructive behavior within a physically and emotionally challenging environment.
Corbis/Bettmann

tween $90 to $99 per day; two reported costs between $80 to $89 per day; four reported $70 to $79; two reported $50 to $59; two reported $30 to $39 per day, while only one reported costs being around $20 per day (Koch Crime Institute, 2000). This suggests that the costs vary widely by state and by program. Although the cost to per day to house a juvenile in a boot camp seems high, on average the cost is approximately $14,000 less per year than housing them in a state residential facility. Primarily the cost savings come from the decreased amount of time youths spend in the program versus the amount of time they spend in an institution (Zaehringer, 1998).

Pros of the Boot Camp Alternative.   There are a variety of pros and cons to maintaining a boot camp program. Proponents of boot camp programs suggest the atmosphere is more positive and conducive to change than a traditional institutionalized setting. Because the programs are short-term in nature, youth are less apt to experience the deleterious effects, such as being victimized, of institutionalization that they may experience by being incarcerated for long periods of time. Proponents further argue the military structure helps to build character and foster camaraderie among program participants (MacKenzie et al., 2001). Some states have begun to utilize the concept of a boot camp in conjunction with the local school system. For example, as Trulson, Triplett, and Snell

Table 8.2 Juvenile Boot Camps by State*

State	No. Boot Camps	Type of Program	Sex	Age	Program Duration	Program Aftercare Duration
Alabama	1	Residential	M	12–18	13 weeks	9 months
Arizona	1 (closed)	Residential	M/F	14–17	1 year (4 months secure, 8 mo. aftercare)	8 months
California	1	Residential	M/F	14+	365 days	7–7.5 months
Colorado	1	Residential	Varies by judicial district	Varies by judicial district	60 days	avg. 90 days
Florida	8	6 Residential (R) 2 Non-Residential (NR)	M/F	14–18 (R) 10–16 (N.R.) 14–17 (NR)	4 mo. boot camp/ 4 mo. transition (R) 22 hours 2 Saturdays (NR) 1 year (NR)	4 months
Georgia	1 open 5 closed	Residential	M	Juveniles	90 days	N/A
Illinois	1	Residential	M	13–19	6 months	6–12 months
Indiana	1	Residential	M	13–17	120 days	Determined by parole services
Kansas	1	Residential	M/F	Juveniles	6 months	Provided by community corrections until released by probation
Kentucky	1	Residential	M/F	14–17	4 months residential, 4 months intensive aftercare	4 months
Louisiana	1	Residential	M	15+	90–120 days	Varies

State	Number	Type	Gender	Age / Selection	Duration	Aftercare
Maryland	2 (closed)					
Michigan	1		M	15–18	18 weeks	4–6 months
Minnesota	1 (closed)					
New Jersey	1	Residential	M/F	13+	6 months	Varies according to length of sentence
New York	1	Residential	M/F	Juveniles	6 months	6 months
North Carolina	2	Residential	M/F	1 designated for 16–30; other open	90–120 days / 81–120 days	15 months / 18 months
Oklahoma	1	Residential	M/F	Level I through L	90 days	Varies
Oregon	1	Residential	M/F	Youth Offenders	4 months	8 months
Pennsylvania	1	Residential	M/F	Juveniles	15 weeks	Varies
South Dakota	1	Residential	M	14–18	120 days	6–12 months
Texas	5 open / 2 closed	All Residential	Court referred / Males	Court referred / 15–17 / 13–17 / Type B violent offenders / Youth	2–12 months / N/A / N/A / 6 months / 9–12 months / 9 months–2+ years	No aftercare / N/A / N/A / 3 months at Halfway House / No aftercare
Virginia	2	Residential	M/F	14–18 / Youth	5 months	6 months
Washington	1		M/F	12–19	120 days / 120 days	6 months / At least 12 weeks or maximum sentence

Information taken from Koch Crime Institute (2000, March). *Juvenile Boot Camps and Military Structured Youth Programs.* Topeka, KS: Koch Crime Institute.

*See the Koch Crime Institute report for a more in-depth discussion of the program selection criteria as well as date program established and costs per day per youth. This table just presents a summary overview of the criteria. For example, many states restrict program participation to type of offense committed as well as sex and age.

(2001) point out, the Texas Department of Corrections has formed a partnership with the local school system for referring youth who have demonstrated disruptive behavior on school campuses. This alternative places youth in a regimented program that incorporates an educational approach. Although this is an innovative approach to handling troubled youth, research comparing recidivism rates of youth referred to an intensive supervision probation program suggests the recidivism rates for ISP participants are lower than for boot camp participants. This study also looked at program participants perceptions of the program and found they believed because of the program they were less likely to get into trouble. This study was a preliminary assessment of the program. Although it did not indicate there was a demonstrable reduction in recidivism by program participants, it did suggest there was a need for continued review and program implementation (Trulson, Triplett, & Snell, 2001).

Cons of the Boot Camp Alternative. Critics of boot camps, however, argue that the confrontational environment is counterproductive to developing interpersonal relationships and building self-esteem in participants (MacKenzie et al., 2001). Others suggest that for boot camps to work they must include a number of offenders. Therefore, a possibility of widening the net to include offenders that otherwise might not have been referred to a confined setting is a realistic possibility (Beyer, 1996). Furthermore, research assessing the effectiveness of boot camps has not demonstrated that boot camps are any more effective in reducing recidivism than traditional institutionalization (Beyer, 1996; MacKenzie et al., 2001; MacKenzie, 1997).

Although juvenile boot camps have been in existence for a decade, very few rigorous assessments of these alternatives have been conducted. The most notable assessment was sponsored by the National Institute of Justice in conjunction with the Office of Juvenile Justice and Delinquency Prevention. These government agencies sponsored an evaluation of three boot camps. Preliminary results from this study suggested that programs incorporating an educational component to the boot camp substantially increased the academic skills of participants. However, there was no way to measure whether these gains were sustained over time. One of the primary goals of any boot camp is to reduce the rate of recidivism for program participants. In two of the sites, findings suggested there was no discernible difference between the control group (youth sentence to the youth department of corrections) and the treatment group (boot camp participants). One study, however, reported that the recidivism rates for boot camp participants were significantly higher than the control group (Peters et al., 1997). These findings suggest that the use of boot camps may be a promising alternative for institutionalized youth, particularly for states wanting to reduce the costs of incarceration. States and programs must continually be aware of issues of net-widening, recidivism, and therapeutic program integrity.

Group Homes

Group homes fall under the umbrella of residential treatment. Although group homes maintain a low level of supervision, residents are still supervised in the community. These facilities may be either publicly or privately ran. **Group homes** are short-term facilities designed to house or detain a small number of youths (typically four to twelve) in a homelike setting. Residents of the group home may include both males and females. They are typically between the ages of thirteen to eighteen (or the state's designated age of majority). Group homes allow the youth to remain in the community, attend school, and therapy sessions (Abadinsky, 2000). There is a concerted effort to maintain some type of control by the juvenile justice system but at the same time allowing the youth an opportunity to participate in community activities and maintain many of the more positive community ties. The facility is typically ran by house parents or counselors. These individuals typically live in the home with the residents. While in the home, they serve as role models to the residents. They may lead group therapy or be responsible for transporting youth to a variety of different treatment programs. For larger programs, there is a small staff who also serve as role models for those living in the home.

Group homes are typically used for youth who fall under one of the following:

- Are in unresolvable conflict with their parents but are not seriously disturbed or psychotic.
- Have inadequate homes and need to develop skills for independent living.
- Need to deal with community social adjustment problems in a therapeutic family environment.
- Need to deal with individual adjustment problems, and to learn about themselves in relation to others.
- Need to develop self-confidence through successful experiences. (Abadinsky, 2000, p. 67)

Group homes are generally treatment-oriented. These programs require youth to participate in group therapy sessions, as well as participate in the community. Many of these programs incorporate the use of behavioral modification techniques to modify behavior. Oftentimes these programs include the use of token economy systems in which points are earned for good (positive) behavior and removed for bad (negative) behavior (Kivett & Warren, 2002). Earned points may be used for a variety of privileges such as extra "talk time" on the telephone, choosing the television program to be viewed by the house for an evening, or even earning extra visitation privileges. For those who lose their points they may be asked to do extra chores or maintenance activities within the house. They may also lose home visitation privileges. If their behavior is to disruptive or extreme, they may be asked to leave the home altogether.

One of the more famous examples of a group home is the Silverlake Experiment. In this experiment, the group home was housed in a residential community of Los Angeles. Residents of the group home were a combination of white, black, and Hispanic males, typically from lower-income communities. The group home itself was located in a predominantly white, middle-class community. "While in the home the youth participated in daily guided-group interaction programs, attended the local high school, performed routine maintenance and housekeeping tasks, and went home on weekends. Residents stayed on average less than six days per week" (Lundman, 2001, pp. 221–222). One important element of not only the Silverlake Experiment but the group home model in general is the linkage to community intervention. Research assessing the effectiveness of the Silverlake Experiment suggested there were a variety of issues confronting the youth. One of the primary issues was a lack of acceptance of the local high school. Evidence suggests that the principal and other members the local high school made the Silverlake residents' time at the school miserable. Truancy rules were more strictly enforced for Silverlake youth. Teachers and staff members complained of the overall appearance and attitude of the residents. Overall, the youths' experiences were not positive. The external pressures from the community resulted in Silverlake being much more punitive in nature than they had originally intended. For example, youth who ran away from the home only once were dropped from the program and recommended for incarceration. In spite of all of this, the residents still went to school (Lundman, 2001, pp. 222–224).

To assess the effectiveness of the Silverlake program, recidivism rates were compared to a control group of youth attending the high school. Results from this study suggested there were no significant differences between the two groups. The control group committed as many offenses as the Silverlake residents (Lundman, 2001, p. 224).

Overall, group homes appear to be a viable alternative, especially for youth who have committed less serious or status offenses. In this instance, group homes allow youth to remain in the community, attend their local school, and receive needed and oftentimes necessary treatment. Group homes are an example of collaborative community efforts to provide youth with rehabilitation, and maintain community safety.

Day Reporting Centers

Day reporting centers (also known as day treatment centers) are another example of an alternative to incarceration that is being used in today's criminal justice system. This option is a more recent correctional innovation and is oftentimes used in conjunction with other alternatives, such as probation and electronic monitoring. **Day reporting centers** are another form of an intermediate sanction. Unlike other options discussed previously, day reporting centers are nonresidential facilities meaning program participants appear at a specific location on a regular basis. Participants are allowed to return home for the evening. While at the facility, offenders participate in a variety of treatment options, including but not limited to group or individual therapies, educational attainment, employment searches, or other tasks that may be identified in the youths' risk or needs assessment. Furthermore, depending upon the adjudication, youths may be asked to participate in other arranged activities such as drug screening, community service, or restitution activities (Abadinsky, 2000; MacKenzie, 1997).

Day treatment programs may be used both as an adjudicatory sanction and as an aftercare program. For example, the Bethesda Day Treatment Center in Pennsylvania provides treatment for both pre-adjudicated and adjudicated youth. This nonresidential option provides up to fifty-five hours of services per week to youth. These services include both school and after-school programs. The average length of stay in the program is six months but can be as long as twelve months. An assessment of the effectiveness at reducing recidivism rates of program participants found that only 5 percent of those who completed the program recidivated within the first year. This finding should be viewed with caution however, because the sample size was very small ($n = 20$) (Krisberg, Currie, Onek, & Wiebush, 1995, p. 154).

Although the use of day reporting centers has grown exponentially over the past ten years, there still have been no extensive impact evaluations conducted assessing the effectiveness of these programs. The continued use of day reporting centers further raises the question of whether their mere existence widens the net of supervision. Since in many of the programs youth may be referred pre-adjudication for issues related to their educational attainment courts and communities must be careful not to sentence youth to this option particularly if the alternative choice would have been no intervention at all (Marciniak, 1999; MacKenzie et al., 2001).

LONG-TERM CONFINEMENT

Long-term confinement is used for those youth who are adjudicated delinquent and sentenced to some term of confinement. In October 2000, there were a total of 110,284 youths held in 3,061 confined juvenile facilities in the United States. The majority of all offenders (70%) were housed in public facilities, while the remainder were housed in private facilities. There were a total 1,203 public facilities and 1,848 private facilities (see Table 8.3) (Sickmund, 2002).

States vary on the upper age level of jurisdiction for dispositional purposes. Ages range from seventeen to twenty-four (see Table 8.4) (Snyder & Sickmund, 1999, p. 93). The majority of all states (66 percent, or thirty-three) designate age twenty as the upper-level age, while three states (Colorado, Hawaii, and New Jersey) maintain jurisdiction until the disposition is complete. Other states may impose a sentence to extend the confinement period beyond the juvenile jurisdiction. This extension is known as a "blended sentence" (Snyder & Sickmund, 1999, p. 93).

The majority of status offenders are housed in private facilities, while most delinquent offenders are housed in public facilities (Sickmund, 2000). In 1997, males accounted for the majority (86 percent) of all offenders housed in some form of correctional institution (Snyder & Sickmund, 1999). Females were more likely to be detained in private facilities 23 percent compared to 17 percent in public facilities. For the committed population, girls were also more likely to be housed in a private facility (17 percent) than a public facility (9 percent) (Snyder & Sickmund, 1999, p. 198).

One issue facing many juvenile correctional facilities is overcrowding. The Juvenile Residential Facility Census (JRFC) is conducted biannually as a way to obtain information on the size, type, structure, security arrangements, and services provided in facilities. Results from this study indicate that four in ten (39 percent) facilities have more residents than bed space (see Table 8.5) (Sickmund, 2002, p. 3).

Reception and Diagnostic Centers

Following the dispositional hearing and being sentenced to the custody of the state, a juvenile will typically be sent to a **reception and diagnostic center**. These centers are designed as short-term facilities where adjudicated juveniles are put through a battery of

Table 8.3   In October 2000, 4 in 10 Juvenile Facilities Were Publicly Operated and Held 70% of Juvenile Offenders in Custody

State	Juvenile Facilities			Offenders Younger than 21		
	All Facilities	Public	Private	All Facilities	Public	Private
U.S. Total*	3,061	1,203	1,848	110,284	77,662	32,464
Alabama	46	12	34	1,583	926	657
Alaska	19	5	14	339	261	78
Arizona	51	16	35	2,248	1,752	398
Arkansas	45	11	34	639	295	344
California	285	116	169	19,286	17,551	1,735
Colorado	73	12	61	2,054	1,112	940
Connecticut	26	5	21	1,360	900	460
Delaware	7	3	4	295	246	49
Dist. of Columbia	17	3	14	272	159	113
Florida	166	53	113	7,278	3,269	4,009
Georgia	50	29	21	3,270	2,593	677
Hawaii	7	3	4	122	107	15
Idaho	22	14	8	580	470	110
Illinois	46	26	20	3,402	3,074	328
Indiana	97	41	56	3,334	2,239	1,095
Iowa	76	16	60	1,166	395	771
Kansas	51	17	34	1,185	831	354
Kentucky	58	31	27	950	757	193
Louisiana	64	20	44	2,663	2,105	568
Maine	17	3	14	300	248	52
Maryland	43	11	32	1,492	690	802
Massachusetts	71	18	53	1,481	567	914
Michigan	108	42	66	3,896	1,782	2,114
Minnesota	121	22	99	1,922	986	936
Mississippi	20	19	1	787	785	2

Note: State is the State where the facility is located. Offenders sent to out-of-State facilities are counted in the State where the facility is located, not the State where their offense occurred.

*U.S. total includes 158 offenders in 10 tribal facilities. These offenders were located in Arizona, Colorado, Montana, Oklahoma, and South Dakota.

Taken from: Melissa Sickmund (2002, December). Juvenile Residential Facility Census, 2000: Selected Findings. *Juvenile Offenders and Victims National Report Series.* Washington, DC: Office of Juvenile Justice and Delinquency Prevention, p. 2.

State	Juvenile Facilities			Offenders Younger than 21		
	All Facilities	Public	Private	All Facilities	Public	Private
Missouri	65	57	8	1,540	1,290	260
Montana	18	8	10	260	173	65
Nebraska	23	6	17	789	577	212
Nevada	15	10	5	1,176	750	426
New Hampshire	8	2	6	193	123	70
New Jersey	57	45	12	2,274	2,171	103
New Mexico	27	19	8	885	838	47
New York	210	59	151	5,081	2,883	2,198
North Carolina	67	27	40	1,555	1,237	318
North Dakota	13	4	9	203	105	98
Ohio	106	71	35	4,890	4,342	548
Oklahoma	52	14	38	1,034	535	479
Oregon	48	27	21	1,637	1,416	222
Pennsylvania	163	29	134	5,085	1,241	3,844
Rhode Island	11	1	10	360	211	149
South Carolina	42	16	26	1,592	1,072	520
South Dakota	22	9	13	646	365	265
Tennessee	63	28	35	1,824	1,041	783
Texas	138	77	61	8,354	6,475	1,879
Utah	51	17	34	1,135	453	682
Vermont	5	1	4	158	26	132
Virginia	74	62	12	2,808	2,615	252
Washington	42	31	11	2,064	1,938	126
West Virginia	27	6	21	381	241	140
Wisconsin	94	27	67	2,017	1,271	746
Wyoming	24	2	22	379	173	206

Table 8.4   Oldest Age Over Which the Juvenile Court May Retain Jurisdiction for Disposition Purposes in Delinquency Matters

Age	State
17	Arizona*, North Carolina
18	Alaska, Iowa, Kentucky, Nebraska, Oklahoma, Tennessee
19	Mississippi, North Dakota
20	Alabama, Arkansas, Connecticut, Delaware, District of Columbia, Florida, Georgia, Idaho, Illinois, Indiana, Louisiana, Maine, Maryland, Massachusetts, Michigan, Minnesota, Missouri, Nevada, New Hampshire, New Mexico, New York, Ohio, Pennsylvania, Rhode Island, South Carolina, South Dakota, Texas, Utah, Vermont, Virginia, Washington, West Virginia, Wyoming
22	Kansas
24	California, Montana, Oregon, Wisconsin
**	Colorado, Hawaii, New Jersey

* Arizona statute extends jurisdiction through age 20, but a 1979 State Supreme Court decision held that juvenile court jurisdiction terminates at age 18.

** Until the full term of the disposition order.

Note: Extended jurisdiction may be restricted to certain offenses or juveniles.

Information taken from: Howard N. Snyder and Melissa Sickmund (1999, September). *Juvenile Offenders and Victims: 1999 National Report.* Washington, DC: Office of Juvenile Justice and Delinquency Prevention, p. 93.

tests including psychological, academic (including IQ tests), and risk/needs assessments to assess the appropriate custody and care level. In some states, the facilities are separate from the training schools. In other states, the reception and diagnostic center is housed on the grounds of the facility. Youths are first sent here for four to six weeks for assessment and recommended placement. Again the battery of structured tests include psychological, emotional, academic, and social history files (Bartollas & Miller, 1998).

Psychological exams are typically conducted by a clinical psychologist. These examinations are conducted in order to make every effort to assess the youth to ensure their emotional, educational, and academic needs are being met. The social history of the youth is also taken. Typically a certified social worker is responsible for conducting this examination. Building off of the social history that was completed prior to the dispositional phase, the social worker will make a recommendation on where to place the youth in an institutional setting, as well as identify potential deficits such as learning problems that may need to be addressed. These deficits may include recommendations on how to deal with visitations for the youth and how to address or deescalate problems with family or living conditions that may exist (Bartollas & Miller, 1998).

Classification instruments assessing the risk and needs of the juveniles are also completed at this time (see Chapter 13 for a more in-depth discussion of classification). Most risk assessment instruments include questions that are predictive of future recidivism. Other classification instruments may be based on the I-level system that assesses the moral development of youth. Unlike the risk assessment instruments, this need assessment is based on seven stages of interpersonal development. Although this classification has been criticized because it solely focuses on the psychological needs of the offender rather than also incorporating the risk for future offending, use of this classification instrument does allow institutional staff to make better decisions in how to house the offenders with one another and to assist in tailoring treatment options with the majority of residents (Guarino-Ghezzi & Loughran, 1996). Once these tests are completed, the youths will be placed in the appropriate facility, unit, cottage, or dormitory. Unlike adult facilities, the juvenile justice system still functions under the basic premise of *parens patriae* and the hope of rehabilitating the offender so he or she will become a productive member of society upon release.

Training Schools

Training schools are the equivalent of an adult prison. They typically house those youths defined as the most serious felony offenders. Falling under a variety of different names, training schools regulate the movement and behavior for youths on a twenty-four-hour-a-day/seven-day-a-week schedule. Juveniles are committed (sentenced) to training schools based on the following criteria:

- A finding of fact occurs indicating that the child has committed an offense that would be punishable by imprisonment if committed by an adult.
- The parents are unable to control their child or provide for his or her social, emotional, and educational needs.
- No other child welfare service is sufficient.
- The child needs the services available at the training school (Abadinsky, 2000, p. 71).

In terms of security, these facilities oftentimes resemble an adult prison. Although not quite as secure, in certain instances you may find constantine wire surrounding the perimeter, towers with armed guards, and strict policies regarding visitation, dress, and program involvement. Other facilities may be less restrictive and resemble a cottage-style environment.

The cottage-style environment resembles a camp-like environment. The cottages themselves are small, youths are typically housed with similar types of offenders. In many instances, youths never have to leave their "cottage" for amenities such as food, and treatment (Whitehead & Lab, 1996). Oftentimes, these facilities will have one central location for academic and vocational education. Programming in a cottage-style setting is typically more liberal than in a closed, confined setting. Many of these facilities incorporate the use of behavior modification techniques such as token economy systems. These systems allow youth to earn points toward home visits, increased opportunities for recreational time, and additional increases in privileges. Like most juvenile facilities, the focus and goals vary by state, institution, and jurisdiction.

Table 8.5 **Nationwide, 39% of Juvenile Facilities Reporting Bed Information Held More Residents than They Had Standard Beds**

State	Facilities Reporting Bed Information			Percent of Facilities with More Residents than Standard Beds		
	All Facilities	Public	Private	All Facilities	Public	Private
U.S. Total*	2,875	1,164	1,704	39%	37%	40%
Alabama	45	11	34	38	73	26
Alaska	15	4	11	27	25	27
Arizona	51	15	32	39	47	41
Arkansas	36	11	25	33	27	36
California	258	115	143	56	37	71
Colorado	70	12	57	31	67	25
Connecticut	23	5	18	30	20	33
Delaware	7	3	4	57	100	25
Dist. of Columbia	11	3	8	18	0	25
Florida	147	53	94	52	47	55
Georgia	50	29	21	42	59	19
Hawaii	7	3	4	43	33	50
Idaho	21	13	8	52	62	38
Illinois	42	25	17	19	16	24
Indiana	95	41	54	23	29	19
Iowa	74	16	58	43	13	52
Kansas	47	16	31	28	25	29
Kentucky	57	30	27	28	30	26
Louisiana	62	20	42	35	30	38
Maine	17	3	14	41	0	50
Maryland	43	11	32	30	36	28
Massachusetts	69	18	51	77	89	73
Michigan	104	39	65	34	21	42
Minnesota	114	22	92	29	45	25
Mississippi	14	13	1	29	23	100

Note: A single bed is counted as one standard bed and a bunk bed is counted as two standard beds. Makeshift beds (e.g., cots, rollout beds, mattresses, and sofas) are not counted as standard beds. Percents are based on facilities reporting bed information. State is the State where the facility is located. Offenders sent to out-of-State facilities are counted in the State where the facility is located, not the State where their offense occurred.

*U.S. total includes seven tribal facilities that reported bed information. These tribal facilities were located in Arizona, Colorado, Montana, and South Dakota.

Taken from: Melissa Sickmund (2002, December). Juvenile Residential Facility Census, 2000: Selected Findings. *Juvenile Offenders and Victims National Report Series.* Washington, DC: Office of Juvenile Justice and Delinquency Prevention, p. 2.

State	Facilities Reporting Bed Information			Percent of Facilities with More Residents than Standard Beds		
	All Facilities	Public	Private	All Facilities	Public	Private
Missouri	63	55	8	25%	27%	13%
Montana	19	9	10	26	25	20
Nebraska	21	6	15	33	50	27
Nevada	15	10	5	33	40	20
New Hampshire	8	2	6	50	50	50
New Jersey	54	45	9	35	38	22
New Mexico	27	19	8	33	37	25
New York	208	59	149	53	37	59
North Carolina	62	24	38	37	38	37
North Dakota	13	4	9	0	0	0
Ohio	106	71	35	35	38	29
Oklahoma	43	14	29	53	57	52
Oregon	44	24	20	30	25	35
Pennsylvania	149	28	121	33	36	32
Rhode Island	10	1	9	80	100	78
South Carolina	37	13	24	38	38	38
South Dakota	21	7	13	24	0	31
Tennessee	58	27	31	52	48	55
Texas	125	73	52	33	37	27
Utah	51	17	34	39	29	44
Vermont	5	1	4	20	0	25
Virginia	74	62	12	41	44	25
Washington	42	31	11	21	19	27
West Virginia	27	6	21	52	67	48
Wisconsin	91	24	67	14	13	15
Wyoming	23	2	21	17	0	19

JUVENILE CORRECTIONAL STAFF AND INSTITUTIONAL LIFE

Working in a juvenile correctional facility may create a different set of conflicts from those found in the adult institution. Correctional staff are perpetually confronted with the issues of adhering to a treatment orientation while still maintaining custody within the institution. There has been a push in the field of corrections to make officers human service–oriented rather than custody-oriented (Hepburn & Knepper, 1993). These roles by mere definition are in conflict with one another. The literature assessing the impact of these potential role conflicts on juvenile correctional staff are essentially void. However, there is a plethora of literature assessing the impact of role conflict and stress on correctional staff in adult facilities.

As defined in Chapter 7, the role of a correctional officer refers to "a unit of culture; it refers to the rights and duties, the normatively approved patterns of behavior for the occupants of a given position" (Walker, 1992, p. 63; Yinger, 1965, pp. 99–100). In a study assessing the level of job stress associated with detention care workers, Liou (1995) found that detention care workers who reported more punitive orientations were more likely to experience role stress, whereas those officers stating they maintained a treatment orientation were likely to experience job stress (p. 434). Liou explains this finding by stating that officers who are punitive-oriented are more likely to experience role stress because they are expected to play the role of counselor and advisor to the youths. Likewise those officers who reported being treatment-oriented were more likely to experience job stress because the juvenile custody and security environment limited their roles as counselors (p. 434). Additionally results from this study suggested that officers who perceived their supervisors to be not only supportive of them but that they had confidence in their abilities were less likely to exhibit job stress. The findings of this study are supported by Gordon's (1999) research. In her assessment of juvenile detention workers, she found differences in commitment to the institution by job roles. For example, she also found support that treatment staff are more likely to support rehabilitation while custody staff are more likely to support punishment (p. 89). Furthermore, research suggests that as correctional officers are more satisfied with their job they are less likely to leave it, therefore, reducing turnover rates (Tipton, 2002).

These findings in addition to others suggest that it is imperative for correctional officers to be trained in the philosophy of the institution. One shortcoming that has been perpetually demonstrated in the literature is the conflict between the primary purpose of the institution (fulfilling custodial needs) and rehabilitating the offender. Therefore, depending upon their exact position within the facility, correctional officers are conflicted with how they are supposed to handle offenders (Rothman, 1980; Mitchell et al., 2001). This becomes evermore present in facilities that incorporate therapeutic communities in their treatment of offenders (see section below for a more in-depth description of therapeutic communities).

These findings are even more disturbing when we consider the impact a correctional officer's orientation or job satisfaction may have on a juvenile. In a study assessing the impact of correctional officers on inmate-on-inmate violence, results suggest that guards had turned a blind eye to inmate violence, they had encouraged violence among inmates, and created an environment of interpersonal violence (Peterson-Badali & Koegl, 2002). It is these findings that provide support that life behind institutional walls for juveniles is oftentimes one of fear, violence, sexual exploitation, victimization, and suicidal behavior (Parent et al., 1994). Research suggests that proper screening tools and placement of juveniles can mitigate some of the negative impacts of juvenile confinement. The literature is replete with studies on the development of inmate subcultures in adult institutions. However, studies assessing the formation of subcultures in juvenile institutions is less forthcoming. There is evidence to suggest however, that facilities with less of a custody orientation and more of a treatment orientation experience reduced levels of aggression and hostility (Regoli & Hewitt, 2000). Furthermore, as Feld (1981) points out, inmate subcultures that form ultimately reflect the institutional values. Therefore, if the facility is more supportive of a custody orientation and less supportive of treatment then the youths are more likely to be violent in nature and less cooperative in a treatment setting.

Overall, the literature assessing the impact of juvenile correctional staff and inmate life suggests a need for more of a treatment orientation. It is imperative, however, if treatment is to be the guiding philosophy behind institutional walls that all staff members are trained in this orientation, and that the training is reinforced by the administrative staff. As we move into the twenty-first century and the continued use of treatment modalities including group approaches to controlling youth behind walls, this reinforcement of skills is not only crucial but necessary.

JUVENILE CORRECTIONAL TREATMENT PROGRAMMING

The issue of the appropriateness of correctional programming or rehabilitation has been met with much debate and criticism since Robert Martinson published his now infamous article in 1974 "What Works?—Questions and Answers About Prison Reform." In his review of 231 evaluation studies that had been conducted in a correctional facility, he found with few and isolated exceptions rehabilitation programs had not achieved their goal of reducing recidivism. This combined with a change in the political context of the 1960s and 1970s spanned a shift in the philosophy from treatment-oriented to a more punitive-based system. This shift was true for both adults and juveniles although it was more predominant in the adult correctional setting.

Since the mid-1970s, we have seen a variety of changes in correctional philosophy and approaches to the handling of juveniles in the criminal justice system. As we usher in the twenty-first century, the approach to juvenile institutional programming is one that combines both a treatment and a custody orientation. Although we have not totally abandoned the premises that were used to create a separate juvenile system, we have continued to get tougher on crime as indicated by the increased use of formally handling youth earlier in the system (refer to Chapter 7 for a more in-depth discussion). Because rehabilitation is still one of the primary goals of the juvenile justice system it is important to understand the different treatment modalities that are being used behind institutional walls. The following treatment modalities will be briefly discussed below: behavior modification or behavior therapy techniques, cognitive techniques, social learning therapies, and group therapies.

Behavior Modification

Behavior modification or behavior therapies seek to either increase or decrease a particular behavior. This treatment does not seek to identify what the source of the problem behavior is, rather it seeks to alter the undesired behavior that is occurring at the present time. Relying on the works of Ivan Pavlov's Classical Conditioning and B.F. Skinner's Operant Conditioning these two models have been used as treatment approaches in both the juvenile and adult settings.

Classical conditioning relies on the identification of two stimuli: the unconditioned stimulus which triggers the unconditioned response; and the conditioned stimulus that triggers the conditioned response. For example, stimuli can produce a variety of different responses such as, fear, anger, crime, obedience. In criminal justice, one of the ways we approach the problem of crime is to create mini-phobias through the process of **aversion therapy** that cause an individual to fear a particular behavior and ultimately response. As Lester, Braswell, and VanVoorhis (1997) point out, a mini-phobia can be created for a person whether adult or juvenile who wants to quit consuming alcohol. "First, we need a stimulus that makes him feel nauseated (unconditioned stimulus). We can use a drug such as apomorphine. We then inject our alcoholic with apomorphine and wait until he is just about to feel nauseated and vomit, and then we give him alcohol to drink. He drinks and vomits. We keep repeating this, and eventually he vomits or feels nauseated at the sight, the smell, and even the thought of alcohol" (Lester, Braswell, & VanVoorhis, 1997, p. 130).

Operant conditioning on the other hand uses the concept of a stimulus with a response which is then reinforced. Relying on the work of B. F. Skinner, juvenile correctional facilities have used this form of behavior modification to create **token economy systems**. The token economy system is used to elicit positive responses and decrease negative behavior. Any response whether it occurs on a regular basis or infrequently is subject to being reinforced. The token economy system builds on this phenomena. Also referred to as contingency management, this system reinforces good behavior (Lester, Braswell, & VanVoorhis, 1997; Alexander, 2000). For example, when using the token economy system there exists a set of structured rules. When the youth follow those rules, they receive a specified token. Once they have received a certain number of tokens they may exchange them for rewards such as extra recreational time or increased visitation. However, should the juvenile not follow the structured rules, tokens will be removed, and the juvenile will have to do extra work or chores, and it would take additional time to proceed through the levels. Token economy systems are used in a variety of different ways. They may be used as tools to provide admittance into programs, or even progression through the programs and ultimately toward release. These **behavior modification** systems allow the youths the opportunity to take responsibility for their own progression through the system. Although there are minimum times for completion, if they behave according to the structured rules, their time may not be extended.

Cognitive Therapies

Cognitive therapies focus on the thinking patterns and behaviors of youth. In order to address the various problem behaviors, the therapist in conjunction with the program participant must identify the thinking errors or cognitive deficits. "Cognitive also refers to the content of our thinking, our attitudes, beliefs, values, and relatively stable manner in which we make sense of our surrounding" (Lester & VanVoorhis, 1997, p. 163). There is agreement in the field that cognitive-behavioral approaches are most frequently identified with a reduction in recidivism. Therefore, there is a movement in both the adult and juvenile systems to incorporate more cognitive based programming both behind institutional walls and in the community (Gaes, Flanagan, Motiuk, & Stewart, 1999).

There are four reasons why cognitive based programming is becoming one of the preferred treatments in juvenile correctional settings:

1. They deal with observable behavior;
2. They do not require hiring of professional staff such as psychologist;
3. They require confrontation of inappropriate behavior, which can occur in a controlled setting;
4. These programs have been shown to be highly effective (Hogan, Barton & Lambert, 2002, p. 3; Andrews, Zinger, Hoge, Bonta, Gendreau, & Cullen, 1990; Izzo & Ross, 1990; Lester & VanVoorhis, 1997; Matthews & Pitts, 1998; Ross & Fabiano, 1985).

According to the propositions put forth in cognitive theories, all persons have the ability to distort reality. It is those, however, who exhibit major distortions that lose touch with reality and create a problem (Freeman, 1983: Alexander, 2000). The therapeutic needs for adults differ from the therapeutic needs for juveniles. For example, when treating an adult offender, the counselor must attempt to address the cognitive distortions that exist. So it is fundamentally essential to redirect this reality into more pro-social attitudes, beliefs, cooperation, flexibility, and an understanding of the consequences of their behavior (Alexander, 2000; Hogan, Barton, & Lambert, 2002; Lester & VanVoorhis, 1997; Reinecke, Ryan, & DuBois, 1998, p. 26). Cognitive problems in juveniles result from cognitive absences. Children do not have the ability to process and control their environment in the same manner as adults. Cognitive skills deficits programs seek "interventions to improve cognitive processes—the structure and form of reasoning, rather than its content" (Lester & VanVoorhis, 1997, p. 164). As Alexander (2000) notes, cognitive programs are effective for children who are "impulsive, not self-controlled, attention-disordered, isolated, withdrawn, and depressed" (p. 63). In order to address the cognitive issues with juveniles, programs must teach problem-solving, self-instruction, discerning correctly physiological arousal and affective state, relaxation techniques to control physiological arousal, and moral reasoning (Alexander, 2000, p. 63). Techniques such as time-out, and environmental manipulation have been used to alter inappropriate cognitive thinking.

One important element with using any form of cognitive programming is it can be conducted in a group. In fact, the techniques learned in a community may be more likely to "stick" if they are reinforced from those around you. There is some evidence to suggest that the inappropriate placement of offenders in a cognitive program may in fact be more detrimental to their attitudes than not placing them in any program. All persons at one point or another distort reality. It is our response to these distortions that may lead to criminal or noncriminal behavior. Research assessing the effectiveness of these programs to reduce recidivism suggests they are most effective in a probation setting, administered to violent offenders over the age of twenty-five. Although there is evidence to suggest modest changes in behavior for all other offenders, programs that focus on screening out the most resistant participants are most likely to be successful (Gaes et al., 1999). Therefore, it is imperative that diagnostic facilities and institutions use the appropriate tools to determine who is displaying either cognitive absences or cognitive distortions so the youth can be placed in the appropriate program.

Social Learning Therapies

As noted in Chapter 4, differential association theory posits that criminal behavior is transmitted from one person to another through the process of learning. As you recall, Sutherland put forth nine propositions to his theory with the most important proposition being that criminal behavior is learned and it is learned in interaction with others. Ron Akers later expanded on Sutherlands theory to include an operant conditioning approach to explain how the learning "sticks." Therefore, Akers purports it is the combination of four concepts that leads to the learning process:

- Differential association—whereby one is exposed to normative definitions favorable or unfavorable to illegal or law-abiding behavior (Akers, 1994, p. 96).
- Definitions—one's own attitudes or meanings that one attaches to given behavior. Definitions are both general and specific. General beliefs can include but are not limited to religious, moral and other conventional values. Specific definitions orient the person to particular acts (Akers, 1994, p. 97).
- Differential reinforcement—the balance of anticipated or actual rewards and punishments that follow or are consequences of behavior. Punishment can be both direct (positive) in which painful or unpleasant consequences are attached to a behavior; or indirect (negative), in which a reward or pleasant consequence is removed (Akers, 1994, p. 98).
- Imitation—refers to the engagement in behavior after the observation of similar behavior in others.

As with Sutherland, Akers points out that learning occurs primarily with those you are closest to, such as, your family, peers, schools, churches, etc. Therefore, for learning to occur or be altered in a correctional setting it is important to include not only macro level elements such as the environment but also cognitive (Bandura, 1977), and behavioral (Akers, 1994) elements.

For social learning models to work in a correctional setting, it is imperative to have good role models for the youth. As Donald Andrews (1980) points out, good role models must be skilled at interpersonal communication. They must be able to be open and understanding to others viewpoints. The role model must also be enthusiastic, open, and flexible, and they must allow their clients the freedom to express their views (VanVoorhis, 1997, p. 148; Andrews & Bonta, 1994). Role models must also be cognizant of the positive behaviors they are modeling as well as the behavior they are trying to discourage. Both positive and negative behaviors must be reinforced. Role models must give praise when someone has demonstrated positive behavior, but they must also immediately voice their disapproval in an empathetic manner (VanVoorhis, 1997; Andrews & Bonta, 1994). It is imperative that counselors provide a clear explanation for their disapproval, otherwise the client will not know how to improve upon his or her behavior. Counselors must also be consistent and clear in their expectations for the clients behavior otherwise the likelihood of success will be compromised.

There are a variety of different programs that have been put into place using the concepts of social learning. One such program is Achievement Place in Lawrence, Kansas. This program targeted delinquent youths between the ages of twelve and sixteen who were failing academically. Youth targeted for this program were placed in a group home setting. While there, the group home was ran by two "parents." They incorporated the use of a token economy system. Each youth had responsibilities in the home, and there were daily conferences. Initial results of an assessment suggested there were significant reductions in recidivism for program participants (VanVoorhis, 1997).

Other techniques for social learning programs include the use of role playing and reinforcing of this behavior. Social learning techniques have become a popular alternative for correctional institutions. They are easily put into action and enhance the accountability of not only the youth participating in the program but the staff as well.

Group Therapies

The use of therapeutic communities and groups have become another popular cost effective alternative for correctional programming. There are a variety of different types of groups that can be used. As Lester (1997) points out, there are two distinct advantages to using group counseling sessions. "First, they are more economic; second, group counseling subjects the offender to input from his or her group" (p. 191). Three specific types of **group therapy** will be discussed: guided group interaction, reality therapy, and therapeutic community (milieu therapy).

Guided group interaction techniques help youths control their future behavior by motivating and teaching them to change. This technique relies very heavily on staff attitude. Staff members set the tone of the group. True change occurs through interaction with other group members. Unlike other therapies that assume there is something "wrong" with the offender or that they are ill, guided group interaction just assumes there are behaviors that are in need of change that may be worked through in group (Lester, 1997).

Reality therapy asserts that individuals are responsible for their own behavior. Therefore, in group, it is the responsibility of the group leader to direct the client(s) to look at their own behavior and take responsibility for their actions. Reality therapy incorporates the use of cognitive theory, behavioral concepts, it is directive, and diadatic (Corey, 1986). The ultimate goal of therapy to help the offender become more emotionally strong and rational in their behavior. The counselor assists the client/program participant in taking responsibility for their behavior. In leading the group, participants can practice the techniques they have learned on a variety of different behaviors. It is imperative they learn to use the techniques in everyday life to assist them in staying out of trouble. This technique can be used in both the individual and group settings (Lester, 1997).

The final form of group therapy to be discussed here is the use of the **therapeutic community/milieu therapy**. In the therapeutic community, the central premise is the entire environment/institution is involved in the administration of the therapy. There are variety of different techniques that can be used, such as cognitive treatments (see Hogan, Barton, and Lambert, 2002). The basic premise is living the treatment on a daily basis. The introduction of the therapeutic community changes the entire structure of the institution. The existence of this form of treatment can be both beneficial and detrimental. It can be beneficial because it relies on the cooperation of all of the actors in the system. It can be detrimental, however, because group members may be reluctant to accept new members (Lester, 1997).

Overall the success of any group therapy relies on the strength of the staff facilitating the program, and the commitment of the participants. Although with proper training both groups can be taught how to properly participate, if they are not cooperative over an extended period of time the integrity of the group could be threatened and the success of the program ultimately compromised.

SUMMARY

To summarize, this chapter reviewed the evolution of childhood and the creation of separate juvenile institutions. As noted in the chapter, the concept of childhood is a relatively new phenomena. The evolution of recognizing children as miniature adults or a potential throw-aways to persons in need of protection is both significant and relevant to our modern day responses to youth in the system. With the passage of legislation such as the Juvenile Justice and Delinquency Prevention Act of 1974 and the subsequent amendments, the focus of attention continues to be placed on not further harming youth who come to the attention of the juvenile justice system. As discussed, many of our alternatives for youth require the interdependence or partnerships with community agencies. Programs such as boot camps, group homes, and day reporting centers are short-term alternatives that are at least showing some minimal promise for future reductions in recidivism.

In spite of these alternatives, there is still a need to house more serious and violent offenders in a confined institutional setting. As noted in the chapter, the number of youths confined in these settings continues to rise as does the harshness of our response to their behaviors. It is important to understand the deleterious effects of this institutionalization on both staff and juveniles. As stated in the chapter, conflict between custodial and treatment orientations towards handling youth continues to exist. Unfortunately, the resulting impact of these conflicts can be distrust of fellow employees and subsequent mistreatment of youth. Many institutions have sought to address the issue by incorporating the use of various treatment modalities within the institution. These therapies include behavior modification, cognitive theories, social learning theories, and group therapies. Overall, the research suggests that the use of any of these treatment modalities is more effective at reducing recidivism than using nothing at all.

CASE STUDY WRAP-UP

Mr. Sinclair does not have an easy job. In addition to being an effective manager, he also should be familiar with juvenile delinquency, various therapies, case management techniques, fundraising, and be involved in the community. His time is taken up with policy, budgeting, programs, and problems, problems, problems. In a time of diminishing resources, greater demand for services, and some public skepticism of the viability of treatment, he must keep his head and plan for the future.

The Gibault program is one that recognizes the corrections continuum, that is, boys and girls are confined to the institution and gradually allowed to assume more and more responsibility as they "mature" under the guidance of educated and dedicated staff. Finally, when ready, they are allowed to live in a less secure setting and attend public school and in general participate in regular community activities while in the group home. Gibault School for Boys is a well-managed and capable program that serves the community and the boys placed there.

STUDY QUESTIONS

1. Discuss the evolution of childhood. What role did the recognition of childhood play in the development of modern day juvenile institutions?
2. How does short-term confinement differ from long-term confinement?
3. How does lock-up differ from the use of jails?
4. What is the Juvenile Justice and Delinquency Prevention Act? What role did this act play in deinstitutionalizing status offenders?
5. What are boot camps? Are they effective alternatives to institutionalization?
6. What are the pros and cons to using boot camps?
7. Define group home. Who are group homes normally reserved for? How do day reporting centers differ from group homes?
8. Describe a training school. Who normally goes to a training school?

9. There are many treatment options available in the juvenile institutional setting. How or why would a juvenile correctional administrator choose one form of treatment over another?

BIBLIOGRAPHY

ABADINSKY, HOWARD (2000). *Probation and Parole: Theory and Practice.* Upper Saddle River, NJ: Prentice Hall.

AKERS, RONALD L. (1994). *Criminological Theories: Introduction and Evaluation.* Los Angeles, CA: Roxbury Publishing.

ALEXANDER, RUDOLPH JR. (2000). *Counseling, Treatment, and Intervention: Methods with Juvenile and Adult Offenders.* Belmont, CA: Brooks/Cole.

ANDREWS, D., ZINGER, I., HOGE, R., BONTA, J., GENDREAU, P., AND CULLEN, F. (1990). "Does correctional treatment work? A psychologically informed meta-analysis." *Criminology, 28,* 369–404.

ANDREWS, DON (1980). "Some experimental investigations of the principles of differential association through deliberate manipulations of the structures of service systems." *American Sociological Review,* 45, 448–462.

ANDREWS, DON, AND BONTA, JAMES (1994). *The Psychology of Criminal Conduct.* Cincinnati: Anderson Publishing.

BALL, RICHARD, A., HUFF, C. RONALD, AND LILLY, ROBERT J. (1988). *House Arrest and Correctional Policy: Doing Time at Home.* Newbury Park, CA: Sage.

BANDURA, ALBERT (1977). "Self-efficacy: Toward a unifying theory of behavioral change." *Psychological Review,* 94, 191–215.

BARTOLLAS, CLEMENS, AND MILLER, STUART J. (1998). *Juvenile Justice in America,* 2nd ed. Upper Saddle River, NJ: Prentice Hall.

BARTON, WILLIAM H., AND SCHWARTZ, IRA M. (1994). "Juvenile Detention: No More Hidden Closets." In Ira M. Schwartz and William H. Barton (Eds.), *Reforming Juvenile Detention: No More Hidden Closets.* Columbus, OH: Ohio State University Press, pp. 1–11.

BECK, ALLEN J., KARBERG, JENNIFER C., AND HARRISON, PAIGE M. (April, 2002). *Prison and Jail Inmates at Midyear 2001.* Washington, DC: U.S. Department of Justice NCJ 191702.

BEYER, MARGARET (1996). "Juvenile Boot Camps Don't Make Sense." *American Bar Association Journal of Criminal Justice,* 10, 20–21.

BLACK, MEGHAN C. (2001). *Juvenile Delinquency Probation Caseloads, 1989–1998: Fact Sheet.* Washington, DC: Office of Juvenile Justice and Delinquency Prevention.

BUSH, J., AND BILODEAU, B. (1993). *Options: A Cognitive Change Program.* Washington, DC: National Institute of Corrections.

CLEAR, TODD R., AND DAMMER, HARRY R. (2003). *The Offender in the Community,* 2nd ed. Belmont, CA: Wadsworth.

COREY, GERALD (1986). *Theory and Practice of Counseling and Psychotherapy,* 3rd ed. Pacific Grove, CA: Brooks/Cole Publishing.

DEMAUSE, LLOYD (1974). "The Evolution of Childhood." In Lloyd deMause (Ed.), *The History of Childhood* (pp. 1–73). New York: Psychohistory Press.

FELD, BARRY C. (1981). "A comparative analysis of organizational structure and inmate subcultures in institutions for juvenile offenders." *Crime & Delinquency, 27,* 336–363.

FOX, K. (1999). "Changing Violent Minds: Discursive Correction and Resistance in the Cognitive Treatment of Violent Offenders in Prison." *Social Problems, 46,* 88–108.

FREEMAN, A. (1983). "Cognitive Therapy: An Overview." In A. Freeman (Ed.), *Cognitive Therapy with Couples and Groups* (pp. 1–9). New York: Plenum Press.

GAES, GERALD G., FLANAGAN, TIMOTHY J., MOTIUK, LAURENCE L., AND STEWART, LYNN (1999). "Adult Correctional Treatment." In Michael Tonry and Joan Petersilia (Eds.), *Prisons: Crime and Justice A Review of Research, volume 26.* Chicago: The University of Chicago, pp. 361–426.

GORDON, JILL A. (1999). "Do Staff Attitudes Vary by Position? A Look at One Juvenile Correctional Center." *American Journal of Criminal Justice, 24*(1), 81–93.

GUARINO-GHEZZI, SUSAN, AND LOUGHRAN, EDWARD J. (1996). *Balancing Juvenile Justice.* New Brunswick, NJ: Transaction Publishers.

HENNING, K., AND FRUEH, B. (1996). "Cognitive-behavioral Treatment of Incarcerated Offenders: An Evaluation of the Vermont Department Corrections' Cognitive Self-change Program." *Criminal Justice and Behavior, 23,* 523–541.

HEPBURN, JOHN R., AND KNEPPER, PAUL E. (1993). "Correctional Officers as Human Services Workers: The Effect on Job Satisfaction." *Justice Quarterly, 10*(2), 315–335.

HOGAN, NANCY L., BARTON, SHANNON M., AND LAMBERT, ERIC G. (2002, August). Evaluation of the CHANGE Program and its Impact on Inmates and Staff at the Michigan Reformatory. Final Report submitted to the National Institute of Justice. Washington, DC.

HOLDEN, GWEN A., AND KAPLER, ROBERT A. (1995, Fall/Winter). "Deinstitutionalizing Status Offenders: A Record of Progress." *Juvenile Justice Journal,* II(2), 3–10.

HOWELL, JAMES C. (1998). "NCCD's Survey of Juvenile Detention and Correctional Facilities." *Crime & Delinquency, 44*(1), 102–109.

IZZO, R., AND ROSS, R. (1990). "Meta-Analysis of Rehabilitation Programs for Juvenile Delinquents: A Brief Report." *Criminal Justice and Behavior, 17,* 134–142.

KAMERMAN, SHEILA, AND KAHN, ALFRED J. (1976). *Social Services in the United States.* Philadelphia: Temple University Press.

KIVETT, DOUGLAS D., AND WARREN, CAROL A. (2002). "Social Control in a Group Home for Delinquent Boys." *Journal of Contemporary Ethnography, 31*(1), 3–32.

KOCH CRIME INSTITUTE (2000, March). *Juvenile Boot Camps and Military Structured Youth Programs.* Topeka, KS: Koch Crime Institute.

KRISBERG, BARRY, CURRIE, ELLIOT, ONEK, DAVID, AND WIEBUSH, RICHARD G. (1995). "Graduated Sanctions for Serious, Violent, and Chronic Juvenile Offenders." In James

C. Howell, Barry Krisberg, J. David Hawkins, and John J. Wilson (Eds.), *Serious, Violent, & Chronic Juvenile Offenders: A Sourcebook.* Thousand Oaks, CA: Sage Publications, pp. 142–170.

LESTER, DAVID (1997). "Group and Mileau Therapy." In Patricia VanVoorhis, Michael Braswell, and David Lester (Eds.), *Correctional Counseling and Rehabilitation* (pp. 189–218). Cincinnati: Anderson Publishing.

LESTER, DAVID, BRASWELL, MICHAEL, AND VANVOORHIS, PATRICIA (1997). "Radical Behavior Interventions." In Patricia VanVoorhis, Michael Braswell, and David Lester (Eds.), *Correctional Counseling and Rehabilitation* (pp. 127–144). Cincinnati: Anderson Publishing.

LESTER, DAVID, AND VANVOORHIS, PATRICIA (1997). "Cognitive Therapies." In Patricia VanVoorhis, Michael Braswell, and David Lester (Eds.), *Correctional Counseling and Rehabilitation* (pp. 163–186). Cincinnati: Anderson Publishing.

LIOU, KUOTSAI TOM (1995). "Role stress and job stress among detention care workers." *Criminal Justice and Behavior* 22(4), 425–436.

LUNDMAN, RICHARD J. (2001). *Prevention and Control of Juvenile Delinquency,* 3rd ed. New York: Oxford University Press.

MACKENZIE, DORIS LAYTON (1997). "Criminal Justice and Crime Prevention." In Lawrence W. Sherman, Denise Gottfredson, Doris Layton MacKenzie, John Eck, Peter Reuter, and Shaw Bushway (Eds.), *Preventing Crime: What Works, What Doesn't, What's Promising.* Washington, DC: U.S. Department of Justice, National Institute of Justice, NCJ 165366. Chapter 8 online @ www.NCJRS.org/works/whitedoc.htm

MACKENZIE, DORIS LAYTON, GOVER, ANGELA R., ARMSTRONG, GAYLENE STYVE, AND MITCHELL, OJMARRH (2001, August). "A National Study Comparing the Environments of Boot Camps with Traditional Facilities for Juvenile Offenders." *National Institute of Justice: Research in Brief.* Washington, DC: U.S. Department of Justice.

MARCINIAK, LIZ MARIE (1999). "The Use of Day Reporting as an Intermediate Sanction: A Study of Offender Targeting and Program Termination." *The Prison Journal,* 79(2), 205–225.

MARTINSON, ROBERT (1974). "What Works?—Questions and Answers about Prison Reform." *The Public Interest,* 35, 22–54.

MATTHEWS, R., AND PITTS, J. (1998). "Rehabilitation, Recidivism, and Realism: Evaluating Violence Reduction Programs in Prison." *Prison Journal,* 78, 390–402.

MAXSON, CHERYL L., AND KLEIN, MALCOLM W. (1997). *Responding to Troubled Youth.* New York: Oxford Publishing.

MITCHELL, OJMARRH, MACKENZIE, DORIS LAYTON, GOVER, ANGELA R., AND STYVE, GAYLENE J. (2001). "The Influences of Personal Background on Perceptions of Juvenile Correctional Environments." *Journal of Criminal Justice,* 29, 67–76.

OFFICE OF JUSTICE PROGRAMS (1995). *Fiscal Year 1995 Corrections Boot Camp Initiative: Violent Offender Incarceration Grant Program.* Program Guidelines and Application Information. Washington, DC: Office of Justice Programs, U.S. Department of Justice.

PALMER, TED (1992). *The Re-Emergence of Correctional Intervention.* Newbury Park, CA: Sage Publication.

PARENT, DALE G., LIETER, VALERIE, KENNEDY, STEPHEN, LIVENS, LISA, WENTWORTH, DANIEL, AND WILCOX, SARAH (1994). *Conditions of Confinement: Juveniles Detention and Corrections Facilities.* Washington, DC: Office of Juvenile Justice and Delinquency Prevention.

PETERS, MICHAEL, THOMAS, DAVID, ZAMBERLAN, CHRISTOPHER, AND CALIBER ASSOCIATES (1997, September). *Boot Camps for Juvenile Offenders: Program Summary.* Washington, DC: Office of Juvenile Justice and Delinquency Prevention.

PETERSILIA, JOAN, AND TURNER, SUSAN (1993). "Intensive probation and parole." In M. Tonry (Ed.), *Crime and Justice: A Review of Research* (Vol. 17, pp. 281–335). Chicago: University of Chicago Press.

PETERSON-BADALI, MICHELE, AND KOEGL, CHRISTOPHER (2002). "Juveniles' experiences of incarceration: The role of correctional staff in peer violence." *Journal of Criminal Justice,* 30, 41–49.

PUZZANCHERA, CHARLES, STAHL, ANNE L., FINNEGAN, TERRENCE A., TIERNEY, NANCY, AND SNYDER, HOWARD N. (2003) Juvenile Court Statistics (2000, May). *Juvenile Court Statistics 1998.* Washington, DC: Office of Juvenile Justice and Delinquency Prevention.

REGOLI, ROBERT M., AND HEWITT, JOHN D. (2000). *Delinquency in Society,* 4th ed. Boston: McGraw Hill.

REINECKE, M., RYAN, N., AND DuBOIS, D. (1998). "Cognitive-behavioral Therapy of Depression and Depressive Symptoms During Adolescence: A Review and Meta-analysis." *Journal of the American Academy of Child and Adolescent Psychiatry, 37,* 26–35.

ROTHMAN, DAVID J. (1980). *Conscience and Convenience: The Asylum and Its Alternative in Progressive America.* Harper Collins Publishers.

ROTHMAN, DAVID J. (1971). *The Discovery of the Asylum: Social Order and Disorder in the New Republic.* Boston: Little, Brown.

ROSENHEIM, MARGARET KENNEY (1962). "Perennial Problems in the Juvenile Court." In Margaret Kenney Rosenheim (Ed.), *Justice for the Child* (p. 5). New York: Free Press of Glencoe.

ROSS, R., AND FABIANO, E. (1985). *Time to Think: A Cognitive Model of Delinquency Prevention and Offender Rehabilitation.* Johnson City, TN: Institute of Social Science and Arts.

SAMENOW, S. (1984). *Inside the Criminal Mind.* New York: Times Books.

SAMENOW, S. (1989). *Before It's Too Late.* New York: Times Books.

SCHWARTZ, IRA M. (1994). "What policymakers need to know about juvenile detention reform." In Ira M. Schwartz and William H. Barton (Eds.), *Reforming Juvenile Detention: No More Hidden Costs* (pp. 176–182). Columbus, OH: Ohio State University Press.

SCHWARTZ, IRA M, AND BARTON, WILLIAM H. (Eds.) (1994). *Reforming Juvenile Detention: No More Hidden Costs.* Columbus, OH: Ohio State University Press.

Schwartz, Ira M., Harris, Linda, and Levi, Laurie (1988). "The Jailing of Juveniles in Minnesota: A Case Study." *Crime and Delinquency,* 34, 146.

Sickmund, Melissa (2002, December). "Juvenile Residential Facility Census, 2000: Selected Findings." *Juvenile Offenders and Victims National Report Series Bulletin.* Washington, DC: Office of Juvenile Justice and Delinquency Prevention.

Sickmund, Melissa (2003). *Juveniles in Court.* Washington, DC: Office of Juvenile Justice and Delinquency Prevention.

Sickmund, Melissa (2000, December). "State Custody Rates, 1997." *OJJDP Juvenile Justice Bulletin.* Washington, DC: Office of Juvenile Justice and Delinquency Prevention.

Siegel, Larry, and Senna, Joseph (1997). *Juvenile Delinquency: Theory, Practice and Law,* 6th ed. St. Paul: West Publishing, Co.

Slingerland, W.H. (1919). *Child-placing in Families.* New York: Russell Sage Foundation.

Snyder, Howard N., and Sickmund, Melissa (1999). *Juvenile Offenders and Victims: 1999 National Report.* Washington, DC: Office of Juvenile Justice and Delinquency Prevention.

Steinhart, David (1988). "California's Legislature Ends the Jailing of Children: The Story of a Policy Reversal." *Crime and Delinquency,* 34, 169–170.

Steinhart, David, and Krisberg, Barry (1987). "Children in Jail." *State Legislature,* 13, 12–16.

Straus, Murray A., Gelles, Richard J., and Steinmetz, Suzanne K. (1980). *Behind Closed Doors: Violence in the American Family.* Garden City, NY: Anchor Books.

Tipton, Jeffrey A. (2002). "Attitudes and Perceptions of South Carolina's Juvenile Correctional Officers, Insight into the Turnover Epidemic." *Journal of Crime & Justice,* 25(1), 81–98.

Tower, Cynthia Crosson (1996). *Child Abuse and Neglect,* 3rd ed. Boston: Allyn and Bacon.

Trulson, Chad, Triplett, Ruth, and Snell, Clete (2001). "Social control in a school setting: Evaluating a school-based boot camp." *Crime & Delinquency,* 47(4), 573–609.

VanVoorhis, Patricia (1997). "Social Learning Models." In Patricia VanVoorhis, Michael Braswell, & David Lester (Eds.), *Correctional Counseling and Rehabilitation* (pp. 145–162). Cincinnati: Anderson Publishing.

Walker, Samuel (1992). *The Police in America: An Introduction,* 2nd ed. New York: McGraw-Hill, Inc.

Whitehead, John T., and Lab, Steven P. (1996). *Juvenile Justice: An Introduction,* 2nd ed. Cincinnati: Anderson Publishing, Co.

Wiehe, Vernon R. (1996). *Working with Child Abuse and Neglect: A Primer.* Thousand Oaks, CA: Sage Publications.

WILLIAMS, G. (1983). "Child protection: A journey into history." *Journal of Clinical Child Psychology*, (12), 236–43.

WOLLONS, R. (Ed.) (1993). *Children at Risk in America: A History Concepts and Public Policy*. Albany: State University of New York Press.

WORDES, MADELINE, AND JONES, SHARON M. (1998). "Trends in juvenile detention and steps toward reform." *Crime & Delinquency*, 44(4), 544–560.

YINGER, J. MILTON (1965). *Toward a Field Theory of Behavior*. New York: McGraw-Hill.

ZAEHRINGER, BRENT (1998, July). *Juvenile Boot Camps: Cost and Effectiveness vs. Residential Facilities*. Koch Crime Institute White Paper Report. Topeka, KS: Koch Crime Institute. [online] Retrieved November 16, 2000. http://www.kci.org/publications/white_paper/boot_camp/index.htm.

ZIGLER, EDWARD, AND HALL, NANCY W. (1989). "Physical Child Abuse in America: Past, Present, and Future." In Dante Cicchetti and Vicki Carlson (Eds.), *Child Maltreatment: Theory and Research on the Causes and Consequences of Child Abuse and Neglect* (pp. 38–75). New York: Cambridge University Press.

GLOSSARY OF KEY TERMS

Aversion therapy.   An approach to therapy in which the therapist attempts to develop a "mini-phobia" as an aversion to a particular behavior.

Behavioral modification.   Behavior modification or behavior therapies seek to either increase or decrease a particular behavior. This treatment does not seek to identify what the source of the problem behavior is, rather it seeks to alter the undesired behavior that is occurring at the present time. Relies on the works of Ivan Pavlov's classical conditioning and B. F. Skinner's operant conditioning these two models have been used as treatment approaches in both the juvenile and adult settings.

Boot camps.   Short-term confinement that are a military-style intermediate sanction used to both punish and rehabilitate offenders who have violated the law.

Cognitive therapy.   Focuses on the thinking and behavior of youth by dealing with observable behavior, it does not require professional staff such as psychologists, and it requires confrontation of inappropriate behavior, which can occur in a controlled setting;

Day reporting centers.   Facilities designed to work with youth during the day and where assigned youth report and receive the benefit of education, counseling, and cultural activities before returning home in the evening.

Deinstitutionalization.   The process of removing youth from long-term facilities as in the case of Massachussets under the guidance of Jerome Miller.

Group homes.   Group homes are either public or private, short-term confinement facilities for small numbers of youth (four to twelve) in a home like setting located in the community.

Group therapy. Working with individual in a group setting of six to eight patients drawing upon the collective insight of all group members to assist in the therapeutic process.

Guided group interaction. A therapeutic process that draws upon group dynamics and techniques to help youths control their future behavior by motivating and teaching them to change.

Juvenile detention. Short-term confinement for youth awaiting a hearing.

Reality therapy. Asserting that individuals are responsible for their own behavior it is the responsibility of the group leader to direct the client(s) to look at their own behavior (in a group setting) and take responsibility for their actions. Reality therapy incorporates the use of cognitive theory, behavioral concepts, it is directive, and didactic. The ultimate goal of therapy is to help the offender become more emotionally strong and rational in their behavior.

Reception and diagnostic centers. These centers are designed as short-term facilities where adjudicated juveniles are put through a battery of tests including psychological, academic (including IQ tests), and risk/needs assessments to assess the appropriate custody and care level before being designated to another facility.

Therapeutic communities/milieu therapy. In the therapeutic community, the central premise is the entire environment/institution is involved in the administration of the therapy and with the use of a variety of techniques the offender learns more responsible ways of behaving.

Token economy systems. An approach to rehabilitation in which the program is designed to reward desired behaviors through awarding of points which can be exchanged for a desirable reward, i.e., a trip to the mall or to see a movie.

Training schools Training schools are the equivalent of an adult prison. They typically house those youths defined as the most serious felony offenders and fall under a variety of different names, training schools regulate the movement and behavior for youths on a twenty-four-hour-a-day/seven-day-a-week schedule.

PART III
MANAGING PROCESSES IN JUVENILE JUSTICE

Part III looks at managing the processes in juvenile justice. Goals and effectiveness of the juvenile justice system, the organization, and how to organize for efficiency and effectiveness are explored as well as decision making, power, and intergroup relations and conflict, as we attempt to understand the successes and failures of the juvenile justice system.

CHAPTER 9

GOALS AND EFFECTIVENESS OF THE JUVENILE JUSTICE SYSTEM

KEY TERMS

Critical task   Organizational goals   Multiple goals
Goals   Real goals   Management by objectives
Formal goals   Stated goals   Total quality management
Informal goals   Operative goals   Planning

CASE STUDY

Evaluation in the Seventeenth Judicial Circuit Court Family Division
Jack Roedema*
Administrator, Family Court

Historically, courts and probably many other social agencies have placed a low priority on the importance of evaluation. There are a number of reasons why courts seldom evaluate their programs and services, despite the fact they have the potential to enhance the quality of life in their communities. First, and for a variety of reasons, most courts have not been required either internally or externally to evaluate what they do. Second, to many it often appears very difficult to evaluate the work of a court or social agency. For instance, in business the bottom line is making a profit, but with a court the end result is not always so clear and is frequently varied and complex. Last, there is a genuine fear of evaluation. Evaluation takes time, expertise, and other resources that normally courts do not have

*Contributed by: Jack Roedema, Court Administrator, Seventeenth Judicial Circuit Court, Family Division, Kent County, Michigan.

available. Also, courts may feel threatened by evaluation and fret about not meeting goals and as a result possibly lose funding.

Times change, however, and most courts and other related social organizations must evaluate what they do. Several reasons prompt this change. More and more funding organizations and elected officials are requiring evaluations to ensure that what they are paying for is really doing what it should. In Kent County, the Seventeenth Judicial Circuit Court Family Division has a rich tradition of providing direct services to children, youth, and families. Many of these services are not mandated by statute. Our local government helps fund these programs but want to be good stewards to their constituency as well. It doesn't help that the criminal justice system in most jurisdictions demands a bigger and bigger share of public dollars. County officials require performance measurement data from all county departments and request the court provide the same. This response flows, in part, from the fact that the general citizenry is becoming more vocal in requesting accountability from courts. In addition, and with the increase of grant funding for programs and services, courts are required to complete a thorough evaluation of the effectiveness of these programs. Finally, courts are discovering that most of their programs are in fact successful and meet the stated needs.

The Seventeenth Judicial Circuit Court Family Division in Kent County tracks over two hundred performance indicators that flow from goals and objectives. We define a performance measure as an indicator of how effective and efficient our services and programs are working. These measurements are compiled quarterly and reported annually to the judges and board of commissioners. The local county administration has played an important role in encouraging departments and courts to compile these statistics and have also provided training and ongoing support. They also recognize that this is a work in progress and refinements will occur along the way. For instance, most of the court's first performance measurements were simply output data. Output data generally is a measure of the number of units produced or services provided. As we refine this process, the court is now measuring more and more outcome data. These measurements generally reflect indicators of timeliness, cost effectiveness, and quality.

Outcome data also measure the extent to which a service or program has achieved its goals and objectives or desired impact on its clients or community. For example, it is fine to measure how many juveniles successfully complete a certain program, but it is much more worthwhile to know how many of these juveniles who successfully complete the program are not involved in a law violation within one year after successful discharge from the program. Also, it is good to know that the intake unit of the court assigned over twenty-eight hundred cases to probation officers in a given year, but even better that it only took probation officers on the average of 7.5 days to see personally these cases once they were assigned. The days of reciting an anecdotal success story to show a program works is no longer valid.

We have begun to require all programs, services, and functions of the court to state goals, objectives to meet these goals, and performance indicators that measure progress toward goals. It is important, however, not to be overwhelmed by the process of collecting and reporting outcome measurements. Innocuous or useless data should not find its way into the process. However, it is acceptable to track output data, since that serves a purpose as well and sometimes provides a backdrop and foundation for outcome data. For instance, it is important to know how much restitution is collected and paid to victims (output). What flows from this information might then be how many juveniles pay total restitution as ordered and what percent pay this amount within six months (outcome).

It is often difficult to get started on the long road to tracking performance and evaluating success. I encourage my staff to view evaluation as a tool for improvement and accountability. I persuade staff to step back and play the role of a citizen or county commissioner. What type of questions would they ask about your program or service? How would you respond to demonstrate that your program is effective and efficient and is doing what it is set up to do? Would our presentation be convincing and lead to support and confidence? And then I tell them a request such as this could be just around the corner. This is a good place to start, and I can guarantee more detailed and valued information will start to follow.

Compiling and tracking performance measurements are here to stay. At our court we measure performance because it improves the delivery of some of our most important services, detects areas that aren't working or need improvement, recognizes success, mobilizes support both from within and without the court, improves accountability for budget expenditures, and certainly improves public communication. We have a long way to go since many of our performance measurements are still output data. However, our court's commitment to performance measurement and evaluation is reflected in the fact we have now assigned one staff person to work in the area of developing new and relevant performance measurements and monitoring and refining existing measurements.

INTRODUCTION

The juvenile court was conceived as an alternative court for children who were felt to be in need of services either because they were delinquent or because of neglect or abuse. The harshness of the adult system with its adversarial nature was felt to be inappropriate for children, to say nothing of the abuse and mistreatment suffered by children who were sent to adult prisons. Today the adult system is still an adversarial system that often pays little attention to treatment or program concerns as opposed to the philosophy of the juvenile justice system that attempts to undo damage done to the child by adults. Over the years, the juvenile court has evolved into an institution that seeks to protect the child and the public, while at the same time offering counseling and treatment to the child and the family. Because of these goals, at least in part, it has come under fire.

The goals of the original reformers and their intent is commendable. Today, however, many goals of the juvenile court, such as a strong emphasis on punishment, were not so prominent twenty or thirty years ago. How has this happened and what are the goals of the juvenile court today? How can the effective juvenile court administrator develop goals that mesh with the needs of the community, the court, and the child? This chapter takes up these questions and attempts to define how goals are established and their relevance to today's society.

THE HISTORY OF JUVENILE JUSTICE

Juvenile delinquency has been around as long as there have been children, but a formal mechanism to deal with juvenile offenders is a fairly recent phenomenon. As early as the sixth century B.C., juvenile misbehavior was noted by the Greeks. Hammurabi who ruled Babylon from 1792 to 1750 B.C. created the first known set of written rules for a kingdom and included a prohibition that was aimed at disobedient children and stated that: *If a son strike the father, one shall cut off his hands* (Regoli and Hewitt, 1994). Children were usually viewed as property, and they had no rights. Over time, as daily life lost some of its harshness and as affluence increased for many families, children began to be viewed differently.

Ultimately, changes in family structure over time assisted in bringing about a change in how children and delinquency were viewed and dealt with (Siegal and Senna, 1997). It is rooted in the decline of marriage as a matter of mutual consent and for convenience, and the growth of marriage based on love and attraction, not parental dominance. This, in turn, created the nuclear family with which we are familiar today.

Early efforts to work with wayward and delinquent youth were largely left up to the family, except in those cases that were thought to be so serious as to require the intervention of the courts, which were geared to dealing with adults. The American innovation of a juvenile court has its antecedents that go back to Roman times, but for the purposes of this text we will begin with the later English common law. Champion (1998) provides an excellent summary of the history of the juvenile court.

Under English law in the sixteenth century, the shire was the lowest governmental unit responsible for preserving the peace. The shire reeve, or the sheriff as we know him (or her) today, was the chief law enforcement officer who was responsible for apprehending law breakers and bringing them before the chancery court. At this time in England, there were no distinctions between youthful offenders over the age of seven and adults. They were administered the same punishments as adults such as stocks and pillories, whipping, branding, and in some cases execution. Incarceration was not used sparingly, and if the youth were sent to prison, the circumstances were particularly grim.

Early immigrants to North America brought those institutions with them with which they were most familiar, and their notions of justice were no exception. However, it was the early Quakers who recognized that changes in the jails were needed. Prior to the American Revolution, they often visited the High Street Jail in Philadelphia to bring food, clothing, and to give religious instruction and counseling. In 1787, the Quakers established the Philadelphia Society for Alleviating the Miseries of the Public Prisons. This group, composed of prominent citizens, were appalled by conditions in the jail and sought to correct what they thought to be an injustice. Through their influence, the Walnut Street Jail was opened in 1776 and transformed into America's first long-term prison. It boasted the first efforts at classification of offenders, rehabilitation programs and meaningful work. The classification of prisoners is especially important, in that children and youthful offenders were segregated from adults in order to protect them.

Immigration and urban migration caused the cities of New York, Boston, Philadelphia, and others to grow at an unmanageable rate, and quite simply they were the barracks of industry. Unsupervised children were abundant because of working and deceased parents, and they were inordinately involved in acts of vandalism and theft. In response to the numbers of unsupervised children, the Child Savers Movement arose as a response by the middle and upper classes to give assistance in many forms. Food and shelter were made available for those who came to the attention of the authorities, and settlement houses were developed to provide educational, social, and recreational activities for idle children (see Regoli and Hewitt, 2003, and Thornton, Jr. and Voigt, 1992).

In 1825, the first House of Refuge was opened in New York City. It was an institution largely for the management of what we call status offenders today. Children guilty only of the "crimes" of running away or of incorrigibility were placed in the House of Refuge, where they were supposed to receive education and training. The House of Refuge soon degenerated into holding facilities for children of immigrants where the atmosphere was less than therapeutic and was often cruel and abusive.

In 1848, the first Reform School was opened in Westboro, Massachusetts, and by the end of the 1800s, all states had reform schools in one form or another. Champion notes that all were characterized by strict discipline, absolute control over behavior, and compulsory work. However, the problem arose that during and because of the Civil War, there were even more orphaned children who were placed in reform school for no other reason than that they had no home. The consequence was that many youth then went on to a career in criminal behavior when all they needed was a secure home, love, and discipline.

There were few legal challenges to the authority of the state over children in the intervening years, but a movement was growing that viewed the adult criminal justice system as too harsh, too confrontive, and as offering few rehabilitative opportunities for children. While similar efforts were underway in many states, reformers in Illinois were successful in persuading the legislature to pass a bill to provide a separate court for children under the age of sixteen. Thus on July 1, 1899, the Illinois legislature passed the Act to Regulate the Treatment and Control of Dependent, Neglected, and Delinquent Children, also known as the Illinois Juvenile Court Act. However, the Governor was not entirely convinced and waited until the last possible day to sign the act into law (Thornton, Jr. and Voigt, 1992). Most states saw the value of such legislation, and by 1945 all forty-eight contiguous states had a juvenile court in one form or another. Since the 1960s, juvenile justice has become more and more oriented to a corporate approach to management, that is attempting to take advantage of what we know about how to effectively manage a pubic organization. This chapter introduces the reader to the importance of goals and how they provide a road map of sorts to guide the organization on to excellence.

GOALS OF THE JUVENILE JUSTICE ORGANIZATION

The juvenile justice organization seems to have lost its moorings in recent years. Conflicting goals, pressure from the public, the media, and the legislature have combined to create an environment characterized by confusion and self-doubt. Nevertheless, each individual and each organization have goals, both formal and informal, that contribute to the success or lack of success) of the organization.

Establishing goals however, is not always that easy for an organization, especially those with multiple constituencies. Wilson (1989) points out that successful organizations learn how to cope with three organizational issues. First, they need to decide on how to perform its **critical task**. For the juvenile justice system, that includes how to protect the public, how to best rehabilitate the child, and how to protect the legal and civil rights of the child while at the same time determining the best disposition for the child.

Second, the successful organization needs to gain "agreement about and widespread (if not enthusiastic) endorsement of the way the *critical task* [is] defined" (Wilson, 1989, p. 26). This is a formidable task for the juvenile justice system indeed. As long as there is confusion over the mission of the juvenile justice system and its various components, then agreement will not be forthcoming.

Third, according to Wilson, each organization must "acquire sufficient freedom of action and external political support (or at least non-opposition) to permit it to redefine its tasks as it saw best and to infuse that definition with a sense of mission" (Wilson, 1989, p. 26). In other words, it acquires a reasonable degree of autonomy. Many juvenile justice organizations today do not have that degree of autonomy. We have discussed the many influences on the organization, and the result is that the juvenile justice system is buffeted by too many influences for any subunit to have much autonomy at all.

We begin with the assertion that effective management is that management that efficiently allocates resources to achieve organizational goals. A **goal** is the desired end result of some exertion of effort. Goals can be either formal or informal. Formal goals are those that are established by organizational members as desired end results. **Formal goals** can also be imposed on the organization by the courts, legislature, or a board of directors. For example, a formal goal of a juvenile court would be to draw families into the rehabilitation process by order of the court (an objective would target a percentage of cases appearing before the court).

Informal goals are those that are more personal or have been agreed upon by organization members without discussion. Informal goals of the juvenile court include keeping adjudicated youth out of further involvement in delinquent behavior and keeping them in school. Hall and Clark (1980), after visiting a number of juvenile courts, determined that the [formal] operational goals were:

1. Determine the best disposition for each child who appears before the court.
2. Protect the civil and legal rights of minors.
3. Protect the community from youths who pose personal threats to the community.
4. Hear and justly dispose of cases before the court.
5. Cooperate with other agencies who deal with problem youths.
6. Remove children from family situations that are damaging to their welfare.
7. Foster acceptance of an individualized rehabilitative treatment philosophy by the general public and other system agencies.
8. Develop more resources and better methods of helping problem youth.

These goals capture the essence of the juvenile court in general. However, there is more to goals than simply stating them. Goals provide a road map to the future in that they point the way. Goals are a means to assess organizational effectiveness, and they provide motivation and direction for staff. Unfortunately, many juvenile justice organizations lurch from crisis to crisis and rarely establish formal goals and objectives. If a court is to effectively serve the needs of the community, leaders in the community such as judges or magistrates as well as the court administrator or chief probation officer must establish both short-term and long-term goals.

TYPES OF GOALS

The effective leader will recognize the value of a vision and goals to work towards. A vision is a picture of the future with some implicit or explicit commentary on why people should strive to create that future (Kotter, 1996). It begins with a vision, which is transformed into goals. As can be seen in the goals identified by Hall and Clark (1980), it is possible to establish a road map to the future. Etzioni (1964) points out that goals set down guidelines for future activity and constitute a source of legitimacy, which justifies the existence of an organization. They also serve as standards by which outsiders can judge the success of an organization.

An **organizational goal** is "a desired state of affairs which the organization attempts to realize" (Etzioni, 1964). For example, controlling juvenile crime through prevention and rehabilitation programs may be the stated goal of the juvenile court, but if that goal is reached, then it ceases to be a stated goal. In fact, as Etzioni points out, in a sense as a goal it never existed, it is a state which we seek, not one we have. As a consequence, the images conjured up by the establishment of goals are a very real sociological force that affects the actions and reactions of actors in the juvenile justice system, but as in the example, eliminating juvenile crime is probably not possible.

Organizations are established to achieve certain goals, and there are many individuals whose personal goals and activities affect organizational goals. Cyert and March (1963) call our attention to the fact that people have goals but that collectivities of people do not have goals. Drawing upon Cyert and March's work, the juvenile court must define a theory of organizational decision making that accounts for organizational level goals, individual goals, and goals of the political subsystem.

Since collectivities of people do not have goals, it is up to the administrator or manager to develop organizational goals in consultation with subordinates. Etzioni (1964) points out that there are two types of goals: real and stated. **Real goals** are those future states toward which a majority of the organization's means and the major organizational commitments of the participants are directed. **Stated goals** are those which are given lip service, but to which few resources are devoted and which have a lower priority. The rub comes, as Etzioni states, with the appearance of unintended consequences. Goals are intended, "unintended consequences are unplanned, unexpected results of action oriented toward some goal" (Etzioni, 1964, p. 7).

There are also organizational goals and individual goals (Houston, 1999). Organizational goals can be either official or operative. Official goals are those put forth for public consumption. **Operative goals** specify what the organization is actually trying to do. The juvenile court has official goals of making the community safer and to rehabilitate children adjudicated guilty of delinquent offenses.

The juvenile court, like many other correctional organizations, serves an integrative function (Houston, 1999) and usually the official and operative goals are congruent. Thus, there is little organizational stress relative to goal incongruence. The problem arises when the political subsystem begins to define goals for the juvenile justice system that may not be attainable given existing official and operative goals.

MULTIPLE AND CONFLICTING GOALS

All organizations have **multiple goals** and some of those goals conflict with each other, with goals of other departments, and with goals of other parts of the system. Daft (1989) offers a good discussion of managing multiple and conflicting goals. He offers four techniques:

- **Satisficing.** The organization accepts satisfactory rather than a superior performance. By accepting satisfactory performance, the organization can achieve several goals simultaniously. A juvenile court satisfices by having multiple goals of supervision of children on the caseload, of offering counseling groups, and of protecting the community. They do not maximize any of these goals and accept mediocrity for all.

- **Sequential attention.** This means that the organization will attend to important goals for a period of time and then turn to other goals. Sequential attention allows the organization to achieve satisfactory levels of performance on one goal before attending to another. This is often found in courts that are particularly political. For example, one juvenile court administrator several years ago found himself held hostage by five judges, each with a different agenda and different demands. Two demanded a just deserts approach to probation supervision and three each thought of themselves as social workers and attempted to micromanage the caseloads of the probation officers. The administrator, after a time, simply pursued the goals of the judges in turn, depending on who was the most vocal and demanding.

- **Preference ordering.** In this technique, top management will establish goal priorities. For example, a juvenile institution will establish a priority of security over rehabilitation programs. It is not that attention will not be given to rehabilitation or education and vocational training and that those goals will not be attained. However, those goals may be difficult to achieve or difficult to measure, or the current level of perfomance may not be adequate. If numbers of youth completing GED or high school goes up, or if personality inventory scores of youth involved in counseling programs go up, goals may be reevaluated and reprioritized.

- **Goal changes.** This means that goal priorities are periodically revised. Not because of satisficing, or because of preference ordering, but because the managers realize that goals are not static. They realize that goals must constantly be reevaluated and changed in light of new information.

Individual and Organizational Goals

We must also pay attention to the fact that there are both individual and organizational goals. Organizations are established to achieve certain goals and organizations are made up of individuals whose personal goals and activities may differ from, but most certainly affect, organizational goals. Thompson and McErven (1958) offer a framework that organizes any discussion of organizational goal setting. They point out that we need to consider goals from three different perspectives: the environmental level, the organizational level, and the individual level.

Environmental Level

Competition between organizations is often intense as resources become more scarce. The various divisions in a State Youth Commission compete for tax dollars, positions, and favorable attention from the legislature and the media. For example, when setting goals, the effective manager will be sure to establish goals that meet high-profile needs and goals that are supported with greater attention to detail. In addition, the supervisor or executive will do what lobbying he or she can in order to press the case for his or her goals that are tied to the budget.

Bargaining between organizations and within organizations is inevitable. A good example of bargaining is that which takes place between the organization and the labor union. Each must modify goals to an extent in order to continue to meet the needs of the public and the members.

Co-optation is defined by Thompson and McErven (1958) as "the process of absorbing new elements into the leadership or policy-determining structure of an organization as a means of averting threats to its stability or existence." In other words, the organization must satisfy the demands of constituencies in its environment whose support is important for its continued survival. Co-optation is not "selling out" but rather an approach that considers the interdependencies of individuals and organizations.

Coalition refers to two or more organizations combining their resources and personnel for the purpose of achieving certain objectives. This approach is primarily political and can be used as a form of co-optation. Public organizations often form a coalition to overcome a particular problem such as increasing educational opportunities, or to get the GED approved for youth under the age of eighteen.

Organizational Level

The juvenile justice organization is a contrived unit whose purpose is to achieve certain goals. For example, a juvenile residential institution pursues the goal of educating the youth while attempting to instill a measure of conformity to community values. In addition, a certain level of security must be maintained in order to protect other youth and the community. Perrow (1961) calls our attention to the difference between official and operative goals. Official goals are those goals put forth for public consumption. They are purposefully vague and general and usually specify what the organization is actually trying to do, regardless of the operational goals.

There are a number of internal as well as external influences that affect the goals and goal setting of an organization. The type of client the organization works with influences the type of goals it establishes and the time frames for establishing them. For example a juvenile court may establish a goal to work more closely with schools as measured by time spent with school counselors and with youth in the school. A juvenile residential institution may establish a goal of increasing the number of hours spent on counseling by staff in the cottages. Thus, the court is interested in interfacing with the community and working with the child. The institution is interested in increasing hours of programs and so on in the cottages.

The education and commitment of staff influence goals and goal setting. Most juvenile courts attempt to hire probation officers with a college degree in the social sciences, but there are those jurisdictions that find it difficult to attract degreed candidates, or the judge, or judges, believes that there are other qualifications that are more important. For example, some jurisdictions will hire retired police officers or sheriff's deputies for the position because of the combination of a lack of degreed candidates and a belief by the hiring authority that police experience is a better qualification for the position.

In institutions, there is a broad range of education achievement among staff, but there are varying levels of commitment to the organization and its goals in both the court and the institution. Finally, because of the diversity experienced in juvenile justice, employees of different agencies will often support conflicting goals. Staff of an institution will support, for example, goals of staff solidarity and custody. Probation officers will value individual effort with youth and the ability to work in neighborhoods. Thus, support of these differing goals could lead to competition between agencies and lead to some animosity if not handled properly.

There are also external influences that are important to consider when establishing goals. Atchison and Hill (1978) call our attention to several external influences on goal setting.

Political.   Today, more than ever, the juvenile justice system is under attack from legislators who want to make the juvenile system more like the adult system in the name of accountability or community safety. While there may be merit for some arguments, and room for improvement, the ramifications are many in terms of policy, employment practices, and programs.

Social.   Over time, social attitudes change and are reflected in the legal code. They informally affect how the organization, employees, and youth in the care and control of the organization are perceived and treated.

Technological.   The great strides made in communications technology and in the social sciences have greatly affected how the juvenile justice organization is managed.

Computers, electronic surveillance, and community policing and community probation have altered the way we manage resources in an organization.

Individual Level

The individual level is composed of the goals of the individual and his or her relationship to the organization. In order to assure organizational excellence, personal and organizational goals must be congruent. Sometimes an organization will develop a means to increase organizational effectiveness, but the unanticipated consequences include a decrease in employee dissatisfaction. For example, implementation of a computerized program to assure efficient case management may take away a measure of individual initiative. Regardless, a strong bond sometimes develops between the individual and the organization. Lorsch and Morse (1979) and Porter and Lawler (1979) found that managers who experience a sense of competency are motivated to achieve organization goals, and have a high degree of satisfaction when the organization is deigned to meet both organizational goals and personal goals. Further, when the organization rewards performance, the employee has a heightened sense of personal satisfaction.

One further note is in order, that is, some individuals put a personal goal ahead of organizational goals resulting in conflict. Robert K. Merton (1968) calls our attention to the fact that some people are affected by bureaucratic organizations and often seek the security of rigid adherence to rules and regulations for their own sake. This results in goal displacement in which adherence to rules becomes an end it itself. It may be unrealistic to expect perfect compatibility between personal and organizational goals; employees must give up a measure of personal autonomy and self-expression in order to gain full benefit from the organization.

Having now discussed the issues and pitfalls of goal setting, we now turn to the real work of developing goals that will guide the juvenile justice organization on to the future.

Creating a Future

Peter M. Senge (1990) points out that we can create our own future by thinking strategically and by rearranging the way people think. Two ways of creating a future that serves our needs and those of the youth we serve are discussed here, MBO (Managing by Objectives) and TQM (Total Quality Management).

Management by Objectives

In any organization, it is important to keep on track and to work toward goals. Whether goals are established by departments, teams, or the organization as a whole, it is important to involve everyone in the process. Once goals or objectives are established, they offer a yardstick against which to measure the organization's progress over time.

Management by Objectives (MBO) is "a well-known philosophy of management that assesses an organization and its members by how well they achieve specific goals that superiors and subordinates have jointly established" (Robbins, 1987). Management by

Objectives can be defined as an attempt to integrate individual and overall organizational goals by involving all levels of staff in a goal-setting process. There is some discussion in the literature in regard to whether or not MBO should be a top-down or bottom-up approach. In a top-down approach, top management formulates objectives, and they are imposed on line and supervisory staff. In a bottom-up approach, objectives are formulated by supervisors and line staff and given to top management.

The consensus seems to be that a compromise is best. Organizations have multiple goals that compete and sometimes appear to be incompatible. This is especially so in a juvenile justice organization where the interests of management, staff, and children often conflict, and those conflicts must be resolved and priorities established. Warriner (1965) concludes, not entirely tongue-in-cheek, that "organizational objectives should be treated as fiction, produced by an organization to account for, explain, or rationalize its existence to particular audiences rather than as valid and reliable indications of purpose." Thus, it is important to involve as many staff as possible and to develop a living document that reflects the real organization and not an organization the manager thinks a particular audience wants to see.

Establishing Objectives

Regardless if one is dealing with a juvenile institution or a community program, the MBO process is a lengthy one that may require years to put firmly in place. Objectives must be reviewed periodically so that progress can be reviewed and, if necessary, changes made. Everyone in the organization, or unit, should feel some ownership of the program.

Establishing organizational objectives is a process that takes a good deal of time. Ideally, the manager should convene the staff away from the regular place of work for a day-long retreat and through the process of brainstorming arrive at a set of objectives that they wish to pursue over the coming year. Through the use of a marking board or flip-chart, ideas can be recorded, refined, and agreed upon. Care must be taken to not let strong personalities impose their ideas on others, and new employees must be drawn into the process. Often newcomers have good ideas, but are hesitant to speak up for fear of making someone angry. Finally, when all is said and done, a document exists that can chart the organizations course for the coming year.

The effective manager should strive to develop objectives in all areas that affect the organization. Drucker (1954) identifies seven key areas important to the business manager; using those as a guide we offer the following areas for juvenile justice mangers:

- **Comparative objectives.** Managers should set objectives that allow it to catch up with other, more progressive agencies, or which would highlight the agencies ability to be a leader in the field or the area in which the organization is located.

- **Innovation.** Management should develop objectives that outline its commitment to sound management and progressive programs for youth.

- **Productivity.** Objectives should be established that provides targets for staff.

- **Physical and financial resources.** Management should set objectives regarding use, acquisition, and maintenance of physical resources.

- **Service.** Objectives should be set for enhanced service to youth and the community.
- **Staff performance and attitude.** Management should set objectives relative to staff "production" and attitude.
- **Public responsibility.** Objectives should be set that outline the agency responsibilities to the public and the community.

According to Certo (1985), managers can increase the quality of their objectives by following the below guidelines:

1. Managers should allow the people responsible for attaining the objectives to have a voice in setting them. In juvenile justice, line staff often have a better feel for conditions than top management; therefore, their input is crucial if work-related problems faced daily by line staff are going to be translated into meaningful objectives.

2. Managers should state objectives as specifically as possible. Precise language minimizes confusion. Further, objectives should be unambiguous, prioritized, measurable, and attainable.

3. Managers should relate objectives to specific actions whenever necessary. Specific actions eliminate the need for guesswork on the part of those responsible for achieving the objectives.

4. Managers should pinpoint expected results. Employees will know when they have achieved results. Completion of a cottage renovation on time is something to celebrate. Likewise the implementation of a new vocational training program will give a boost to the spirits of staff.

5. Managers should set goals high enough that employees will have to work hard to achieve them, but not so high that employees become discouraged and give up trying.

6. Managers should specify when they expect goals to be achieved. Stated time frames are important so that employees can pace themselves.

7. Managers should set objectives (with staff) only in relation to other organization objectives. Keeping a close eye on the larger picture will keep conflicting objectives to a minimum.

8. Managers should write out the objectives clearly and simply. Understandable and concise language should be used when communicating a goal to the organization.

There often are problems in developing an MBO program, Kast and Rosenzweig (1979) point out that

> Management by objectives programs have been used successfully by a number of business organizations to integrate organizational and individual goals. The most successful programs appear to be those that emphasize a total systems approach to MBO and take into consideration its impact on all of the organization's subsystems (p. 168).

Total Quality Management

Total quality management (TQM) is a means of assuring quality in an organization. At the same time it allows the organization to prioritize services in terms of value, and at the same time it often radically alters the way the organization goes about its daily business. Unlike MBO, which is both a pre-control and post-control mechanism, TQM builds quality into the culture.

Understanding TQM in the context of juvenile justice means that everyone involved must understand that all work in the organization is part of a process. What goes on in one part of the organization or institution affects what goes on in other parts of the system. One way to assure the quality of services is to build quality into every step of the work process. In many public agencies, including adult and juvenile corrections, TQM has been the catalyst to propel the organization from mediocrity to excellence.

Morgan and Murgatroyd (1994) point out that TQM:

TQM and the Florida Department of Juvenile Justice

Florida has worked hard to build quality into the programs of the Department of Juvenile Justice. In 1994, the Department of Juvenile Justice established the quality assurance (QA) system as part of the Juvenile Justice Reform Act. An approach was developed to review programs that encompass the principles of total quality management (TQM). The approach is innovative and the Florida Department of Juvenile Justice Services has received wide acclaim for its efforts.

The QA program uses a team approach that provides a broad and balanced perspective for program evaluation. The reviewer not only asks if something is being done, but also asks, "How well is it being done?" Answers rely on the professional judgment of the individuals who are familiar with the job or task.

In addition, the QA process also emphasizes using multiple data sources to document policy, procedure, and practice. QA reviewers examine program records and files to document policy, conduct interviews with managers, line staff, youth, parents, and others to document program operations over an extended period of time. Rating decisions are thus based on substantiated conclusions from three separate data sources: policy, procedure, and practice.

Approximately 85 percent of the Department of Juvenile Justice are contacted. QA documents the quality of the programs, and the annual reviews have made a positive difference in the juvenile justice system and over five years' review have markedly improved the system. During the 1999 cycle, 523 programs were reviewed during the year. The distribution of scores illustrate a bell-shaped curve with 4 percent of programs rated as superior, 31 percent as high satisfactory, 47 percent satisfactory, 15 percent marginal satisfactory, and 3 percent below satisfactory.

Clearly, the Florida Department of Juvenile Justice has put the principles of TQM to work for the youth and taxpayers of Florida. Continued monitoring and review will assist programs in maintaining or achieving excellence and in building quality into the programs.

1. Involves everything an organization, a society, or a community does, which in the eyes of others determines its reputation on a comparative basis with the best alternatives.

2. Is a total system of quality improvement with decision making based on facts—data collection—not opinion or impression.

3. Embraces not only the quality of the specific product or service which the end-user or the customer purchases or receives, but everything an organization does internally to achieve continuing performance improvement.

4. Assumes that quality is the outcome of all activities that takes place within an organization, that all functions and all employees have to participate in the improvement process, and that organizations need both quality systems and a quality culture.

5. Is a way of managing an organization so that every job and process is carried out right, first time every time. It affects everyone.

Perhaps no name is associated with TQM more than that of W. Edwards Deming. Dr. Deming is best known for his *14 Points* and his *Deming Wheel*. The *14 Points* express his methods and philosophy for managers, which he saw as necessary to the transformation of businesses and manufacturing. Over time, his approach evolved from one of strictly product to one where the worker and consumer were important parts of the quality process. The Deming Wheel is a systematic approach to problem solving, and its format assures quality built into every step of the manufacturing process.

Deming also identified "five deadly diseases" that need to be dealt with if the manager is to be successful in transforming the culture of an organization.

- A general lack of constancy and purpose.
- Too much emphasis on short-term profit.
- A lack of or unsuitable evaluation of performance, merit rating, or annual review.
- Management too mobile.
- Management decision making too readily relies on quantitative data without paying due consideration to less tangible or hidden factors.

There are a number of tools available to the manager who wants to improve problem analysis and management. The Fishbone (see Figure 9.1) allows the manager to determine cause and effect, flowcharts allows one to challenge the process, arrow diagrams are useful to show the time required to solve a problem, and so on.

Total quality management is a means to continuously improve services within the juvenile justice organization. It is not so much a technique as much as it is a paradigm shift. That is, it is a shift from making one or two persons responsible for quality within an organization, to making all members of an organization responsible for quality. True quality begins at the top of the organization and continues down the organizational ladder where it finally impacts the quality of services and life for youth charged to the care of the organization.

Deming's 14 Points

1. Create constancy of purpose toward improvement of product and service, with the aim of becoming competitive and staying in business and providing jobs.

2. Adopt the new philosophy. We are in a new economic age. Western managers must awaken to the challenge, must learn their responsibilities and take on leadership for change.

3. Cease dependence on inspection to achieve quality. Eliminate the need for inspection on a mass basis by building quality into the product in the first place.

4. End the practice of awarding business on the basis of price tag. Instead, minimize total cost. Move toward a single supplier for any one item, in a long-term relationship of loyalty and trust.

5. Improve constantly and forever the system of production and service to improve quality and productivity and thus to constantly decrease costs.

6. Institute training on the job.

7. Institute leadership (see Point 11). The aim of leadership should be to help people and machines and gadgets do a better job. Leadership of management is in need of overhaul, as is leadership of production workers.

8. Drive out fear so that everyone may work effectively for the company.

9. Break down barriers between departments. People in research, design, sales, and production must work as a team, to foresee problems of production and use that may be encountered with the product or service.

10. Eliminate slogans, exhortations, and targets for the work force. Ask for zero defects and new levels of productivity.

11. a. Eliminate work standards (quotas) on the factory floor. Substitute leadership.
    b. Eliminate management by objective. Eliminate management by numbers, numerical goals. Substitute leadership.

12. a. Remove barriers that rob the hourly worker of his or her right to pride of work. The responsibility of supervisors must be changed from sheer numbers to quality.
    b. Remove barriers that rob people in management and engineering of their right to pride of work. This means, among other things, abolishment of the annual or merit rating and of management by objective and management by number.

13. Institute a vigorous program of education and self-improvement.

14. Put everybody in the company to work to accomplish the transformation. The transformation is everybody's job.

Adapted from: Mary Walton, W. Edwards Deming. *The Deming Management Method.* NY: Perigee, 1986.

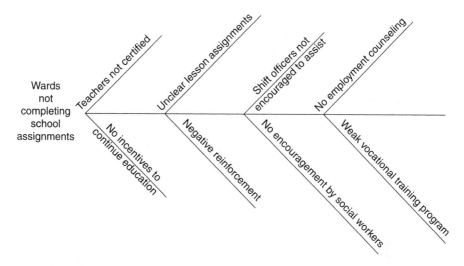

Figure 9.1   Fishbone Diagram

GOALS AND ORGANIZATIONAL EFFECTIVENESS

Every manager and leader of an organization must eventually ask how he or she can evaluate the effectiveness of the organization. The first way the manager will seek to determine effectiveness is by asking, "Did we achieve the specified goals of the organization?" At first glance, this may be the sole criterion of success, but there are other measures that we use as well.

Before we examine the characteristics that determine the effectiveness of a juvenile justice organization, we need to ask some questions:

1. What is the growth trend of the organization? Will it increase in number of service units provided, or will it remain about the same over time?

2. In what way is the organization's environment changing? Has the introduction of new approaches to "doing business" created change?

3. Is the morale of staff a goal of the organization? Is it a goal in the same sense of service to the community?

4. Are the subunits in competition with each other? Do they all subscribe to the same set of objectives?

Goal Approach

The goal approach to organizational effectiveness consists of identifying an organization's goals and determining how well the organization is achieving those goals. The important issue here is that the organization must strive to achieve operational goals identified through the process outlined above, rather than more abstract official goals. Operative goals reflect the values of the organization and what staff feels are important.

Internal Criteria Approach

Richard Daft (1989) points out that in the internal approach, effectiveness is measured as internal organizational health and efficiency. An effective organization is a smoothly running entity where employees are happy and satisfied and departmental activities mesh to ensure high productivity. He states that the important element in effectiveness is what the organization does with the resources it has as reflected in internal health and efficiency.

There are certain indicators to determine whether or not the organization is effective or not. They include:

1. Supervisor interest and concern for workers
2. Team spirit, group loyalty, and teamwork.
3. Confidence, trust, and communication between workers and management.
4. Decision making near sources of information, regardless of where those sources are on the organizational chart.
5. Undistorted horizontal and vertical communication, sharing of relevant facts and feelings.
6. Rewards to managers for performance, growth, and development of subordinates, and for creating an effective working group.
7. Interaction between the organization and its parts, with conflict that occurs over projects resolved in the interest of the organization.
8. Are indicators of economic efficiency at a high level and does management communicate that fact with employees?

A Contemporary Approach

The goal approach seems to be the most logical, but there is an argument for combining the two approaches to determine organizational effectiveness. Perhaps many competent managers do combine the two instinctively, but we need to be aware that it is important that we not only establish organizational goals and strive to achieve them, but that we also monitor the internal health of the organization. The effective manager will spend time moving about the organization, keeping a high profile, listening to staff and sitting in on meetings and keeping them informed of issues and occurrences that affect their work and personal lives.

The effective manager will establish a system of rewards for all levels of staff and see to it that competence and loyalty to the organization are rewarded. One way to do so is by breaking the organization up into smaller, more manageable pieces, each one supervised by someone with the authority to make decisions and supervise the day-to-day activities of the unit. Often an organization is broken up into smaller units, but the top executive will not let go and attempts to micromanage the units from afar, thus creating terrible bottlenecks and seriously affecting morale.

Smaller organizations such as group homes and small probation departments are unable to break up into smaller units, but the supervisor can see to it that the above criteria for internal effectiveness are met. In larger community programs, departments and institutions, the organization can be broken up and discretion and authority given to supervisors for greater decision making and supervision responsibility. Cottages in institutions and caseload distributed by zip code, for example in a probation department, are one way to attending to internal health. Once internal health measures are attended to, the implementation of an MBO program is not difficult, and the operational goals of the organization can be met and striven for with a more productive and agreeable work force.

Keep in mind that the juvenile justice organization is a social unit constructed by the government to accomplish some end such as holding youth in secure custody or provide guidance and counseling in a group home. Employees and residents react to and are a part of relationships in the organization, thus one measure of effectiveness should be, how well does the manager use the social forces at work to achieve established objectives.

Planning for the Future

Maintaining maximum organizational effectiveness and quality is a function of a future-oriented manager. As noted by Jack Roedema in the introductory essay, the Seventeenth Judicial Court (Family Division) tracks over two-hundred performance indicators that flow from goals and objectives. A manager, such as Jack Roedema, who wants to lead an organization on to success does so through effective and thoughtful planning. **Planning** can be defined as the process of arranging future activities in order to accomplish a particular objective. Certo (1985) defines planning as the "process of determining how the organization can get where it wants to go." Gibson, Ivancevich, and Donnelly, (1979) point out that "the planning function includes all the managerial activities which lead to the definition of goals and the determination of appropriate means to achieve these goals." They also assert that the planning function can be broken into four parts:

- Establishing goals and fixing their priority.
- Forecasting future events that can affect goal accomplishment.
- Making the plans operational through budgeting.
- Starting and implementing policies that direct the organization's efforts toward the desired ends.

Generally speaking, all planning is directed toward improved decision making and is the first step in the decision-making process. Improved planning and the resultant improvement in decision making has several benefits:

1. Programs and services are improved. The ultimate goal of any juvenile justice organization, is service—service to the community and children and youth under the care, custody, and control of the agency.

2. The ability to identify and analyze problems is improved. Adequate planning generates data and information that can be used to improve decision making.

3. Planning demands that clear and attainable objectives be established. Once objectives are established, the procedures to attain them can be specified, as can the linkages between the objectives.

4. Cooperation and coordination between the various units or departments are improved.

5. Planning allows for effective allocation of resources. In an often resource-scarce environment, it is imperative that the manager establishes priorities for the allocation of resources.

Effective planning precedes policy formulation. The planning process lays the groundwork for policies that meet the needs of the organization and the target group. In addition, planning decreases risk within the organization and ensures the safety and well-being not only of the community, but of line staff and support staff as well. It decreases the risk that requested funds will be cut for the coming year and planning decreases risk that stated objectives will not be met.

Planning allows the chief executive in the position of commissioner of youth services, director, superintendent, chief probation officer or court administrator to push decision making further down the organizational ladder and still maintain effective coordination. Many juvenile justice institutions are custodially-oriented institutions where all decisions are made with a view to security. Juvenile probation officers also make decisions with public safety in mind, but planning is often put on the back burner because of more pressing problems such as lack of budgetary resources or lack of time.

Planning also forces the executive staff to formulate objectives as discussed earlier. Pursuing those objectives requires a coordinated effort throughout the organization, with thought given to decisions that affect the organization. Finally, planning forces the staff to be future-oriented. The advantage of planning is that staff are required to look to the future, anticipate problems or issues, and ponder possible solutions before problems erupt.

Mintzberg (1994) points out that planners, and by implication, CEOs and directors of large agencies, have been notably reluctant to study their own efforts. They have been so busy calling on others to gather data that they are uncertain as to whether or not they are hitting the mark. Further, he points out, planning can be inflexible and stifle creativity and breed resistance to strategic thinking and novel ideas.

SUMMARY

Juvenile delinquency has been with us forever, but a separate formal system for handling juvenile delinquents has been with us only since 1899. In the years since 1899, the juvenile justice system has grown from a few reformers interested in assisting children to a system that critics fear is not doing its job effectively. One way to enhance system effectiveness is to establish goals that serve the youth, the public, and the community. There can be multiple and conflicting goals, and there are ways to handle them. Perhaps the most effective way is through management by objectives (MBO). Establishing goals as a means to guide the organization can only result in measurable and specific results. Another means to assure the effective distribution of resources and quality of programs and services is total quality management. TQM builds quality into the culture of the organization. In the end, the public will have greater confidence in the organization if they feel that results are being accomplished.

CASE STUDY WRAP-UP

Mr. Rodema clearly understands the importance of having goals and measures to determine how established goals are achieved. He works with members of the court to determine what the goals are for the coming year and then uses performance indicators to measure progress in achieving those goals. As Mr. Roedema points out, it is important for the employee to put himself or herself in the place of the county commissioner in order to fully understand the importance of goals.

STUDY QUESTIONS

1. What goals do you think are important for a juvenile court? Why?
2. How do you define goals?
3. Why is satisficing not a proper goal of a juvenile justice organization?
4. How does an MBO program help the manager of a juvenile justice organization create a future?
5. Should individual and organizational goals be congruent? Why?
6. Total quality management is a means to continuously improve services within the juvenile justice organization. Would you say it is a technique or paradigm shift? Why?

BIBLIOGRAPHY

ATCHISON, THOMAS, AND HILL, WINSTON W. (1978). *Management Today: Managing Work in Organizations.* New York: Harcourt Brace Jovanovich, p. 63.

CERTO, SAMUEL (1985). *Principles of Management,* 3rd ed. Dubuque, IA: William C. Brown.

CHAMPION, DEAN J. (1998). *The Juvenile Justice System: Delinquency, Processing, and the Law,* 2nd ed. Upper Saddle River, NJ: Prentice-Hall, Inc.

CYERT, RICHARD, AND MARCH, JAMES G. (1963). *A Behvioral Theory of the Firm.* Englewood Cliffs, NJ: Prentice-Hall, Inc., p. 26.

DAFT, RICHARD L. (1989). *Organization Theory and Design.* St. Paul, MN: West Publishing Company.

DRUCKER, PETER F. (1954). *The Practice of Management.* New York: Harper and Row.

ETZIONI, AMITAI (1964). *Modern Organizations.* Englewood Cliffs, NJ: Prentice-Hall, Inc.

GIBSON, JAMES L., IVANCEVICH, JOHN M., AND DONNELLY, JAMES H., JR. (1979). *Organization: Behavior, Structure, Processes,* 3rd ed. Dallas: Business Publications.

HALL, RICHARD H., AND CLARK, JOHN P. (1980). "An Ineffective Effectiveness Study and Some Suggestions for Future Research." *The Sociological Quarterly, 21,* 119–134.

HOUSTON, JAMES (1999). *Correctional Management: Functions, Skills, and Systems,* 2nd ed. Chicago: Nelson-Hall Publishers.

KAST, FREMONT E., AND ROSENZWEIG, JAMES E. (1979). *Organization and Management: A Systems and Contingency Approach.* New York: McGraw-Hill Book Company.

KOTTER, JOHN P. (1996). *Leading Change.* Boston: Harvard Business School Press.

LORSCH, JAY W., AND MORSE, JOHN J. (1979). "Organizations and Their Members: A Contingency Approach," in Fremont E. Kast and James E. Rosenzweig (Eds.), *Organization and Management,* 3rd ed. (p. 163). New York: McGraw-Hill.

MERTON, ROBERT K. (1968). *Social Theory and Social Structure,* enlarged edition. New York: The Free Press, pp. 186–214.

MINTZBERG, HENRY (1994). *The Rise and Fall of Strategic Planning.* New York: The Free Press.

MORGAN, COLIN, AND MURGATROYD, STEPHEN (1994). *Total Quality Management in the Public Sector: An International Perspective.* Buckingham, England: Open University Press.

PERROW, CHARLES (1961). "The Analysis of Goals in Complex Organizations." *American Sociological Review 26:* 854–66.

PORTER, LYMAN W., AND LAWLER III, EDWARD E. (1979). "Managerial Attitudes and Performance" in Fremont E. Kast and James E. Rosenzweig (Eds.), *Organization and Mangement,* 3rd ed. (p. 163). New York: McGraw-Hill.

REGOLI, ROBERT M., AND HEWITT, JOHN D. (2003). *Delinquency in Society,* 5th ed. Boston: McGraw-Hill.

ROBBINS, STEPHEN P. (1987). *Organization Theory: Structure, Design, and Application,* 2nd ed. Englewood Cliffs, NJ: Prentice-Hall.

SENGE, PETER (1990). *The Fifth Discipline: The Art and Practice of the Learning Organization.* New York: Doubleday.

SIEGAL, LARRY, AND SENNA, JOSEPH (1997). *Juvenile Delinquency: Theory, Practice, and Law,* 6th ed. St. Paul: West Publishing Company.

THOMPSON, JAMES G., AND MCERVEN, WILLIAM J. (1958). "Organizational Goals and Environment: Goal Setting as an Interactive Process." *American Sociological Review,* (February): 23–31.

THORNTON, WILLIAM E., JR., AND VOIGT, LYDIA (1992). *Delinquency and Justice,* 3rd ed. New York: McGraw-Hill, Inc.

WARRINER, CHARLES K. (Spring 1965). "The Problem of Organizational Purpose." *Sociological Quarterly, 6,* 140.

WILSON, JAMES Q. (1985). *Thinking About Crime* (Rev. Ed.) New York: Vintage Books.

WILSON, JAMES Q. (1989). *Bureaucracy: What Government Agencies Do and Why They Do It.* New York: Basic Books.

GLOSSARY OF KEY TERMS

Critical task.   The focus of the organization, its reason for existence.

Formal goals.   Formal goals are those that are declared and publicly noted. They can be established by organizational members, a board of directors, or a central office.

Goals.   A goal is the desired end result of some exertion of effort. Formal goals can also be imposed on the organization by the courts, legislature, or a board of directors.

Informal goals.   Goals that are not formally sanctioned, but are recognized as a goal.

Management by objectives.   A management approach defined as an attempt to integrate individual and overall organizational goals by involving all levels of staff in a goal setting process.

Multiple goals.   Many organizations have several goals and some, or all, may conflict with each other, with goals of other departments, and with goals of other parts of the system.

Operative goals.   Specify what the organization is actually trying to do.

Organizational goals.   A desired state of affairs which the organization attempts to realize.

Planning.   A task that can be defined as the process of arranging future activities in order to accomplish a particular objective

Real goals.   Those future states toward which a majority of the organization's means and the major organizational commitments of the participants are directed.

Stated goals.   Those which are given lip service, but to which few resources are devoted and which have a lower priority.

Total quality management.   TQM is a means of assuring quality in an organization by building it into the process rather than as an afterthought.

CHAPTER 10

ORGANIZATION, BUREAUCRACY, AND SYSTEMS

KEY TERMS

Production organizations	Division of work	Span of management
Political goals	Unity of command	Formal group
Integrative organizations	Centralization	Command group
Prevention programs	Scalar chain	Task group
Aftercare	Departmentalization	Informal group

CASE STUDY*

Summit View, a private youth facility north of Las Vegas, Nevada announced that it is pulling out of its contract with the state two years before the contract expires. Designed to hold the most serious of offenders between ages thirteen and eighteen, it is the first secure youth prison in the state and the first privately managed facility.

The facility had a history of problems, but had completed 96 percent of an action plan written in May 2001 by the state to correct ongoing problems. Nevertheless, Youth Services International wants out of the contract and plans to be gone by mid-March. The facility gained national attention in summer of 2001 when twenty inmates escaped onto a rooftop and held the police at bay for several hours in 100-degree-plus heat. More problems were brought to light when two former employees were arrested on charges of having sex with two inmates ages seventeen and eighteen.

The corrective plan worked out by the state with YSI administrators included:

*Condensed from: Kim Smith, "Operator of privatized youth prison calls it quits." *Las Vegas Sun,* September 24, 2001, p. B1.

- The development of a youth rights system.
- Implementation of programming and case management standards.
- The establishment of procedures in the event of escape.
- The training of all staff before they receive work assignments.
- The development of an effective grievance system.
- The development of a way to track allegations of mistreatment.

Officials concluded that a facility like Summit View is needed in order to separate violent youth from the majority of kids who are successfully rehabilitated and willing to follow the rules.

INTRODUCTION

Amitai Etzioni (1964) points out that we are an organizational society. This is true because without formal organizations to provide the structure for managing our daily lives, we could not survive as a modern society. For example, we are born in a hospital, which is organized to deliver health care. We are educated in a school, which is organized to deliver education. Our church, temple, or mosque are organizations. We work in an organization, and our personal and community safety is assured by organizations. Thus, without organizational skills, our life would be considerably more complicated, not easier.

Organizations in criminal justice are not modern inventions. The early prisons of the Romans required a degree of organization to at least guard the prisoners, keep them alive, and keep straw on the floor. Things became a little more complicated during the Cromwellian Period when Oliver Cromwell first organized a police force to keep the peace, but upon his departure from power, keeping the peace reverted to the crown. It was up to Sir Robert Peel, however, to bring order and organization to policing. Prisons and corrections continued to follow the military model without much attention to detail other than guarding the prisoners. Finally, during the past century, juvenile justice has organized itself to deal with issues of juvenile crime through the implementation of aftercare, diversion programs, group homes, and so on.

In 1870, the Congress on Penitentiary and Reformatory Discipline (Wines, 1970) convened in Cincinnati, Ohio. By 1870, those involved in positions of importance began to examine and clarify the formal and informal roles of school volunteers, volunteers in general, the organization of religious instruction, and training of staff. However, juvenile corrections had not quite reached that level of sophistication. In 1899, a great leap forward was taken for the protection of children with enactment of the *Act to Regulate the Treatment and Control of Dependent, Neglected, and Delinquent Children,* also known as the *Illinois Juvenile Court Act.* This act proved to be the impetus for the juvenile justice system as we know it today.

TYPES OF ORGANIZATIONS

In criminal justice and juvenile justice in particular, we think of organizations in terms of community corrections and institutional corrections. But we can look at organizations even more closely than simply defining them by their mission. Richard H. Hall (1991) discusses organizational typologies and summarizes what we know about them.

He notes that Talcott Parsons (1960) distinguishes between production organizations, political organizations, integrative organizations, and pattern-maintenance organizations. The first, **production organizations,** are those that make things consumed by society. That is factories and plants that make such things as automobiles, refrigerators, and televisions. The second type of an organization is that which is oriented toward **political goals**. That is, the organization seeks assurance that society attains valued goals and it allocates power within the society. Such an organization would be a legislature or a watch dog group. The third type, **integrative organizations**, have as their purpose settling conflicts within society, directing motivations toward the fulfillment of institutionalized expectations, and ensuring that parts of society work together. Such an organization could be the courts or an administrative organization such as the Interstate Transportation Commission. The fourth type of organization is those which attempt to provide societal continuity through educational, cultural, and expressive activities. This type of an organization could be a public school corporation or a university.

Hall notes that while each of these activities are important, the type of classificatory scheme offered by Parsons is lacking because it doesn't say much about the organizations themselves. For example, the 3M Corporation not only manufactures a number of important items for our society, including handy "Post-It™ Notes," they also are an important research organization; they allocate power within the corporate world, and through philanthropic giving and so on, fall into some of the other categories.

Etzioni (1961) offers another typology based upon compliance. In his scheme, compliance is the way in which members lower in the organization respond to the authority system of the organization. According to Etzioni, there are three bases of authority—coercion, utilitarian or remuneration, and normative. In addition, there are three types of compliance—alienative, instrumental/calculative, and moral. The result is a three-by-three classificatory scheme that yields nine possible types of organizations. Most fall into the "congruent" types, which are *coercive-alienative, remunerative-calculative,* and *normative-moral* types. Figure 10.1 illustrates types of organizations by example.

Coercive organizations are those that rely mainly upon coercion to gain and maintain control. Etzioni points out that typical examples are concentration camps, prisoner of war camps, prisons, correctional institutions, mental hospitals, and relocation centers. The greater the amount of coercion used, the higher the level of alienation among the inmates. Etzioni's focus is on the inmates found in prisons, hospitals, or concentration camps. If, as Etzioni asserts, coercion breeds alienation, then it is not difficult to comprehend why the work force in those institutions is alienated and why workers so often express a low level of loyalty to the organization.

Authority

	Coercion	Utilitarian Remuneration	Normative
Compliance	Reform schools	Day reporting centers	Some private long-term residential facilities
	Many state residential facilities without razor wire	Group homes	Group homes
	Group homes	Run-away shelters	Alternative public schools

Figure 10.1   Authority/Compliance Organizations
Adapted from: Amatai Etzioni. *A Comparative Analysis of Complex Organizations.* NY: The Free Press. 1975.

Utilitarian organizations are "organizations in which remuneration is the major means of control over lower participants and calculative involvement (i.e., mild alienation to mild commitment) characterized the orientation of the large majority of lower participants" (Etzioni, 1975, p. 31). These organizations are usually industries; lower participants include blue-collar workers in factories and mines and white-collar workers in banking, finance, and so on. Also considered lower participants are professionals in, for example, research organizations and even law firms.

Normative organizations are "organizations in which normative power is the major source of control over most lower participants, whose orientation to the organization is characterized by high commitment" (Etzioni, 1975, p. 40). Normative power is defined as the allocation and manipulation of symbolic rewards and deprivation by leaders. Such organizations include religious organizations, hospitals, universities, and professional organizations.

According to Hall et al. (1967), it is difficult to also place some organizations into Etzioni's typology. For example, public schools can yield alienative, calculative, and moral compliance on the part of various students. While this discussion of organizational typologies is not complete, it sheds light on the difficulties one faces in attempting to identify the type of organizations we see in juvenile justice. However, light is shed on how juvenile justice organizations fit into American society, largely in terms of the compliance of those who come under its sway.

JUVENILE JUSTICE ORGANIZATIONS

We discuss juvenile programs later in this chapter, but it is useful if we briefly examine them in terms of their level of coerciveness. Juvenile justice organizations are not either/or types of organizations, but rather fall along a continuum from least coercive to most coercive. At one end of the continuum, we find low coercive organizations such as those working with at-risk children in the community. At the other end of the continuum, we find secure juvenile facilities; prisons, actually, for those children who pose a risk to themselves and to the community.

In this sense, if we view juvenile correctional programs in light of coercion, we begin to sense the reason for the relative alienation on the part of staff and youth who are in their care. Clearly, greater coercion is used by the superintendent of a secure youth institution to achieve organizational goals than is used by the administrator of a juvenile court in working with youth placed on probation.

We can examine juvenile correctional organizations in light of their function. We must remember that organizations often serve a variety of purposes, the typology noted below is useful for discussion.

Prevention Programs

Prevention programs are those efforts that attempt to keep youth from engaging in delinquent behavior before they come to the attention of the authorities. Such programs seek to improve school performance, build or rebuild stronger families, provide counseling in schools, keep youth from joining gangs, improve living conditions, and the like. Such programs can be managed by organizations such as the Boys and Girls Clubs of America, Boy and Girl Scouts, police departments and courts. They can also be stand-alone programs that are either funded by grants or by a philanthropic organization.

The Juvenile Justice and Delinquency Prevention Act of 1974 and subsequent renewals establish prevention as a national priority. There are three levels of delinquency prevention (Newton, 1978):

- **Primary prevention.** Aims to modify conditions in the physical and social environment at large,
- **Secondary prevention.** Is directed at early identification and intervention in the lives of youth or groups in criminogenic circumstances,
- **Tertiary prevention.** Aims at the prevention of recidivism. They can also be rehabilitation programs. See later comments on Intensive Supervision Programs.

Primary prevention can be illustrated by the Shoplifting Diversion Program in Davenport, Iowa. This program is offered to juvenile shoplifters and their parents as a one-time event in lieu of prosecution. Presenters include police, adult court workers, and local merchants, and the aim is to raise awareness of the consequences of shoplifting. According to Director Kathy Biscontine, the program is twenty years old and processes about thirty offenders per month. Research reflects a 90 percent success rate for any crime.

Secondary prevention is illustrated by D.A.R.E., a drug education program designed to educate middle-schoolers about drugs. G.R.E.A.T. (Gang Resistance Education and Training) does the same thing in regard to street gangs. Tertiary prevention aims at the prevention of recidivism after youthful delinquency has been detected. Scared Straight is one program that attempted to prevent delinquency recidivism by acquainting youth with the harshness of prison life and by convicts "telling it like it is." Scared Straight type of programs are no longer as popular as they used to be as the effectiveness of such an approach has been disputed (Finckenauer and Gavin, 1999).

However, the Western Youth Correctional Institution at Morganton, North Carolina, manages a similar program called "Final Step." This program is similar to Scared Straight in that juveniles on probation are brought to the institution for a tour and then participate in a group session where inmates harangue them in a session not unlike a Synanon Game. In spite of research, the local authorities like the program, and it continues on as an example of the interplay between politics and practice.

There are a number of notable prevention programs that have withstood the test of time and research, and one of the more enduring programs is the Chicago Area Project (CAP), often called Community Action Programs. Bartollas and Miller (1998) sum up CAP very nicely. Founded by Clifford Shaw and Henry McKay in 1934, the original CAP were started in three areas: South Chicago, the Near West Side, and the Near North Side. Local leaders were recruited to promote the welfare of local youth who, in turn, involved organizations and individuals including those with a criminal record.

There are three primary goals to Community Action Programs:

- Provide a forum allowing local residents to become acquainted with up-to-date techniques on child rearing and welfare and juvenile delinquency.
- Initiate new channels of communication between residents and representatives of the larger community who have influence over the life of the child.
- Bring adults in contact with local youth, particularly those in danger of law-breaking.

Tertiary prevention programs are those that attempt to prevent recidivism of youthful delinquency. In an ideal world, we could say that juvenile probation, or even institutional placement are forms of tertiary prevention. However, life is not perfect, and while some probation departments are excellent and well-staffed, many are not. Some residential facilities are excellent and do a good job at therapeutic intervention; many are not. Consequently, we look to other programs, or devise special programs, to work with youth and guide them to a law-abiding life.

One such program is the Intensive Aftercare Supervision Program of the Delaware County Juvenile Court in Delaware, Ohio. Key elements of the program include in-home family counseling, community monitoring, behavior management and linkages to community resources.

Started in 1988, the program was aimed at keeping youth on **aftercare** from committing delinquencies that would cause them to be returned to the institution. It was patterned after the Delaware County Juvenile Court intensive probation program, which was the first in the State of Ohio for juveniles. The Assistant Court Administrator, Ed Uhlman, credits much of the program success to Reclaim Ohio, which provided cash incentives to counties to work with youth in their home community. Such innovations as in-home counseling and the Wrap-around Program provide assistance, counseling, and mentoring to the youth and family members.

Diversion Programs

Diversion is a process in which offenders are not allowed to penetrate the juvenile justice system any further than they have already penetrated, be it at the time of arrest, intake, or hearing. Informal diversion efforts aside, such as a police officer opting to warn a juvenile rather than transport him or her to the juvenile detention center, diversion programs can take several forms. One diversion program is foster care, in which the child is placed with a family by the court for a period of time in order to sort out issues relevant to the safety and care of the child. Another diversion program could be a drug treatment program, and another could be a mental health program. All are used rather than formally entering the youth into the juvenile justice system.

Regoli and Hewitt (1997), in earlier editions of their text, provide an excellent summary of what we know about diversion. They point out that a number of critics assert that diversion is nothing more than widening the juvenile justice net for alleged offenders who have not been found guilty of a crime. Further, the stigmatizing effect on youth so identified labels them as delinquents, thus causing them further harm.

Youth can be diverted at several points in the juvenile justice system: at the time of apprehension, during intake, by the prosecutor, or at the time of the formal hearing. However, as Regoli and Hewitt point out, if diversion is to minimize penetration of the system, then the earlier diversion occurs, the better for the youth.

At the end of the day, we are left with a conundrum; if we refer the child or youth to a diversion program, he or she may be labeled as a delinquent and liberties may be taken with the constitutional right to be regarded as innocent. On the other hand, failure to refer a child or youth and allowing him or her to be processed by the juvenile justice system may cause even further harm. In any case, great care must be exercised.

One final point is there is often an overlap between prevention and diversion programs. While prevention programs rely upon their own search for program participants, diversion programs receive referrals from competent authorities such as police or the prosecutor's office. One program can serve as both prevention or diversion.

Community Programs

Just like prevention and diversion programs, community programs have at their heart the goal of keeping troubled youth from being placed in residential programs. They take many forms: probation, aftercare, group homes, day treatment centers, wilderness survival programs, community service, and so on. We can generally state that the first community program for youth was the implementation of probation in Cook County, Illinois. However, other than isolated attempts to do something other than probation, there were no noteworthy programs until the early 1950s when programs such as the Highfields experiment introduced the concept of guided group interaction.

In that project, delinquent boys were placed in a small group home, formerly the home of Col. and Mrs. Charles Lindbergh, accommodating about twelve boys. They were provided a "treatment diet" consisting of group therapy in the evenings, work, and school. Don C. Gibbons (1976) summed up the Highfields program very well by pointing out that the boys were not required to work, as they might have been in a more conventional setting as the architects of the program viewed the youth as normal youngsters with antisocial attitudes and self-images. The entire program of guided group interaction with related work experiences and peer interaction was directed toward pressuring the boys into new perspectives and improved work habits.

Initial research indicated that the Highfields boys did better after release than did the boys released from the Annandale Reformatory. However, subsequent research by Lerman (1968) indicates that the results are less impressive than originally believed. Lerman reanalyzed the data and found that 18 percent of the Highfields subjects did not complete the program and were returned to the court as unsuitable. When the returned boys were included in the data, the results of the training school and Highfields were similar. Thus, as Lerman points out we need to exercise caution before making grand statements about success of community programs because the luxury of returning "unsuitable" clients is one not enjoyed by public agencies.

Aftercare Programs

Aftercare programs are the equivalent of parole for juveniles released from secure residential placement. Most casework methods, counseling techniques, and community efforts to keep the youth from recidivating are the same as for probation, including intensive supervision as developed by the Delaware County, Ohio Juvenile Court. Group homes are another example of attempts to work with troubled youth short of placement in a residential facility away from the area of residence. Group homes rely upon a close-knit family type of atmosphere that fosters conforming behavior. Some rely on the principles of guided group interaction, others on a token economy, and others are somewhat eclectic. The aim of all is to teach the child ways of behaving that will keep him or her out of further trouble with the court.

Wilderness Survival Programs

These programs are another attempt to remove the youth from the community for a short period of time as an ancillary to probation or perhaps aftercare and provide an opportunity for success. These are not programs as we may have become familiar with on commercial television, but rather planned, coordinated programs that give each youth the chance to test himself or herself and to learn to work as a team in an atmosphere of camaraderie and friendship. Outward Bound and Vision/Quest are two of the better-known programs. Vision/Quest is rather controversial in that it is a very rigorous program that critics claim places youth in dangerous situations. Nevertheless, it is a program that some view as successful.

Day treatment programs, restitution, and community service are programs that attempt to work with youth in the community while allowing them to live at home. Day treatment programs require the youth to report to a location early in the morning as if attending school. Indeed, that is what the youth will do most of the day, attend school, participate in enrichment activities and counseling/therapy sessions and perhaps some work in the community. The youth is then allowed to go home for the night, sometimes for the evening meal, sometimes after the evening meal. The rationale for day treatment programs is that they are cheaper than group homes and do not require twenty-four-hour supervision.

Restitution and community service are aimed at in some way reconnecting the youth to the community and to gain an understanding of the victims plight by requiring the delinquent to pay back the victim or community for his or her transgressions. Restitution is simply outright payment for damages suffered by the victim in the form of money or in the form of work. Community service allows the youth to serve in some capacity by working for an agency. Work can be manual labor such as lawn work or cleaning up an area or park of litter. Whatever the work, it must be supervised by an employee of the agency under the oversight of an officer of the Court in order to document hours worked.

Diversion is discussed at greater length in Chapter 7; however, it is an issue with which all juvenile justice practitioners must be aware. The Courts, the county commission, and the public expect diversion programs and the expectations of these constituencies must be dealt with knowledgeably and with sensitivity.

Institutional Corrections

Juvenile institutions also take several forms: group homes, boot camps, minimum-, medium-, and close-custody facilities. All are designed around a specific mission and a particular type of offender. Many juvenile institutions are designed along the cottage system, which, in many ways, was the forerunner of unit management as developed by the U.S. Bureau of Prisons in the 1960s.

The Cottage System

This system was introduced in the mid-1800s and was offered as an alternative to the large industrial training schools that were viewed as demeaning and even brutal. Children were, and still are, housed in separate units of twenty to fifty children with its own staff, including a unit supervisor, counselors, and around-the-clock supervisors. Originally the cottage was staffed by a married couple who lived in the cottage, and it was believed that such an arrangement fostered a more homelike atmosphere and facilitated rehabilitation. There is more on the subject of institutions in Chapter 11.

ORGANIZING FOR SUCCESS

Achieving excellence as a probation officer, counselor, or institutional case manager is critical to achieving the goal of successfully working with at-risk or delinquent youth. It is also critical that as the juvenile justice practitioner advances up the organizational ladder, he or she understands how the organization must be managed to achieve organizational goals. This brief introduction to organizations and their function examines how the administrator can assure success. Many probation officers move up the organizational ladder to become chief probation officer or juvenile court administrator and many boys reformatory case managers become superintendents.

Organizing the juvenile justice organization depends on three things: the type of organization and its mission, the size of the organization, and the number of employees. These three issues will determine the organizational structure and overall approach to achieving organizational objectives. Certain assumptions are made when one considers how an organization should be structured (Boleman and Deal, 1984).

Organizations exist primarily to accomplish established goals.

1. For any organization, there is a structure appropriate to the goals, the environment, the technology, and the participants.
2. Organizations work effectively when environmental turbulence and the personal preferences of participants are constrained by norms of rationality.
3. Coordination and control are accomplished best through the exercise of authority and impersonal rules.
4. Structures can be systematically designed and implemented.
5. Specialization permits higher levels of individual expertise and performance.
6. Organizational problems usually reflect an appropriate structure and can be resolved through redesign and reorganization.

ORGANIZATIONAL STRUCTURE

Henri Fayol (1984) made a significant contribution to management theory with his "general principles of management." Several of these "general principles" are relevant to organizational structure in juvenile justice.

Division of Work

According to Fayol, the object of division of work is to produce more and better work with the same effort. In a juvenile institution or juvenile court, there must be a **division of work** if youth are to be kept secure and safe, probationers worked with and supervised, problems and paperwork attended to, and payroll maintained. However, since the safety and security of an institution is every employee's job, or the effective supervision of youth

Fayols 14 Principles of Management

1. *Division of Work.* The object of division of work is to produce more and better work with the same effort. Work specialization promotes skill, confidence, and accuracy, which increase output.

2. *Authority and Responsibility.* According to Fayol, authority is the right to give orders and the power to exact obedience. Authority and responsibility are two sides of the same coin; responsibility means accountability. Authority is sought after as much as responsibility is feared.

3. *Discipline.* Fayol was convinced that discipline is essential for the smooth running of an enterprise. It requires common effort and agreement as well as sanctions judiciously applied.

4. *Unity of Command.* Dual command is a perpetual source of conflict. Thus, workers should receive orders from only one person.

5. *Unity of Direction.* A group of activities having the same objective and plan. The same department head or supervisor gives unity of direction.

6. *Subordination of Individual Interests to the General Interests.* The interests of one employee or group of employees should not take priority over the interests of the organization as a whole.

7. *Remuneration of Personnel.* In determining fair compensation for services employees render, several things need to be considered, such as cost of living, abundance of personnel, and general business conditions.

8. *Centralization.* Centralization as a system is neither good nor bad. The issue of centralization or decentralization is one of proportion and the extent of one or the other that will yield the highest productivity.

9. *Scalar Chain.* The scalar chain, according to Fayol, is the chain of supervision from the top to the bottom. Each level possesses more authority than the position below it. The scalar chain is necessary if organizations are to be successful, and adherence to it is necessary if superiors are to be kept informed of each person's work activity.

10. *Order.* There is both a social order and a material order. There must be an appointed place for every person and item in the organization.

11. *Equity.* Employees should be treated fairly and equally.

12. *Stability of Tenure for Personnel.* It costs money to train personnel, and less successful firms have a high turnover of personnel. Therefore, the retention of good personnel should be a high priority for a manager.

13. *Initiative.* Management should give personnel the freedom to initiate, propose, and execute ideas.

14. *Espirit de Corps.* Management should promote harmony and prevent dissension among subordinates.

Source: Henri Fayol, "General Principles of Management" in D.S. Pugh, ed., *Organization Theory,* 2nd ed. New York: Penguin Books, 1984, pp. 135–56.

in community programs attended to, it is sometimes necessary for many people to be able to do other tasks. Nevertheless, all employees have a specialty, and they must perform that specialty effectively.

Unity of Command

Unity of command dictates that employees should receive orders from one superior only. If this rule is violated, according to Fayol, discipline and authority are undermined and order and stability threatened.

Centralization

Fayol believed that **centralization** is a part of the natural order. In small organizations, centralization is greater, but in large organizations the scalar chain is interposed between the superintendent or court administrator and those in the lower echelons who are responsible for executing the orders of the CEO.

Scalar Chain

The **scalar chain** is the chain of command ranging from the highest authority to the lowest rank. The line of authority is the route followed by all formal commands and communications. Suppose, for example, that the court administrator takes a call from a victim of an offense. The court administrator will ask the supervisor or probation officer to speak to the victim and attempt to ease his or her fear or anger. The organization chart in Figure 10.2 illustrates the scalar chain and the formal lines of communication. Traditionally organizational charts are pyramidal, illustrating that most authority rests at the top and the least authority resting at the bottom. In addition, the chart illustrates the departmental form of an organization and the working relationship between those responsible for executing the mission of the organization.

DEPARTMENTALIZATION

A department can be viewed as a unique group of organizational resources established by management to perform specific organizational tasks. The process of establishing departments is called **departmentalization**. The creation of a department is based upon either tasks to be accomplished (grouping similar functions together) or the target group of the department.

One example of departmentalization by tasks to be accomplished is the education department of a youth institution. This department is responsible for the delivery of education and related services to youth confined at the institution. It is composed of several subunits: remedial education, secondary education (or GED), and vocational training. In some institutions the recreation unit is included in education.

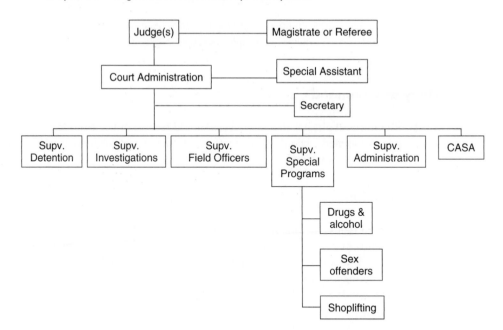

Figure 10.2   Organization Chart: Traditional Court Organization

Departmentalization based on target groups is not uncommon in juvenile courts. For example, in a large court there might be a special unit responsible for completing pre-hearing reports. There might be a unit designated to work with gang members or youth placed on probation who have a history of drug abuse. The possibilities are limited only by the creativity and resources of the court administrator and the court.

SPAN OF MANAGEMENT

The term "span of control" is frequently used in the literature and in casual conversation, but a more accurate term is "span of management." The term can be defined as analyzing the number of organizational personnel reports to one superior. As Koontz and O'Donnell (1984) point out, "The span is one of management not merely of control."

Today if an organization is to be successful, the **span of management** must be appropriate for the tasks and management style of the chief executive officer. Henry Albers (1965, pp. 85–87) summarizes a report by the American Management Association that attempts to shed light on the question of how many employees a manager can effectively supervise. The study included a sample of 141 companies "with good management practices." Data were obtained from one hundred large companies with over five thousand employees each and forty-one medium-sized companies with five hundred to five thousand employees. The researchers found that the:

number of subordinates reporting to the president ranged from one to twenty-four. In nine out of 141 companies only one executive, usually an executive vice president, reported to the president. The presidents of fifty-five companies had a span of ten or more. The median for the one hundred large organizations surveyed was between eight and nine; for the forty-one medium-sized concerns, between six and seven.

The results of the survey are clear. Only six large companies reported more than seven subordinates reporting to the president and only one small company reported more than seven reporting to the president. The ideal number of subordinates reporting to an executive is between five and seven (Urwick, 1938). Generally speaking, the principle of span of control, or span of management as it is now called, indicates that efficiency is increased by limiting the manager's number of subordinates. Any more than that creates communication problems. Put another way, the more levels of the organization communication must pass through, the less responsive lower levels of the organization are to the manager's direction.

SPAN OF MANAGEMENT IN JUVENILE JUSTICE

In juvenile justice, the span of management varies from agency to agency. Few guidelines are available for the juvenile justice manager, but the American Correctional Association somewhat obliquely addresses this issue in its Standards for Juvenile Probation and Aftercare Services (1983) as well as other standards manuals. However, the reader should note that while the below discussion of the standard does acknowledge span of control, it does not state what an appropriate span of control should be.

> There is a written organizational plan and chart reflecting the current structure of authority, responsibility and accountability within the field agency which is reviewed at least annually and updated as needed.
>
> *Discussion:* A signed and dated plan of organization and current chart provide the employees with a clear picture of the field agency administration. Names of units and duties should reflect precisely what is entailed. Similar functions should be grouped. Span of control, lines of authority and orderly channels of communication should be noted. Updating should be made as changes occur, and a regular review should be made to be certain that the plan is appropriate for agency functions.
>
> An organizational chart also presents an overview of the agency to other private and public organizations.

Most mangers in juvenile justice, as well as other fields of endeavor, will admit that any more than six or seven subordinates are too many. For example, the superintendent of a medium to large juvenile facility will have six, seven, even ten subordinates reporting directly to him or her. They include such diverse positions as locksmith, secretary, and treatment director, as well as the assistant superintendents. Given the many roles the superintendent must play, he or she must delegate as much responsibility as possible in order to effectively carry out the daily routine.

THE INFORMAL ORGANIZATION

The above discussion about the formal organization illustrates how we often want it to work. However, the informal organization is perhaps the most important aspect of organizational life. Several years ago, one of the authors took a job as the juvenile court administrator of a small court consisting of four probation officers, a detention chief, and several detention officers and related office staff. The new administrator was aware of the influence of the informal organization, but naively went on his way attempting to bring new life and programs to a court disparaged by the media and public as incompetent and as a dumping ground for political friends. A little more than a year later, the administrator was fired because he was not part of the informal organization composed of those who had a vested interest in maintaining the status quo. Unfortunately, he believed that competence and integrity would prevail.

Stojkovic, Kalinich, and Klofas (1998) point out that nearly all organizations have an informal side, but that the structure of the informal organization differs from the formal organization to the extent that the top management is able to control the behaviors of staff and to the extent that the staff buy into the mission, policies, and procedures. In the above example, the new administrator tried to mold a new culture, but one individual in the organization was able to persuade the five judges to align themselves against the administrator because she was the chairwoman of the county democratic party. After that, it was just a matter of time.

Examination of the formal organization chart of any agency will reveal the formal lines of communication and authority. The informal organization can only be known after becoming familiar with the organization. Lines of communication do not necessarily follow the formal lines of communication. Lines of authority are meaningless, and the skillful manager will be able to take advantage of the informal organization to accomplish the organizational mission.

Informal organization is related to groups within the organization. These groups are usually based upon relationships that have built up over the years and rely on informal leadership. Informal leaders are those people who do not have formal authority, but because of respect of peers, are able to exercise informal leadership within the organization. That is, they are perceived as individuals who can get something done.

GROUPS IN JUVENILE JUSTICE ORGANIZATIONS

In terms of staff in a youth institution, there are two kinds of groups to be found: formal and informal.

Formal Groups

A **formal group** is one that is established to further the mission of the organization. In a residential facility for youth, there is a group who identify themselves as officers. Their job is to provide security and to maintain institutional tranquility. Another example is that of the juvenile court administrator who forms a standing committee to keep him or her informed of community sentiment and concerns. Thus, the demands of the organization lead to the formation of different types of formal groups: command groups and task groups.

Command Group

The **command group** is specified by the organization chart. Members of such a group report to a supervisor, who, in turn, reports to someone else. The authority relationship between the shift supervisor and his or her subordinates constitutes a command group.

Task Group

Members of a **task group** work together to complete a particular task or project. In the above example with the court administrator, he or she will ask that a number of probation officers and staff meet with him or her once a month to discuss the organization and the attitudes, perceptions, and juvenile justice needs of the community. The court administrator will then be able to discuss programs and problems more intelligently with the judges and to gauge the impact of programs more accurately. Task groups are often called committees. They are valuable for four reasons (Koontz and O'Donnell, 1984). First, they allow organization members to exchange ideas; second, they allow members to generate suggestions and recommendations for other organizational units; third, they encourage members to develop new ideas for solving existing organizational problems; and fourth, they assist in the development of organizational policies.

Informal Groups

Informal groups arise naturally as a result of the work situation and in response to social needs. Until the late 1920s, the importance of the social experience of work was largely unrecognized. Based upon Abraham Maslow's (1954) hierarchy of needs model (see Figure 10.3) Maslow asserts that human needs are arranged in a hierarchical order, beginning with the basic needs for air, food, and water. At the other end of the continuum is the need for self-actualization. Thus, according to Maslow, as one fulfills lower-order needs, one is then free to fulfill the next higher-order need.

We see that there is a social need for humans to fill after the security needs are fulfilled. As a consequence, employees will seek to fulfill that need in the work place and two types of informal groups have been identified that attempt to fulfill the need for social ties.

Interest Groups

Employees may band together to address a particular issue; for example, to press for higher wages or better benefits. Once that need is met, such groups often disband.

Friendship Groups

Many groups form because of common interests such as hobbies, or age of children, or of similarity in age. Friendship groups extend their activities to off-work hours and tend to change over time.

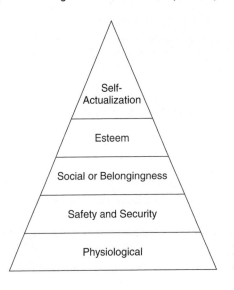

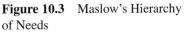

Figure 10.3   Maslow's Hierarchy of Needs

SUMMARY

Talcott Parsons (1960) distinguishes between production organizations, political organizations, integrative organizations, and pattern-maintenance organizations. The juvenile justice organization is an integrative organization and exists to deal with youth who come before the court and are adjudicated as delinquent. Organizations may be structured several ways, but usually they are organized along departmental lines, that is, like functions are grouped together. The span of management is important because the CEO or chief administrator can be stretched too thin by having too many employees reporting directly to him or her. Delegation is important.

Informal groups exist in an organization and influence how successfully the organization achieves organizational goals. Informal groups can be either interest groups or friendship groups. The effective manager will accept the presence of informal groups and work with them to drive the organization onward.

CASE STUDY WRAP-UP

Summit View seems to have ignored principles of sound management. Many, or most, of their problems could have been avoided if the management had constructed the institution according sound principles of managing a youth institution. To begin, they should have developed some variation on the cottage system, with an adequate staffing pattern. The development of sound policies and procedures would have avoided the problems surrounding the escape and the staff sexual involvement with inmates. Finally, one does not open an institution for youth without being aware of the dynamics of the informal work group, the importance of departmentalization, and of hiring staff who are willing to abide by the scalar chain. Clearly, Summit View did not pay attention to sound management.

STUDY QUESTIONS

1. Etzioni identifies three bases of authority. What are they?
2. Why is delinquency prevention a national priority? What are the types of prevention programs?
3. What is a community action program?
4. What are the three things that determine how to organize a juvenile justice organization?
5. From a staff perspective, what are the two types of groups found in an organization?

BIBLIOGRAPHY

ALBERS, HENRY (1965). *Principles of Organization and Management,* 2nd ed. New York: John Wiley and Sons.

AMERICAN CORRECTIONAL ASSOCIATION (1983). *Standards for Juvenile Probation and Aftercare Services,* 2nd ed. Laurel, MD: American Correctional Association.

BARTOLLAS, CLEMENS, AND MILLER, STUART J. (1998). *Juvenile Justice in America,* 2nd ed. Upper Saddle River, NJ: Prentice-Hall.

BOLEMAN, LEE G., AND DEAL, TERRENCE E. (1984). *Modern Appraches to Understanding and Managing Organizations.* San Francisco: Josey-Bass.

ETZIONI, AMITAI (1975). *A Comparative Analysis of Complex Organizations.* New York: The Free Press.

ETZIONI, AMITAI (1964). *Modern Organizations.* Englewood Cliffs, NJ: Prentice-Hall, Inc.

FAYOL, HENRI. (1984). "General Principles of Management." In D. S. Pugh (Ed.), *Organization Theory,* 2nd ed. (pp. 135–156). New York: Penguin Books.

FINCKENAUER, JAMES O., AND GAVIN, PATRICIA W. (1999). *Scared Straight: The Panacea Phenomenon Revisited.* Prospect Heights, Ill: Waveland Press, Inc.

GIBBONS, DON C. (1976). *Delinquent Behavior,* 2nd ed. Englewood Cliffs, NJ: Prentice-Hall, Inc.

HALL, RICHARD H., HAAS, J. EUGENE, AND JOHNSON, NORMAN (1967). "An Examination of Blau-Scott and Etzioni Typologies." *Administrative Science Quarterly, 12,* No. 2 (June): 118–139.

HALL, RICHARD H. (1991). *Organizations: Structures, Processes, and Outcomes.* Englewood Cliffs, NJ: Prentice-Hall, Inc.

KOONTZ, HAROLD, AND O'DONNELL, CYRIL (1984). *Principles of Organization and Management,* 3rd ed. New York: McGraw-Hill.

LERMAN, PAUL (July 1968). "Evaluative Studies of Institutions for Delinquents: Implications for Research and Social Policy," *Social Work,* XIII: 55–64.

MASLOW, A. H. (1954). *Motivation and Personality.* New York: Harper Brothers.

NEWTON, ANNE M. (June 1978). "Prevention of Crime and Delinquency." *Criminal Justice Abstracts,* 4.

PARSONS, TALCOTT (1960). *Structure and Process in Modern Society.* New York: The Free Press. In Richard H. Hall (Ed.), *Organizations: Structures, Processes, and Outcomes.* Englewood Cliffs, NJ: Prentice-Hall, Inc., 1991, p. 39.

REGOLI, ROBERT M., AND HEWITT, JOHN D. (1997). *Delinquency in Society,* 3rd ed. New York: McGraw-Hill Companies, Inc.

STOJKOVIC, STAN, KALINICH, DAVID, AND KLOFAS, JOHN (2003). *Criminal Justice Organizations.* 3rd ed. Belmont, CA: West/Wadsworth Publishing Company.

URWICK, L.F. (1938). *Scientific Principles and Organization.* Institute of Management Series, No. 19. New York: American Management Association.

WINES, E.C. (Ed.) (1970). *Transactions of the National Congress on Penitentiary and Reformatory Discipline.* Albany, NY: Weed, Parsons, and Company, Printers. 1871, reprinted by the American Correctional Association.

GLOSSARY OF KEY TERMS

Aftercare.   Much like parole for adults.

Centralization.   The tendency for an organization to have all power and authority located at the top of the organization with communication and decisions flowing downward.

Command group.   A group of employees identified on the organization chart and responsible for a specific task in the organization.

Departmentalization.   The process of dividing work in an organization by task. A department can be viewed as a unique group of organizational resources established by management to perform specific organizational tasks.

Division of work.   According to Henri Fayol, the object of a division of work is to produce more and better work with the same effort. For example, instead of having a staff member guard, counsel, do paperwork, conduct therapy groups, and so on, the institution hires a specialist in each area.

Formal group.   A formal group is one that is established to further the mission of the organization.

Informal group.   A group that arises naturally as a result of the work situation and in response to social needs. Such groups can be based on propinquity, shared interests, and so on.

Integrative organizations.   Their purpose is to settle conflicts within society, directing motivations toward the fulfillment of institutionalized expectations, and ensuring that parts of society work together.

Political goals.   An organization oriented to political goals seeks assurance that society attains valued goals and it allocates power within the society.

Prevention programs.   Those efforts that attempt to keep youth from engaging in delinquent behavior before they come to the attention of the authorities.

Production organizations.   Those organizations that make things consumed by society.

Scalar chain.   The chain of command ranging from the highest authority to the lowest rank.

Span of management.   The term can be defined as analyzing the number of organizational personnel reports to one superior.

Task group.   An ad hoc group appointed by the CEO and responsible for completing a specific task. The task group is disbanded upon completion of the task.

Unity of command.   Employees should receive orders from one superior only.

CHAPTER 11
DECISION MAKING

Decision
Programmed decisions
Nonprogrammed
   decisions

Case management
   decisions
Agency decisions
Risk assessment

Needs assessment
Scenario writing
Decision tree

CASE STUDY

Decision Making in the Courtroom
Marie Kessler[*]

As an attorney referee in the juvenile division of the circuit court, I find myself making immediate decisions that are based on what I am told by the probation officer, the child's attorney, the parent, and even the child.

I have to rely on my past experiences, my knowledge of the law, my insight into human nature, and my observations of what unfolds in front of me. And I have to trust my instincts.

I need to keep all of these points of information in perspective and in my thoughts as I watch the story open up in front of me. I also have to remember that I have a child in

---

[*]Marie Kessler is an attorney referee with the Kent County Circuit Court Family Division, Grand Rapids, Michigan, in both the Juvenile and Family Court for the last five years. She graduated from Aquinas College in Grand Rapids, Michigan, with a Bachelor of Arts in Communications and Theatre and earned her Juris Doctorate from Detroit College of Law. Prior to her current position, she practiced law in Grand Rapids in the areas of criminal and insurance defense, family law, and general civil litigation. She was born in Dayton, Ohio, and raised in Omaha, Nebraska.

front of me who has found his or her way to my courtroom through a series of events that many of us as adults would find overwhelming if not devastating to our lives.

I am concerned about sending a child back home with a parent who appears to have a half-hearted commitment to the problem of the child and working with the system. I worry if a parent has the capability to deal with a child who is defiant in all that he or she says and does and seems bent on self-destruction. My heart hurts for the child who is crying uncontrollably because he can't go home. I am confused and angry with parents who tell me that they have done all that they care to do for their child, and it is now up to the court system to fix their broken child.

My job is to try and make the right decision for all concerned; to listen to the recommendation of the probation officer and the police officers and the attorneys and the parent. I have a limited relationship with the child in front of me and I have to do the best for that child in a short period of time.

I have to rely on my probation officers, the social workers, the attorneys, and all the other people in the system to follow through with my decisions. All these people are relied on to work with the families. It is assumed that the members that make up the juvenile system have the best interest of the child as their main objective.

In one of my hearings, I had a ten-year-old little boy who was in foster care. He was in front of me for a preliminary hearing because his foster mother was considering returning him to the system and getting him out of her home. At times, he would become disruptive and almost impossible to control. She said that he was usually a very nice little boy who did little boy things when it came to following or not following the rules of the home, but at times he would begin to act in such a way in which she was concerned for herself and the other children in the home.

During the course of the hearing, foster mother said that his mother was supposed to show up weekly for visits with her son. His mom was neither consistent nor reliable in her visits. More times than not, she would not show, and the little boy would go into his room at the foster home, take off his good clothes and proceed to be as disobedient, foul-mouthed, and mean as he could be.

The child sat in front of me with his probation officer, his foster mother (birth mother had been informed of the hearing but did not attend), his attorney, and a social worker. The little boy was defiant, insolent, and angry.

All I saw at that point was a child who was out of control and ready to argue with whatever was said and whoever said it. Foster mother explained her position with the afterthought that his behavior seemed worse after a missed visit from his mom. I asked the child what the problem was in the foster home. His reply was that nothing was wrong. I made the comment that it must be very disappointing when his mother doesn't show for her visits.

This churlish child began to sob uncontrollably. He tried to tell me something and could not be understood. He could not be consoled. We had to take the child out of the hearing. If I had not spoken to the child, or asked him questions, I would have followed the request of the foster parent to remove him from her home and placed back in detention until we could find yet another home for him. I also suspended birth mother's parenting time with the child. He no longer had to wait for the visits that never happened. Foster mom agreed to work with him at her home on this issue and give the placement one more try.

The point of the story is that you can depend on your plans, your routines, the information presented to you by the experts, and the grown-ups, but in the end you are still dealing with a little boy who thinks and responds as if he is at the center of the world. He is at the center of his world, and he is most often out of control of that world. You have to ask one more question. You have to be willing to listen with the heart, not just the head. We deal with broken children, and they will hide their pain as best they can to avoid being hurt even more.

People will always ask how one can do this kind of work; that it must be sad or depressing or just maddening in general to see all the bad things children do every day. I do it because, more often than not, I think we actually accomplish more good than we realize, just by listening with our eyes and our ears and our heart.

INTRODUCTION

In juvenile justice, it is critical that managers and counselors exercise sound judgment and effective decision making. The public relies on the juvenile justice bureaucracy to promote rationality in the organization, and the effective probation officer, counselor, and manager must rely on rational, comprehensive decision making that specifies objectives and the most satisfactory means to achieve them. Some practitioners state that this approach is not always compatible with today's conditions and that juvenile justice practitioners, including managers, must be capable of making decisions quickly. While this is true, most decisions are made in offices or committee meeting rooms. The task is difficult but as Klofas et al. point out:

> Attempting to impose rational decision-making procedures and techniques on an organization without considering implicit and hidden constraints are doomed to failure. Organizations, individual decision makers, and information itself constrain decision making and assure that a purely rational mode of decisions is not possible under the conditions of ambiguity that exist in criminal justice (Stojkovic, Kalinich, & Klofas, 1998).

Indeed, ambiguity and the juvenile justice system seem to be synonymous. The pressures of overcrowding in our institutions, gangs, waivers to adult court, and an avalanche of clients in our probation and aftercare systems appear to render rational decision making most difficult, if not impossible. In addition, pressure from the courts, the legislature, special interest groups, and the media have created a climate capable of giving heartburn to the most seasoned decision maker.

DECISION DEFINED

A **decision** is a judgment. It is a choice between two or more alternatives (Certo, 1986). It is rarely a choice between right and wrong, but as Drucker points out, "it is at best a choice between (almost right) and (probably wrong) but much more often a choice be-

tween two courses of action neither of which is probably more nearly right than the other"
(Drucker 1973).

Those involved in juvenile justice make decisions every day. Some of those decisions are significant and alter the course of an organization or impact the community in significant ways. Most are relatively insignificant, but necessary, consider the example noted below.

An article published in the *Los Angeles Times* in February 2000 related the incident of a 14-year-old boy who walked into a Yuba City, California convenience store and stabbed the co-owner to death. He was arrested while running from the market and driven to the police station where he confessed to slaying the woman. After a hearing, the judge ruled that he should be tried as an adult.

Not long afterwards on March 7, 2000, Californians voted to take such decisions out of the hands of judges and turn them over to prosecutors in the state's 58 counties. Proposition 21, as it was called, increased penalties for youthful offenders, particularly gang members. In addition, passage requires that more than $1 billion be spent on additional correctional facilities. The incident in Yuba City highlights the passions and feelings on both sides of the debate. The boy must be held accountable for his crime. Even though it was an adult crime, should the punishment meted out be for an adult and result in spending most, if not all of his life behind bars (Gladstone, 2000)?

Proposition 21 was passed by the voters on March 7, 2000. The incident in Yuba City as illustrated above calls our attention to the many decisions that must be made in the juvenile justice system. In this instance, the police who heard the boy's confession face decisions on how to handle the confession; the prosecutor, judges, and other actors in the juvenile justice system have decisions to make relative to placement, sentencing, classification, housing, and eventually even the potential for supervised release as the boy progresses through the system and on into adulthood. None of these decisions are easy, but they can be made easier by use of various devices that allow conformity of decision making. These are termed **programmed decisions** and **nonprogrammed decisions**. They will be discussed at greater length later, but briefly a programmed decision is one that is repetitive in nature and made by an employee relatively low in the organization. A nonprogrammed decision is a unique decision often reflecting changes in policy and is usually made at the executive level.

DECISION MAKING IN GENERAL

Johnson (1992) identifies four models for decision making; the rational-decision making model, the organizational process model, the governmental politics model, and the garbage can model.

The Rational Decision-making Model

Rational decision making requires first that the goals be clearly specified, next that all evidence and alternatives be considered, and finally that the best alternative be selected. Simon (1976) and others point out that this model is an ideal the decision makers should adhere to as closely as possible.

There are several deliberate steps in this process. First, one identifies the goals to be achieved by the selected alternative. They should be ranked in order of priority. Second, alternative means of reaching each goal should be clearly defined. Third, the costs, risks, and consequences for each alternative should be listed, as well as the probability of whether the chosen alternative will achieve the goal. Fourth, alternatives should be compared to determine the relative costs of achieving each goal. Fifth, the optimum alliterative should be chosen on the basis of cost and its likelihood of achieving the goal(s). Sixth, the chosen alternative should be implemented.

This approach's applicability to juvenile justice is questionable. A great deal depends on the accuracy of information and the context of the decision. The rational decision-making model is contrasted with the incremental model of decision making. This less formal procedure "is a means of proceeding when the goals are not precise, the evidence and alternatives incomplete, and when political controversy inevitably shapes the final decisions" (Johnson 1992). Lindbolm (1959) calls our attention to the incremental method and criticizes the *rational-decision making model* and points out that it is "impossible to take everything important into consideration unless 'important' is so narrowly defined that analysis is in fact quite limited" (1959). His incremental model stresses a short-term horizon and is a means of attaining consensus among a group of people who do not agree on the goals or the means of achieving them. Thus, the incremental method stresses small victories and incremental steps in decision making rather than the grand, sweeping decision that immediately alters the course of an organization.

The Organizational Process Model

The organizational process model is a variation of the incremental model. In this model, choices are less the product of rational thought than the output of a large organization behaving in an accustomed manner. Organizations have an established job to do, and given normal circumstances, certain decisions are made in the same manner day after day. For example, employees of a youth institution are responsible for the safety of the youth entrusted to their care and effective programming. Therefore, each youth must be assigned to the appropriate housing unit and receive the benefit of a program that meets his or her needs. Those decisions may have originally been a rational selection, but sticking to that decision and subsequent changes need not take much thought. The aim is to minimize the time and effort necessary to make the decision as well as the tendency for staff members to bargain among themselves. This is accomplished by using computerized decision-making aids that accept information and then provide a guide to the staff member to make a decision, be it custody, housing, or involvement in certain programs. (For example, refer ahead to Figure 12.3.)

The Governmental Politics Model

The governmental politics model of decision making views decision making as the product of bargaining among the participants. It focuses on "the perceptions, motivations, positions, power and maneuvers of the players" (Allison 1992). In a sense, governmental politics decision making is a struggle for governance as much as it is a decision-making model. Competing actors have their own ideas of the right decision and compete to assert their view over others.

The Garbage Can Model

The garbage can model (Cohen, March, & Olson 1992) is the opposite of the rational decision-making model:

> Choices emerge from a highly diverse network of decision makers that could be called "organized anarchy." Its members are many and changing. Its processes are not well grasped even by its regular participants, and they do not hold agreed-upon or consistent preferences. It lacks all of the qualities needed to sustain the rational process. . . . The "garbage can" itself does not really contain garbage but rather a collection of ideas about problems and solutions from which participants can draw depending on their interests and opportunities (p. 323).

Current debate about the effectiveness of the juvenile justice system illustrates the garbage can model. There are many views of what the highest priority of the juvenile justice system should be: building more institutions and group homes, home detention, waiver to adult court, intensive probation, boot camps and so on. Each is a goal and a means to other goals, including the reelection of the legislator making the proposal. The various levels of government pick ideas out of the garbage can, which leads to conflicting decisions.

DECISIONS IN JUVENILE JUSTICE

Gottfredson and Gottfredson (1988) point out that "if a more rational decision making in corrections is to be achieved, data concerning offenders, treatments and outcomes must be more systematically reliably collected and analyzed than heretofore." Indeed, if we are to adequately serve the public and fellow staff members, corrections managers must use all the information and tools at their discretion to make rational decisions.

Gottfredson and Gottfredson (2000) advocate a decision-making system in juvenile justice that:

- Acknowledges the distinction between policy and case decisions.
- Recognizes the need to treat.
- Facilitates comparisons among decision makers within a particular setting to examine and encourage consistency.

- Provides those outside the system with a set of explicit purposes and rules that govern decision making, thus promoting visibility.
- Seeks to maximize the efficiency and effectiveness of decisions by giving explicit attention to decision-making goals and systematically gathering information about performance.
- Has within itself the capacity to evolve.
- Is a system that will actually be used by those it is designed to serve.

There are two kinds of decisions in juvenile justice: ward or client decisions, usually called **case management decisions**, and organizational or **agency decisions**. As in most other organizations, the position one holds determines the type of decisions one makes on a regular basis. Thus, case managers and probation/aftercare officers make case management decisions that directly effect the community, the youth, families of the youth involved, and the safety of the community. Supervisors, department heads, and executives make decisions more directly related to policy and planning.

Separating case management decisions from organizational decisions is sometimes difficult. For example, how does one categorize the psychologist's decision to recommend that a youth he or she has determined is dangerous to himself or others should be transferred to a more secure facility? Or the Court Administrators decision to create a special unit to supervise drug offenders or those who have a history of abuse? Clearly these decisions affect the children and the organization.

Figure 11.1 illustrates the overlap in case management and organizational decisions. Some of these decisions are programmed, that is they are routine, repetitive decisions often made with the aid of a matrix of some sort or computer program. Others are nonprogrammed, that is, they are novel, one-time occurrences. For example, a programmed case management decision would be a decision about where to designate a youth for institutional placement if there is more than one institution in the state. A nonprogrammed organizational decision could be one that relates to a decision on whether or not to rehabilitate an existing detention center or build a new one. Additionally, some case management treatment decisions affect, or are affected by, organizational decisions.

Figure 11.1   Organizational and Case Management Decisions

Programmed Decisions	**Nonprogrammed Decisions**
Classification	Build a new Detention
Security level	Center
Housing assignments	Some personnel decisions
Budgetary	

Figure 11.2 Examples of Programmed and Nonprogrammed Decisions

Earlier we discussed the fact that programmed decisions are usually made by those farther down in the organization and that nonprogrammed decisions are usually those made by executives. Figure 11.2 illustrates this characteristic; review of the figure reveals that as one goes up the organizational chart, the greater the propensity for nonprogrammed decisions to be made by first supervisors and then executives.

Case Management Decisions

Case management decisions are those decisions that are made relative to custody or levels of supervision, programs, housing assignments, and the like. Case management decisions are based upon a classification system whose most important goal is to maintain institutional (and by inference in the case of juvenile probation, community security) security. Apao (1984) points out that in prisons, traditional approaches to classification rely heavily on the clinical judgment and experience of corrections staff. This is also typically true in juvenile institutions. Usually the newly arrived ward undergoes a battery of educational, medical, and psychological tests. He or she is interviewed, watched, and often kept apart from the general population until a complete case summary or classification packet is completed. Often, the classification is completed in a diagnostic and reception unit or center where the ward is kept until the classification process is completed. At that time, he or she is transferred to the appropriate cottage or institution. In the case of a juvenile being placed on probation, the classification is comprised of a program plan, and a risk and needs assessment.

Obviously, most of the classification work is an attempt to predict future behavior. Decisions are made relative to the following questions:

- Will the youth attempt to escape or abscond?
- Will the youth exhibit episodes of violent behavior?
- Will the youth be involved in misconduct in the institution or in the community?

Thus, predictive validity is important. Apao asserts, however, that predictive validity is difficult to achieve and that few, if any, instruments are of value in predicting an (adult) inmate's behavior while in prison. In his study of the National Institute of Corrections'

(NIC) Custody Classification System, he concluded that the accuracy of the model's predictions remain to be determined.

Specifically he found that:

- Only five of the nineteen classification items were positively related to misconduct. The other fourteen were either negatively correlated or uncorrelated with misconduct.

- More of the needs assessment variables were significantly related to misconduct than were the custody classification variables.

- Correlations between total risk scores and misconduct indicated that attempts to discriminate between high- and low-risk inmates were useless. (Apao, 1984).

Predictive validity is important in that the staff must be assured that what they observe is a reasonable indication of future conduct. The absence of reliability in case management decisions leads to arbitrary and capricious decisions, which, in turn, lead to sagging morale among the youth, litigation, and perhaps an increase in impulsive, acting-out behaviors. It should also be pointed out that overcrowding may completely invalidate classification procedures.

Thus, case management decision making is an imperfect science. The attempt to objectify the classification process is an illustration of the organizational process model, in which the organization attempts to minimize time and effort in making decisions relative to such things as custody, housing assignments and programs in a residential facility. A community programs organization such as a juvenile court must make decisions such as level of need, level of supervision, and intensity of effort to make in working with parent(s). For example, the Kent County, Michigan, Family Court requires a **risk assessment** on all children under the age of ten in order to identify high-risk youth at an early age and provide court intervention. Any youth who receives a score of thirty-five or more receives special attention. Figure 11.3 illustrates the risk assessment instrument used by Kent County, Michigan.

The Michigan Family Independence (FIA), the state department responsible for juvenile facilities and aftercare in Michigan, also uses a classification instrument that uses the same additive scoring system in an effort to properly place youth out of home upon adjudication.

In addition a **risk and strengths/needs assessment** is completed in order to support recommendations relating to youth. The value of the use of the instruments is that they provide a uniform checklist of critical factors relative to placement decisions. Thus, we see here the organizational process model at work, that is a large organization behaving in an accustomed manner. There are other forms to further that objective.

The Classification Report is prepared on each youth in an effort to determine program needs while confined. The Reassessment Quarterly Report is used to guide continued placement in programs and other relevant decisions. The Risk of Youth Re-offending Reassessment Quarterly Report—Youth in Community Supervision (Figure 11.4) is used for much the same purpose, but in addition the aftercare officer must keep a keen eye on the possibility of the youth reoffending.

DELINQUENT YOUTH RISK REASSESSMENT QUARTERLY REPORT
Youth In Residential Placement
Family Independence Agency

Case Name		DOB	FIA Case Number			

FIA Worker Name		Date of Reassessment	County	District	Unit	Worker

Provider Number CA (If applicable)	Most Recent Risk Level
	☐ Low ☐ Moderate ☐ High

Initial Risk Level	Current Security Level
☐ Low ☐ Moderate ☐ High	☐ Low ☐ Moderate ☐ High

ODS Case Number	Site Number	File Number

REASSESSMENT FACTORS

	SCORE
1. Overall Adjustment to Residential Care	
Positive 0	
Satisfactory 1	
Fair 2	
Poor 4	
2. Furlough / Escape Violations	
None 0	
Late return from leave 2	
Attempted escape 3	
Escape 6 or more hours.. 4	
3. Assault on Staff or Other Youth	
None 0	
One or more... 6	
4. Response to Treatment	
Positive, youth engaged, progress in all areas 0	
Positive, youth engaged, progress in several areas 1	
Some resistance or problems, some progress 2	
Poor or negative response, some resistance, minimal progress 3	
Poor or negative response, denial, no response 4	
TOTAL SCORE	

Risk Level	Risk Level Override Reason(s)	**Final Risk Level:**

Is the youth eligible for Security Level Change?   Reason:
Recommended Security Level:
Estimated completion date of current residential treatment plan

Worker Name	Worker's Signature	Date
Supervisor's Name	Supervisor's Signature	Date

The Family Independence Agency will not discriminate against any individual or group because of race, sex, religion, age, national origin, color, marital status, political beliefs or disability. If you need help with reading, writing, hearing, etc., under the Americans with Disabilities Act, you are invited to make your needs known to an FIA office in your county.

AUTHORITY: P.A. 280 of 1939.   COMPLETION: Is Voluntary.
CONSEQUENCE IF NOT COMPLETED: None.

Residential_Risk_Revised.doc   1 of 1

Figure 11.3 Delinquent Youth Risk Reassessment Quarterly Report
Youth in Residential Placement

DELINQUENT YOUTH RISK REASSESSMENT QUARTERLY REPORT
Youth In Community Supervision
Family Independence Agency

Case Name		DOB	FIA Case Number				
FIA Worker Name		Date of Reassessment		County	District	Unit	Worker
Provider Number CA (If applicable)		Initial Risk Level ☐ Low ☐ Moderate ☐ High					
ODS Case Number	Site Number		File Number				

Rate the first four questions the same as rated on the initial risk assessment	SCORE
1. Age At First Adjudication 　　16 or over .... 0 　　15 .... 1 　　12 - 14 .... 2 　　11 or under 3	
2. Is Either the Current or Most Serious Prior Adjudication for a Robbery or Burglary Offense? 　　None .... 0 　　One .... 1 　　Both 2	
3. Youth has Exhibited Physically Assaultive Behavior 　　No .... 0 　　Yes 1	
4. Placed on Probation by Court Prior to FIA Commitment 　　No .... 0 　　Yes 1	
When scoring the items below, use information and observations made since last assessment.	
5. Arrests 　　None .... 0 　　Yes, status offense/misdemeanor .... 1 　　Yes, felony offense 3	
6. Response to Supervision 　　Positive response; cooperates with worker .... 0 　　Some problems; occasionally uncooperative .... 1 　　Major problems; uncooperative 3	
7. Runaways From Home or Community-Based Placement 　　None .... 0 　　One or more 2	
8. Current School ☐ or Employment ☐ Adjustment 　　No problems, or problems of a minor nature .... 0 　　Some attendance problems, short-term suspension/loses job .... 1 　　Major Problems, suspended, fired, does not make effort 2	
9. Current Drug/Alcohol Use 　　No known use or experimentation; use may be suspected but not verified .... 0 　　Occasional use; causes some disruption in functioning .... 1 　　Major problems functioning at school, work, or in home 3	
10. Current Peer Relationships 　　Good support and influence .... 0 　　Not peer-oriented, or some companions with delinquent orientations .... 1 　　Most companions involved in delinquent behavior or gang involvement/membership 3	
TOTAL SCORE	

Risk Level Final Override Level	Risk Level Override Reason(s)	Recommended Security Level:

Worker Name	Worker's Signature	Date
Supervisor's Name	Supervisor's Signature	Date

The Family Independence Agency will not discriminate against any individual or group because of race, sex, religion, age, national origin, color, marital status, political beliefs or disability. If you need help with reading, writing, hearing, etc., under the Americans with Disabilities Act, you are invited to make your needs known to an FIA office in your county.

AUTHORITY: P.A. 280 of 1939.　　COMPLETION: Is Voluntary.
CONSEQUENCE IF NOT COMPLETED: None.

community_Revised.doc　　　　　　　　　　　1 of 1

Figure 11.4   Delinquent Youth Risk Reassessment Quarterly Report
Youth in Community Supervision

Organizational Decisions

The difference between case management decisions and organizational decisions lies in the kind of job one has in the organization and the manager's level in the organization. As a rule, the higher the manager, the greater discretion she or he is able to exercise. The higher one goes in the managerial hierarchy, the more frequently broad, complex problems "that defy routine or detailed solutions are encountered. Decision criteria are vague, and solutions to decision problems are ordinarily given in terms of policy guidelines" (Haimann, Scott, & Connor, 1978).

While the counselor or probation officer is primarily concerned with case management decisions, correctional managers are concerned with nonprogrammed decisions relating to policy, budget and personnel. Further, the type of organizational structure has a great deal to do with who participates in what decisions (Haimann, Scott, & Connor 1978).

Who Makes Decisions?

Decisions are made in groups as well as alone, and often the manager makes the mistake of making a decision alone when she or he should have solicited help in making the decision. The reverse is true as well. We all have been in meetings with the "boss" who asks for help on a matter on which we either had no real input or saw no real reason why the "boss" could not just have made the decision alone. Rowe and Boulgiardes (1992) point out that when one is faced with a decision-making situation, the manager can chose from several alternatives in "deciding" how to decide:

- Make the decision alone.
- Make the decision and inform subordinates.
- Consult subordinates before making the decision.
- Consult other managers before making the decision.
- Depend on staff for input to the decision.
- Make the decision jointly with subordinates.

If the quality of the decision is affected by whether or not the manager makes the decision alone, then involving others in the decision-making process is a good idea. If the decision depends on acceptance by others, then involving others higher up in the chain of command is a good idea. In addition, if acceptance by others is important, then involving others at the operational level, including line staff, union and department head levels is a good idea.

There are also many different kinds of decisions to be made in a juvenile justice organization, ranging from what supplies and equipment should be purchased to whether or not to recommend a youth for early discharge from aftercare. Other decisions involve policy, budget, and personnel. The unifying goals of such diverse decisions are safety to the community, service, and management of organizational resources. With such variety in types of decisions, there must be some rationale for who makes what decision.

One approach to decision making is based upon two factors: the scope of the decision and the level of management. The scope of the decision refers to how much of the management subsystem is involved in the decision, and the level of management refers to the lone, mid-level, or executive management.

At the line level, the probation officer or the institutional counselor and the team, which usually includes other staff such as psychologists, officers, cottage manager, or the probation officer, decide who is to be recommended for involvement in a program or for aftercare. The mid-level manager, such as the cottage manager or supervisor in a large probation department, will determine who to recommend for promotion and whether to purchase a piece of equipment or machinery (if budgeted). The executive will decide on programs and policy.

In most of these decisions, the manager can ask for group input and solicit the advice of others. This is the point at which the style of leadership and type of organization enter into the process. Recall Figure 11.2 in which programmed and nonprogrammed decisions were discussed. The same concept can be applied to managerial responsibility in decision making. Figure 11.5 illustrates the levels of management and the responsibility for making decisions. Note that as one climbs higher in the organization, decisions become broader in scope. That is, more decisions are unique to the moment and require a certain amount of authority to make.

In many instances leadership and decision making are linked.

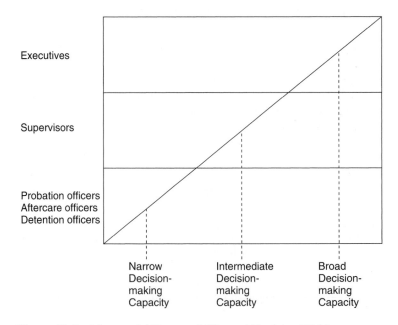

Figure 11.5   Managerial Responsibility and Decision Making

Continuum of Leadership Behavior

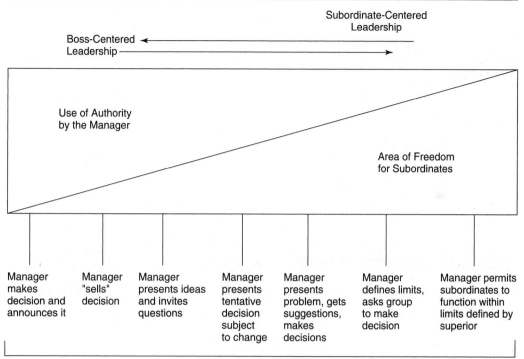

Figure 11.6   Continuum of Leadership Behavior

Source: Reprinted by permission of *Harvard Business Review.* Continuum of Leadership Behavior. From Robert Tannenbaum and Warren H. Schmidt, "How to Choose a Leadership Pattern," *Harvard Business Review* (March/April 1958), p. 96. Copyright © 1973 by the Harvard Business School Publishing Corporation; all rights reserved.

Figure 11.5 illustrates the fact that there is no one best way to lead. In fact, much of being an effective leader lies in determining how much freedom to give subordinates in making decisions on their own. Figure 11.6 illustrates a continuum in which leadership behavior is linked to the amount of freedom given to subordinates.

Managers to the left of the model exercise high control and allow subordinates little freedom in decision making. Managers to the right exercise little control and allow subordinates maximum freedom in decision making. One should not infer from the model that some managers always announce a decision and other simply announce limits and then let subordinates make decisions. Quite the contrary, it should be obvious that different styles are appropriate for different situations.

We can illustrate this point by stating the formula

$$SL = f(L, F, S)$$

Where *SL* (situational leadership) is a function of the leader, the followers, and the situation. Since the manager spends a great deal of time making decisions, it makes good sense to allow subordinates freedom to make decisions in areas covered by their job description, thus freeing the manager for more strategic concerns.

Types of Decisions

Decisions are of two types: programmed and nonprogrammed. A programmed decision is routine and usually the organization has developed ways to make it. For example, when a youth requests a lower security rating or permission to leave the district with his or her parent(s), a routine procedure allows the matter to be considered. A nonprogrammed decision is unstructured, novel, and often one-time. For example, opening a new group home involves a nonprogrammed decision. Other nonprogrammed decisions include whether to start a new education program or alter visiting hours in an institution.

THE DECISION-MAKING PROCESS

To divorce the planning process from the decision-making process is impossible. Planning is the premise. Once we are certain of our goals, the next step is to develop alternatives. There are always alternatives to every situation that must be discussed. Perhaps, this is the process that sets Japanese business organizations apart from their U.S. counterparts. In Japanese organizations, no one is forced to take sides during the debate; thus, defeat for one side or the other is ruled out. Consensus is obtained, but at the expense of time. Westerners find this frustrating.

David Halberstam points out that during the early 1970s, the Japanese had to be "dragged kicking and screaming into the American automobile market" (Halberstam 1986). One suspects that Halberstam misinterpreted this reluctance and that it signified not so much a fear of defeat, as he noted, but the Japanese approach to decision making. However, once the goal was clarified and the question defined, it did not take long for the Japanese to corner a large share of the U.S. automobile market, thus illustrating the value of planning, discussions, and thoughtful decision making.

There are four identifiable steps in rational decision making; premising (planning), identifying alternatives, evaluating alternatives in the light of the goal, and choosing an alternative (making a decision) (Koontz, O'Donnell & Weirich 1986).

Identifying Alternatives

Once the goal is identified, the decision maker must identify alternatives. If no alternatives have been identified, then perhaps the manager has not thought hard enough or has surrounded him- or herself with "yes men." Alfred P. Sloan, famed CEO and chairman of the board of General Motors from 1937 to 1956, is reported to have said at a committee meeting, "Gentlemen, I take it we are all in complete agreement on the decision here."

Everyone present nodded in agreement. "Then," continued Mr. Sloan, "I propose we postpone further discussion of this matter until our next meeting to give ourselves time to develop disagreement and perhaps gain some understanding of what the decision is all about" (Drucker 1973). One of Sloan's strengths was in his refusal to arrive at a conclusion and then cast about for facts and/or supporters to back it up.

There are several reasons why dissent is necessary.

- It safeguards the decision maker from becoming a prisoner of the organization. Everyone wants something from the manager, and the only way to avoid preconceived notions and pressure from special interests is to encourage thoughtful and well-documented disagreement.
- Disagreements alone can provide alternatives to a decision. For example, a decision to open a group home in a small county can generate a great deal of discord. The use of lively discussions can lead to a more sound decision based on fact and not ideology or philosophy.
- Disagreement is necessary to stimulate the imagination. Bureaucracies are known for their stifling of imagination and creativity. If we are to find creative solutions, we need to step outside of traditional ways of looking at problems and solutions and find or develop new paradigms (Barker 1989).

Evaluation of Alternatives

A manager must accept "limited rationality": that is, the limitations of information, time, and certainty. He or she must recognize that one is not always able to choose the best of all alternatives. Often, one must settle for the best alternative possible under the circumstances. Simon calls this "satisficing" (Simon 1976). For example, a juvenile court administrator wants to create a new position for a probation officer who will supervise and counsel youth with a history of truancy and other status offenses. Since it is a small, rural county, the county council will not approve the new position. However, after some negotiation, the council does set aside a lesser amount of money for limited counseling for youth. Satisficing is a reality all too familiar to juvenile justice managers.

In another work (Houston and Parsons, 1999), the Quantitative Strategic Planning Matrix (QSPM) is discussed as a way to assess policy alternatives. The QSPM is merely a more elaborate process of one that we often carry out in our daily lives. This is rational decision making in a simplified form. We break the process into three steps: we list the alternatives; we assign a level of probability for success to each alternative; and we select the alternative that represents the best chance for achieving the stated goal.

TOOLS FOR SPECIFYING ALTERNATIVES

There are several methods to help the manager evaluate alternatives. Two of these methods are scenario writing and simulation.

Scenario Writing

Scenarios are descriptions of future conditions and events (Gershuny 1982). When we make a decision, we are attempting to shape the future. However, the future is not only unknown, it is also subject to external events and conditions. **Scenario writing** is an attempt to predict the future based upon known quantities. That is, we try to make the incomprehensible comprehensible.

Since our knowledge of the future is imperfect, we attempt to improve our understanding through the modeling technique; that is, a method of showing causal relationship between two events:

$$Y \rightarrow Z$$

Simply stated, a change in Y leads to a change in Z.

Hirshorn (1982) offers a typology of scenarios. Two are offered below:

- State Scenarios—These are broken into end-state and process scenarios. An end-state scenario is based upon an imagined condition in the future; a process scenario specifies a chain of events that leads up to a particular future state.
- Predictive/Planning Scenarios—These scenarios are used primarily for planning. Emphasis is on accuracy and validity. The decision maker can also use the scenario to stimulate further discussion and to provoke unexpected ideas.

Simulation

Computers are indispensable to simulation. The technique is frequently performed when there are a large number of variables, making exploration of each variable impracticable. The decision maker or analyst must have a good grasp of the factors involved and how they interact:

> Like scenario writing, the process of constructing a simulation reveals the interrelationships among variables, some of which are presumably under the analyst's control. The effect of changing some of these variables can be predicted by changing the computer program accordingly. Assuming that the model is an accurate representation of the way in which factors produce outcomes, the policy consequences of various administrative action can be predicted with the simulation. The technique is thus particularly valuable when actual experiments on target populations are impractical, unethical or too slow to be of practical benefit (Bingham & Ethridge 1982).

CHOOSING AN ALTERNATIVE

Many managers rely heavily on intuition and other subjective means (Michalasky, 1975) to make decisions. However, two of the more popular objective means of decision making are probability theory and decision trees.

Probability Theory

Quantifying variables is very difficult, and some managers rebel at attempts to quantify relationships (Kast & Rosenzweig 1979). We use statistics to describe a sample population, and we say that, for example, probationers in our court are on average 15.4 years of age, and they are on average in the ninth grade.

On the other hand, "probability is the 'reverse' of statistics: in probability we use the population information to infer the probable nature of the sample" (McClane and Benson 1985). Probability is important in decision making. For example, do you allow a youth to participate in a community program to help clean state parks when he absconded from probation and aftercare? Your answer should be an emphatic "No!" If the youth has demonstrated that he or she has been unwilling in the past to stay home while on probation or aftercare and even walked away from a group home, we say that it is improbable that he will refrain from further attempts just a few months after the last episode.

In juvenile justice, we face two types of situations relative to decision making: deterministic situations and stochastic situations. The former are situations in which the environment approached certainty; that is, before the decision is made, all relationships relevant to the decision problem are known precisely, as well as the values of all relevant variables. In this instance, we are often able to make the best possible decision. The latter are situations in which the environment is uncertain. In other words, relationships relevant to the decision problem and values of relevant variables are unknown. Thus, in a stochastic situation, we do not know whether we have made the right decision until the decision has been implemented (Simone 1967).

For example, if we flip a two-headed coin, we can say with certainty that if we call heads, we will be correct 100 percent of the time. In other words, out of ten tosses of the coin we will get ten heads. On the other hand, using a conventional coin we have a 50 percent chance of getting heads on any given toss. Thus, we say that in all probability we have a fifty-fifty chance of getting heads. No matter how many times we toss the coin, we still have a probability of fifty-fifty coming up heads.

The same process, albeit much more sophisticated, is used to examine many variables for many cases in developing the actuarial tables called sentencing guidelines used by judges and parole guidelines used by boards of parole. Thus we can see that there is a certain power of quantitative techniques in managerial decision making.

Decision Trees

The most important decisions facing the juvenile justice practitioner will not be made right away. Rather, the manager will take the time to gather information, develop alternatives, and evaluate the alternatives. One tool available to managers is the **decision tree**. A decision tree is a "graphical model that displays the sequence of decisions and the events that comprise a sequential decision situation" (Huber 1980). The value of the decision tree is that it enables the manager to construct a model to identify the inadequacies in his or her mental model, helps the manager to determine whether additional information is needed, and serves as an organized external memory and helps the manager communicate with subordinates.

Constructing a Tree—the Branches

Begin at the left and work to the right:

- Lay out the alternatives like branches. In Figure 11.7, the decision maker lays out as branches the alternatives of building a new detention center, renovating the old center and doing nothing. The square from which the fork originates is called a *choice fork.*
- Choosing an alternative leads to one or more outcomes. This is represented by the decision maker's drawing of a circle at the end of each alternative branch. The circles represent outcome forks. The decision maker may then draw branches corresponding to various positive or negative outcomes of the alternatives.

Constructing a Tree—the Leaves

- For each alternative, indicate the costs of implementation (see Figure 11.8). Some costs can be calculated, such as the cost of building a new detention center or renovating the old center. Other costs associated with outcomes can only be estimates.
- For each outcome indicate the probability of its occurrence.
- If applicable, indicate the gross payoff (in dollars) at the end of the outcome branch.

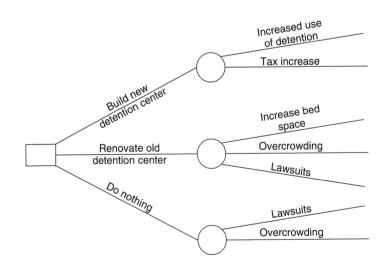

Figure 11.7   The Branches

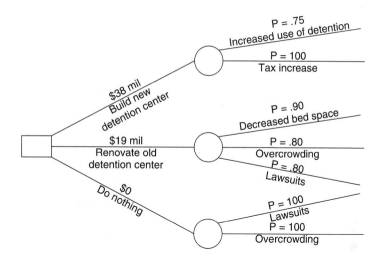

Figure 11.8 The Leaves

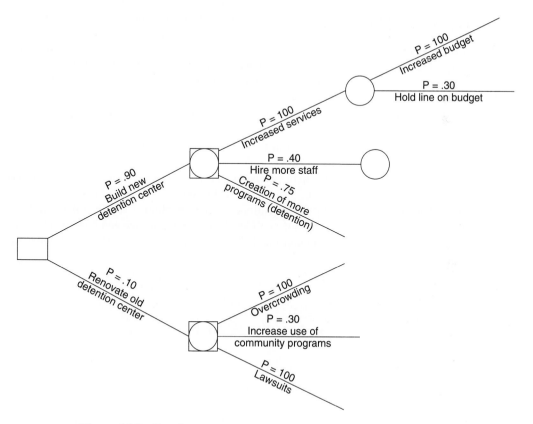

Figure 11.9 Pruning

Constructing a Tree—Pruning

Once the information has been gathered, it may be necessary to aggregate the information and construct a new tree (see Figure 11.9). To do this:

- Compute the net expectation at each outcome fork in terms of probability. In our example, we conclude that the only feasible alternatives are to either build a new detention center or renovate the old one.
- Estimate the expected probability for each outcome.
- If applicable, estimate the dollar payoff each alternative provides.

SUMMARY

A decision is a judgment, a choice between alternatives. Every day, juvenile justice practitioners make critical decisions that affect the safety and well-being of the community. In juvenile justice, there are two types of decisions: case management decisions and organizational decisions. What decisions one makes depends upon the position one holds in the hierarchy. The higher the practitioner is in the organization, the more likely it is that he or she will be concerned primarily with organizational decisions.

Decisions are of two types: programmed and nonprogrammed. Programmed decisions are those that are routine and for which the organization has a procedure that allows all similar decisions to be handled in the same way. Nonprogrammed decisions are unstructured, novel, and often one-time.

Two tools available to help the decision maker are scenario writing and simulations. Both tools attempt to make the incomprehensible comprehensible. Finally, probability theory and decision trees help the practitioner choose an alternative. It is important to remember that the decisions are made at all levels in juvenile justice and that all are important to the safety of the community and the well-being of the youth placed under our supervision.

CASE STUDY WRAP-UP

Ms. Kessler has an awesome job. She is the one who makes the decision regarding where a child will be placed and can have a serious impact on the life course of the child. It is a job that must be taken seriously and one that is all too often overlooked in terms of importance. It is therefore important that she have at her beck and call tools and individuals that can help her make the best decision possible.

STUDY QUESTIONS

1. What is a decision? How do you define the term?
2. Is the garbage can model of decision making one you see in organizations with which you are familiar?
3. What is a nonprogrammed decision? Give an example.
4. Should the boss be the only one making decisions in an organization?
5. When would you use a decision tree to assist you in making a decision?

BIBLIOGRAPHY

ALLISON, GRAHAM T. (1992). "Essence of Decision: Explaining the Cuban Missile Crisis." In William C. Johnson (Ed.), *Public Administration: Policy, Politics and Practice.* Guilford, CT: Dushkin, p. 32.

APAO, WILLIAM K. (1984). *Improving Prison Classification Procedures: Application of an Interaction Model.* Washington, DC: National Institute of Corrections, 84-IJ-CX4027.

BINGHAM, RICHARD D., AND ETHRIDGE, MARCUS E., Eds. (1982). *Reaching Decisions in Public Policy and Administration.* New York: Longman.

COHEN, MICHAEL D., MARCH, JAMES G., AND OLSON, JOHAN P. (1992). "A Garbage Can Model of Organization." In William C. Johnson (Ed.), *Public Administration: Policy Politics and Practice.* Guilford, CT: Dushkin.

CERTO, SAMUEL (1986). *Principles of Management: Functions and Systems,* 3rd ed. Dubuque, IA: William C. Brown.

DRUCKER, PETER (1973). *Management: Tasks, Responsibilities, Practices.* New York: Harper & Row.

GERSHUNY, J. (1982). "The Choice of Scenarios." In Richard D. Bingham & Marcus E. Ethridge (Eds.), *Reaching Decisions in Public Policy.* New York: Longman, pp. 77–123.

GLADSTONE, MARK (February 1, 2000). "Youth Crime Crackdown Up to Voters." *Los Angeles Times.* B2.

GOTTFREDSON, MICHAEL R., AND GOTTFREDSON, DON M. (1988). *Decision Making in Criminal Justice: Toward the Rational Exercise of Discretion,* 2nd ed. New York: Plenum Press.

GOTTFREDSON, MICHAEL, AND GOTTFREDSON, DON M. (2000). "Decision Guidelines." In Don M. Gottfredson (Ed.), *Juvenile Justice with Eyes Wide Open: Methods for Improving Information for Juvenile Justice.* Pittsburgh, PA: National Center for Juvenile Justice.

HAIMANN, THEO, SCOTT, WILLIAM G., AND CONNOR, PATRICK E. (1978). *Managing the Modern Organization,* 3rd ed. Boston, MA: Houghton Mifflin.

HALBERSTAM, DAVID. (1986). *The Reckoning.* New York: William Morrow.

HIRSHORN, LARRY (1982). "Scenario Writing: A Developmental Approach." In Richard D. Bingham and Marcus E. Ethridge (Eds.), *Reaching Decisions in Public Policy and Administration.* New York: Longman.

HOUSTON, JAMES, AND PARSONS, WILLIAM W. (1999). *Criminal Justice and the Policy Process.* Chicago: Nelson-Hall.

HUBER, GEORGE P. (1980). *Managerial Decision Making.* Greenview, IL: Scott Foresman.

JOHNSON, WILLIAM C. (1992). *Public Administration: Policy, Politics and Practice.* Guilford, CT: Dushkin.

KAST, FREMONT E., AND ROSENZWEIG, JAMES E. (1979). *Organization and Management: A System's and Contingency Approach.* San Francisco, CA: McGraw-Hill.

STOJKOVIC, STAN, KALINICH, DAVID, AND KLOFAS, JOHN (1998). *Criminal Justice Organizations: Administration and Management,* 2nd ed. Pacific Grove, CA: Brooks/Cole.

KOONTZ, HAROLD, O'DONNELL, CYRIL, AND WEIRICH, HEINZ (1986). *Essentials of Management.* New York: McGraw-Hill.

LINDBOLM, CHARLES E. (1959). "The Science of Muddling Through." *Public Administration Review,* 19, 79–88.

MCCLANE, JAMES T., AND BENSON, GEORGE P. (1985) *Statistics for Business and Economics,* 3rd ed. San Francisco, CA: Dellen.

MICHALASKY, JOHN (1975). "ESP in Decision Making." *Management Review,* 32–37.

ROWE, ALAN J., AND BOULGIARDES, JAMES D. (1992). *Managerial Decision Making.* New York: Macmillan.

SIMON, HERBERT A. (1976). *Administrative Behavior,* 3rd ed. New York: The Free Press.

SIMONE, ALBERT J. (1967) *Probability: An Introduction with Applications.* Boston: Allyn and Bacon.

GLOSSARY OF KEY TERMS

Agency decisions.   Decisions made by agency heads or supervisors that are not case management decisions, but affect the overall agency and its direction.

Case management decisions.   Decisions made by juvenile workers on behalf of a youth that directly effect the community, families of the youth involved, and the safety of the community.

Decision.   A judgement, a choice between two or more alternatives.

Decision tree.   A graphical model that displays the sequence of decisions and the events that comprise a sequential decision situation.

Needs assessment.   A tool used by youth workers to identify those youth most in need of services and what those services should be.

Nonprogrammed decisions.   An unstructured, novel, and often one-time decision.

Programmed decisions.   A routine, structured decision.

Risk assessment.   A tool used by youth workers to identify high-risk youth, those most in danger of absconding, participating in assaultive behavior, drug use or any other behavior that is detrimental to the well-being of the youth.

Scenario writing.   Scenario writing is an attempt to predict the future based upon known quantities.

CHAPTER 12
INTERGROUP RELATIONS AND CONFLICT

KEY TERMS

Groups
Intergroup conflict
Horizontal conflict

Vertical conflict
Custody/treatment
dichotomy

Cottage system

CASE STUDY

Are There Answers for Embattled New Jersey Juvenile Detention Center?*

Among the 270 youth in the Essex County Juvenile Detention Center (New Jersey) are 120 confirmed members of the Bloods, Crips, and Latin Kings. This spells severe heartburn for Director Joe Clark and his staff. According to Clark, a hard-core group of about twenty leaders were hurling feces and urine at the officers and, in general, doing their best to disrupt the order of the institution. This included putting some officers in the hospital after beatings, breaking the jaws of other detainees in fights, and committing hundreds of thousands of dollars in vandalism.

Director Clark states he was forced to resort to twenty-three-hour lock-downs and physical restraints. However, an eight-page report by the state Juvenile Justice Commission issued in December 2001 stated that long-term isolation, strait-jackets, and restraint "mittens" are prohibited. Clark said they were used only for short periods in order to restore order and accused the commission of encouraging violence by the enforcing the prohibition of restraints.

*Source: Adapted from "Joe Clark lashes out at critics of his tactics: Essex detention director says he intended to stop gang violence." *The Star-Ledger* (Newark, NJ). Dec 7, 2001, p. 37

Clark further stated that the commission standards are for smaller rural or suburban counties and that Essex County Juvenile Detention Center is one of the toughest juvenile detention facilities in the nation. He belittled Mr. Burke, the commission investigator, as a "low-level" minion who is trying to boost a sagging ego at the expense of the facility and Essex County.

In addition to the new problems, the detention facility has operated for a decade under a federal consent decree resulting from a lawsuit against the facility. Soon after Joe Clark took over as director he ran afoul of the consent decree when he ordered a dozen youth cuffed to their beds. It seems that Mr. Clark is doing all he can to stem the violence and work with various groups, but can he succeed?

INTRODUCTION

The Hawthorn Studies (Mayo, 1984) clearly reveal the importance of groups in the workplace. Every organization is a patchwork of groups and an individual can belong to several groups at the same time (Gibson, Ivancevich, and Donnelly 1979). For example, a counselor is a member of a cottage unit, serves on a task force for the superintendent, a member of an informal group who like to play golf together, and a member of the union. His or her role in each group is different. There are formal groups and informal groups, and in each group the members interact and influence each other and sometimes there is conflict between groups. How to recognize and work within the formal and informal system along with how to resolve conflict is the subject of this chapter.

GROUPS DEFINED

The effective juvenile justice manager must have a good understanding of the group and how it relates to the organization. For purposes of this chapter, a **group** is understood to be made up of two or more people who interact and mutually influence each other. Gibson, Ivancevich, and Donnelly (1979) point out that there is no generally accepted definition of "group," however, they surveyed the literature and found that understandings of what a group is fall into four categories:

1. Perception—group members perceive that they are members of that group.
2. Organization—the group is viewed relative to organizational characteristics. That is, there is a set of standard set of role relationships among members, and the group has a set of norms that guide conduct.
3. Motivation—the group is viewed as an entity that satisfies certain needs of its members.
4. Interaction—the group is characterized by face-to-face communication, and the group is small enough that each person is able to communicate with all other members over a period of time.

Thus, we arrive at a more specific definition of group as "two or more employees who interact with each other in such a manner that the behavior and/or performance of a member is influenced by the behavior and/or performance of other members" (Shaw, 1981, p. 8).

KINDS OF GROUPS IN JUVENILE JUSTICE ORGANIZATIONS

We will discuss inmate groups and conflict later in the chapter, but in regard to staff, there are basically two kinds of groups in juvenile justice organizations: formal groups and informal groups.

Formal Groups

A formal group is one that is established to further the mission of the organization. In a juvenile detention center, for example, one group is composed of employees who work various shifts and are combination security officers, counselor, and even in some instances case managers. Their job is to keep the children safe and maintain security. Another example is that of a Juvenile Court Administrator who forms a task force to review the risk assessment form. Thus, the demands of the organization have led to the formation of two different formal groups, one a command group and the other a task group (Gibson, et al. 1979).

Command Group

The command group is specified by the organization chart. Members of such a group report to a supervisor, who in turn reports to someone else. The authority relationship between the shift supervisor and his or her subordinates constitutes a command group. Figure 12.1 illustrates an organization chart that depicts command groups by departmentalization.

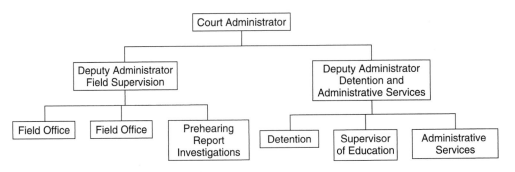

Figure 12.1 Organizational Chart

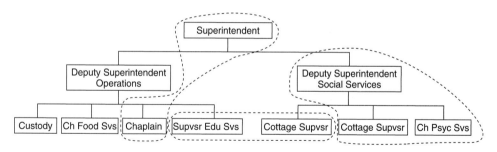

Figure 12.2   Informal Groups

Task Group

Members of a task group work together to complete a particular task or project. For example, an institutional superintendent will assign five or six staff members to review and rewrite, if necessary, visitation policy and procedures for the institution. In the introductory essay at the beginning of the chapter, the director could establish a group to look into the causes of gang conflict and submit a list of solutions. Task groups are often called committees, and they are valuable for at least four reasons (Management Review 1957). First, they allow organization members to exchange ideas; second, they allow members to generate suggestions and recommendations for other organizational units; third, they encourage members to develop new ideas for solving existing organizational problems; and fourth, they assist in the development of organizational policies.

Informal Groups

Informal groups arise naturally as a result of the work situation and in response to social needs, see Figure 12.2. Two types of informal groups have been identified:

Interest Group

Employees may band together to address a particular issue; for example, to press for higher wages or to change a procedure. Once the need is met, such groups often disband.

Friendship Groups

Many groups form because of common interests such as church and hobbies or because of a similarity in age. Friendship groups extend their activities to off-work hours and tend to change over time.

THE NATURE OF INTERGROUP CONFLICT

The field of criminal justice is difficult enough to work in without the creation of conflict among groups in the organization. Several years ago, the juvenile court in a populous midwestern county experienced a period when they hired four consecutive court administrators in as many years. Problems included some of the old veterans who resisted a more get-tough approach, a sense of elitism on the part of some of the newer probation officers, a judge who kept stirring the pot, and finally there were some racial overtones. Each administrator resigned after about one year of service because of strife and conflict in the court among the two groups who held a great deal of animosity towards one another. It seemed that no amount of energy invested, or despite what creative approaches were used to try to draw the two groups together, seemed to work. One administrator would be hired who was attractive to one group, and he or she was pilloried by the other group, then an administrator who was more attractive to the "other side" was hired and the same thing happened.

Finally, the fifth administrator, who evidently had a high tolerance for pain, stayed the course and was able to bring the two groups together in order to accomplish the goals of the court. He did this by opening lines of communication, forging a shared vision, and through small groups, which included youth on probation who were able to share their frustrations and hopes for the future. It wasn't perfect, but the organization was moving forward again.

There are a number of definitions of the term conflict. Thompson (1960) defines conflict as "that behavior by organization members which is expended in opposition to other members." Deutsch (1966) simply defines conflict as "whenever incompatible activities occur." Regardless of who is defining conflict, we know what it is when we see or experience it. The common theme running through all definitions is that all parties concerned perceive conflict to exist. Other key words or concepts that occur include: *opposition, incompatible goals,* and *divergence of interests.*

Intergroup Conflict

Daft (2000) points out that **intergroup conflict** requires three ingredients: group identification, observable group differences, and frustration. Usually, employees perceive themselves as part of an identifiable group, as social workers or correctional officers for example. Second, there has to be an observable group difference of some sort, which is necessary for conflict to exist. Third, frustration must be present. Frustration stems from the belief that if one group achieves its goal, the other will not. Frustration need not be severe, even minimal frustration can promote conflict. On the other hand, intergroup conflict will occur when one group tries to advance at the expense of the other.

There are two kinds of conflict in organizations: horizontal and vertical (Daft 1989). **Horizontal conflict** occurs between groups or departments on the same level on the organizational chart, for example, between the security staff and social work staff in a state youth institution. The correctional officers may believe that the social workers are not backing them up in their efforts to maintain institutional tranquility and that the social workers are too "soft." Social workers, on the other hand, feel that the correctional officers are too rigid and not understanding enough of the needs of the youth.

In the example cited at the beginning of the chapter, one group, mostly African Americans, believed that the other group was prejudiced and insensitive to the needs of youth (mostly African American) on probation who needed the benefit of counseling. The

Detention
Director

Shift   Shift   Shift
Supervisor ◄─────────► Supervisor   Supervisor

Counselor   Counselor ◄─────────► Counselor   **Figure 12.3**   Horizontal Conflict

other group believed that "leniency" was not the answer and that strict accountability is the key to conforming behavior. The fact that most youth on probation were African American was simply incidental. Figure 12.3 illustrates horizontal conflict.

Vertical conflict also occurs between hierarchal levels or between those at the top of the hierarchy and those further down the hierarchy. Usually conflict occurs over issues of control, goals, power, and wages and benefits (Daft, 2000). A typical conflict occurs between the union and the administration over wages and benefits or between the central office and a field office over police. Figure 12.4 illustrates the conflict in relationship to other organizational units.

According to Nye (1973) conflict results from either intentional provocation or unintentional provocation. In reducing intentional provocation, the supervisor or executive can reduce conflict by decreasing the frustrations produced by the environment. That is, if people can feel free from, and are thus unable to learn, defensiveness, prejudice, aggressiveness, and other conflict-producing characteristics then cooperation, equality, and civility will predominate.

However, according to Nye, unintentional provocation is more difficult to deal with because conflicts will still be with the organization since they are accidental. Nye offers two suggestions: first, many accidental provocations are unintentional and are simply inconsiderate behavior. Thus, it stands to reason that if sensitivity can be increased, then civility and cooperation will follow. This can be carried out by promoting sessions designed to acquaint staff with such issues as cultural awareness, gender sensitivity, and team building. Second, if defensiveness, prejudice, and so on are reduced, it decreases the likelihood that individuals will react with blind hostility to provocation and reasons for the provocation will be sought.

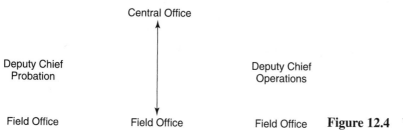

Central Office

Deputy Chief   Deputy Chief
Probation   Operations

Field Office   Field Office   Field Office   **Figure 12.4**   Vertical Conflict

GANGS AND CONFLICT

There is rich and varied literature on the subject of street gangs (some of which was covered in Chapter 4). While this issue was covered earlier, it is important to review it here as gangs are a continual source of conflict with which the juvenile justice practitioner must contend. Gangs are not a new phenomenon and Sheldon, Tracey, and Brown (1997) and Yablonsky (1997) provide a good summary of street gangs and their growth.

Gangs are noted as early as fourteenth-century England as a result of the decline of the manorial system. Due to the high death rate, there were thousands of orphans on the streets, and gangs offered a measure of protection and a way to survive. Gangs were noted for fighting each other in London for various reasons, usually related to issues of turf. The battles between gangs did not let up as London, and the emerging cities of Manchester and Birmingham, entered the industrial age. In general, mayhem, robbery, and burglary were the main offenses of these gangs.

It wasn't until the nineteenth century that gangs were noted in the new United States, although Sanders (1970) asserts that there were gangs during colonial times. The larger cities of New York, Boston, and Philadelphia saw the growth of street gangs, and the battles described by Herbert Asbury (1928, 2003) were usually a result of conflict between immigrant groups, for example, Irish against the Germans and Italians against the Jewish gangs. Their influence extended to control of certain areas of the city, and the adult gangs were used as a model for youth gangs. In New York, at about the time of the Civil War, the Pug-Uglies, Bowery Boys, Dead Rabbits, and others in and around the notorious Five Points area of New York ruled the area and contributed significantly to the draft riots of that time.

Under the stress of rapid urbanization and industrialization, the cities grew at an alarming rate with a host of social, health, and immigration problems. In the end, as Thrasher (1927) and Shaw and McKay (1942) found, immigration contributed to the formation of gangs as cities such as Chicago became a mosaic of cultures, each with conflict around the edges of neighborhoods. World War II saw a decrease in youth gangs as the military absorbed young men for the war in Europe and the Pacific. It wasn't until the 1950s that youth gangs again began to be noticed as a significant social problem.

During the 1960s, life in the inner cities began to change. The construction of the interstate highway system meant it became convenient for city dwellers to move to the suburbs and commute to work. The availability of affordable housing in the inner city was an attraction for rural migrants seeking better employment and a better way of life. It was this migration that changed the composition of the nation's cities and ultimately the fabric of the nation's prisons.

The change resulted in an increase in the number of impoverished citizens living in the inner cities and a declining tax base caused by the flight of the middle class from the city. As the cities began a downward spiral to decay and dependence upon federal largess, employers began to follow the middle class to the suburbs and beyond to the sunbelt and offshore sites. In addition, the civil rights movement and the anti-war movement coalesced to foster civil disobedience and to raise the expectations of those at the bottom of the economic heap, often beyond the point of fulfillment. The result was a vacuum waiting to be filled.

Gangs filled the void and served to meet the economic, social, and cultural needs of adolescents and youth who were the product of decay, despair, and often hopelessness (Jackson, 1991). Children raised on the street by mothers just out of childhood used each other for role models. Adolescents with no sense of community ownership, responsibility, or a moral rudder began to join together in order to obtain a sense of community and belonging. The resultant street gangs used an abundant supply of drugs for sale and resale in order to build a financial foundation that contributed to the super gangs we know today as the Gangster Disciples, Vice Lords, Latin Kings, Bloods, Crips, and so on.

STREET-LEVEL WORK AND GANG CONFLICT

Gangs have become a major impediment to successful efforts with youth who have come to the attention of the juvenile justice system. In the preceding pages, we provided a brief history of gangs, and this is not the place for an in-depth review of the dynamics of gangs, but a brief review of gang intervention programs may be helpful to understand how the probation officer, aftercare officer, and other youth workers can deal more effectively with conflict caused by gang involvement.

The Problem of Definition

Miller (1975) asserts that there are five components of gang activity and structure: criminal behavior (including violent behavior), group organization, identifiable leadership, continuing interaction among members, and cohesion. Conforming to Miller's components is perhaps the most widely accepted definition of a gang as defined by the California State Task Force on Youth Violence:

> A gang is a group of people who interact at a high rate among themselves to the exclusion of other groups, have a group name, claim a neighborhood or other territory and engage in criminal and other anti-social behavior on a regular basis (Destro, 1993).

Not long ago, the popular notion of youth gangs or street gangs was that of groups of adolescent males involved in delinquent activity (mostly gang fights and turf battles with each other) as part of their everyday lives. That is no longer the case, and we now must view gangs on at least two levels: youth gangs and organized crime groups such as the KKK, Aryan Brotherhood, and Skinheads. The new term security threat groups (STGs) seems to meet the needs of gang researcher and practitioners more adequately (Trout, 1992). In the case of juvenile justice worker, youth gangs are of greatest interest, but not exclusively.

There has been an ongoing debate over intervention programs for some years and Goldstein (1993) neatly summarizes what we know about those efforts. Thrasher (1927) learned that the gang promoted agreeable activities even though they were a platform for delinquent activities. His approach to meeting the needs of youth in gangs was that of social worker, and he urged social intervention in the family, alleviating poverty, improving education, and recreational outlets for youth. While the conditions noted by Thrasher did not go away, WWII intervened and absorbed many young men who otherwise would have been involved in gang activities.

Following WWII, a generation of bright, capable, and dedicated men and women began to filter into blighted neighborhoods armed with degrees in social work, sociology, and psychology, and they began to formulate programs that they hoped would intervene in the conflict that was a result of gang activity and steer youth from gang membership. One such approach was that of the detached worker, as discussed by Lewis Yablonsky (1962). Yablonsky identifies the violent gang as a force to be reckoned with and asserts that the gangs he worked with were "near groups," that is they were continually in the process of becoming organized. Klein (1971) defines the detached worker approach thusly, "Detached work programs are grounded in one basic proposition; because gang members do not ordinarily respond well to standard agency walls, it is necessary to take the program to the gangs."

Goldstein (1993) points out that while the detached worker approach was popular from the mid-nineteenth century through the 1950s and 1960s, it began to fall into disrepute during the 1970s. The goals of the detached worker program were to make referrals of gang members into treatment opportunities, to provide assistance when necessary including the provision of assistance and guidance in vocational education and employment choices, and in the instance of fighting gangs, redirect them in a positive direction. Unfortunately, the detached worker appears to not work as supposed (see for example Mattick and Kaplin, 1962; Quicker, 1993; Goldstein, 1993, and Klein, 1971). In the end it appears that the detached worker, instead of separating the youth from the gang and successfully diminishing the gang's importance in the life of youth, attention paid to the gang actually had the unanticipated effect of increasing the gang's cohesiveness and making the gang more attractive. Thus, conflict continued and defeated the efforts of juvenile justice workers and the police. Perhaps the lesson here for the street-level practitioner is to work with the individual or the community, while trying to avoid any kind of special attention to the gang as an entity.

One closely held notion by experts in delinquency prevention is that delinquency, and particularly gang delinquency, is a function of a lack of opportunity within the general opportunity structure of American society. Morales (1981) captures the thinking on this subject when he notes that the gang is a symptom of certain conditions found in the United States, including low wages, unemployment, lack of suitable recreation opportunities, inadequate school, poor health, deteriorated housing, and urban decay.

Street-level juvenile justice practitioners, as well as supervisors and executives in juvenile justice, can benefit from a national survey by the National Gang Crime Research Center in 1995 (Knox et al., 1995). Houston (1996) further refined the data and revealed what gang members and former gang members think about treatment and prevention efforts in regards to gangs. Knox and his colleagues surveyed twenty-four sites including alternative schools in the midwest, juvenile correctional institutions in seven states, jails in

Illinois and North Carolina, a state boot camp in Texas, and private residential facilities for at-risk youth in Iowa, Indiana, and Ohio. A usable sample of 3,348 was obtained with 1,994 self-admitted gang members completing the questionnaire. Overall validity is rated as high as a staff member or Gang Crime Research Center member was either in the room or watched on closed-circuit TV as the responders filled out the questionnaire.

Ninety-one percent (91.3 percent) of the respondents were male and 88 percent (88.8 percent) of the respondents were between the ages of fourteen and eighteen. Ninety-five percent had not yet completed high school, 88 percent had been suspended from school at least once, and two-thirds had been expelled from school. About one-half agreed that prevention efforts can effectively prevent youth from becoming involved in gangs, but there is dispute in what is effective even though three-fourths (74.7 percent) state that sooner or later gang members do want out of the gang. In addition, nearly all (93.5 percent) state they would like to get married, get a legal job, and have children.

Of particular interest to juvenile justice practitioners as they search for ways to deal with conflict between gangs and gang members, in addition to efforts to develop effective programs, are the responses by the gang members surveyed for this project. Surprisingly, half (49.1 percent) state that suppression efforts by the police are important in order to deter the spread of gangs. Beyond that, the programs seen by the respondents with the largest number in agreement was the statement in regard to employment. Thirty-nine percent (39.4 percent) stated that employment and employment services are important to keep youth out of gangs. Second in ranking is residential programs, that is, group homes or halfway houses. Third (20.3 percent) is the use of social workers who work with youth in the neighborhood. This is a surprising finding as it flies in the face of Klein's (1968) observations. Last in ranking of effective gang prevention programs are recreation programs, wilderness programs, and mentoring.

Using the above data, Houston (1996) compared the gangsters rankings of effective programs to the number of programs cited by the Office of Juvenile Justice and Delinquency Prevention (OJJDP) as programs that work. Programs cited as effective are social skills/nonresidential (8), social skills/residential (6), special education (11), individual/family/group counseling (24). On the other hand, looking at effective programs from the viewpoint of the survey respondents, only one program was cited in the area of vocational training/nonsecure residential, one secure residential and nine nonsecure residential. Perhaps before the juvenile justice worker attempts to develop a program to deal with gangsters and conflict, he or she should talk to known gangsters.

What Works and the Practitioner

Conflict resolution and juvenile justice go hand in hand. Gangs and conflict are two sides of the same coin; if you can eliminate gangs, you eliminate a good deal of conflict. Gangs fight over turf, drugs, and simply for the sake of fighting (see Sanders, 1994). It falls to the probation officer, aftercare officer, and other street workers to defuse situations and restore a degree of calm. As a consequence, the effective juvenile justice practitioner would be wise to look closely at what gangsters say works and to devote a great deal effort to see that some of the above effective programs are established in their jurisdiction.

In developing an approach to working with gangs and other adjudicated delinquents who are in conflict with other youth or groups, we can take a page from Spergel, Curry, Ross, and Chance (1990). They assert, based on their research, that the programs investigated in their research fell into one of four categories: (1) community organization, (2) social intervention, (3) opportunities: jobs, job training, and education, and (4) suppression.

Community organization is the hardest and perhaps outside the realm of the role of juvenile justice practitioners. However, it is an approach that the director or administrator of a juvenile justice organization can support and lend informal support. An example would be a grass roots organization, such as a CAP, discussed earlier, whose goal is to keep neighborhood youth out of gangs and provide opportunity and role models for wanna-bes and gangsters. The administrator can provide information about estimated numbers of youth involved in gangs or she or he can assign a probation officer to be the liaison with the group.

Social intervention is what the juvenile justice organization is about. The primary efforts are directed to youth and to keep him or her from reoffending or, in some instances, prevent youthful involvement in delinquency. Exposing the youth to opportunities is another way of dealing with delinquency and conflict. If youth have a sense of future and believe that they will not be excluded from the legitimate opportunity structure, they will be less likely to come to the attention of the juvenile justice system. Finally, it is important that suppression continue to be pursued in order to bring to justice and apprehend youthful offenders.

Clearly, conflict in the juvenile justice system comes in many forms, from the gangs and other groups that the probation officer must deal with on the street to staff conflicts. One area of staff conflict is the treatment/custody dichotomy that is prevalent in some institutions.

CUSTODY/TREATMENT DICHOTOMY

Most juvenile institutions are well-managed, and the staff work well together. In a few others, there is a good deal of conflict between those who supervise the daily activities of the inmates, or wards, as some states call them, and the staff who are responsible for programs or rehabilitation. The **custody/treatment dichotomy** is mostly present in state institutions and is characterized by disdain of one group towards the other group, and often there is a display of animosity and occasional difficulty in working together as a unit.

There is usually justification for animosity on the part of one group towards the other. Stitt (1998) calls our attention to the fact that there are four basic ways in which membership in different groups can create conflict:

   a. Different characteristics are identified as inherently attractive or unattractive. Conflict arising from this point is related to prejudice: education level, gender, racial, or sexual orientation. While it is a gross stereotype, we can say that criminal justice employees are usually strong personalities with definite opinions on just about any subject, but in particular on what characteristics make a good employee and how to handle lawbreakers. For example, many in the field of juvenile justice believe that there is a place for women and that does not include a tough boys reform school. Racial prejudice often raises its ugly head, but it usually does not interfere with getting the job done.

b. See as legitimate different equations for determining how much reward—either in terms of status or goods—a person should have. Many times the custody staff feel they do the bulk of the work, and the treatment staff sit around and drink coffee all day. Often the treatment staff see the bulk of the custody staff as ignorant of the principles they are trying to implement in therapy and counseling and believe that their work is often undone by the custody staff. The differences in salary then are amplified by the custody staff who feel they should get a greater salary and the treatment staff feel the custody staff hardly earn what they take home.

c. Feel that different kinds of procedures and different interpretations of the same data [or ways of dealing with the youth] make more sense when performing different tasks. This usually is a major area of differences. Custody staff often feel the treatment staff are too lenient on the youth, and the treatment staff often feel the custody staff are too harsh. Whenever an incident occurs where an officer must interfere, the treatment staff may be too quick to criticize and thus contribute to the chasm between the two groups. After the incident, the custody staff may be too critical of the way the treatment staff handled the situation after the fact and feel that the social worker or case worker didn't lay down the law sternly enough and they will have to reprise the incident again.

d. Feel that the other group's control over certain resources will be detrimental to their own group's interests. Most juvenile workers inherently feel that the budget reflects the priorities of the organization. As a result, if one group or the other is believed to be getting too much in the way of resources, conflict is bound to follow. Certainly the custody staff need radios and to purchase new ones as technology improves and vehicles to transport youth is necessary. On the other hand, the treatment staff need room to conduct therapy groups, and computers are necessary in each social worker's office to prepare paperwork and keep up with his or her caseload. But sometimes one group or the other believes the other is gaining access to resources at their expense.

Dealing effectively with this type of conflict is difficult, but if the various department heads work closely together, there will be a trickle-down effect. In addition, properly designed cottage management is the most effective way of dealing with organizational conflict. Most juvenile institutions are organized according to the cottage system and thus, conflict is held to a minimum. On the other hand, if all staff in each cottage are not reporting to the cottage supervisor, there is plenty of room for staff conflict to develop.

THE COTTAGE SYSTEM

Not long before the Civil War, reformers began to realize that their efforts to rehabilitate youth were not working in the institutions of the time and, as a consequence, developed reformatories whose purpose was to train and rehabilitate wayward youth. Many were organized around a cottage system that was supposed to imitate home life and a married couple was retained to live in the cottage and provide support and discipline to the youth.

Today many juvenile institutions reflect a campus-like setting with a relatively small number of youth housed together in "cottages." At the heart of the **cottage system** is the notion that a decentralized organization and smaller living groups are better able to quickly respond to the needs of the youth and to draw staff into the daily decision-making necessary to manage the youth's program.

Cottage Management Defined

There may be as many definitions of the cottage system as there are institutions that use the concept (for a more complete discussion of unit management which the authors use as a guide for this discussion, see Levinson, 1999; and Houston, 1999). Drawing on the defi-

Figure 12.5   The cottage system allows the staff to work closely with youth and to see each youth daily in a more intense relationship. Staff also benefit in that they all play a part in decision making.
Billy E. Barnes/PhotoEdit

nition of unit management as a guide (Gerard, 1971), we can define the cottage system as a small, self-contained, living and staff office area that operates semi-autonomously within the larger institution.

The essential components of a cottage are:

- A small number of youth (twelve to twenty-five) who are permanently assigned together,

- A multidisciplinary staff (unit manager, social workers(s), counselor(s), full- or part-time psychologist, clerk-typist, and officers whose office or work station is located within or adjacent to the housing area and are permanently assigned to work with the youth of that cottage).

- A cottage manager who has administrative authority and supervisory responsibility for the cottage staff.

- A cottage staff that has administrative authority for all within-unit aspects of youth living and programming.

- Youth who are assigned to a cottage because of age, prior record, specific behavior typologies, need for a specific type of program such as drug abuse counseling, or random assignment.

It is no accident that Gerard, Levinson, and Norman Carlson implemented unit management at the new Kennedy Youth Center in Morgantown, West Virginia for the U.S. Bureau of Prisons. Levinson had experimented with the concept at the National Training School for Boys in Washington, D.C., in the 1950s where it was deemed a success but was dropped because of budget concerns. The effective cottage follows certain guidelines critical for its success. The effective cottage must have the support of top management, there must be a cottage plan, the cottage manager must be, at least, on the same level as other department heads on the organization chart, and the cottage manager must have administrative and supervisory authority over staff working in the cottage.

Advantages of Cottage Management

The advantages of cottage management are many. It allows staff to take as much responsibility as they wish or are able to handle. It makes achievements visible, enabling the cottage manager to recognize subordinate's good work. Further, the work itself is considered more satisfying. Shared decision making and participation in the policy process are also advantages. In short, staff feel that they are involved in the total workings of the institution and the cottage, resulting in a sense of cohesiveness and staff and ward conflict is greatly reduced.

The multidisciplinary nature of unit management improves communication between staff and youth and allows for discussion while making both program decisions and organizational decisions. Other advantages include:

- Cottage management divides the youth population into small, well-defined, and manageable groups whose numbers develop a common identity and close association with each other and their cottage staff.

- It increases the frequency of contacts between staff and youth and the intensity of their relationships, resulting in:
  a. Better communication and understanding between individuals.
  b. More individualized program planning.
  c. Better observation of youth, enabling early detection of problems before they reach critical proportions.
  d. Development of common goals that encourage positive cottage cohesiveness.
  e. Generally a more positive living and working environment for youth and staff.
- Decisions are made by the cottage staff who are closely associated with the youth, which increases the quality and swiftness of decision making.
- Program flexibility is increased because special areas of emphasis can be developed to meet the needs of the youth in each unit, and programs in a unit may be changed without affecting the total institution.
- Finally, and perhaps most importantly, the cottage provides an effective program to develop and deliver effective therapeutic programs, be it a therapeutic community, guided group interaction, a token economy, skill development or even specialty units for substance abuse.

Clearly, the cottage system is the most effective way to manage a youth institution. Implementation is sometimes difficult, it rearranges the lines of power and communication, and threatens individuals more comfortable with the more traditional pyramidal organization. It is an approach that the director of the Essex County detention center should consider if he wants to put an end to the violence. In the end, youth are more effectively served and conflict is held to a minimum when cottage management is implemented.

SUMMARY

A group is defined as two or more people who mutually influence each other. That influence can be either positive or negative and will interfere with the achievement of organizational goals. There are both formal and informal groups and the effective juvenile justice worker must be able to use each to the benefit of the organization or the youth under his or her supervision.

It is not uncommon for conflict to erupt between staff, and the supervisor must act quickly to deal with the situation in order to defuse future conflict. Conflict between youth, and youth and the community is common, and it is up to the institutional worker, probation officer, or aftercare worker to work with the youth in order to teach him or her how to fit into the community without resorting to conflict.

At the institutional level, the cottage system is an effective way to manage an institution and control conflict. Implementation of the cottage system will enhance communication between staff and between staff and youth. In addition, the cottage offers an effective platform for the delivery of services to youth assigned to the cottage.

Conflict will occur as long as humans work together and as long as we attempt to work with those who violate the law. It is important that the juvenile justice worker immediately and effectively deal with conflict when it occurs.

CASE STUDY WRAP-UP

Director Joe Clark has his hands full. The introductory essay began with the question, "Are there answers for embattled New Jersey Juvenile Detention Center?" Conflict dominates Mr. Clark's life: gangs fighting each other, other detainees, and staff; the state Juvenile Justice Commission is critical of center operations and can decertify the center; and the federal government is involved through a consent decree with a special master who oversees the entire operation. Mr. Clark probably needs a Palm Pilot just to keep the players straight.

There may be other options to consider, first perhaps the organization of the detention center is too rigid, and Clark needs to think about cottage management approach or unit management in order to increase supervision and increase staffing. He can also think about programs to occupy the time of the detainees, and finally, there is always the option of transferring the major troublemakers to another facility. Whatever he does, staff should be involved, and he should not shoulder the decision alone.

STUDY QUESTIONS

1. Define conflict and explain one way to deal with institutional conflict.
2. What is the difference between a formal group and an informal group?
3. How would horizontal conflict interfere with the smooth management of the organization?
4. Identify one advantage of cottage management.
5. Why does Klein assert that the detached worker approach does not work with street youth, and how would a detached worker contribute to conflict?

BIBLIOGRAPHY

ASBURY, HERBERT (1928, 2003). *The Gangs of New York: An Informal History of the Underworld.* New York: Wheeler Publications, Inc.

DAFT, RICHARD L. (2000). *Organization Theory and Design,* 3rd ed. St. Paul, MN: West Publishing Company.

DESTRO, ROBERT A. (1993). "Gangs and Civil Rights." In Scott Cummings and Daniel Monti (Eds.), *Gangs: The Origins and Impact of Contemporary Youth Gangs in the United States.* Albany, NY: State University of New York Press, pp. 277–304.

DEUTSCH, KARL W. (1966). *The Nerves of Government: Models of Political Communication and Control,* 2nd ed. New York: The Free Press.

GERARD, ROY, AND GERARD, ROY E. (April 1971). "The Ten Commandments of Unit Management." *Corrections Today,* 32, 34, 36.

GIBSON, JAMES L., IVANCEVICH, JOHN M., AND DONNELLY, JR., JAMES H. (1979). *Organizations: Behavior, Structure, Processes,* 3rd ed. Dallas, TX: Business Publications.

GOLDSTEIN, ARNOLD P. (1993). "Gang Intervention: A Historical Review." In Arnold P. Goldstein and C. Ronal Huff (Eds.), *The Gang Intervention Handbook.* Champaign, IL: Research Press. pp. 21–51.

HOUSTON, JAMES (Spring 1996). "What Works: The Search for Excellence in Gang Intervention Programs." *Journal of Gang Research, 3*(3): 1–16.

———— (1999). *Correctional Management: Functions, Skills, and Systems,* 2nd ed. Nelson-Hall Publishers.

JACKSON, PAMELA IRVING (1991). "Crime, Youth Gangs, and Urban Transition: The Social Dislocations of Postindustrial Economic Development." *Justice Quarterly, 8,* 3: 379–397.

KLEIN, MALCOLM W. (1993). "The Ladino Hills Project" (Final Report). In Arnold P. Goldstein, "Gang Intervention: An Historical Review." In Arnold P. Goldstein and C. Ronald Huff (Eds.), *The Gang Intervention Handbook.* Champaign, IL: Research Press, p. 27.

KLEIN, MALCOLM W. (1971). *Street Gangs and Street Workers.* Englewood Cliffs, NJ: Prentice Hall.

KNOX, GEORGE W., TROMANHAUSER, EDWARD D., HOUSTON, JAMES G., MARTIN, BRAD, MORRIS, ROBERT E., MCCURRIE, THOMAS F., LASKEY, JOHN L., PAPACHRISTOS, DOROTHY, FEINBERG, JUDITH, AND WAXMAN, CHARLA (1995). *The Economics of Gang Life: A Task Force Report.* Chicago: National Gang Crime Research Center.

LEVINSON, ROBERT B. (1999). *Unit Management in Prisons and Jails.* Landham, MD: American Correctional Association.

MAYO, ELTON. (1984). "Hawthorn and the Western Electric Company." In D.S. Pugh (Ed.), *Organizational Theory,* 2nd ed. New York: Penguin.

Management Review. (Oct. 1957). "Committees: Their Role in Management Today." 46: 4–10.

MATTICK, HANS W., AND CAPLIN, K.N.S. (1962). *Chicago Youth Development Project: The Chicago Boys Club,* Ann Arbor, MI: Institute for Juvenile Justice and Delinquency Prevention, LEAA, U.S. Department of Justice. Washington, D.C.: U.S. Government Printing Office.

MILLER, WALTER B. (1975). *Violence by Youth Gangs and Youth Groups as a Crime Problem in Major American Cities.* National Institute for Juvenile Justice and Delinquency Prevention, LEAA, U.S. Department of Justice. Washington, D.C.: U.S. Government Printing Office.

MORALES, A. (1981). *Treatment of Hispanic Gang Members.* Los Angeles: University of California, Neuropsychiatric Institute.

NYE, ROBERT D. (1973). *Conflict Among Humans.* New York: Springer Publishing Company.

QUICKER, KAMES C. (1993). "Seven Decades of Gangs." Sacramento, CA: State of California Commission on Crime Control and Violence Prevention. In Arnold P. Goldstein, "Gang Intervention: An Historical Review," in Arnold P. Goldstein and C. Ronald Huff (Eds.), *The Gang Intervention Handbook.* Champaign, IL: Research Press, 1993.

SANDERS, WILLIAM B. (1994). *Gangbangs and Drive-bys.* Hawthorne, NY: Aldine DeGruyter.

SANDERS, W.B. (1970). *Juvenile Offenders for a Thousand Years.* Chapel Hill, NC: University of North Carolina Press.

SHAW, CLIFFORD, AND McKAY, H.D. (1942). *Juvenile Delinquency in Urban Areas.* Chicago: University of Chicago Press.

SHAW, MARVIN E. (1981). *Group Dynamics: The Psychology of Small Group Behavior,* 3rd ed. New York: McGraw-Hill.

SHELDON, RANDALL G., TRACEY, SHARON K, AND BROWN, WILLIAM B. (1997). *Youth Gangs in American Society.* Belmont, CA: Wadsworth Publishing Company.

SPERGEL, IRVING A., CURRY, GLEN DAVID, ROSS, R.E., AND CHANCE, RON (May 1990). "Survey of Youth Gang Problems and Programs in 45 Cities and 6 Sites," National Youth Gang Project, University of Chicago, School of Social Service Administration. OJJDP, U.S. Department of Justice.

STITT, ALLEN J. (1998). *Alternative Dispute Resolution: How to Design a System for Effective Conflict Resolution.* New York: Wiley.

THOMPSON, JAMES D. (March 1960). "Organizational Management of Conflict." *Administrative Science Quarterly,* p. 389.

THRASHER, FREDERICK (1927). *The Gang.* Chicago: University of Chicago Press.

TROUT, CRAIG H. (1992). "Taking a New Look at an Old Problem." *Corrections Today,* (February): 62, 64, 66.

YABLONSKY, LEWIS (1962). *The Violent Gang.* New York: McMillan.

——— (1997). *Gangsters: Fifty Years of Madness, Drugs, and Death on the Streets of America.* New York: New York University Press.

GLOSSARY OF KEY TERMS

Cottage system.   A philosophy of management that breaks an institution into small, self contained, living and staff office areas that operates semi-autonomously within the larger institution.

Custody/treatment dichotomy.   A condition that exists in many adult and youth institutions in which the officer force and the case management/social work force are at odds over philosophical differences. The result can be animosity and feelings that are often directed at the youth.

Groups.   A group is understood to be made up of two or more people who interact and mutually influence each other.

Horizontal conflict.   Conflict between groups who appear on the same level on an organizational chart.

Intergroup conflict.   A social condition that requires three ingredients: group identification, observable group differences, and frustration.

Vertical conflict.   Conflict between hierarchal levels or between those at the top of the organizational hierarchy and those further down the hierarchy.

PART IV
INTEGRATING THE JUVENILE JUSTICE SYSTEM

Part IV pulls what we have learned together in terms of how the chief executive officer operates as the major coordinating influence in the organization and as a consequence has a great deal of influence on where the juvenile justice system is going. His or her power, responsibility for budgeting, planning, and organizing subordinates to strive for excellence and to achieve organizational objectives are examined in light of what we know about organizational management and the juvenile justice system. Finally, we peer into our crystal ball and discuss the future of juvenile justice. Whatever the future holds, we know that it will be an exciting time and one that is ready for competent and concerned practitioners to take the reins and lead us on to excellence of service.

CHAPTER 13
POWER AND POLITICS
IN JUVENILE JUSTICE

KEY TERMS

Power	Power core	Legal authority
Authority	Traditional authority	Politics
Power cone	Charismatic authority	

CASE STUDY

Juvenile Justice and Gubernatorial Politics in Oregon*

Oregon's gubernatorial election of 2002 was a tough one, and the two candidates were at opposite ends of the continuum on crime and juvenile justice. One candidate had a reputation for toughness on lawbreakers, and the other candidate's best-known work was in trying to revamp the juvenile justice system to try to balance punishment with reformation.

In the time leading up to the election, both candidates knew the winner would face pressure to keep up spending for youth and adult prisons and the police despite budget problems. The president of Crime Victims United, an outspoken advocate group for victims of crime stated, "What the vast majority of Oregonians hope is that whoever the next governor is, they don't turn back the clock to the days when we had accelerating crime rates and a lack of respect for victims' rights."

Both candidates pledged that there would be money for state police and for prevention programs for youth. Democrat Kulogoski stated that he had no plans to rework Measure 11, which established mandatory minimums for murder, robbery, and rape, even

*Source: Adapted from David Steves. *The Register-Guard* (Eugene, OR) Oct 30, 2002, p. A1, State of Oregon website: www. governor.state.or.us/.

though there was a push to require a second look at juveniles sentenced as adults for those crimes. Kulogoski was in support of former governor Kitzhaber's work to direct services to at-risk families, and he stated that he planned to continue youth-crime prevention programs.

Republican candidate Mannix clearly stated that Measure 11 is an "outstanding success," but he was willing to consider proposals from second-look advocates if they could make a case for a shortened sentence. Mannix also called himself a major proponent of youth crime-prevention programs. Both candidates rejected any call for decreasing the state police budget.

The political fight was tough, and while there were many other issues to be considered as voters went to the polls, juvenile crime was at the top of the list. Governor Kulogoski has now finished his first term and his pledge for children is

> I believe that it isn't enough to assure our citizens that "no child will be left behind." In my administration, children will go to the head of the line. That is both an economic imperative and a moral necessity. My budget invests in health care, education and other programs for the children of Oregon. By shoring up our youngest citizens, we invest in Oregon's future.

INTRODUCTION

Stojkovic, Kalinich, and Klofas (2003) point out that "power and politics are inseparable in the criminal justice system." They go on to assert that power seems to be used inappropriately and often to the detriment of the organization. Unfortunately, until recently this subject was ignored in criminal justice literature (see Stojkovic, et al., 2003, and Houston, 1999), and the student was forced to learn the hard way as a new employee that power is often abused and is often used to the benefit of the individual instead of the organization.

Power is often thought of as an individual characteristic and we are apt to say, "She has a lot of power," or "He can get things done." But power in an organization is often a function of structural characteristics (Brass, 1984). Juvenile justice organizations range from the small to the very large. For example, a juvenile court in a rural area might have four probation officers and a supervisor or chief. On other hand, in a large, populous county such as Cook County, Illinois; Los Angeles; or Wayne County, Michigan, one will find a large number of probation officers, perhaps hundreds, and a very large detention center often employing more than three-hundred officers and counselors. The smaller system will be characterized by face-to-face encounters, and the supervisor will be able to see daily all employees in the system and take a hands-on approach to supervision. The administrator of a large organization such as Cook County, Illinois, will not know many front-line employees, and the court will be arranged hierarchically, usually with like functions grouped into the same departments. Thus, in the small department, power will usually be vested in the administrator who has daily contact with the judges and Board of Commissioners. In the large department, not only will the court administrator have power, but power will also flow to the one with contacts and to the department that controls resources or is indispensable to the operation of the organization.

POWER DEFINED

Bierstedt (1950) defines **power** as the force or the ability to apply sanctions. That is, it is potential force, not actual force and is not to be confused with the application of sanctions. Power is inherently coercive. Dahl (1957) defines power as the ability to get people to do something they would not have otherwise done. Daft (1989) states that power is an intangible force in organizations, and while it cannot be seen, its effects can be felt.

While power can be acquired or conferred, authority, on the other hand, is narrower in scope and is a function of the hierarchy. That is, authority is vested in organizational positions, is accepted by subordinates, and authority flows downward in the organization. In order not to confuse power with **authority**, it is useful to conceptualize power as taking the shape of a cone. One does not have to hold a formal position in the organizational hierarchy to hold power; various individuals throughout the organization can, and do, hold informal power. The **power cone** can be viewed as representing the organizational structure, as well as the distribution of power in the organization. The superintendent or court administrator, for example, sits at the top of the cone with the various department heads positioned on the outside of the cone in a ring at equal distance from the court administrator. On down the outside of the cone are arranged various subunits reporting to the department heads, and last the line staff at the bottom of the power cone. Down the center of the cone exists a core, called the **power core**. The closer one is to the power core, the more power one has, even without the authority. It is easy to see that one can move closer to the power core without acquiring authority. This concept can be illustrated by looking at the secretary to the superintendent of a large juvenile residential facility. Because she, or he, is in close proximity to the superintendent day after day and because the superintendent relies heavily on the secretary to keep him or her organized, the secretary has a lot of informal power, but no authority.

Another example is that of a teacher in the same facility. Perhaps the teacher and superintendent attended college together and both obtained jobs at the reform school at the same time. While the teacher remained a teacher, by choice, the other individual moved up from counselor to department head and ultimately to superintendent. All the while the two former classmates remained friends and associated together outside of work. Clearly, the teacher has no authority except in the classroom, but he has access to the superintendent and thus a measure of power.

TYPES OF POWER

There are several ways to distinguish between types of power, but probably the best known is that of Weber (1947). Hall summarizes Weber's views on power and authority (1991). Weber makes a distinction between power and authority, and he points out that

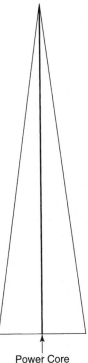

Power Core   **Figure 13.1**   Power Cone

power involves force or coercion, while authority is a form of power that does not imply force. It involves a "suspension of judgment" on the part of its recipients. Thus, as Figure 13.1 illustrates, one can have power and no authority, as does our hypothetical secretary or teacher. On the other hand, one can also have authority and be powerful because authority implies power. Weber's typology is helpful at this point in order to understand issues of authority.

Traditional authority is based on belief in the established traditional order and is best exemplified by the example of a court administrator who has held the position for many years. Terms such as "the old man wants it that way" are thrown about, and no one objects to his demands. Conformity to the wishes of "the old man" is expected. **Charismatic authority** stems from devotion to a particular individual and is based on certain personal characteristics. This is often found in organizations, and the leader who holds charismatic authority can often extend legal powers through the exercise of personality. **Legal authority** is based on the belief in the right of those in higher office to have power over subordinates. Most of us who work in criminal or juvenile justice are familiar with all three types of authority, but we are most comfortable with legal authority because that allows the organization to continue no matter who is in charge. That is, as Weber (1947) asserts, we are all part of a bureaucracy and are interchangeable.

Weber's study of bureaucracy has been interpreted in ways that promote a conservative view of power (Mumby, 1988). Mumby goes on to point out that Weber's notion of

Figure 13.2   It is important for the superintendent or director to not be aloof from staff, but to communicate openly and sincerely with staff and inmates.
Dorling Kindersley Media Library

purposive-rational action has permitted organizational structuring to be conceived of as a largely rational process that has little to do with the exercising of power by social actors. Weber links power to the personality of individuals and authority is associated with social roles or positions in formal hierarchies. This, in turn, permits a view of organizational power as the legitimate exercising of authority by virtue of one's position in the hierarchy (the power cone).

Mumby (1988) makes an interesting connection between Clegg (1975) and Weber (1947). Clegg reconceptualizes Weber's notions of power and authority into a more radical idea of the relationship between power and organizational structuring. Clegg reinterprets Weber's *Herschaft* (power) as "rule" in order to emphasize the interpretive mental gymnastics people go through when they try to make sense of the social world. All authority is dependent on the concept of rule-governed behavior. That is, different types of "rule" provide differing types of orders to which people orient their behavior. Domination is socially significant as a structural phenomenon because people orient their behavior towards it.

Clegg makes a clear connection between "power as domination," organizational structure, and interaction. He articulates a relationship in which the organizational structure acts as a mediator between interaction and domination. In other words, an organization's mode of rationality is embodied in both its structure and in the way in which this structure is manifested in interaction. Domination occurs when the rules of organizational rationality are structured to favor vested interests and to militate against others. Power is both a product of organizational activity and the process by which activity becomes institutionally legitimated. It is both medium and outcome; enabling and restraining. Thus, organizational interaction is not something that takes place within the (power) structure of an organization, but is rather the process through which structure is created, reproduced, and changed (Clegg, 1975).

This concept can be illustrated by a small midwest juvenile court that hired a new administrator because of years of criticism by the media and recent revelation of corruption and incompetence. The court was comprised of the administrator, magistrate, five probation officers, a detention center, and various office staff. The administrator reported to five county judges who attempted to work as a governing board and the magistrate also reported to the judges and was not responsible to the administrator. Obviously the juvenile court was small enough to be characterized by face-to-face relationships and a hands-on approach by the administrator. However, he viewed the staff as members of one of three different departments for budgetary and management purposes: field supervision, detention, and administrative support.

This arrangement clearly upset the status quo in that the staff were now sheltered by a department that acted as a mediator between them and the judges who were highly political (rationality). Since the administrator attempted to inject rationality into the management of the court, the judges were greatly concerned as this clearly interrupted their domination over line staff. Further, the new structure threatened vested interests in that the court had traditionally been used as a place to reward political loyalists with a job of some sort. The end of this story is that the administrator was fired, the court went back to business as usual with the judges able to protect their vested interest and maintaining power over all employees in the court.

DEPARTMENTALIZATION

Clearly, departmentalization is in the best interests of line staff as it is a buffer against domination, and it clearly lays out lines of communication and authority. An organization is structured in ways that will best achieve organizational objectives. For example, a juvenile court will be structured with a judge, or magistrate, serving to listen to cases and make decisions relative to attorney requests and adjudication. In addition, there is a court administrator who manages the day-to-day affairs of the court and who assures that the orders of the judge or magistrate are carried out. From there the court fans out below the administrator organized along departmental lines. Or does it?

A department can be viewed as a unique group of organizational resources established by management to perform specific tasks. The creation of a department is based upon either tasks to be accomplished (grouping like functions together) or the target group. Many times, however, a judge or administrator will structure the organization according to his or her preferences, and sometimes that structure defies logical explanation. However, in light of Clegg's (1975) assertions there is logic, we just have to look for it. For example, it makes sense for the CASA (Court Appointed Special Advocate) program to report to the court administrator. But, occasionally a judge will insist that the supervisor of the CASA program report directly to him or her. The reasoning is usually justified

CASA

The Court Appointed Special Advocate (CASA) program has its beginnings in Seattle in 1976 when Superior Court Judge David Soukup realized a recurring problem in his courtroom. He was troubled by a lack of information about many of the children he saw in his courtroom and to ensure he was getting all the facts and the long-term welfare of each child was being represented, he came up with an idea that would change America's judicial procedure and the lives of thousands of children. He obtained funding to recruit and train community volunteers to step into courtrooms on behalf of the children: the Court Appointed Special Advocate (CASA) volunteers.

This unique concept was implemented in Seattle as a pilot program in January 1976, and during that first year, the program provided 110 trained CASA volunteers for 498 children in 376 dependency cases. The idea caught on, and in 1978, the National Center of State Courts selected the Seattle program as the "best national example of citizen participation in the juvenile justice system." This recognition, along with a grant from the Edna McConnell Clark Foundation of New York City (one of CASA's earliest and strongest supporters), resulted in the replication of the Seattle CASA programming courts across the country.

By 1982, it was clear that a national association was needed to direct CASA's emerging national presence. The National Court Appointed Special Advocate Association was formed that year, and by 1984 the National CASA Association had received financial support from several significant sources: a grant from the National Council of Juvenile and Family Court Judges, under the direction of the U.S. Department of Justice, Office of Juvenile Justice and Delinquency Prevention; funding from the U.S. Department of Health and Human Services; and two one-year grants from the Edna McConnell Clark Foundation. The Association opened its national headquarters office in Seattle, Washington, in the summer of 1984, and launched a membership and fundraising drive.

In 1985, President Ronald Reagan presented the National CASA Association with the President's Volunteer Action Award for "outstanding volunteer contribution, demonstrating accomplishment through voluntary action."

National CASA has also received support from the Kappa Alpha Theta Foundation since 1989. This international women's fraternity selected CASA as its philanthropy and has provided funds for a variety of projects, including start-up grants and a public awareness video.

In 1989, the American Bar Association officially endorsed the use of CASA volunteers to work with attorneys in order to speak for abused and neglected children. In 1990, the National Council of Juvenile and Family Court Judges named CASA "Outstanding Volunteer Program" in America's juvenile and family courts. Also during that year the U.S. Congress authorized the expansion of CASA with the passage of the "Victims of Child Abuse Act of 1990" (P.L. 101–647), so that a "court-appointed special advocate shall be available to every victim of child abuse or neglect in the United States that needs such an advocate."

(continued)

CASA *(Continued)*

The Office of Juvenile Justice and Delinquency Prevention (OJJDP), named CASA an "Exemplary National Program in Juvenile Delinquency Prevention." Finally in December of 1992, David Soukup, founder of CASA, was recognized with an award from the Caring Institute of Washington, D.C. Also in 1992, Congress initiated funding of a grants program to expand CASA representation of abused and neglected children.

The National CASA Association has helped more than a million children since it first started in 1976. Today, the National CASA Association represents over 950 CASA programs across the country in every state, including Washington, D.C. and the U.S. Virgin Islands. It provides support for starting programs, technical assistance, training, and fundraising, media, and public awareness services.

Source: Web page of the CASA Association, www.nationalcasa.org. With permission.

along the lines of a need to directly supervise volunteers or to personally assure the well-being of neglected and dependent children. On the other hand, how does the administrator control the budget of the program, assure adequate training of the volunteers, and coordinate the efforts of child welfare workers volunteers to his or her satisfaction?

One example of departmentalization by tasks to be accomplished is the psychological services department in a boys or girls state residential school. This department is responsible for all psychological testing, group and individual therapy, family therapy and so on. The department could be composed of small subunits responsible for working with cottage supervisors, testing, and therapeutic services. The chief psychologist will appear on the organizational chart on the same level as cottage supervisors and supervisor of education. Departmentalization can occur in regard to the target group. This is not unusual in larger juvenile probation courts where the probation officers may be assigned by zip code, or to children by age or sex. In addition, there may be a unit exclusively for investigating and writing pre-hearing reports and one for youth with drug problems or who live in a particular housing project.

Clearly, departmentalization militates against the meddling of others within and without the organization and allows the concentration of authority in the hands of the department heads and his or her superiors. Next we take up the issue of politics and juvenile justice is one area where nearly every citizen has an opinion and those opinions are often translated into politics both from the community and within the organization.

POLITICS IN AND OUT OF THE ORGANIZATION

Politics in the organization is ephemeral and difficult to measure. On the other hand we recognize it when we experience it and it often touches our lives in a host of ways. A manager who believes in a particular project can find himself or herself against a coalition that is determined to stop the project. The line staff member passed over for a choice assignment in favor of someone who is close to the deputy superintendent recognizes power. As researchers or managers, we are unable to measure "politics" and as a consequence devise ways to mitigate its effects.

Daft (1989) provides an excellent discussion of politics and political behavior. He calls our attention to two surveys that reveal the reactions of managers toward political behavior (Gantz and Murray, 1980 and Madison et al., 1980).

- Most managers have a negative view towards politics and believe that politics will more often hurt than help an organization in achieving its goals.
- Managers believe that political behavior is common to practically all organizations.
- Most managers think that behavior occurs more often at upper rather than lower levels in organizations.
- Political behavior arises in certain decision domains, such as structural change, but is absent from other decisions, such as handling employee grievances.

If power is the use of force for achieving certain outcomes, we can then define politics as the use of power to influence decisions in order to achieve those outcomes. Again Daft (1989) provides further explanation. He states that the exercise of power and influence leads to two ways to define politics: "as self-serving behavior or as natural organizational behavior" (Daft, 1989, p. 416). The first definition emphasizes the self-serving nature of politics and involves activities that are not in the best interests of the organization. Further, politics involves a good deal of deception and dishonesty for the purpose of individual self interest. This view is widely held and may explain the negative attitudes revealed in the research noted above.

The second view states that politics is a natural organizational process for resolving differences between interest groups in the organization. Hallmarks of this view are the bargaining and negotiation process that tends to overcome conflicts and differences of opinion. That is, it is no different than coalition building for decision-making. For certain issues the political decision-making approach is necessary in order to muster support for organizational actions. On the other hand, many people (too many it seems) use politics to acquire resources and power to achieve their preferred choice when there is a great deal of uncertainty or disagreement about choices.

To illustrate this point, a midwest organization faced a challenge in that the organization had been going nowhere for several years and had gone through four directors in five years. A national search was conducted to find someone to fill the position. The person was hired with full knowledge of the history of the organization and with a promise of any and all assistance from the chairman of the board.

Things went smoothly for over a year until it began to dawn on the chairman of the board and three favored subordinates that the new director had his own idea of where the organization should be headed. In the meantime, the chairman of the board had forced the director to hire two employees who were friends and who he knew would support his ideas. In addition, two other subordinates with a history of troublemaking in the organization were upset over the style of the director. Ultimately, a coalition was forged between the two troublesome employees, the three favored employees, and the chairman of the board. Unknown to the director, the three favored employees and the chairman of the board met several times to plot the unseating of the director. The showdown came over the hiring of three new employees. The conspirators panicked, as they realized that three additional employees who favored the director and his vision for the future would forever tip the program away from where they wanted it to go. Thus, the qualifications desired and some procedures were changed in order to hire still others that the chairman of the board knew would support him. As a consequence, the director, knowing that he would never be able to rehabilitate the organization, resigned in protest, leaving the organization to remain satisfied with mediocrity.

The lesson here is that in spite of our best intentions, things do not always go the way we want them to go. In this instance, the director had to contend with two employees who were largely ignorant of effective management, but knew that they didn't want any part of a change; an organizational culture that favored the way things had been done for many years; and a coalition of old-timers and the disgruntled faction. Without support from a champion or a sovereign, the director was certain to be unable to turn the organization around and develop one that would be a credit to the taxpayer.

The above example is illustrative of the political model which was used for negative purposes in the long run. However, political behavior can be a positive force (Daft, 1989). Politics is the use of power to get things done, be they good or bad. Since conflict and uncertainty are assured, politics is sometimes the way to achieve some kind of agreement. That is, informal discussions are held that allows participants to arrive at an agreement and to make decisions that might not otherwise be made.

While research on organizational politics is scanty, one such project is nicely summarized by Ivancevich and Mattison (2002). Madison et al. (in an earlier project) queried 142 purchasing agents revealing that a variety of political tactics are used by employees. Adapting those findings to a juvenile justice organization, they include:

- **Rule evasion.** Evading the formal procedures in the organization. This can take the form of a probation officer doing most of his or her investigation on a prehearing report on the telephone rather than getting out into the community to talk to family, teachers, and so on. Another example would be the institutional employee taking youth to unauthorized locations while on an outing.

- **Personal-political.** Using friendships to facilitate or inhibit the implementation of a new program or procedure. For example, shift officers decide among themselves that a new therapy program is too lenient, or they suspect that the "touchy-feely" approach is not harsh enough to get the attention of "hard-core" youth. They arrange to get the inmates to the sessions late, or "forget" altogether to allow the youth to attend the sessions.

- **Educational.** One department attempts to persuade other staff that a more focused approach to therapy is necessary to be more effective.

- **Organizational.** Attempting to change the formal or informal interaction between treatment and custody.

These political tactics are outside the legitimate power system, benefit the actor involved in, or who initiated, the act, and were intentionally initiated or developed in order to increase the influence of the actor in the decision-making process. Clearly, research and personal experience indicates that politics exists in organizations and that some employees are quite good at playing politics. Mintzberg (1983) describes these individuals as playing a game. The games are intended to accomplish at least five goals: 1) resist authority (the insurgency game), 2) counter the resistance to authority (the counter insurgency game), 3) build power bases (the sponsorship game and the coalition-building game), 4) defeat rivals (the line versus staff game), and 5) effect organizational change (the whistle-blowing game).

The Insurgency Game

This game is played to resist authority. For example, a supervisor is instructed to develop a drug program for youth held in detention. If the program is developed half-heartedly, it will fail, as the youth will see that no one really cares how well the program is doing. On the other hand, if the program is developed with enthusiam, the youth will pick up on the enthusiasm of staff and participate more fully and attempt to gain something from the program.

The Sponsorship Game

A subunit such as a field office may be able to increase its power by forming a coalition with other field units or the head of the field unit forms a close friendship with the head of the organization or elected official who controls policy or budget. When such coalitions or friendships are formed in the organization, there is an emphasis on common goals or personal advancement (Ivancevich and Mattison, 1990). Typically field units do not have much power by themselves, but with an emphasis on supervision of youth on probation, they become increasingly important and the coalition is able to bolster its power and demand greater resources. They can also form a coalition with the gang unit or juvenile unit of the local police department and acquire even more power.

Line versus Staff Game

The dichotomy between treatment and custody in correctional institutions has existed for many years. In essence, the line versus staff game is one that pits older, more sophisticated officers against younger staff. In addition, the custody force is more experienced in making decisions and, as a consequence, more able to garner valuable resources. On the other hand, treatment staff are younger, and better educated and more analytical decision-makers. As a result, the two groups see the institution, if not the world, quite differently. Withholding information, having access to authority figures, creating favorable impressions (often at the expense of the other) are tactics used by both groups.

The Whistle-blowing Game

Whistle-blowing is becoming more frequent as more and more employees are coming forward both in the private sector as well as the public sector to reveal mismanagement or corruption. Whistle-blowing is the leaking of information about mismanagement or corruption to an elected official or news source. They often do so after attempting to call management's attention to the fact with no success.

Politics is the expenditure of effort to control scarce resources. Bacharach and Lawler (1980) assert that the greater the resource scarcity within an organization, the greater likelihood that interest groups will coalesce with other interest groups as they attempt to exert power over the decision making that allocates the resources. This seems to be the immutable rule of organizations and the reason why political infighting is so often the source of great concern to managers and executives.

POLITICAL TACTICS FOR USING POWER

The chief executive of an organization wears many hats and must work effectively with a host of individuals both within the organization and in the community. He or she is the representative of juvenile justice in the community and often the most visible representative of juvenile justice in the community. As a consequence, he or she must know the ways of political maneuvering and how to judiciously use power for the benefit of youth and staff who have been entrusted to his or her care.

Earlier we discussed the tactics for increasing one's power base. Daft (1989) provides tactics for using power in order to influence decision outcomes.

- **Build coalitions.** This includes the necessity of talking with other managers, as well as others in one's department or organization. Most important decisions are made outside of formal meetings. The effective manager will huddle with others in the organization in groups of two or three to discuss important issues. In other words, build good relationships.

- **Expand networks.** Networks can be expanded by reaching out to others and by coopting dissenters. The first approach includes using the hiring, promotion, and transfer process in order to achieve your objectives. Placing key people in key positions who are sympathetic to your agenda goes a long way. Cooptation is the act of bringing dissenters into the network. One example involves a superintendent who wanted to develop a group home to supplement program efforts and to aid in the transition of boys into the family, school, and society. The superintendent knew the supervisor of security was opposed to the measure. The superintendent put the supervisor on the committee responsible for developing the program, and he became a strong supporter.

- **Control decision premises.** Controlling decision premises means to limit or restrict the boundaries of a decision. One way is to limit information provided to others or to choose what is provided to others. A common method is to always put the most favorable information out in order to make oneself or the organization look good. Statistics are useful tools to support the organizational point of view or showcase accomplishments.

Decision premises can be limited further by controlling the decision process. For example controlling what is put on the agenda for a meeting or by controlling the sequence items to be discussed are effective means of controlling the decision process.

- **Enhance legitimacy and expertise.** Managers can exert the greatest expertise in areas in which they have recognized legitimacy and expertise. Thus, it is difficult for an institutional superintendent who was appointed because of political connections to have the necessary legitimacy to carry the organization on to excellence. In addition, without legitimacy, the superintendent will have a harder time establishing credibility with the media, other juvenile justice organizations and the general public with whom he or she is supposed to work.

- **Make preferences explicit, but keep power implicit.** It is difficult for managers to achieve their agenda if they do not make it plain. Thus, explicit promotion of one's vision for the organization is important if that vision is to be realized. The manager should aggressively sell his or her ideas in small group discussions and in large meetings. An assertive pursuit of a recognized agenda is important because other proposals may not be so clear and alternatives may be ambiguous and less well defined. Power should always be implicit. Calling attention to one's power is to lose it. Organizational members know who has power, thus the quiet application and use of power will obtain greater results.

POLITICS OUTSIDE THE ORGANIZATION

Many harsh words and speeches have been uttered by politicians about the "broken" juvenile justice system. Politics outside the organization have had their effect, and today we have more referrals to adult court than ever before, more politicians are calling for "accountability" in the juvenile system, which is code for harsher sentences and less time spent on probation and aftercare. More and more youth are being placed in secure institutions, and more and more youth are not benefiting from the meager resources allotted to the juvenile justice system.

We can break down the external politics into four categories: partisan politics, attempts to gain name recognition, in the name of higher abstractions, and competition for scarce resources.

Partisan Politics

This is highly political and is usually related to elections and is an attempt to advance a political agenda. For example, in the Iowa general election of 1988 one candidate for state attorney general in his attempt to unseat the incumbent, pointed out that during the incumbent's tenure juvenile crime had increased in the Des Moines area. He never did explain how the incumbent had caused juvenile crime to increase. In another incident, one of the authors was a juvenile court administrator, and one candidate for circuit court judge inferred that the administrator had somehow deviously caused problems at the court when just the opposite had occurred and troublemakers had been discharged.

Attempts to Gain Name Recognition

Since about 1988, crime has become increasingly important as a campaign issue. The juvenile justice system has been pilloried for problems not within its control such as problems caused by absentee parents, toxic neighborhoods, and dysfunctional families. As a consequence, if a political candidate can raise an issue that will get his or her name before the electorate, then name recognition will follow.

In the Name of a Higher Abstract

Occasionally a citizen will identify a fault in an organization and attempt to do something about the problem, and sometimes the system just will not listen. When this happens, the persistent individual will campaign with neighborhood groups until a group of concerned citizens will be large enough to have the status of an interest group, or several interest groups will coalesce into a coalition to bring pressure on the organization to make a change.

Competition for Scarce Resources

This kind of political behavior usually emanates from other governmental agencies in the fight for scarce resources and in order to have a say in budgetary decisions. Usually these kinds of conflicts are a zero sum game and the gain of one group or agency is at the expense of another. At present, nearly all states and local jurisdictions are facing serious budget shortfalls, and all government agencies are facing cutbacks. As a result, great competition results and political activity increases as each agency strives to hold on to its share of the budgetary pie.

SUMMARY

Power is defined as the force or the ability to apply sanctions in order to achieve a goal. That is, it is potential force, not actual force and is not to be confused with the application of sanctions. Power is inherently coercive, but it is not to be confused with authority. While power is the ability to apply sanctions, authority is a part of the position and is conferred.

Authority is based on tradition, charisma, or it is legal authority. Departmentalization allows the organization to clearly define lines of authority and departmentalization acts as a buffer to domination. The use of power and attempts to dominate are often identified as politics. Politics exist inside the organization and outside the organization. In any case, politics is the use of power to increase one groups influence in decision making. The effective juvenile justice manager will recognize political activity and be able to blunt its effects through effective communication and the judicious use of executive power.

CASE STUDY WRAP-UP

Clearly juvenile crime was a hot topic for the 2002 gubernatorial election in Oregon. Both candidates pledged to be tough on crime, but each had a different record in regard to his approach to crime. During the election, various advocacy and interest groups came out for one candidate or the other. As a result, voters had a difficult choice on election day. Newly elected Governor Kulogoski knows that he now controls resources to achieve the end that he desires. He will also appoint those who will carry out his agenda without a lot of questions. Juvenile justice executives should be aware of how to use this system in order to get their ideas on the agenda to further their aims for the rehabilitation of children.

STUDY QUESTIONS

1. How do you define power?
2. What is the difference between power and authority?
3. How does departmentalization militate against politics in the organization?
4. Identify two ways to use politics to your advantage.

BIBLIOGRAPHY

BACARACH, SAMUAL B., AND LAWLER, EDWARD J. (1980). *Power and Politics in Organizations.* San Francisco: Jossey-Bass Publishers.

BIERSTEDT, R. (1950). "An Analysis of Social Power." *American Sociological Review,* 730–738.

BRASS, DANIEL J. (1984). "Being in the Right Place: A Structural Analysis of Individual Influence in an Organization." *Administrative Science Quarterly,* 29: 518–539.

CLEGG, S. (1988). "Power and Domination." London: Routledge and Kegan Paul. 1975. In Mumby, Dennis K. *Communication and Power in Organizations: Discourse, Ideology, and Domination.* Norwood, NJ: Ablex Publishing Corporation.

DAFT, RICHARD L. (1989). *Organization Theory and Design,* 3rd ed. St. Paul, MN: West Publishing Company.

DAHL, ROBERT A. (1957). "The Concept of Power." *Behavioral Science,* 2: 201–215.

GANTZ, JEFFERY, AND MURRAY, VICTOR V. (1980). "Experience of Workplace Politics." *Academy of Management Journal, 23:* 237–251.

HALL, RICHARD H. (1991). *Organizations: Structures, Processes, and Outcomes.* Englewood Cliffs, NJ: Prentice-Hall, Inc.

HOUSTON, JAMES G. (1999). *Correctional Management: Functions, Skills, and Systems,* 2nd ed. Chicago: Nelson-Hall Publishers.

IVANCEVICH, JOHN M., AND MATTISON, MICHAEL T. (2002). *Organizational Behavior and Management.* Columbus, OH: McGraw-Hill Companies.

MADISON, DAN L., ALLEN, ROBERT W., PORTER, LYMAN W., RENWICK, PATRICIA A., AND MAYES, BRONSON T. (1980). "Organizational Politics: An Exploration of Managers' Perceptions." *Human Relations, 33:* 79–100 in Daft (1989) op cit.

MINTZBERG, HENRY (1983). *Power In and Around Organizations.* Englewood Cliffs, NJ: Prentice-Hall Publishers.

MUMBY, DENNIS K. (1988). *Communication and Power in Organizations: Discourse, Ideology, and Domination.* Norwood, NJ: Ablex Publishing Corporation.

STOJKOVIC, STAN, KALINICH, DAVID, AND KLOFAS, JOHN (2003). *Criminal Justice Organizations: Administration and Management,* 3rd ed. Belmont, CA: Wadsworth/Thomson Learning, p. 244.

WEBER, MAX (1947). *The Theory of Social and Economic Organization,* trans. A. M. Parsons and T. Parsons. New York: The Free Press.

GLOSSARY OF KEY TERMS

Authority.   Narrower in scope and is a function of the hierarchy. Authority is vested in organizational positions, is accepted by subordinates, and authority flows downward in the organization.

Charismatic authority.   Stems from devotion to a particular individual and is based on certain personal characteristics.

Legal authority.   Based on the belief in the right of those in higher office to have power over subordinates.

Politics.   Is the expenditure of effort to control scarce resources.

Power.   The force or the ability to apply sanctions, that is, potential force, not actual force and is not to be confused with the application of sanctions.

Power cone.   A means of illustrating authority. Power is seen as running down the core of a cone, the further outward one is from the power core, the less power one has.

Power core.   In the power cone, there is a core that runs from the top of the cone to the bottom. The closer to the power core the employee is located, the more power he or she has, whether or not he or she has authority.

Traditional authority.   Is based on belief in the established traditional order.

CHAPTER 14

THE EXECUTIVE
IN JUVENILE JUSTICE

KEY TERMS

Planning	Influencing	Motivation
Management by objectives	Communication	Hierarchy of needs
Organizing	Leadership	Needs-goal model
Policy	Transactional leadership	Vroom expectancy model
Procedure	Transformative leadership	

CASE STUDY*

Sometimes it is a mystery to citizens how governors and other high officials pick individuals to fill important posts. Such was the case with the Virginia Department of Juvenile Justice. The Rev. Gerald O. Glenn was such a selection, and his time as Director of the Virginia Department of Juvenile Justice caused the governor some embarrassment. Mr. Glenn decided to step down from his post, thus sparing the administration any further problems, such as when he defended officers who kicked and hit their charges in extreme situations.

Mr. Glenn's commitment to improving the lives of troubled youth is unassailable, but the post of director of the Department of Justice Services is not a "good heart and seat-of-the-pants" type of job. At least it shouldn't be.

One Virginia state government observer noted that there has been far too long an endemic mediocrity with the Department of Juvenile Justice and what is needed is someone

---

Source: Adapted from "Juvenile Justice Time for Cleaning House as Director's Departure Creates Opportunities" (editorial), *The Virginian Pilot.* Nov. 18, 1999, p. B10.

who can set high standards and who has a zero tolerance for sloppy performance. The entire department needs to understand that the state's commitment to reforming troubled youth and to supporting them in their communities whenever possible is more than rhetoric. The legislature and the governor need to re-enforce that understanding. Mr. Glenn's departure is an opportunity for all those associated with the Department of Juvenile Justice to reassess directions and perform some badly needed housecleaning.

INTRODUCTION

It is the juvenile justice executive who is responsible for maintaining the organization and overseeing the achievement of the stated mission. The chief executive and his or her immediate subordinates are also responsible for forging a shared vision, working with rank and file to develop objectives, and working with the community and elected officials to assure them that community safety is of paramount importance, youth are well cared for and that programs are implemented to improve future opportunities for adjudicated youth.

Chester Barnard (1938, 1968) notes that the executive functions serve to maintain a system of cooperative effort and that they are impersonal. Further, Barnard did not think that a correct understanding of executive work could be had. Barnard identified a number of executive functions that are covered in other portions of this text and are further explored in this chapter. However, his comments are important as an introduction to the functions of the juvenile justice executive. First is the *maintenance of organization communication.* That is, the need of a definite system of communication creates the first task of the organizer and is the "immediate origin of executive organization" (p. 217). Second, *the scheme of organization* is usually reduced to organizational charts, specifications of duties, and descriptions of divisions of labor. Primarily, the executive is responsible for coordinating the efforts of organizational personnel. Finally, Barnard identifies *personnel* as key to the success of the organization. Not only is the executive responsible for choosing responsible, competent individuals to fill positions, he or she is required to make the contribution of loyalty and submission; loyalty to the organization and submission to the responsibilities of leadership.

Barnard's contribution to our understanding of the executive in the organization is immense and serves as a valuable springboard for understanding how the executive in juvenile justice is critical to the success of one of the most important aspects of the entire criminal justice system.

MANAGEMENT RESPONSIBILITIES AND ACTIVITIES

For the purposes of this chapter, we reduce the functions of the executive to that of planning, organizing, influencing, and controlling (Certo, 1986). The four areas are important in that employees want to know where the organization is going and how it will get there. It is important to organize resources to achieve organizational resources, including time of employees. The executive is responsible for forging a shared vision and for influencing others to do their best to achieve organizational objectives. He or she can do so through formal or informal groups that exist in the organization. Finally, the effective executive needs to exercise a measure of control: pre-control, concurrent control, or feedback control.

Planning

Planning is defined as the process of arranging future activities in order to accomplish a particular objective. Hudzik and Cordner (1983) view planning as deliberately linking present actions to future conditions. Certo (1986) defines planning as the process of determining how the organization can get where it wants to go and Ivancevich (1971, p. 57) states that "the planning function includes all the managerial activities which lead to the definition of goals and the determination of appropriate means to achieve these goals." Ivancevich also asserts that the planning function can be broken into four parts:

- Establishing goals and fixing their priority.
- Forcasting future events that can affect goal accomplishment.
- Making the plans operational through budgeting.
- Stating and implementing policies that direct the organization's activities toward the desired ends.

Generally speaking, planning is directed towards improved decision making. Improved planning and the resultant improvement in decision making have a number of benefits:

- Programs and services are improved. The ultimate goal of all juvenile justice executives is service; service to the community and youth charged to the care of one's organization, service in regard to security of an institution and general protection of the community, and the delivery of effective programs.
- The ability to identify and analyze problems is improved.
- Planning demands that clear and attainable objectives be established, procedures to attain them be specified, and to be able to link objectives to one another.
- Cooperation and coordination between the various units or departments are improved.
- Planning allows for effective allocation of resources. In an often resource-scarce environment, the executive has to establish priorities for the allocation of those resources.

Overall, planning decreases risk within the organization. Planning ensures the safety and well-being not only of staff and inmates, but also of the community. It decreases the risk that requested funds will be cut for the coming year, if cutting them would be detrimental to the organizational mission. Planning also decreases the risk involved in accomplishing stated goals.

Overall, planning decreases risk within the organization. Planning ensures the safety and well-being not only of juvenile justice employees, but also the youth under the care and supervision of the juvenile justice system, as well as the community. It decreases the risk that requested funds will be cut for the coming year, if cutting them would be detrimental to the organizational mission. Planning also decreases the risk involved in accomplishing stated goals; and finally, planning decreases the risk that the career of the organizational chief will not be cut short because of problems.

There are other reasons for planning. As previously pointed out, planning allows the chief executive to coordinate decision making. Many times, juvenile justice organizations follow the paramilitary model just as the adult system where decisions are subordinated to a custody model. On the other hand, in the juvenile system we find more examples of the corporate model of management and a more "client-centered" approach that takes the overall needs of the child into consideration. Thus, in the "client-centered" organization, planning is easier and one finds more examples of court administrators and others easily including staff into the planning process.

Planning also forces the executive staff to formulate objectives. Pursuing those objectives requires a coordinated effort throughout the organization, with thought given to decisions that affect the organizations. Finally, planning forces the staff to be future-oriented. So many times in a juvenile justice organization, such as a court, one hears the comment that "It will work out." Not so! If proper attention is not given to the direction to which the CEO wants to lead, the road will be bumpy indeed.

Planning is important in order to garner administrative support for organizational direction. In addition, if the judges, county commission, board of directors (in the case of nonprofit organizations) and state-level administrators in the case of state agencies understand that the juvenile justice executives plan for the future and work at being good stewards of the public purse, they can be less obstreperous at budget time. Krisberg, Neuenfeldt, Wiebush, and Rodriguez (1994) postulate four questions that are important for planning purposes and once these questions are answered to the CEOs satisfaction, he or she can then proceed:

- Do the top administrators [judges] within the agency understand and support the program premise?
- Do they support pursuing program development?
- Do they support the program [direction] design (and in the case of futures planning do they support the stated means to get there?)
- Are they willing to secure resources for the program?

Thus, if the management of the agency is based on an MBO approach, the support of top management is easier to obtain if they see how budget requests fit with planned activities and future directions.

Management by Objectives

So many times the organization will find itself reacting to crises and not taking time to plan and, consequently, keeping on track is difficult. When that happens, the public, through the media, will soon know. Whether goals are established by work teams, departments, or the organization as a whole, involving everyone in the process is crucial. Once goals or objectives are established, they offer a yardstick against which to measure the organizations progress through time.

Management by objectives (MBO) is "a well-known philosophy of management that assesses an organization and its members by how well hey achieve specific goals that superiors and subordinates have jointly established" (Robbins, 1987, pp. 31–32). There is some discussion in the literature in regard to whether or not MBO should be a top-down or a bottom-up approach. In a top-down approach, the objectives are formulated by top management and then imposed on line and supervisory staff. In a bottom-up approach, objectives are formulated by supervisors and line staff and given to top management.

The consensus seems to be that a compromise is best. Organizations have multiple goals that compete and sometimes appear to be incompatible. This incompatibility is especially true in the state reformatory for boys for example, where the interests of youth, management, and line staff often conflict, and those conflicts must be resolved and priorities established. One author has concluded that organizational objectives should be treated "as fiction produced by an organization to account for, explain, or rationalize its existence to particular audiences rather than as valid and reliable indications of purpose" (Warriner, 1965, p. 140). Therefore, it is imperative to involve as many staff as possible and to develop a living document that reflects the real organization and not an organization the managers think a particular audience wants to see.

Establishing Objectives

The MBO process is a lengthy one that may require years to put firmly in place. Objectives need to be reviewed periodically so that progress or attainment can be ascertained, and everyone in the organization should feel some ownership of the program.

According to Samuel Certo (1986), managers can increase the quality of their objectives by following certain guidelines:

- Managers should allow the people responsible for attaining the objectives to have a voice in setting them. In juvenile justice, staff often have a better feel for conditions than top management: therefore, their input is crucial if work-related problems faced daily by line staff are going to be translated into meaningful objectives.

- Managers should state objectives as specifically as possible. Precise language minimizes confusion. Further, objectives should be unambiguous, prioritized, measurable, and most of all, attainable.

- Managers should relate objectives to specific actions whenever necessary. Specific actions eliminate the need for guess work on the part of those responsible for achieving the objectives.

- Results should be specified. Staff will know when they have achieved results. Completion of a cottage renovation before a deadline is to be celebrated, increased personality inventory scores after completion of a therapy program is something for which staff can be proud.

- Managers should set goals high enough that employees will have to strive to meet them but not so high that employees become discouraged and give up trying. Supervisors, court administrators, superintendents, and directors urge their staff to work hard, but they do not want them to burn out trying to achieve goals.

- Time frames for the achievement of goals should be identified in order to allow staff to pace themselves.

- Goals should only be set in relation to other organizational goals. Keeping a close eye on the larger picture will keep conflicting goals to a minimum.

- State objectives clearly and simply.

One can expect some problems in developing an MBO program. Many organizations in both the public and private sector use management by objectives in order to integrate both individual and organizational goals. The most successful programs are those that emphasize a total systems approach and take the entire organization into consideration (Kast and Rosenzweig, 1979).

Organizing

Organizing is the process of establishing effective uses for all resources in the organization (Certo, 1986). These uses include the attainment of objectives and assisting managers in their role as cheerleaders and coaches.

The Process of Organizing

There are five steps to the organizing process as illustrated in Figure 14.1.

The first step is that of developing good policies and procedures. Policies and procedures serve several purposes: Among them are that they provide a guide to staff training; second, everyone is on the same page when it comes to staff behavior in the organization; third, they shield the organization from grievances and adverse court action against staff. A **policy** is defined as a broad, general guideline for directing management thinking towards a certain objective (Certo, 1986). It is also a standing decision characterized by behavioral consistency and repetitiveness on the part of both those who make it and those who abide by it (Eulau and Prewit, 1973). The effective juvenile justice organization will have established policies and procedures arrived at through a form of consensus, and they will be in the hands of all staff with additional copies available for all concerned. In addition, each policy will be accompanied by a thorough procedure that explains how the policy is to be implemented.

A **procedure** is defined as a standing plan that identifies what sequential actions to take to implement a policy. For example, a policy for intake of newly arrived youth at a state boys reform school will state something like the following:

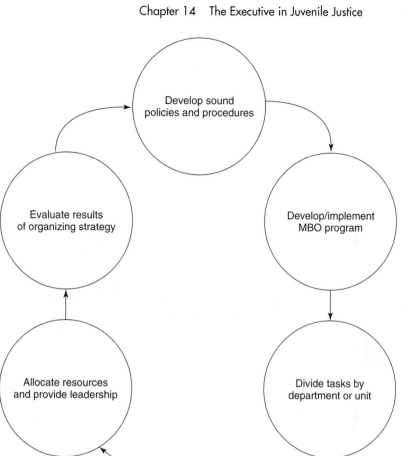

Figure 14.1   Steps in the Organizing Process

All newly arrived youth will complete the intake process in an efficient, compassionate, and humane manner.

The above policy states the desired state of intake, but provides little guidance to the counselor who must accompany the youth through the intake procedures. The procedure will provide a step-by-step guide to the intake process.

1. The counselor will meet the youth at the reception desk.
2. The counselor will accompany the youth to the intake unit in order to answer any questions and to allay any fears the youth may have.
3. While standing by as the youth is processed, the counselor will continue to answer questions and will verify commitment papers and review all material contained in the packet from the court.

4. Once the intake staff have completed all tasks, the counselor will escort the youth to his assigned cottage and introduce him to the unit staff.

Clearly, the procedure provides the "how to" information necessary to implement the policy.

Developing and Implementing a Management by Objectives Program

While this task is covered earlier in the chapter, the effective executive should begin his or her MBO program through a vigorous education program with staff in order that they do not think of MBO as the "fad of the month." Once he or she is comfortable with the level of staff maturity on MBO, the executive can move on to the next stage, which is to train the department heads and other top-level executives on how to develop objectives. Once that goal is reached, the department heads should be charged with the task of meeting with members of their department or cottage/unit to develop objectives for the coming fiscal or physical year. Ideally, that process will be completed by December of that year of working with a fiscal calendar, and the executive will gather the department heads together in an out-of-the-way location such as a state park lodge or resort and begin the process of developing organizational goals for the coming year. These goals will then drive budget formulation.

Divide Tasks by Department or Unit

Chester I. Barnard (1938, 1968) calls our attention to the "scheme of the organization," which he states is the aspect of organization which receives a lot of attention and which can be reduced to charts, specifications of duties, job descriptions and so on (p. 219).

Since a department or unit is a unique collection of individuals and resources established to perform a specific organizational task it should be created to address a specific need or target group. For example, in juvenile court a specific unit or department can be created for field supervision and work areas assigned by zip code or census tract, or any other convenient method. Or, a unit can be created to address the need of drug offenders or sex offenders. The idea is to be able to effectively marshal resources to meet the need of that particular locale or target group.

Allocating Resources and Providing Leadership

The budget is perhaps one of the most important documents in the organization (after the policies and procedures manual). The budget will clarify where organizational priorities lie and is key to achieving organizational objectives. Once the executive has determined what the departments are and developed objectives for the coming year, he or she knows how to allocate financial resources within the organization.

There are several ways to develop a budget (see Houston, 1999), but in the view of the authors the most efficient way is to use the zero-based budget (ZBB) approach. In a literal sense, ZBB implies constructing a budget without considering what went on in the past. While this has been criticized as naïve and simplistic (see Taylor, 1978), its value is believed in by most street level bureaucrats.

It was developed by Peter Pyres at Texas Instruments in the 1970s and there are three basic elements: (1) the identification of "decision units," (2) the analysis of decision units and (3) formulation of "decision packages." The decision units are the lowest level of the organization for which a manager is responsible. The manager must have the authority to establish priorities and prepare a budget for each decision unit. Presumably the decision unit manger asks questions such as: "Can this program be eliminated?" "Can I cut back in this area?" "Do we need to add more resources to this program?" and "How can we be more cost effective?" The decision unit mangers then prepare a series of packages. The first package contains those programs or part of programs that are deemed to be of the highest priority. The second package contains those of the second-highest priority, and so forth. The packages are then passed on to a higher-level manager, who is responsible for establishing priorities for all decision packages from all subordinate decision unit. The entire ranking is then reviewed with an eye to probable funding.

Providing leadership is important if the juvenile court or institution is to attain a level of excellence in service. It takes a manager to effectively allocate resources, but it takes a leader to develop a forged vision and to communicate that vision. The effective leader will gain a level of consensus within the organization, serve as coach and cheerleader, and provide resources that allow all members of the organization to serve to the best of their ability.

Evaluating the Results of the Organizing Strategy

Evaluating the results of one's efforts in organizing the organization can take many forms. The simplest way is to determine certain benchmarks and then track progress over time. For example, effectiveness of a unit created to work with drug offenders in a juvenile court can be assessed by determining numbers of technical violations, program completions, successful discharges from supervision, or all the above. The best strategy would before the executive to have the manager of the unit solicit advice from subordinates before deciding what criteria determines success.

Influencing

Influencing is the art of working with and through people. It includes communicating, leadership, and motivation. All are necessary in order to move the organization on to excellence and to serve youth who come under our supervision. In addition, since juvenile justice does not exist in a vacuum, the skills noted above (effective communication, leadership, and motivation) are necessary to work effectively with community groups and elected officials.

Influencing is the process of "guiding the activities of organization members in appropriate directions" (Certo, 1986, p. 289). Thus, the purpose of influencing is to enhance the achievement of organizational objectives and to complete the mission of the organization.

Communication

Communication is the sharing of information through the spoken or written word. It is the transmission of ideas, information, skills, and emotions through symbols such as words, pictures, gestures, and body language. It is communication that makes us human and allows us to communicate abstractions.

Clampitt (1991) asserts that many managers are what he calls "arrow" managers: That is, they tend to be straight forward and results-oriented. To these managers, communication is something like shooting an arrow at a target—they attempt to imbed a message in a target. They see communication as a one-way activity based primarily on the skills of the sender. In other words, the focus is on the sender, rather than the receiver.

Many times one finds organizational members who do not feel the need to receive communications or they attempt to dominate all communications (they "take up a lot of space"). These subordinates are the most difficult to work with, and they often exert a corrosive influence that is difficult to overcome. It takes a lot of patience to work around this type of individual as they are often very skillful at manipulating others and may seem to border on the psychopathic. The problem with this type of individual is that they often see arrow communicators as a challenge to their hegemony and as ignoring their "good" advice. One can easily see the problems in communication with this type of individual.

Clampitt also identifies two other approaches to communicating: The "circuit" approach and the "dance" approach. In the former, the managerial approach to communicating is on "networking," "going with the flow," and making "connections." Circuit communicators stress feedback over response, relationships over content, and understanding over compliance. They view communication as a two-way process involving an active sender and receiver. Those who use the dance approach to communication believe that effective communication can only be determined in light of the communicator's goals, whatever they may be. They view communication as a patterned activity involving the coordination of meaning, and co-orientation (one's ability to anticipate another's cues, actions, and responses) and as a set of skills, some of which are not a part of one's consciousness.

The effective communicator uses all three methods of communication in attempting to further the mission of the juvenile justice organization. For example, in making a presentation at a staff meeting or before the county council, he or she will primarily use the arrow approach, but will also draw upon skills in the circuit and dance approach.

Leadership

Leadership is difficult to define, but we know it when we experience it. Generally speaking, leadership is defined as the art of motivating people to strive willingly and enthusiastically toward the attainment of an objective. Burns (1978) identifies two types of leadership: transactional and the transforming.

Transactional leadership is an exchange of one thing for another: a promotion for a job well-done, a transfer to another (more desirable) department for putting in extra effort over time, and so on. This type of leadership comprises the bulk of relationships between leader and follower. **Transforming leadership** is quite another thing. It is more complex and more potent:

> The transforming leader recognizes and exploits existing need or demand of a potential follower, but beyond that, the transforming leader looks for potential motives in followers, seeks to satisfy higher needs, and engages the full person of the follower. The result of transforming leadership is a relationship of mutual stimulation and elevation that converts followers into leaders and may convert leaders into moral agents. (Burns, 1978).

Kouzas and Posner (1986) point out that leaders establish and maintain credibility by their actions. They discovered five fundamental practices that enable leaders to earn the respect of followers:

- **Challenge the process.** Leaders innovate and experiment and are willing to change the status quo in order to improve the organization.

- **Inspire a shared vision.** Leaders are able to look over the horizon and to envision a future pregnant with possibilities. They have good communication skills and are able to share that vision with others.

- **Enable others to act.** Leaders stress collaborative goals and infuse people with a strong sense of responsibility. They foster spirit-developing relationships based on mutual trust. They involve others and make them feel strong and capable.

- **Model the way.** Simply put, leaders are role models who are clear about their values and beliefs. They are able to keep people and projects on course by behaving consistently, making it easier for others to achieve goals.

- **Encourage the heart.** Leaders encourage people by recognizing contributions to the common vision. They recognize accomplishments and find ways to celebrate them.

Motivation

The juvenile justice executive is responsible for motivating a host of people to action, including members of his or her organization, elected officials, police, other juvenile justice and adult agencies, families of adjudicated youth, and teachers and officials of the educational subsystem. The effective executive must work effectively with all of the above in order to motivate them to work diligently toward the best interests of delinquent and pre-delinquent youth.

Motivation is generally defined as a motive with strong emotional association that arises from the individual's reaction to anticipated goal attainment and is based upon past association of certain cues with pleasure or pain. From the preceding definition, it can be seen that various levels of motivation are necessary in order to be effective in the field of juvenile justice. For example, it is doubtful that the executive can cause pain to an elected official; probably the reverse can happen. But the elected official can be motivated to experience the pleasure of being associated with a winning program that is known to be effective in working with delinquent youth. It's always good to be reelected. Therefore, the effective executive will know how to spread the credit for good programs around in order to advance his or her organization.

Abraham Maslow's **hierarchy of needs** rests on the assumption that people have a number of needs and that unsatisfied needs motivate behavior. These needs are arranged in a hierarchy where the lowest level need must be fulfilled before a higher level need can be fulfilled. Recall Figure 10.3 which illustrates Maslow's hierarchy of needs and the lowest-level needs, including shelter, food, clothing, and sex must be fulfilled before the needs of safety and security can be attended to and so on, right up the hierarchy to the need for self-actualization, which Maslow defined as the need for personal growth.

Two Models of Motivation

For this discussion, two models of motivation are discussed: the **needs-goal model** and the **Vroom expectancy model**. The needs-goal model of motivation is rather simple in that it only focuses on the need of the organism and the fulfillment of that need. Motivation begins with a need, and the need is then transformed into behavior directed at fulfilling that need. For example, a department head wishes to advance to assistant superintendent. He or she will then enroll in a master's degree program at a nearby university in hopes that attainment of the advanced degree will put him or her in a favorable position for the assistant superintendent's job.

The Vroom expectancy model is somewhat more complicated. Vroom (1964) posits that felt need causes behavior. However, he further suggests that motivation strength (valence) is base not on desired goals, but on the "anticipated satisfaction or dissatisfaction associated with other outcomes to which they are expected to lead" (Vroom, 1964, p. 15).

Thus, motivation is based on a number of variables that must be taken into account. The elected official desires to be reelected; the probation officer desires a pay raise; the school official wishes to be of service to wards of the court, but at minimal expenditure of resources to the system; and the taxpayer wants to be protected. All are challenges to the juvenile justice executive when it come to motivating others to work for the betterment of youth.

In the end, the juvenile justice executive is responsible for getting the job done by working with and through others. This is not an easy task, and it requires much patience and the attention to details that are beyond the reach of some people. One further word, juvenile justice professionals are not working with "small" adults. They are working with humans who have not had the time to develop good decision making skills, to know how to make an ethical decision, or even sometimes the difference between right and wrong. It is the responsibility of the juvenile justice executive to see to it that all resources possible are directed towards working with youth so that they do learn skills necessary to fit into today's society. Often those efforts are expended while under attack from within and without the organization. It is never easy being in charge.

Controlling

Control is a primary function of the executive. He or she is charged with the direction of the organization and the control of resources, including staff time, is of utmost importance. In a broad sense, much of what we have discussed so far relates to control, but "the measurement and correction of performance in order to make sure that enterprise objectives and the plans devised to attain them are accomplished" is how the executive's performance is measured by the public and by superiors (Koontz, O'Donnell, & Weihrich, 1986 p. 447).

The control process is a sequential chain of events. Objectives are established, programs developed, workloads determined, and so on, all with an eye on excellence of service. Step one is the establishment of plans as discussed earlier. But the manager should establish standards to determine whether or not plans are being adhered to. Standards are criteria of performance and the yardstick against which we measure performance. In a group home, for example the director can control performance through direct observation, but in a large reform school, the superintendent must establish a variety of standards.

There are a number of standards including:

Physical standards which are nonmonetary standards used to measure consumption of materials.

Cost standards are a computation of daily costs for service for example.

Capital standards relate to capital invested such as in construction.

Program standards are the effort to measure progress toward objectives established for youth or performance standards for staff to look to for guidance in carrying out their job.

Goal standards are those included in the MBO program and which enable the executive to quantify progress.

There are also three types of control: precontrol, concurrent control, and feedback control. Precontrol occurs before work is begun. Policies, procedures, and rules are examples of precontrol aimed at directing the activities of staff and eliminating undesirable work results.

Concurrent control occurs while work is being performed. For example, rules for staff to work in pairs when involved in a dangerous part of the city is concurrent control. In an institution, on-time inventory is another example of concurrent control

Feedback control focuses on work that has already been completed. That is, the executive will require periodic reports on activities, such as numbers of hearings each month or in an institution the number of runaways and disciplinary reports. Another form of feedback control is that of periodic audits of performance by a team of staff from another unit in the organization.

Employee performance evaluations are another form of control. The evaluation should be used to give the employee feedback on his or her performance and not as a tool to threaten the staff member. If used properly they can be used to guide staff training and as a tool to increase retention of staff.

SUMMARY

The effective juvenile justice executive is responsible for the development and implementation of programs and activities necessary to rehabilitate and supervise adjudicated youth. This includes the community and in institutions. A major task for the executive is that of planning. The key is to draw everyone into the process in order to assure input from all levels of the organization. From the planning process flows well-written policies and procedures that are necessary to effectively carry out the mission of the organization. Thus, careful attention to keeping them up-to-date is important.

From the policies and procedures flow the MBO program, which will identify priorities and objectives for the organization for the short-term and long-term. Drawing upon the polices and procedures, the budget will be developed.

To accomplish the above, the executive must be able to work through and with others, if he or she is to influence the direction of the organization. One goes about this task through effective communication, leadership, and motivation. One's effectiveness at working with and through others is often influenced in turn by others up the chain of command, but through it all, the executive must persevere for the youth under his or her direct or indirect influence.

CASE STUDY WRAP-UP

It appears that the time for opportunity and change arose when Mr. Glenn made his departure. His replacement had an excellent opportunity to demonstrate effective leadership and bring the staff into the process of changing the Department of Youth Services into one that stressed excellence in service. He could begin by establishing a planning bureau or department in the central office that would conduct research and find opportunities to advance the cause of youth. He also needed to learn where the deficiencies were in terms of organizational control and programs. Next he could implement a Management by Objectives program that would keep the department moving forward and at the same time begin an effort to build quality into the culture of the department and implementing a TQM approach.

STUDY QUESTIONS

1. What is planning and who should do it?
2. Define MBO and explain how it informs policies and procedures.
3. Identify the functions of the executive.
4. Do you think people can learn how to be a leader? Why or why not?
5. Explain why you think a sound ethical foundation is important to a juvenile justice executive.

BIBLIOGRAPHY

BARNARD, CHESTER (1938, 1968). *The Functions of the Executive: Thirtieth Anniversary Edition.* Cambridge, MA: Harvard University Press.

BURNS, JAMES MACGREGOR (1978). *Leadership.* New York: Harper Torchbooks.

CERTO, SAMUEL (1986). *Principles of Modern Management: Functions and Systems,* 3rd ed. Dubuque, IA: W. C. Brown Publishers.

CLAMPITT, PHILLIP G. (1991). *Communicating for Managerial Effectiveness.* Newbury Park, CA: Sage Publications.

EULAU, HEINZ, AND PREWITT, KENNETH (1973). *Labyrinths of Democracy.* Indianapolis: Bobbs-Merrill.

HOUSTON, JAMES (1999). *Correctional Management: Functions, Skills and Systems,* 2nd ed. Chicago: Nelson-Hall Publishers.

HUDZIK, JOHN K., AND CORDNER, GARY W. (1983). *Planning in Criminal Justice Organizations and Systems.* New York: Macmillan Publishing Company, Inc.

IVANCEVICH, JOHN M. (1971). *Fundamentals of Management.* Dallas, TX: Business Publications.

KAST, FREEMONT, AND ROSENZWEIG, JAMES E. (1979). *Organization and Management: A System and Contingency Approach,* 3rd ed. New York: McGraw-Hill.

KOONTZ, HAROLD, O'DONNELL, CYRIL, AND WEIHRICH, HEINZ (1986). *Essentials of Management,* 4th ed. New York: McGraw-Hill.

KOUZAS, JAMES M., AND POSNER, BARRY Z. (April 1986). "Eye of the Follower." *Administrative Radiology,* pp. 55–56, 58, 63–64.

KRISBERG, BARRY, NUENFELDT, DEBORAH, WIEBUSH, RICHARD, AND RODRIGUEZ, ORLANDO. (October 1994). *Juvenile Intensive Supervision: Planning Guide: Program Summary.* Washington, DC: OJJDP Grant # 87-JS-CX-K101.

ROBBINS, STEPHEN (1987). *Organization Theory: Structure, Design, and Application,* 2nd ed. Englewood Cliffs, NJ: Prentice-Hall.

TAYLOR, GRAEME M. (1978). "Introduction to Zero-Base Budgeting." In Albert C. Hyde and Jay M. Shafritz (Eds.), *Government Budgeting: Theory, Process, and Politics.* Oak Park, IL: Moore Publishing, pp. 265–284.

WARRINER, CHARLES (Spring 1965). "The Problem of Organizational Purpose," *Sociological Quarterly, 6:* 140.

VROOM, VICTOR H. (1964). *Work and Motivation.* New York: John Wiley and Sons.

GLOSSARY OF KEY TERMS

Communication.   Communication is the sharing of information through the spoken or written word.

Hierarchy of needs.   Abraham Maslow proposed that people have a number of needs and that unsatisfied needs motivate behavior. However, lower-order needs must be fulfilled before higher-order needs can be fulfilled.

Influencing.   The art of working with and through people.

Leadership.   The art of motivating people to strive willingly and enthusiastically toward the attainment of an objective.

Management by objectives.   A well-known philosophy of management that assesses an organization and its members by how well they achieve specific goals that superiors and subordinates have jointly established.

Motivation.   A motive with strong emotional association that arises from the individual's reaction to anticipated goal attainment and is based upon past association of certain cues with pleasure or pain.

Needs-goal model.   Focuses on the need of the organism and the fulfillment of that need.

Organizing.   The process of establishing effective uses for all resources in the organization.

Planning.   The process of arranging future activities in order to accomplish a particular objective.

Policy.   A broad, general guideline for directing management thinking towards a certain objective.

Procedure.   A standing plan that identifies what sequential actions to take to implement a policy.

Transactional leadership.   A form of leadership that includes the exchange of one thing for another in order to gain compliance.

Transformative leadership.   A form of leadership that looks for potential motives in followers, seeks to satisfy higher needs, and engages the full person of the follower. The result of transforming leadership is a relationship of mutual stimulation and elevation that converts followers into leaders and may convert leaders into moral agents.

Vroom expectancy model.   Victor Vroom feels that need causes behavior. However, he further suggests that motivation strength (valence) is based not on desired goals, but on the "anticipated satisfaction or dissatisfaction associated with other outcomes to which they are expected to lead."

CHAPTER 15

JUVENILE JUSTICE:
AN OVERVIEW
AND ASSESSMENT

Retributive sentence   Blended sentence   Determinate sentence

INTRODUCTION

As we have seen throughout the text, the juvenile justice system functions as a loose con-federation of organizations that is reliant upon a variety of entities to make it run smoothly and to provide justice for those youth who come in contact with it. As we enter the twenty-first century, there have been a number of debates among scholars concerning the role of the present-day juvenile justice system. Questions such as what purpose should the modern ju-venile justice system serve? And do we even need a separate system? Are those elements that were present over one hundred years ago that caused reformers such as the Progressives to call for the creation of a separate system still in existence today? Or, as many have argued, have we become too lenient on the youth of today who (as critics claim) believe that violat-ing the law and getting caught will result in nothing more than a slap on the wrist? Further-more, has society as a whole strayed from the moral foundations we were founded on so much so that it is necessary to take a step backwards in an attempt to regain lost control?

As society has clamored for a tougher stance on crime, legislators and policy-makers have responded by saying yes, we should begin getting tougher on crime at a much younger age. We should hold youth accountable for their crimes by using **retributive sentences** rather than rehabilitative responses. Responses such as providing statutory avenues for judges and prosecutors to transfer youth to the adult system, or the creation of a system based on determinate sentencing policies has allowed society to move away from the original intent of the juvenile justice system which was to focus on rehabilitating juveniles. These conservative policies are a direct result of society's increased fear of crime, particularly random violence, the apparent failure of rehabilitation, and the concern for increased exposure to and use of drugs.

On the other side of this debate, however, is the call for maintaining a separate juvenile justice system. There are those reformers who argue that in keeping with the intent of the original juvenile court system, we should focus on rehabilitating and preventing future criminal and delinquent acts from occurring. As stated in the Illinois Court Act of 1899, hearings were to be held to determine "the treatment necessary for rehabilitation rather than 'trials' to determine guilt" (Binder, 1984, p. 358).

In 1998, juvenile courts handled approximately 1.8 million (1,757,400) delinquency cases. This is an increase of 44 percent between 1989 and 1998 (Sickmund, 2003, p. 12). These changes to the court system have caused an increased strain and burden to an already overworked system. What is even more disturbing is the rate at which the juvenile caseload for female delinquents grew. Between 1989 and 1998, the female caseload grew 83 percent compared with a 35 percent increase for males (Sickmund, 2003, p. 14). In addition, the number of cases formally processed by the juvenile court increased from 50 percent to 57 percent between 1989 and 1998 (Sickmund, 2003, p. 20). However, males (60 percent) were still more likely to have their cases formally petitioned than females (48 percent).

These statistics suggest that we are getting tougher on crime. We are processing more and more youth through the system. Yet our fear of crime continues to be high, and our responses seem to resemble the criminal court rather than the juvenile court system.

The purpose of this chapter is to summarize the material that has been presented. Furthermore, an overview of the debate concerning the purpose of the juvenile justice system will be presented. Ultimately we must question whether these policies are helping or hurting future generations. What should be the purpose of the juvenile justice system? Should it exist at all? These questions are left up to the individual to decide.

In making these decisions, the reader must keep in mind that the system is a loose confederation of organizations. Each part relies on the other. The courts cannot be effective without good policing. Law enforcement officers work best when they have the cooperation of the community and its members, as well as the cooperation of the prosecutor. Judges make decisions based upon the information gathered by the intake or probation officers. The system is interdependent upon itself. It works when there are collaborative efforts. Oftentimes it fails because of the lack of resources available within the community to adequately administer rehabilitative efforts, duplication of services, and society's continued desire to get tough on crime.

Therefore, there are two possible avenues we can follow when dealing with youth of today and tomorrow. First, we can continue down the path of getting tough on juveniles. We can continue to muddy the waters by incorporating more policies waiving youth to the adult court system or we can incorporate blended or determinate sentences such as those found in Texas. Or, second we can take what we know about violent juvenile offenders and use this information to focus our efforts on preventing delinquency and treating those who slip through the cracks.

These efforts, however, cannot be unidimensional. The efforts must focus on strengthening families, enhancing educational opportunities, positive peer cultures, and mentoring. We must focus on using diversionary programs and get back to creating a less formal system. We must also focus on reducing the fear of crime by citizens and instead making the best use possible of available resources which can include the elderly to assist with mentoring youths.

ALTERNATIVES TO THE JUVENILE JUSTICE SYSTEM

The increase in juvenile violent crime during the late 1980s and early 1990s served as the impetus for a major shift in the overall handling of youths in both the juvenile and adult court systems. This shift towards getting tough on crime began with many states lowering the minimum age of eligibility for transferring a youth to the adult court, criminalizing juvenile behavior, and altering the purpose of the juvenile court from rehabilitation to punishment and community safety.

The idea of using retributive responses to juvenile behavior has gained a lot of public support because it is viewed as a way for policy-makers and the public to hold juveniles accountable for their actions while affirming the communities disapproval of their behavior (Bazemore, & Umbreit, 1995). Many states began to seek or enhance existing alternatives to the juvenile court system. These alternatives include transferring the jurisdiction of the child from the juvenile to adult court systems and the imposition of a **blended sentence**, which allows juvenile court judges to impose both a juvenile and criminal sentence (Podkopacz & Feld, 2001). This sentence is sometimes referred to as a **determinate sentence**, which was designed to deal with violent juvenile offenders who were not eligible to be transferred to the adult court system but were deemed to be serious enough to maintain supervision over for an extended period of time (Mears & Field, 2000). These alternatives reflect the desires of Americans to hold juveniles accountable for their behavior at a younger age. Each of these alternatives for dealing with juveniles in the system will be briefly discussed below.

TRANSFERRING YOUTH TO THE ADULT COURT SYSTEM

The U.S. Supreme Court set the impetus for waiving juveniles to the adult court system in two relevant Supreme Court cases *Kent v. the United States* (1966) and *Breed v. Jones* (1975). As you recall from Chapter 6, the U.S. Supreme Court established in *Kent v. the United States* that juveniles could not be transferred to the adult court system without a procedural due process hearing. In *Breed v. Jones,* the U.S. Supreme Court ruled that juveniles could not be tried in the juvenile court system and then transferred to the adult court system for a subsequent hearing on the same case even if during the predispositional hearing the court deems the youth unsuitable for rehabilitation in the juvenile system. To try the youth in both courts violates the fifth amendment protections against double jeopardy. These cases framed the ability to transfer juveniles to the adult court system in terms of either the amenability to treatment or dangerousness.

As previously presented in Chapter 6, there are three categories of waivers (five distinct types of waivers) to the adult court system. These include judicial waivers (discretionary, presumptive, and mandatory), direct file waivers, and statutory exclusions. These waivers differ by the level of responsibility and influence the judge or prosecutor has in

---

Kent v. United States (1966) Waiver Criteria

In an appendix to its opinion, the Court in *Kent* detailed the following "criteria and principles concerning waiver of jurisdiction":

An offense falling within the statutory limitations . . . will be waived if it has prosecutive merit and if it is heinous or of an aggravated character, or—even though less serious—if it represents a pattern of repeated offenses which indicate that the juvenile may be beyond rehabilitation under Juvenile Court procedures, or if the public needs the protection afforded by such action.

The determinative factors which will be considered by the Judge in deciding whether the Juvenile Court's jurisdiction over such offenses will be waived are the following:

1. The seriousness of the alleged offense to the community and whether the protection of the community requires waiver.

2. Whether the alleged offense was committed in an aggressive, violent, premeditated or willful manner.

3. Whether the alleged offense was against persons or against property, greater weight being given to offenses against persons especially if personal injury resulted.

4. The prosecutive merit of the complaint, i.e., whether there is evidence upon which a Grand Jury may be expected to return an indictment (to be determined by consultation with the [prosecuting attorney]).

5. The desirability of trial and disposition of the entire offense in one court when the juvenile's associates in the alleged offense are adults who will be charged with a crime in [criminal court]).

6. The sophistication and maturity of the juvenile as determined by consideration of his home, environmental situation, emotional attitude, and pattern of living.

7. The record and previous history of the juvenile, including previous contacts with [social service agencies], other law enforcement agencies, juvenile courts and other jurisdictions, prior periods of probation to [the court], or prior commitments to juvenile institutions.

8. The prospects for adequate protection of the public and the likelihood of reasonable rehabilitation of the juvenile (if he is found to have committed the alleged offense) by the use of procedures, services and facilities currently available to the Juvenile Court.

Information taken from: Snyder, Howard, Sickmund, Melissa, Poe-Yamagata, Eileen (2000, August). *Juvenile Transfers to Criminal Court in the 1990's: Lessons Learned from Four Studies.* Washington, D.C.: Office of Juvenile Justice and Delinquency Prevention (p. 3).

deciding to transfer the juvenile case to the adult court system. As you recall judicial waivers refer to those cases falling within the specified criteria of the court (typically age of the offender, offense category, previous record, or some combination of the three), that the judge considers in deciding to transfer the offender to the adult court system. There are three different forms of judicial waivers: discretionary waiver (judges have the discretion to waive the case to the adult court system); presumptive waivers (in these cases the juvenile rather than the state assumes the burden of proof to show why he or she should not be transferred to the adult court system); and mandatory waivers (cases meeting certain age, offense, or other criteria have their cases initiated in the juvenile court then the decision is made to transfer the case to the adult court). The second form of waiver is the direct file waiver. With the direct file waiver (sometimes known as the prosecutorial waiver), the prosecutor makes the decision of whether the case should be tried in the juvenile or adult court system. The third form of waiver is the statutory exclusion. This waiver is similar to the mandatory waiver except that the prosecutor makes the decision to file the case directly in the adult court system (Griffin, Torbet, & Szymanski, 1998).

Discretionary waivers are the most frequently used form of waiver in the judicial system. Currently, forty-six states use some form of discretionary waiver (Griffin, Torbet, & Szymanski, 1998). Typically those youth who have committed a very serious crime (as defined by state statute) and those who have a longer criminal history are more likely to be waived. The presence of a weapon and the injury of the victim from the weapon also strongly impacts the decision to waive youth to the adult court system (Sickmund, 2003, p. 8). The number of cases waived to the adult court system have fluctuated throughout the years. For example, "the number of delinquency cases waived to criminal court grew 51% between 1989 and 1994, from 8,000 to about 12,000. By 1998, waived cases were down 33%, nearly to the 1989 level" (Sickmund, 2003, p. 26).

The age at which a juvenile can be transferred to the adult court system varies by state. In twenty-three states and the District of Columbia, there is no minimum age specified in at least one of the transfer provisions. As Table 15.1 indicates, the ages when

Table 15.1   Minimum Transfer Age Specified in Statute

Age	State
None	Alaska, Arizona, Delaware, District of Columbia, Florida, Georgia, Hawaii, Idaho, Indiana, Maine, Maryland, Montana, Nebraska, Oklahoma, Oregon, Pennsylvania, Rhode Island, South Carolina, South Dakota, Tennessee, Texas, Washington, West Virginia, and Wisconsin
10	Kansas and Vermont
12	Colorado and Missouri
13	Illinois, Mississippi, New Hampshire, New York, North Carolina, and Wyoming
14	Alabama, Arkansas, California, Connecticut, Iowa, Kentucky, Louisiana, Massachusetts, Michigan, Minnesota, Nevada, New Jersey, North Dakota, Ohio, Utah, and Virginia
15	New Mexico

Source: Sickmund, Melissa (2003, June). "Juveniles in Court." *Juvenile Offenders and Victims National Report Series.* Washington, D.C.: Office of Juvenile Justice and Delinquency Prevention, p. 9.

specified range from ten to fifteen. As noted for those states who specify the minimum age, age fourteen is the most commonly cited (Sickmund, 2003, p. 9).

As Feld (1999) points out, there are four distinct characteristics of youth who are most likely to be waived to the adult court system: First, juveniles who are tried in rural court systems are more likely to be transferred to the adult court system than youth who are tried in urban courts. This differentiation can be explained by a variety of factors including community disapproval of the behavior, particularly when it is viewed as something extreme or out of the ordinary. Additionally, the interpretation of the law by the individual judge may impact the handling of the case (Podkopacz & Feld, 2001). For example, if a judge adheres to a more retributive ideology rather than rehabilitation they will be more likely to waive the juvenile to the adult court system. The caseload size and available resources of the court may also impact the decision to transfer. For example, a judge or prosecutor in a rural court may believe there are fewer resources in their community to adequately handle a violent youth, therefore, they will process them through the adult court system. The court system itself may also want to send a message to other youth throughout the community that the behavior is not acceptable and will be prosecuted to the fullest extent of the law. Because youth living in rural communities are more inclined to communicate with one another on a less formal, personal basis, the ruling is more likely to be heard by more individuals in the community than may be possible in an urban area.

The second characteristic of youths who are most likely to be waived to the adult court system is the race of the offender and the victim. As Feld (1999) indicates, black offenders with white victims are more likely to be waived to the adult court system than any other offender-victim racial composition (p. 217). These effects, however, are not always direct. For example, in a study conducted by Podkopacz and Feld (2001), they found that the effects were oftentimes indirect in that prosecutors were more inclined to charge minority youths with violent crimes and white defendants with property crimes when they had the same offense criteria. So in studying the relative impact or decision-making process, it becomes less clear whether the race of the offender ultimately impacts the judges decision to waive. Rather the differences are occurring in a less visible arena, the charging of the offender.

The third characteristic of youths who are most likely to waived to the adult court system includes the idiosyncratic differences of the courts. These differences refer to the absence of guidelines for waiving youth to the adult court system. As Feld (1999) suggests, "The subjective nature of waiver decisions, the absence of effective guidelines to structure outcomes, and the lack of objective indicators or scientific tools with which to classify youths allow judges to make unequal and disparate rulings without any effective procedural or appellate limitations" (p. 216). Many states have begun to call for a regimented approach in deciding which cases should be waived to the adult court system. Although this approach would objectify the decision-making process and make it similar to the sentencing guidelines that have been instituted at the Federal level and in many states, it would violate the sanctity of the juvenile court process and eliminate the ability for judges to adhere to the original concept of *parens patriae* and the need for individualized justice.

The final characteristic of youth who are most likely to be waived to the adult court system is the organizational politics that exist within the communities. The political climate of the community will directly impact whether the court itself should be getting tough on crime (Feld, 1999). For example, if a highly publicized violent crime occurs during an election time period, the judge and prosecutor may be more inclined to "get tough" on the offender.

One question that has arisen is whether these transfer provisions are effective at reducing recidivism and deterring future delinquent activity? Although hotly debated amongst legislators the effectiveness of these provisions has not been fully explored.

Studies assessing the effectiveness of transfer provisions for youth from the juvenile to the adult court system during the 1970s and through the mid-1980s suggests that youth who were transferred were treated more leniently than if they were in juvenile court. Some have argued these differences could be explained because it was their first appearance in the criminal court system, therefore, they had relatively short offending histories. Also, some researchers have argued this could be symptomatic of the age of the offenders when they appeared in the court room (Snyder, Sickmund & Poe-Yamagata, 2000). For example, many of them were younger when they first appeared in front of a jury, which could have accounted for them being sympathetic to their needs.

The research assessing whether criminal courts were more likely than juvenile courts to incarcerate juvenile offenders has found mixed results. For example, Hamparian and collegues (1982) found that 46% of cases judicially waived and of cases directly filed in the adult court system were likely to be incarcerated. Fagan (1991), in his study of juveniles waived to the adult court system in New York and New Jersey, found that youths tried in criminal court in New York were twice as likely to receive incarceration as those youths tried in juvenile courts in New Jersey (Snyder, Sickmund, & Poe-Yamagata, 2000).

Furthermore, one of the primary arguments for maintaining and enhancing the transfer provisions of the juvenile court is for community safety as well as punishment. In their study of three-thousand juveniles transferred to the adult court system in Florida compared to juveniles who were handled in the juvenile court system, Bishop and colleagues (1996) found that those youth who were transferred to the adult court system were more likely to be rearrested, rearrested for more serious offenses, and rearrested within a shorter time frame than those youths who were handled in the juvenile court system. After six years, the juvenile court comparison group caught up to the rearrest rates of the transferred youth (Winner, et al., 1997). One important finding of this study was that youths who were transferred overall were more likely to reoffend more frequently and to commit more serious offenses than those handled in the juvenile court system. The only exception to this finding was with those youth who were transferred and charged with a property offense were less likely to be rearrested than those youth handled in the juvenile court system (Snyder, Sickmund, & Poe-Yamagata, 2000).

Snyder, Sickmund, and Poe-Yamagata (2000), in an effort to compare the use and effects of transfer provisions, identified three different states for assessment: South Carolina, Utah, and Pennsylvania. In this study, they looked at the criteria for transfer; whether the criteria for transfer had changed during the study time frame; and what the impact of the new legislation was on juveniles that may be transferred to the adult court system. Findings from their study suggested that there were two primary criteria used to transfer youth to the adult court system in both South Carolina and Utah: offense seriousness and extent of previous criminal record. They did find within these studies that the decision to waive a juvenile was influenced by the local concerns, such as in Utah judges were less likely to waive a youth if they did not have an extensive juvenile history. In South Carolina, however, they were more inclined to waive youth if they had committed an offense with a weapon. In Pennsylvania, it appeared that the number of youths waived to the adult court system between 1986 and 1994 dramatically increased.

One reason for this increase in the number of youths transferred has been attributed to the change in the waiver statutes and the increase in the number of youths who were convicted of committing drug offenses. Overall, findings from these studies suggest that juveniles who have a history of delinquent activity, who have committed a serious offense with a weapon, or those who have committed drug offenses are most likely to be transferred to the adult court system. These findings are important given the fact that previous studies have suggested that youth who are waived to the adult court system are more likely to recidivate sooner and for more serious offenses than those youth who are handled in the juvenile court system.

BLENDED SENTENCING/DETERMINATE SENTENCING

Blended sentencing, in some states known as determinate sentencing, strategies allow the juvenile court judge to impose both juvenile and adult sanctions specifically for dealing with violent or chronic offenders (Feld, 1999). The impetus for adopting and utilizing blended sentences (determinate or mandatory sentences) is the focus on punishment rather than treatment. Many states have begun to adopt the use of fixed sentences in adult prisons to deal with juveniles in the adult court system. These sentences usually function within specified age ranges but some states allow for no minimum age requirements (Bazemore & Umbreit, 1995). These statutes allow for judges to sentence juveniles to adult prisons. In some states, the courts allow the judge to suspend the adult sentence but initiate the sentence should the juvenile violate the conditions of the original juvenile disposition. In 1999, there were a total of twenty-two states allowing for some form of blended sentencing. (See Table 15.2 for an overview of the blended sentencing authority specified by statute.)

The blended sentence is viewed as middle ground or intermediate sanction for the offender. This serves as one last chance before being waived to the adult court system (Sickmund, 2003, p. 7). Below are two examples of states that have begun to utilize the

Table 15.2   Blended Sentencing Authority Specified by Statute, 1999

Court	State
Juvenile	Alaska, Colorado, Connecticut, Illinois, Kansas, Massachusetts, Michigan, Minnesota, New Mexico, Rhode Island, South Carolina, Texas
Criminal	Arkansas, California, Colorado, Florida, Idaho, Iowa, Michigan, Missouri, Oklahoma, Vermont, Virginia, West Virginia

Taken from: Sickmund, Melissa (2003, June). "Juveniles in Court." *Juvenile Offenders and Victims National Report Series.* Washington, D.C.: Office of Juvenile Justice and Delinquency Prevention, p. 7.

blended sentencing and determinate sentencing structures. First will be a discussion of the state of Minnesota, which modified their statute in 1995 to expand and bridge the gap between the juvenile and adult court system with the passage of the Minnesota's Extended Jurisdiction Juvenile Prosecution blended sentencing law. During that same year, the state of Texas enacted legislation to extend the control of the juvenile court system through determinate sentencing policies. Each of these programs will be briefly reviewed below.

Minnesota's Extended Jurisdiction Juvenile Prosecution (EIJ)

In 2001, Podkopacz and Feld reviewed the implementation of Minnesota's Extended Jurisdiction Juvenile Prosecution (EIJ) blended sentencing law which passed in 1995. During the late 1980s and early 1990s, the state of Minnesota, like many other states throughout the United States experienced an increase in the amount of violent juvenile crime. The legislature, in response to this increasing concern over violence, chose to look at the existing waiver statutes, as well as focusing on the creation of new statutes to deal with those youth who fell in between the cracks. In other words, those youth who did not quite meet the eligibility criteria to be waived to the adult court system, but at the same time they were in need of additional supervision that the juvenile court alone may not be able to provide. One of the first things the state of Minnesota did was to reconsider and amend the present waiver statutes. The primary change came with the amendment of the waiver criteria from "amenability to treatment" to the concern for "public safety" (p. 1007). Under this new law the juvenile court judge must decide whether the child's offense severity, criminal history, and "unamenability to probation" warrant adult imprisonment (p. 1008). The second approach to handling the juvenile offenders came with the creation of a new law that called for the enactment of a new intermediary sentencing option for judges where they could take youths who committed a felony offense and seek to extend the juvenile court jurisdiction beyond the youth's nineteenth birthday, which was when the prior juvenile court disposition authority ended. In order to prosecute under the EIJ law, the prosecutor must file a motion stating that the youth is eligible for this option and they are electing not to transfer the youth to the adult court system. There are four different ways youth may qualify for the EIJ processing:

1. There was an unsuccessful attempt to certify a youth as an adult.
2. A sixteen or seventeen year old may qualify for presumptive certification for which the sentencing guidelines presume commitment to prison. If the judge does not certify the youth, they may file under the subsequent EIJ statutes.
3. A prosecutor charges a youth sixteen or seventeen years of age with a presumptive-certification offense and designates the case as an EIJ prosecution automatically without any further judicial review.
4. Prosecution for other serious and younger offenders. Instead of filing a certification motion against a non-presumptive-certification youth, a prosecutor may file a motion for the court to designate the youth for EIJ prosecution (pp. 1011–1013).

Under this intermediate court, the youth receives greater procedural protections, such as a right to trial by jury. If the jury trial convicts the child of a lesser nonpresumptive offense then they must sentence them to the delinquency offense. This finding indicates that the prosecutor incorrectly charged the youth as an EIJ. On the other hand, the juvenile may plead guilty to a nonpresumptive sentence but still receive an EIJ disposition. There are also provisions to restrict prosecutorial overcharging of juveniles as presumptive-certification EIJ's (Podkopacz & Feld, 2001, pp. 1014–1015). Although this option provides an intermediate status for the courts to deal with juveniles who would have otherwise been waived to the adult court system allowing them to remain out of adult prisons, many argued that this still could result in the youths being housed in adult prisons if their probation was revoked.

Overall, an assessment of the implementation of this new law suggested that instead of providing an option for prosecutors and judges to keep felony offenders in the juvenile court system but utilizing more retributive methods for dealing with the offenders, they widened the net and prosecuted more youths under the certification (waiver) proceedings, as well as prosecuting a number of youths under the EIJ statute who would have ordinarily received a delinquency rather than criminal disposition. The biggest differences between youth whom the prosecutors decided to file certification provisions against versus those who they filed EIJ's against was the age of the offender. The prosecutors were more likely to file certification motions on older youth and more likely to file EIJ's on younger offenders. The findings of this study suggests that the EIJ intermediate sanction has "become the youth's 'first and last chance' for treatment, widened the net of criminal social control, and moved larger numbers of younger and less serious or chronic youths into the adult correctional system indirectly through the 'back door' of probation revocation proceedings rather than through certification hearings" (Podkopacz & Feld, 2001, p. 1070).

Determinate Sentencing in Texas

During 1995, Texas was also concerned about the continuing trend towards violence by youth. In order to address the problem of how to deal with those youth who are not eligible to be waived to the adult court system but are also not eligible to be handled by the juvenile court system, the state legislator passed and implemented the use of determinate sentencing for juveniles. Under the determinate sentencing statutes enacted in the state of Texas, juveniles regardless of age can be sentenced up to 40 years to the Texas Youth Commission (TYC) (Mears and Field, 2000, p. 986).

The determinate proceedings are separate from waiver proceedings. Similar to the blended sentencing models, determinate sentencing was designed to address the issue of violent juvenile offenders who were not eligible to be transferred to the adult court system. In 1995, Texas increased the number of offenses eligible for determinate sentencing from five to approximately thirty. They also modified the conditions under which parole can occur. Juveniles were also afforded the same rights and procedural safeguards afforded adults including the right to trial by jury.

To study the impact of the new determinate sentencing policies on the handling of juveniles in the system, Mears and Fields (2000) reviewed the factors that would make youths eligible for either a determinate sentence or whether they would be waived to the adult court system. They particularly wanted to focus their attention on whether legal factors (e.g., offense severity, prior history of offending), extralegal factors (e.g., age, gender, race/ethnicity) or processing (e.g., plea bargaining) played a role in determining whether youths would receive a more serious sanction. There were a total of 1,430 youths ($n = 530$ waiver ineligible youths, and $n = 906$ waiver eligible youths) identified for participation in the study. A review of the data revealed that the most important characteristic for the decision to process a youth were legal factors such as offense severity, although this relationship differed for waiver eligible versus waiver ineligible youth. For those youth who were classified as waiver eligible, offense severity played a greater role in predicting the outcome of their case, where as it did not always for the waiver ineligible group. Additionally, those youth who were older were considered to be less amenable for treatment than were the younger offenders. There were examples of "youth discounts" for younger offenders. These juveniles were also more likely to receive the benefit of treatment than older offenders. There were also many examples of the use of plea bargaining as a tool for handling and processing youth through the system, therefore, allowing for more rehabilitative measures to be used (Mears & Fields, 2000).

Overall, the use of both blended sentences and determinate sentences point to the move towards getting tough on crime. In addition, these responses to the juvenile crime problem have resulted in the shifting of the discretionary powers from the judges, which was the intent of the original court, to the prosecutors. There has been a narrowing of the gap between the juvenile and adult court systems. As we have begun to further criminalize the juvenile justice system, we have essentially witnessed the increased use of procedural safeguards which were once only afforded to adults. This movement has led to the argument by many scholars that there is no longer a need for a separate juvenile court. Rather the systems should be blended together to provided for more protections of chronic or serious offenders and to protect against the widening of net or the inclusion of youths who would not otherwise have come to the attention of the juvenile court system.

PREDICTORS OF YOUTH VIOLENCE

As we enter the new millennium, concern over youth crime and violence has led to the creation of policies that call for getting tough on crime. As we have already seen, these policies focus on the retributive philosophy of just deserts (punishment should be just greater than the harm that was caused by the offense) we have turned to reducing the rehabilitative role of the juvenile court and begun to focus on a more punitive orientation towards handling these offenders. One area that has recently generated a lot of attention and focus is on understanding the causes and correlates of juvenile crime particularly violence. It is the belief that in understanding the causes of crime we can focus our resources and efforts on preventing the delinquency and violence from occurring, therefore, providing us many more rehabilitative options which was included in the original intent of the juvenile court.

The argument has been made that violence itself does not occur within a vacuum, rather it is a product of cultural and social conditions that must be addressed if violence is to be adequately addressed and ultimately prevented. Violence is something we are all familiar with. As a society we seek to eliminate the most intimate exposure to violence yet we allow it into our homes on a daily basis through popular media, which includes television, movies, and video games. We in many ways have an obsession with violence. The more violent and graphic a movie is, the more likely the public is to attend. Additionally, the increase in violence on the news cannot be dismissed. For example, the graphic images such as the destruction that was experienced with the terrorist attacks on September 11, 2001 continue to be replayed in the minds of the citizens who watched in horror as the Twin Towers came down. Exposure to such violence cannot be dismissed. So what causes our youth to be more violent, and how should we respond?

Society's concern over violence by youth alarmed citizens, as well as policymakers and legislators so much that the Office of Juvenile Justice and Delinquency Prevention created the OJJDP Serious Violent and Chronic Offenders Study Group Project led by Rolf Loeber and David Farrington. During the course of this research, three study sites were identified: Pittsburgh, Rochester, and Denver. This study group was charged with understanding and identifying the predictors of youth violence and we present a summary of those findings below.

A plethora of literature assessing the factors that contribute to violence and violent behavior can be found in the psychological, sociological, criminology, criminal justice, and health professional literature. The issue of violence has been studied for a number of years. So what do we know? In essence we know a lot. As the literature suggests, we can divide the risk factors for participating in violent behavior and activities into three primary categories: community, family, and school (Howell, 1997). Each of these risk factors will be briefly reviewed below.

Community

The community as a risk factor has its origins in the works of Shaw and McKay (1969). As Shaw and McKay pointed out, communities characterized by diminished social control in socially disorganized areas were more likely to experience delinquency which seems to hold true as much today as it did eighty years ago. Specific neighborhood risk factors for juvenile violence include: availability of firearms and crime, transitions and mobility, low neighborhood attachment, community disorganization, and extreme economic and social deprivation (Howell, 1997, p. 136; Huizinga et al., 1995, p. 35). Additionally, children growing up in underclass neighborhoods are more likely to participate in delinquency than those youths growing up in advantaged neighborhoods.

Firearm availability in the community has shown to be a strong predictor of future delinquent activity. As Howell (1997) points out, there are seven contributing factors related to firearm availability and violence.

1. There is evidence that homicides increase because of the greater lethality that results from gun use.

2. Guns bought for family protection represent a greater threat to members of the household than to outsiders.

3. Guns kept in the home for self-protection are thirty-seven times more likely to be used in a suicide as in the killing of an intruder.

4. Guns are readily available to adolescents. In a study by Sheley and Wright (1993), they found that most incarcerated youth reported having a firearm in their home at the time of their incarceration and 65 percent of them reported owning three or more guns.

5. Gangs are more likely to recruit adolescents who own firearms.

6. Drug trafficking is associated with firearm possession.

7. Firearms are increasingly the weapon of choice in homicides, whereas use of other weapons is decreasing (Howell, 1997, pp. 137–139).

Furthermore, neighborhoods that experience a high rate of residential mobility are more likely to experience and increase in institutional disruption and weaken community controls, which leads to community disorganization. Therefore, the social controls, such as church, school, neighbors, that may have once prevented a youth from participating in delinquent activity no longer exist. This breakdown in controls increases the probability that youth will run free in the streets unsupervised which presents them with more opportunities to commit delinquent and criminal acts. Furthermore, these factors or weakened controls lead to low neighborhood attachment as well as extreme economic and social deprivation (Sampson, 2002).

Family

The research suggests that families play an integral role in the behavior of youth. A number of research studies have been conducted addressing these issues. Some of the most important areas that have been identified in the literature are low family income. As previously suggested, juveniles growing up in economically disadvantaged families are more likely to participate in delinquent activities than those youth growing up in advantaged families. Furthermore, income shapes where a family lives. Therefore, if a family is economically disadvantaged they may have no other choice than to live in a violent community where the school system is inadequate (Howell, 1997; National Research Council, 1993). There is also a growing body of literature that suggests youths growing up in structurally weak families, meaning those growing up in homes of divorce, are more likely to participate in delinquent activity (Farrington, 1996; Eggebeen & Lichter, 1991). Other issues such as family size (children reared in larger families are more likely to experience delinquency than children reared in smaller families), poor prenatal care, and poor child-rearing methods are related to later delinquent involvement (Farrington, 2002). Overall, this literature suggests that the family plays a real and integral role in the child's later delinquent involvement.

School

The influence of schools and school factors in predicting future delinquent activity is one that does not function alone. The school environment and the relative success of juveniles in school has been shown to be an important factor in contributing to future delinquent activity. As the research suggests, children who fail to succeed academically are more likely to participate in later delinquent activity (Hawkins et al., 1998). In addition, "students who are impulsive, are weakly attached to their schools, have little commitment to achieving educational goals, and whose moral beliefs in the validity of conventional rules for behavior are weak are more likely to engage in crime than those who do not possess these characteristics" (Gottfredson, Wilson, & Najaka, 2002, p. 149). As Howell (1997) indicates, school failure is not unidimensional. Children whose families experience economic deprivation, as well as experience a lower educational background themselves, are more likely to participate in delinquent activity than those youths who are from families with higher income levels and have parents who have achieved academically. In addition, poor academic performance is not only related to delinquent activity but it is also a strong predictor of early onset of delinquent activity as will as the escalation in frequency of delinquency (Howell, 1997, p. 142).

PREVENTING YOUTH VIOLENCE

Now that we have a better understanding of the causes of violent offending, legislators and policy-makers alike have begun to focus on what can be done to prevent youth violence. The following section presents an overview of some of the efforts of both legislators and researchers to respond to preventing violent delinquent offenses.

In June 1999, the U.S. House of Representatives formed a Bipartisan Working Group on Youth Violence. This working group was charged with exploring six main issues related to juvenile violence: parents and families, law enforcement, school safety, community programs, pop culture and media, and health. There were seven themes identified by the working group:

1. Prevention and early intervention programs are essential.
2. Parents and communities must play active and positive roles in children's lives.
3. Youth health programs and mental health services must be accessible.
4. The juvenile justice system should treat youth individually with the goal of rehabilitation.
5. Sharing of information among educators law enforcement, judges, and social services is essential.
6. Schools are prime locations to identify at-risk youth.
7. Congress should fund only programs showing effective outcomes and demonstrating continuous benefit (Steinberg, 2000, p. 31).

As we can see, in this instance, legislators have made a conscientious effort to incorporate the research into understanding and creating policies that address the issues of violence committed by youth. These findings are further articulated by the OJJDP Study group. Many of these efforts are interdependent on the system. As Thornberry, Huizinga, and Loeber (1995) point out that there are a number of characteristics of effective prevention programs. These elements can be summarized or collapsed into three categories: early intervention, comprehensive interventions, and long-term interventions. Each of these categories will be briefly addressed below.

Early Intervention

Research suggests that delinquency does not begin in mid-adolescence, rather the foundation for the onset of delinquency occurs early on in a childs life. Therefore, it is imperative to begin efforts to address family concerns as well as the individual childs concerns. These efforts can include parenting programs, prenatal care, as well as providing avenues for the parents to educate themselves and provide job training for the parents so the issues of economic deprivation can be addressed. If these cooccurring problems are not addressed at an early age they may manifest themselves later on as serious or violent offending (Thornberry, Huizinga, & Loeber, 1995).

Comprehensive Interventions

As Thornberry, Huizinga, and Loeber (1995) suggest, the interventions themselves must be comprehensive. When developed, the programs need to address the particular risk factors, such as school problems, or familial problems that the child may be experiencing. They must also address the issue of cooccurring behaviors such as those youths who are not only participating in violent behavior for example, but that behavior may be occurring because of a drug use. Therefore, it is important to identify, understand, and address the multitude of problems youths may be experiencing in their lives. To address only one of the issues or problems the youth is experiencing may only result in tapping into the surface rather than responding to the multitude of problems that may exist. Youths may also exhibit a number of protective factors that programs may need to tap into. Although they may be associating with known delinquents, which results in their own delinquent activity, they may also come from a family that is intact and may be the nexus for stopping the delinquent behavior. Therefore, it is important for program personnel to identify the characteristics that may protect or prevent a youth from participating in later delinquent activity and to capitalize on them.

Long-term Interventions

Finally, the interventions should not solely focus on the immediate alteration of the behavior. In order to prevent future delinquent activity, the programs that are put into place should be made available to the youths on a long-term basis, which is defined as years rather than months. Traditionally, most programs are only offered on a short-term basis. The research informs us, however, that violent behavior typically persists over time therefore, it is important to implement programs that not only address the multitude of problems juveniles experience but that these programs can be sustained over a long period of time (Thornberry, Huizinga, & Loeber, 1995).

CHALLENGES OF THE FUTURE

Now that we've come to the end of the text, it is apparent that the issue of handling juveniles within the present system is complex at best. There is an ongoing debate about how juveniles should be handled. Should they be treated as miniature adults or should they be treated as individuals who are in need of protection through the maintenance of a separate juvenile justice system? These are all important issues that are driven primarily by public opinion. Myths about juvenile crime have further demonstrated the need to merge the gap between public opinion and reality. These myths include:

1. Compared to the past, there is a new and more serous "breed" of child delinquents and young murderers, as is evident from the spate of recent killings by school-aged children.

2. Today's child delinquents are destined to become tomorrow's "super-predators."

3. Most delinquent acts and problem behavior of child delinquents should be ignored because children will "grow out of it."

4. There is little that can be done to prevent child delinquency or escalation afterward into chronic criminal careers.

5. Incarceration is the best justice response to serious child offenders.

6. A single agency (e.g., juvenile justice system, schools) can reduce the prevalence of child delinquents (Loeber & Farrington, 2001, pp. 5–6)

The existence of these myths, although they have been proven to be false, create a variety of different challenges researchers, practitioners, and legislators must confront.

Lloyd Ohlin (1998) states that the focus of attention on addressing the issue of youth crime and violence in the future should be on six issues. Each of these issues will be summarized. First, Ohlin argues we need to confront the issue of alienation of youth. As we know, youth who feel alienated from their communities are more likely to participate in delinquent activity. So in preventing juvenile delinquency, communities need to make valiant efforts to keep youth involved in community related activities (Ohlin, 1998, p. 148).

Second, Ohlin argues communities should focus on building community resources. Therefore, it is important for community members, which includes not only those working within the criminal justice system but also those who provide resources, to communicate with one another to address the issue of crime and delinquency. This communication is especially important in areas that experience very high rates of crime and yet are also suffering from access to limited resources. By working in conjunction with one another, communities can decrease the amount of duplication of services and yet capitalize those resources that have been shown to effectively reduce crime and delinquency.

Third, Ohlin argues there needs to be an adequate allocation of federal, state, and local resources. The effective allocation of resources does not have to be in the form of reactive services. Rather, government officials need to focus on the literature that addresses how we can prevent future delinquent activity. These resources could include education, employment, welfare, adequate housing, and adequate medical care. As noted in the previous sections, juveniles that suffer from inadequate controls such as educational failure are more likely to participate in later delinquent or criminal activity.

Fourth, Ohlin argues there needs to be a focus on adequate employment and education. He argues when there is a reduction in employment and education opportunities it results in and contributes to further isolation of youth. Schools need to work in conjunction with the workforce to teach job skills and career-oriented exercises.

Fifth, communities must focus on reducing fear of crime. As stated earlier, the fear of crime by the American public has resulted in policies focused on getting tougher on crime. Inaccurate information has been disseminated in the popular media which has resulted in increasing the fear of crime. Furthermore, it is those individuals who are least likely to be victimized (the elderly) who have voiced their concerns the loudest that something needs to be done to address the issue of juvenile delinquency.

Sixth, Ohlin argues, new policy needs to focus on creating cooperation between juvenile justice agencies. This can be reflected in an attempt to coordinate efforts between agencies. Efforts such as those put forth by the OJJDP Study Group can help initiate coordinated responses to the issue of juvenile delinquency.

Overall, these challenges as presented by Ohlin further point to the need for a collaborative response to dealing with juvenile justice in the new millennium. As we consider whether we should maintain the present day juvenile justice system or whether we should abolish it in its current form, we must also look for alternative ways to prevent future delinquency from occurring. These are not impossible tasks. We know more now than ever before. It is the continued search for the causes of delinquency and the responses that will serve as the future challenge. The question remains, as a system, are we capable of effectively addressing the problem of delinquency in the twenty-first century?

CONCLUSION

Now, here, you see, it takes all the running you can do, to keep in the same place. If you want to get somewhere else, you must run at least twice as fast as that!

Lewis Carroll, Through the Looking-Glass *(1872)*

Change has a considerable psychological impact on the human mind. To the fearful it is threatening because it means that things may get worse. To the hopeful it is encouraging because things may get better. To the confident it is inspiring because the challenge exists to make things better.

King Whitney, Jr.

The quotes above are inspirational to the both of us. As the rabbit pointed out, you must run twice as fast as usual to get someplace else and it seems as if we have been running in place for the past twenty-five years. We have continued to implement the same old solutions, and when they fail, we throw up our hands and state that the youth are so terrible today that we must get even more punitive without investigating systemic causes for delinquency. For many of us, change is also threatening, because we believe that if we try something and it fails, then things can only be worse. However, we are hopeful, and inspired, because change is a challenge, change is to embraced warmly and with anticipation.

This text is the elucidation of our hope. We both know that the majority of staff responsible for the welfare and programming of youth are dedicated, ethical, and hard-working people. Thus, it is our collective responsibility to be sure they have the resources and tools necessary to do the best possible job.

We have attempted to share with the reader the fact that the juvenile justice system and the other institutions that are a part of our community are so interrelated that it is impossible to untie the knot. Juvenile justice workers must have a knowledge of juvenile delinquency and how the system works, but if there is to be hope for the future they need to know how to make the system work effectively, and we cannot wait for them to marinate for years in order to learn how to make it work. The juvenile justice practitioner must know how to manage resources, work with groups, be a leader, and understand how policy affects his or her daily life as well as the lives of youth he or she supervises. In addition, legislators and the public must be willing make a commitment to long term change by allocating the necessary resources for change to occur. That is the aim of this text.

We hope we have succeeded.

STUDY QUESTIONS

1. Discuss Lloyd Ohlin's six issues for youth. Why do you think they are important and how might they be implemented for the sake of future generations?

2. What do you think is in the future for delinquent youth?

   a. Waivers

   b. Rehabilitation

   c. Gangs

   d. Military service

   e. Less of a safety net

   f. Jobs

BIBLIOGRAPHY

BAZEMORE, GORDON, AND UMBREIT, MARK (1995). "Rethinking the Sanctioning Function in Juvenile Court: Retributive or Restorative Responses to Youth Crime." *Crime & Delinquency, 41* (3), 296–316.

BINDER, ARNOLD (1984). "The Juvenile Court, the U.S. Constitution and When the Twain Meet." *Journal of Criminal Justice, 12,* 355–366.

BISHOP, DONNA M., FRAZIER, CHARLES E., LANZA-KADUCE, LONN, AND WHITE, H. (1996). "The Transfer of Juveniles to Criminal Court: Does It Make a Difference?" *Crime & Delinquency, 42,* 171–191.

EGGEBEEN, DAVID, AND LICHTER, DANIEL (1991). "Race, Family, Structure, and Changing Poverty among American Children." *American Sociological Review, 56,* 801–817.

FAGAN, J. (1991). *The Comparative Impacts of Juvenile and Criminal Court Sanctions on Adolescent Offenders.* Washington, DC: National Institute of Justice.

FARRINGTON, DAVID P. (2002). "Families and Crime." In James Q. Wilson and Joan Petersilia (Eds.), *Crime: Public Policies for Crime Control* (pp. 129–148). Oakland, CA: ICS Press.

FELD, BARRY C. (1999). *Bad Kids: Race and the Transformation of the Juvenile Court.* New York: Oxford Publishing.

GOTTFREDSON, DENISE C., WILSON, DAVID B., AND NAJAKA, STACY S. (2002). "The Schools." In James Q. Wilson and Joan Petersilia (Eds.), *Crime: Public Policies for Crime Control* (pp. 149–189). Oakland, CA: ICS Press.

GRIFFIN, PATRICK, TORBET, PATRICIA, AND SZYMANSKI, LINDA (1998, December). *Trying Juveniles as Adults in Criminal Court: An Analysis of State Transfer Provisions.* Washington, DC: Office of Juvenile Justice and Delinquency Prevention.

HAMPERIAN, D., ESTEP, L., MUNTEAN, S., PREISTINO, R., SWISHER, R., WALLACE, P., AND WHITE, J. (1982). *Major Issues in Juvenile Justice Information and Training Youth in Adult Courts—Between Two Worlds.* Washington, DC: Office of Juvenile Justice and Delinquency Prevention.

HAWKINS, J. DAVID, HERRENKOHL, TODD, FARRINGTON, DAVID P., BREWER, DEVON, CATALANO, RICHARD F., AND HARACI, TRACY W. (1998). "A Review of Predictors of Youth Violence." In Rolf Loeber and David P. Farrington (Eds.), *Serious & Violent Juvenile Offenders: Risk Factors and Successful Intervention* (pp. 106–146). Thousand Oaks, CA: Sage Publications.

HOWELL, JAMES C. (1997). *Juvenile Justice & Youth Violence.* Thousand Oaks, CA: Sage Publications.

HUIZINGA, DAVID, LOEBER, R., AND THORNBERRY, TERRANCE (1995). *Recent Findings from the Program of Research on Causes and Correlates of Delinquency.* Washington, DC: Office of Juvenile Justice and Delinquency Prevention.

LOEBER, ROLF, AND FARRINGTON, DAVID P. (2001). "The Significance of Child Delinquency." In Rolf Loeber and David P. Farrington (Eds.), *Child Delinquents: Development, Intervention, and Service Needs* (pp. 1–24). Thousand Oaks, CA: Sage Publications.

MEARS, DANIEL P., AND FIELD, SAMUEL H. (2000) "Theorizing Sanctioning in a Criminalized Juvenile Court." *Criminology, 38*(4), 983–1019.

NATIONAL RESEARCH COUNCIL (1993). *Losing Generations: Adolescents in High Risk Settings.* Washington, DC: National Academy Press.

OHLIN, LLOYD E. (1998). "The Future of Juvenile Justice Policy and Research." *Crime & Delinquency, 44*(1): 143–153.

PODKOPACZ, MARCY R., AND FELD, BARRY C. (2001). "The Back-door to Prison: Waiver Reform, 'Blended Sentencing,' and the Law of Unintended Consequences." *The Journal of Criminal Law & Criminology, 91*(4), 997–1071.

SAMPSON, ROBERT J. (2002). "The Community." In James Q. Wilson and Joan Petersilia (Eds.), *Crime: Public Policies for Crime Control* (pp. 225–252). Oakland, CA: ICS Press.

SHAW, CLIFFORD R., AND McKAY, HENRY D. (1969). *Juvenile Delinquency and Urban Areas,* rev. ed. Chicago: University of Chicago Press.

SHELEY, J.F., AND WRIGHT, J.D. (1993). *Gun Acquisition and Possession in Selected Juvenile Samples (Research in Brief).* Washington, DC: National Institute of Justice and Office of Juvenile Justice and Delinquency Prevention.

SICKMUND, MELISSA (2003, June). "Juveniles in Court." *Juvenile Offenders and Victims National Report Series.* Washington, DC: Office of Juvenile Justice and Delinquency Prevention.

SNYDER, HOWARD, SICKMUND, MELISSA, AND POE-YAMAGATA, EILEEN (2000, August). *Juvenile Transfers to Criminal Court in the 1990's: Lessons Learned from Four Studies.* Washington, DC: Office of Juvenile Justice and Delinquency Prevention.

STEINBERG, LAURENCE (2000, April). "Youth Violence: Do Parents and Families Make a Difference?" *National Institute of Justice Journal.* Washington, DC: National Institute of Justice.

THORNBERRY, TERRENCE P., HUIZINGA, DAVID, AND LOEBER, ROLF (1995). "The Prevention of Serious Delinquency and Violence: Implications from the Program of Research on the Causes and Correlates of Delinquency." In James C. Howell, Barry Krisberg, J. David Hawkins, and John J. Wilson (Eds.), *Serious, Violent, & Chronic Juvenile Offenders* (pp. 213–237). Thousand Oaks, CA: Sage Publications.

WINNER, LAWRENCE, LANZA-KADUCE, LONN, BISHOP, DONNA M., AND FRAZIER, CHARLES E. (1997). "The Transfer of Juveniles to Criminal Court: Reexamining Recidivism over the Long Term." *Crime & Delinquency, 43,* 548–563.

GLOSSARY OF KEY TERMS

Blended sentence.   This sentence strategy allows juvenile court judges to impose both a juvenile and criminal sentence.

Determinate sentence.   Determinate sentences allow for youth to be sentenced to a specified amount of time under court supervision, less good time. These strategies have been used in the juvenile court system as a way for the juvenile court to extend the supervisory authority of youth who were not eligible to be transferred to the adult court system.

Retributive sentence.   This framework focuses on the punishment of the offender rather than their rehabilitative needs.

INDEX